MW01174396

£9.99.

Studies in the History of Medieval Religion

VOLUME XXXIII

RELIGIOUS LIFE IN NORMANDY, 1050–1300
Space, gender and social pressure

The religious life was central to Norman society in the middle ages. Professed religious and the clergy did not and could not life in isolation; the support of the laity was vital to their existence. How these different groups used sacred space was central to this relationship.

Here, fascinating new light is shed on the reality of religious life in Normandy. The author uses ideas about space and gender to examine the social pressures arising from such interaction around four main themes: display, reception and intrusion, enclosure and the family. The study is grounded in the discussion of a wide range of sources, including architecture, chronicles and visitation records, from communities of monks and nuns, hospitals and the parish, allowing the people, rather than the institutions, to come to the fore.

DR LEONIE V. HICKS teaches at the University of Southampton.

Studies in the History of Medieval Religion

ISSN: 0955–2480

General Editor
Christopher Harper-Bill

Previously published titles in the series
are listed at the back of this volume

RELIGIOUS LIFE IN NORMANDY, 1050–1300

Space, gender and social pressure

LEONIE V. HICKS

THE BOYDELL PRESS

First published 2007
The Boydell Press, Woodbridge

ISBN 978-1-84383-329-1

The Boydell Press is an imprint of Boydell & Brewer Ltd
PO Box 9, Woodbridge, Suffolk IP12 3DF, UK
and of Boydell & Brewer Inc.
668 Mt Hope Avenue, Rochester, NY 14620, USA
website: www.boydellandbrewer.com

A CIP record of this publication is available from the British Library

This publication is printed on acid-free paper

Typeset by Carnegie Book Production, Lancaster
Printed in Great Britain by
Antony Rowe Ltd, Chippenham, Wiltshire

Contents

Maps

For Ian Hawke

Acknowledgements

The completion of this book would not have been possible without the help and support of a number of people and institutions. Elisabeth van Houts supervised my thesis and has been unfailing in her support, help and encouragement while I was a student and beyond. I owe her a huge debt of gratitude. Along with David Bates, she has always been convinced that this project would see the light of day. Both of them have read drafts of various chapters, and their comments have ensured that this is a much better book than it otherwise would have been and I thank them. The origins of this book lie in my doctoral thesis 'Women and the Use of Space in Normandy, c.1050–1300'. Financial assistance was provided for that initial project by what was then the Arts and Humanities Research Board, Emmanuel College, Cambridge and the Lightfoot Fund administered by the History Faculty, Cambridge University.

Many other people have been generous with their time. Max Satchell and John Walmsley both read sections of the original thesis, and John Walmsley allowed me to use unpublished material, which is duly acknowledged. Laura Napran has given me a great deal of help with Latin translations, provided hospitality, as well as proofreading (any errors remain my own) and I thank her for her company and good advice. I would also like to thank the participants of the Centre for Antiquity and the Middle Ages research seminar at the University of Southampton who helped me to clarify my conclusions, especially Brian Golding, who has also read drafts of this work.

The staff of the Inter-Library Loans departments of the University Library, Cambridge and Hartley Library, Southampton have been unstinting in their pursuit of obscure French references for which I am very grateful. I would also like to thank Caroline Palmer and the staff at Boydell and Brewer for all their advice. Tehmina Goskar and Tom Goskar helped in the production of the maps as well as providing good company since moving to Southampton.

My friends and family have borne the brunt of the associated agonies and anxieties of my work with great patience and I thank them here, especially Barbara, Trevor and Siân Hicks. Finally, but by no means least, thanks to Ian Hawke whose faith in me and the merits of medieval Norman history has been absolute. This book is dedicated to him.

Abbreviations

AA SS	*Acta sanctorum quotquot toto orbe coluntur*, 67 vols (Antwerp, 1643–1940)
AD	Archives départementales
AN	*Annales de Normandie*
ANS	*Anglo-Norman Studies: Proceedings of the Battle Conference*
L'architecture normande	*L'architecture normande au Moyen Age: actes du colloque de Cerisy-la-Salle*, ed. Maylis Baylé, 2 vols, 2nd edn (Caen, 2001)
Arnoux	M. Arnoux, 'Les origines et le développement du mouvement canonial en Normandie', *Des clercs au service de la réforme*, 11–172
arr.	arrondissement
Barlow	Arnulf of Lisieux, *The Letters of Arnulf of Lisieux*, ed. F. Barlow, Camden third series 61 (London, 1939)
Bonnin	Eudes Rigaud, *Regestrum visitationum archiepiscopi Rothomagensis: journal des visites pastorals d'Eude Rigaud (1248–69)*, ed. T. Bonnin (Rouen, 1852)
BSAN	*Bulletin de la Société des Antiquaires de Normandie*
cant.	canton
comm.	commune
Cottineau	J. Cottineau, *Répertoire topo-bibliographique des abbayes et prieurés*, 3 vols (Macon, 1939)
Decrees	*Decrees of the Ecumenical Councils: vol. 1 Nicaea I to Lateran V*, ed. and trans. N. P. Tanner (London, 1990)
dép.	Département
Des clercs au service de la réforme	*Des clercs au service de la réforme. Études et documents sur les chanoines réguliers de la Province de Rouen*, ed. M. Arnoux (Turnhout, 2000)
Fauroux	*Recueil des actes des ducs de Normandie, 911–1066*, ed. M. Fauroux, MSAN 36 (Caen, 1961)
Fröhlich	Anselm of Canterbury, *The Letters of Anselm of Canterbury*, trans. W. Fröhlich, Cistercian Studies 96–7 and 142 (Kalamazoo, 1990–95)
GC	*Gallia Christiana in provincias ecclesiasticas distributa*, ed. D. Ste-Marthe, 16 vols (Paris, 1715–1874, repr. Farnborough, 1970)
GND	*The gesta Normannorum ducum of William of Jumièges, Orderic Vitalis and Robert of Torigni*, ed. and trans. E. van Houts, OMT, 2 vols (Oxford, 1992–95)
Haimon	L. Delisle, 'Lettre de l'abbé Haimon sur la construction de l'église de Saint-Pierre-sur-Dives en 1145', *Bibliothèque de l'École des Chartes*, 5e série, 1 (1860), 113–39
JMH	*Journal of Medieval History*
Mansi	*Sacrorum conciliorum nova et amplissima collection*, ed. J. D. Mansi, 31 vols (Venice, 1759–98)

Miracula e. Constantiensis	E. A. Pigeon, 'Miracula ecclesiae Constantiensis', Histoire de la cathédrale de Coutances (Coutances, 1876), 367–83
Monastic Constitutions	The Monastic Constitutions of Lanfranc, ed. and trans. D. Knowles and C. N. L. Brooke, OMT (Oxford, 2002)
Monasticon	M. Germain, Le monasticon Gallicanum, 2 vols (repr. Paris, 1882), vol. 2
MSAN	Mémoires de la Société des Antiquaires de Normandie
Normans in Europe	The Normans in Europe, ed. and trans. E. van Houts, Manchester Medieval Sources (Manchester, 2000)
OMT	Oxford Medieval Texts
OV	Orderic Vitalis, The Ecclesiastical History, ed. and trans. M. Chibnall, OMT, 6 vols (Oxford, 1969–80)
PL	Patrologia latina, ed. J.-P. Migne, 221 vols (Paris, 1844–64)
Platelle	H. Platelle, 'Les relations entre l'abbaye Saint-Amand-de-Rouen et l'abbaye Saint-Amand-d'Elnone', La Normandie Bénédictine, ed. Daoust, 104–6
Regesta regum	Regesta regum Anglo-Normannorum: the Acta of William I (1066–1087), ed. D. Bates (Oxford, 1998)
Register	The Register of Eudes of Rouen, ed. J. F. O'Sullivan and trans. S. M. Brown, Records of Civilisation Sources and Studies 72 (New York, 1964)
Registrum epistolarum	Stephen of Lexington, Registrum epistolarum Stephani de Lexinton Pars II. Epistolae et tempus regiminis in Savigniaco pertinentes (1230–1239), ed. P. Bruno Greisser, Analecta Sacri Ordinis Cisterciensis, 8 (1952), 181–378
RS	Rolls Series
Rule	The Rule of St Benedict: a Guide to Christian Living, ed. G. Holzherr and trans. the monks of Glenstal Abbey (Dublin, 1994)
Schmitt	Anselm of Canterbury, S. Anselmi Cantuariensis archiepiscopi opera omnia, ed. F. S. Schmitt, 6 vols (Edinburgh, 1946–61)
Schriber	Arnulf of Lisieux, The Letter Collections of Arnulf of Lisieux, trans. C. P. Schriber, Texts and Studies in Religion 72 (Lampeter, 1997)
Statuta	Statuta capitulorum generalium ordinis Cisterciensis 1116–1786, ed. J.-M. Canivez, 8 vols (Louvain, 1933–41)
Statuts	Statuts d'hotels-Dieu et de leprosaries, ed. L.-F. Le Grand (Vernon, 1901)

Introduction

In September 1087, William the Conqueror died. His body was taken to his own foundation of St-Etienne in Caen whereupon 'Dom Gilbert the abbot came out reverently in procession with all his monks to meet the bier, and with them came a great multitude of clergy and laity, weeping and praying.'[1] Allowing for the twelfth-century chronicler Orderic Vitalis's rhetorical flourishes, the burial of the duke of Normandy was an occasion for a great gathering of monks, clergy and laity. They assembled to bury their leader at the site of a significant monastic foundation, underlined by its magnificent architecture. It is this interaction of laity and religious within the context of sacred space that forms the basis for this consideration of space, gender and the religious life in central medieval Normandy.[2]

Attempts by the Church to maintain a clear distinction between religious, clergy and laity form the backdrop to this discussion. In the wider historical context our period begins with the Gregorian reform: a movement which sought among other things to free the Church from lay control and, as far as possible, to define a separate sacred space within society.[3] Reform of the institutional Church had wide-ranging ramifications for the relationship between the clergy and professed religious on the one hand and the laity on the other. Central to our understanding of this relationship is the use of sacred spaces, defined here to include churches, monasteries, leper houses and hospitals, along with their precincts. Both groups had a claim on these areas and so they became contested spaces, where conflicting needs met and had to be reconciled.

---

[1]   OV, vol. 4, pp. 104–9.

[2]   There is a rich and varied historiography on this subject. See, for example, C. N. L. Brooke, *Churches and Churchmen in Medieval Europe* (London, 1999); P. Brown, *The Cult of Saints: its Rise and Function in Latin Christianity* (Chicago and London, 1981) and *Society and the Holy in Late Antiquity* (London, 1982); A. Vauchez, *The Laity in the Middle Ages: Religious Beliefs and Devotional Practice*, ed. D. E. Bornstein (Notre Dame, IN and London, 1993).

[3]   See for example, H. E. J. Cowdrey, *Pope Gregory VII 1073–1085* (Oxford, 1998); I. S. Robinson, 'Church and Papacy', *The Cambridge History of Medieval Political Thought c.350–c.1450*, ed. J. H. Burns (Cambridge, 1988), pp. 252–305; and *Crises et réformes dans l'église de la réform grégorienne à la préréforme*, Actes du 115e congrès national des sociétés savantes (Paris, 1991).

In this book, the subject is tackled through four key areas in spatial practice, accommodation and conflict: display on the part of the religious; reception of and intrusion by the laity and other religious into demarcated sacred space; contemporary interpretation of the requirement for religious communities to be enclosed ones; and the relationship between religious and their families left behind in the world. Thus the experiences of the laity and religious are situated within the context of their use of sacred space and gender differences. This book is not, therefore, an institutional and economic history of the Norman Church, but concentrates instead on the people it comprised.

Theory: space, gender and the body

My analysis of the Norman evidence concerning the religious life is under-pinned by theories of space, gender and the body. This approach sets my work within a growing area of historical enquiry based on the assumption that social relations between men and women were to a real extent determined, enacted, reinforced and, in some instances challenged, by the spaces in which they moved.[4] Both historians and archaeologists have employed theories emanating from the fields of social anthropology and sociology to create a theoretical framework that enables consideration of day-to-day spatial contexts in a meaningful way. Chief among these theories are those of Henri Lefebvre and Pierre Bourdieu. In *La production de l'espace*, Lefebvre sees the concept of space, specifically social space, as a means of analysing society embodied in a Marxist perspective. The idea of space is a triad involving spatial practice, representations of space and representational spaces. Spatial practice is defined as a perceived space including the production and reproduction of each social formation and thus is concerned with the function of space. Representations of space are conceptual spaces which 'are tied to the relations of production' of society 'and to the order, hence knowledge, that these relations impose'; they embody space as a codified language. Representational spaces, the third angle, are the lived everyday experience of space, including non-verbal symbols, which embody a complex symbolism, dominating all senses and bodies by containing them.[5] In other words, these different concepts of what constitutes space combine together to produce a knowledge of how physical and symbolical space is constructed and how space affects those people who use it by the rules it imposes on them.

---

[4]   For the use of space as a challenge to what is perceived as normal see T. Cresswell, *In Place/Out of Place: Geography, Ideology and Transgression* (Minneapolis and London, 1996).

[5]   Trans. as H. Lefebvre, *The Production of Space* (Oxford, 1991), pp. 33, 38–9, first published in 1974. See also *Medieval Practices of Space*, ed. B. Hanawalt and M. Kobialka, Medieval Cultures 23 (Minneapolis and London, 2000), p. ix. For a critique of Lefebvre's Marxist approach see M. Cassidy-Welch, *Monastic Spaces and their Meanings: Thirteenth-Century English Cistercian Monasteries*, Medieval Church Studies 1 (Turnhout, 2001), pp. 2–4.

Lefebvre's ideas have been related to Bourdieu's theory of *habitus*, a system of rules which governs social behaviour and which provides the knowledge of how to proceed in different spaces.[6] *Habitus* is essentially an unconscious phenomenon which is possessed by the individuals who make up communities, thus helping to maintain a social identity. Architecture, art, the use of space, and movement through space combine with other factors, for example, dress codes, to formulate ideas of how we should act in a given context. Thus, not only is space divided by gender, but also by the value judgements which people put on the spaces men and women occupy. Of course, one of the ways in which spatial practice might be challenged is by acting contrary to *habitus*. Barbara Hanawalt highlights the usefulness of the juxtaposition of Lefebvre's notions of space and Bourdieu's idea of *habitus* in relation to medieval beguines and prostitutes. Beguines were viewed with suspicion because they did not fit into medieval society's conception of strictly enclosed female religious. Whilst prostitutes who worked in brothels were tolerated, those who walked the streets were not. Both beguines and street walkers had taken themselves out of an acceptable bounded space with its own set of behavioural rules (*habitus*).[7] In considering the function of space, spatial order and the everyday experience of spatial practices, we shall see that, at times, both the laity and religious in Normandy acted contrary to their social rules and thus contrary to *habitus*.

Once a use had been created for a given space, it prescribed behaviour within it: this is particularly marked in the context of monastic communities and hospitals. Both Barbara Hanawalt and Michal Kobialka nonetheless underline the fluidity of spatial practice.[8] Like modern spaces, medieval spaces were rarely static and constantly developed.[9] One also has to remember that there were gradations of sacredness in conceptions of medieval space: for example, some parts of the church like the sanctuary were considered more sacred than others like the nave.[10] As Roberta Gilchrist has recently shown, the most sacred space in the diocese was located at the high altar of the cathedral church.[11] Richard Berkhofer has demonstrated that twelfth-century monks were well aware of these gradations, which extended beyond the church to encompass the monastic patrimony as a whole shown through the organisation

---

6   P. Bourdieu, *Outline of a Theory of Practice* (Cambridge, 1977), pp. 72–95. See also R. Gilchrist, *Gender and Material Culture: the Archaeology of Religious Women* (London, 1994), pp. 14–17.

7   B. Hanawalt, 'At the Margin of Women's Space in Medieval Europe', *Matrons and Marginal Women in Medieval Society*, ed. R. Edwards and V. Ziegler (Woodbridge, 1995), pp. 14–15.

8   *Medieval Practices of Space*, ed. Hanawalt and Kobialka, p. x.

9   This point is highlighted by Mayke de Jong and Frans Theuws in 'Topographies of Power: Some Conclusions', *Topographies of Power in the Early Middle Ages*, ed. M. de Jong and F. Theuws, The Transformation of the Roman World 6 (Leiden, 2001), p. 541.

10   D. M. Hayes, *Body and Sacred Place in Medieval Europe, 1100–1389*, Studies in Medieval History and Culture 18 (New York and London, 2003), p. 17. See the discussion of Marsilia of St-Amand's letter in chapter two below.

11   R. Gilchrist, *Norwich Cathedral Close: the Evolution of the English Cathedral Landscape*, Studies in the History of Medieval Religion 26 (Woodbridge, 2005), p. 11

of cartularies spatially, beginning with relics and moving outwards.[12] That conceptions of geographical space were important in the Middle Ages is also a central feature in the work of Dick Harrison and Laurence Jean-Marie.[13] Barbara Rosenwein has considered political space from the perspective of the demarcation of protected and prohibited areas in her work on immunities and exemptions in the early Middle Ages.[14] We must remember, however, that space in the Middle Ages, in particular sacred space, cannot merely be defined as the physical world. Lefebvre attempts to distinguish between material space and abstract space by defining the latter as 'absolute space'. According to his analysis, medieval space was absolute space as it was characterised by links between the real and imagined: medieval minds were fixed not only on the physical space of the earth but also the world beyond which transcended the earth.[15] In this context, to try to separate and rigidly define concepts of 'space' and 'place' as some scholars have done, may be counterproductive.[16] It is possible that the people of central medieval Normandy did discriminate between spaces and places, but as Harrison has acknowledged, the sources do not allow us to recognise this: consequently 'sacred place' and 'sacred space' are used as synonyms here.[17]

Any analysis of the relationship between lay people and those professed to a religious vocation requires a consideration of gender. Although many of the communities studied here were founded for the benefit of one sex, this did not preclude members of the opposite sex living or working within them. Like space, gender is a concept that is socially constructed and historically specific. As such, gender is both personal to each individual and a structuring principle of society; it is also a reflection of how these two perceptions interact. To put it another way, gender 'is a result of the ways we live together and construct a universe around us and through this gender is an inconsistent but permanent part of history and life'.[18] There are no universal ideas of masculine and feminine, as each society invests these words with meanings specific to its own circumstances. The interpretation of evidence using gender as a category of

---

[12]   R. Berkhofer III, *Day of Reckoning: Power and Accountability in Medieval France* (Philadelphia, 2004), pp. 81–3.

[13]   D. Harrison, *Medieval Space: the Extent of Microspatial Attitudes in Western Europe during the Middle Ages*, Lund Studies in International History 34 (Lund, 1996), p. 17 and L. Jean-Marie, *Caen aux XIe et XIIe siècles: espace urbain, pouvoirs et société* (Condé-sur-Noireau, 2000).

[14]   B. Rosenwein, *Negotiating Space: Power, Restraint and Privileges of Immunity in Early Medieval Europe* (Manchester, 1999).

[15]   Lefebvre, *Production of Space*, pp. 234, 254–5.

[16]   See, for example, M. Camille, 'Signs of the City: Place, Power and Public Fantasy in Medieval Paris', *Medieval Practices of Space*, ed. Hanawalt and Kobialka, p. 9; Hayes, *Body and Sacred Place*, p. xix and p. 105 note 1; Y.-F. Tuan, *Space and Place: the Perspective of Experience* (Minneapolis, 1977), pp. 12, 199; and M. de Certeau, *The Practice of Everyday Life* (Berkeley, 1984), p. 117.

[17]   Harrison, *Medieval Space*, p. 17.

[18]   M. L. S. Sørensen, 'Is there a Feminist Contribution to Archaeology?', *Archaeological Review from Cambridge*, 7 (1998), p. 17 and *Gender Archaeology* (Cambridge, 2000), pp. 52–4.

analysis is, therefore, not only a way of exploring relationships between men and women, but also a means of elucidating difference between them as well as between people of the same biological sex in different contexts. This is especially relevant when considering professed monastics, as these people may have had different gendered identities during the course of their lives: for example, widows who became nuns after previous roles as wives and mothers, and men who entered the cloister after an active military life. Nursing sisters who served in leper houses or hospitals may have taken on board the attributes of the sick poor for whom they cared: sick and poor men and women were gendered differently from nobles as Sharon Farmer has recently shown for thirteenth- and fourteenth-century Paris.[19] It is conceivable therefore that we should not talk of 'men' or 'women' so much as individuals who were located in specific situations which may have a greater affect on their identity than biological sex.[20] When discussing the religious life in a gendered context, however, it is virtually impossible to remove fully the dichotomy between male and female, as the nature of the sources renders the debate as one of the relationship between the general (men) and the particular (women).[21]

In recent years, there has been a growing recognition of the need to include the study of masculinities within gender history in order to elucidate fully the relationship between men and women in the Middle Ages, but this work is still very much under-represented.[22] It is crucial to understand how men were gendered and the implications for their identity as, after all, men surely defined themselves in a manner that went beyond their identification as 'not women'.[23] Most important for this work is the consideration of clerical celibacy in relation to gender, both with regard to the priests themselves and their wives and concubines.[24] Questions arise as to how priests perceived their masculine

[19] S. Farmer, *Surviving Poverty in Medieval Paris: Gender, Ideology and the Daily Lives of the Poor* (Ithaca and London, 2002), p. 2.

[20] *Gender in Debate from the Early Middles Ages to the Renaissance*, ed. T. S. Fenster and C. A. Lees, The New Middle Ages (New York and Basingstoke, 2002), p. 1.

[21] *Gender in Debate*, ed. Fenster and Lees, p. 2.

[22] This point was highlighted by Pauline Stafford and Anneke Mulder-Bakker when they expressed regret that men and masculinity were not as well represented in a recent issue of *Gender and History* as women and femininity: *Gendering the Middle Ages*, ed. P. Stafford and A. B. Mulder-Bakker, special issue *Gender and History*, 12 (2000), (Oxford, 2001), p. 2. Recent collections of essays incorporating ideas about masculinity include *Becoming Male in the Middle Ages*, ed. J. J. Cohen and B. Wheeler, The New Middle Ages (New York and London, 1997); *Masculinity in Medieval Europe*, ed. D. Hadley, Women and Men in History (Harlow, 1999); *Medieval Masculinities Regarding Men in the Middle Ages*, ed. C. A. Lees, Medieval Cultures 7 (Minneapolis and London, 1994) and *Medieval Memories, Men, Women and the Past 700–1300*, ed. E. van Houts, Women and Men in History (Harlow, 2001).

[23] J. A. McNamara, 'The *Herrenfrage*: the Restructuring of the Gender System, 1050–1150', *Medieval Masculinities*, ed. Lees, p. 4.

[24] See, for example, D. Elliott, *Fallen Bodies: Pollution, Sexuality and Demonology in the Middle Ages*, The Middle Ages (Philadelphia, 1999), especially pp. 81–106 and R. N. Swanson, 'Angels Incarnate: Clergy and Masculinity from Gregorian Reform to the Reformation', *Masculinity in Medieval Europe*, ed. Hadley, pp. 160–77.

identity in a world that defined as manly those aspects of life that priests had theoretically renounced, particularly fatherhood and martial prowess.

The third theoretical category that underpins this book is that of the body.[25] The sacred spaces I consider here were most definitely inhabited by various bodies, both living and dead. As Henri Lefebvre states, spatial practice presupposes the uses of the body: it is after all bodies that inhabit space and help to give it meaning.[26] In a study of lay and religious within the context of sacred space, bodies were subject to various forms of social control in order to differentiate groups, for example through clothing regulations.[27] In the field of religious practice, Caroline Walker Bynum's work has highlighted the importance of control of the body through penitential food practices, especially with regard to non-contemplative religious women.[28] For women like Mary of Oignies and Catherine of Siena, extreme fasting coupled with devotion to the Eucharist was not only a means of controlling their own bodies, but also wider corporate bodies such as the family and the Church, and was thus a means of renegotiating their relationships with them.[29] Bynum's women are, however, exceptional. More important for this book is Hayes' work on Chartres cathedral.[30] Chartres housed the Holy Tunic allegedly worn by the Virgin Mary when she gave birth to Jesus. It was the only sacred relic that had touched both Mary and Jesus and so was doubly significant as both Jesus and, according to Catholic tradition, Mary were assumed into heaven, leaving very little of their bodies on earth.[31] Chartres became a major pilgrimage centre as the power of the Virgin manifested in the presence of the tunic was deemed to be particularly efficacious in the restoration of damaged and diseased bodies.[32] Here, one can see a strong connection between a particular place, Chartres cathedral, and both heavenly and earthly bodies. The pilgrimage to Chartres also became a model for similar exercises elsewhere, notably, as we shall see below, at St-Pierre-sur-Dives in Normandy.

---

[25] For an overview of the theory of the body, see *Framing Medieval Bodies*, ed. S. Kay and M. Rubin (Manchester, 1994), pp. 1–9 and *Bodies and Disciplines: Intersections of Literature and History in Fifteenth-Century England*, ed. B. A. Hanawalt and D. Wallace, Medieval Cultures 9 (Minneapolis and London, 1996), pp. ix–xii.

[26] Lefebvre, *Production of Space*, p. 40.

[27] Hanawalt, 'At the Margins of Women's Space', pp. 7–8. For medieval clothing more generally see F. Piponnier and P. Mane, *Dress in the Middle Ages* (New Haven and London, 2000).

[28] C. W. Bynum, *Holy Feast and Holy Fast: the Religious Significance of Food to Medieval Women* (Berkeley and London, 1997).

[29] Bynum, *Holy Feast and Holy Fast*, especially 'Food as control of circumstance', pp. 219–44.

[30] Hayes, *Body and Sacred Place*.

[31] Hayes, *Body and Sacred Place*, pp. 33–6. The exceptions to this are, of course, Christ's foreskin, strands of hair and drops of the Virgin's milk.

[32] Hayes, *Body and Sacred Place*, pp. 42–8.

The religious life in Normandy

By c.1050, the religious life in Normandy had been firmly re-established following the upheavals of the ninth and tenth centuries.[33] In 1087, around forty Benedictine houses were in existence, including at least seven houses of nuns.[34] The twelfth century saw the introduction of new orders to the duchy including the Savignacs (later Cistercian), Cistercians, Augustinians and Premonstratensians. These orders differed in character: the Savignacs and Cistercians sought out secluded locations and a greater separation from the secular world, whereas the Augustinian and Premonstratensian canons maintained greater contact with the laity through pastoral work, though the Premonstratensians lived according to a more austere rule akin to the Cistercians.[35] In addition, four houses of the order of Fontevraud were established between c.1120 and c.1190.[36] The twelfth century also saw an

[33] For the early history of the re-establishment of the religious life in Normandy see C. Potts, *Monastic Revival and Regional Identity in Early Normandy*, Studies in the History of Medieval Religion 11 (Woodbridge, 1997), pp. 13–35. An overview is also given in D. Bates, *Normandy Before 1066* (London, 1982), pp. 31–3, 218–25 and D. Knowles, *The Monastic Order in England*, 2nd edn (Cambridge, 1963), pp. 83–100. See also L. Musset, 'Les abbayes normandes au moyen âge: position de quelques problèmes', *Les abbayes de Normandie, actes du XIIIe congrès des sociétés historiques et archéologiques de Normandie*, ed. L. Andrieu et al. (Rouen, 1979), pp. 13–26 and S. N. Vaughn, *The Abbey of Bec and the Anglo-Norman State 1034–1136* (Woodbridge, 1981), pp. 4–7.

[34] P. Bouet, 'Le patronage architectural des ducs de Normandie', *L'architecture normande*, vol. 1, p. 351, fig. 1 and p. 359. The dates of foundation for various houses cannot be given accurately in most cases, hence the need for qualification. In addition to the seven nunneries founded by the ducal house and its supporters of Almenèches, Montivilliers, St-Amand in Rouen, St-Sauveur in Évreux, St-Désir in Lisieux, St-Léger-des-Préaux and La Trinité in Caen, John Walmsley lists an eighth house in his unpublished list of nunneries: La Caine, probably founded in 1066. I am grateful to Dr Walmsley for permission to use this list.

[35] For Savigny, see C. Auvry, *Histoire de la congregation de Savigny*, Société de l'histoire de Normandie, 3 vols (Rouen, 1896–98). For the Cistercians, see L. J. Lekai, *The Cistercians: Ideal and Reality* (Kent, Ohio, 1977); T. N. Kinder, *Cistercian Europe: Architecture of Contemplation*, Cistercian Studies 191 (Kalamazoo, 2002); D. H. Williams, *The Cistercians in the Early Middle Ages* (Leominster, 1998) and C. Berman, *The Cistercian Evolution: the Invention of a Religious Order in Twelfth-Century Europe* (Philadelphia, 2000). For the Augustinians, see *Des clercs au service de la réforme. Études et documents sur les chanoines réguliers de la province de Rouen*, ed. M. Arnoux, Bibliotheca Victorina 11 (Turnhout, 2000). For the Premonstratensians, see B. Ardura, *Abbayes, prieurés et monastères de l'ordre de Prémontre en France des origines à nos jours. Dictionnaire historique et bibliographique*, Collection Religions (Nancy, 1993).

[36] Acquigny, Chaise-Dieu-Du-Theil, Clairruissel and Fumechon. See J.-M. Bienvenu, 'L'ordre de Fontevraud et la Normandie au XII siècle', *AN*, 35 (1985), pp. 3–15 and J.-C. Martin, 'Un couvent des femmes, le prieuré de la Chaise-Dieu', *La femme en Normandie. Actes du XIXe congrès des sociétés historiques et archéologiques de Normandie* (Caen, 1986), pp. 287–96. These houses are not well documented in either the archaeological or documentary record and in the case of Acquigny, short-lived. Bouet

increase in the number of hospitals founded for the care of the sick poor and lepers.[37]

The religious life in Normandy was not just confined to single-sex houses of monks and nuns. The Fontevraudine priories housed sisters and brothers who owed obedience to a female superior and most hospitals and leper houses had both men and women as inmates, professed religious, and lay staff.[38] Some women also sought a vocation living in obedience in a male community, for example, the widows of Bec.[39] In addition to those individuals who took solemn vows, there also existed in Normandy chapters of canons within the cathedral churches of Rouen, Avranches, Bayeux, Coutances, Évreux, Lisieux and Sées, and in some collegiate churches throughout the regions, for example, Les Andelys.[40] Every parish, at least in theory, had its own priest to provide the day-to-day pastoral care in the localities. Each group of religious, whether living in community or as secular priests, had some contact with the laity and will be examined during the course of this book. Due to the survival of evidence, the bulk of the material concerns monasticism as practised by Benedictines, Augustinians and Cistercians; the lives of parish priests; and the experiences of brethren and patients in hospitals and leper houses.

There is no general synthesis on the history of Norman monasticism and little published work exists regarding the history of hospitals and leper houses. Research into hospitals in the region is still in its infancy and often we are still reliant on work done in the nineteenth century.[41] More recent work, some of which is not yet published, has concentrated on single houses, for example,

does not include them in his maps of the Norman foundations with the exception of Chaise-Dieu-Du-Theil which he lists as Benedictine.

[37] For the European context see J. Henderson, *Piety and Charity in Late Medieval Florence* (Oxford, 1994); M. Rubin, *Charity and Community in Medieval Cambridge*, Cambridge Studies in Medieval Life and Thought, 4th series 4 (Cambridge, 1987) and P. Richards, *The Medieval Leper and his Northern Heirs* (Cambridge, 1977). For France see F. Bériac, *Histoire des lépreux au moyen âge une société d'exclus* (Paris, 1988) and *Des lépreux aux cagots: recherches sur les sociétés marginales en Aquitaine médiévale* (Bordeaux, 1990); J. Mundy, 'Hospitals and Leprosaries in Twelfth- and Early Thirteenth-Century Toulouse', *Essays in Medieval Life and Thought*, ed. J. H. Mundy, R. W. Emery and B. N. Nelson (New York, 1965), pp. 181–205 and F.-O. Touati, *Maladie et société au moyen âge. La lèpre, les lépreux et les léproseries dans la province ecclésiastique de Sens jusqu'au milieu du XVI siècle*, Bibliothèque du Moyen Âge 11 (Paris and Brussels, 1998).

[38] For the organisation of the order of Fontevraud see P. S. Gold, *The Lady and the Virgin: Image, Attitudes and Experience in Twelfth-Century France* (Chicago and London, 1990), pp. 93–113 and B. Venarde, 'Praesidentes negotiis: Abbesses as Managers in Twelfth-Century France', *Portraits of Medieval and Renaissance Living: Essays in Memory of David Herlihy*, ed. S. K. Cohen and S. A. Epstein (Ann Arbor, 1996), pp. 189–205. For leper houses and hospitals see notes 41–44 below.

[39] The widows of Bec are discussed fully in chapter four.

[40] For the organisation of Norman cathedrals see Bates, *Normandy Before 1066*, pp. 213–16.

[41] Arnoux, p. 119. See also M. A. Léchaudé d'Anisy, 'Recherches sur les léproseries et maladreries dites vulgairement maladreries qui existaient en Normandie', *MSAN*, 17 (1847), pp. 149–212 and M. Renault, 'Nouvelles recherches sur les léproseries et maladreries en Normandie', *MSAN*, 28 (1871), pp. 106–48.

St-Gilles in Pont-Audemer and St-Nicolas in Évreux, or individual dioceses like Bayeux.[42] So far no major study encompassing the entirety of Normandy has been undertaken akin to Touati's work on the province of Sens.[43] In addition, archives survive only for a very small minority of houses and there has been little extensive archaeological investigation, though some excavations have been carried out in major urban centres, for example Bayeux and Sées, and comparative material exists from England.[44]

Although the issue of priestly celibacy and the attendant developments in canon law have been extensively studied in the context of the Church as a whole, little work has been published on the Norman experience.[45] The other major group under consideration here, namely parish priests and their wives and concubines, also suffers from a lack of published research. Little work has been done anywhere from the point of view of the wives and concubines.[46]

[42] S. C. Mesmin, 'The Leper House of Saint-Gilles de Pont-Audemer: an Edition of its Cartulary and an Examination of the Problem of Leprosy in the Twelfth and Thirteenth Centuries', 2 vols (Ph.D. thesis, University of Reading, 1978) parts of which are published as 'Waleran, Count of Meulan and the Leper House of St-Gilles de Pont-Audemer', AN, 32 (1982), pp. 3–19 and 'Du comté la commune: la léproserie de Saint-Gilles de Pont-Audemer', AN, 37 (1987), pp. 235–68; B. Tabuteau, 'Une léproserie normande au moyen âge. Le prieuré de Saint-Nicolas d'Évreux du XII–XVI siècles. Histoire et corpus des sources' (Ph.D. thesis, Université de Rouen, 1996) and D. Jeanne, 'Exclusion et charité: lépreux et léproseries dans le diocèse de Bayeux aux XII–XV siècles', 3 vols (mémoire de maîtrise, Université de Caen, 1990–92).
[43] F.-O. Touati, Maladie et société.
[44] F. Bériac, Histoire des lépreux au moyen âge, p. 152. For work in Normandy see D. Jeanne, 'Quelques problématiques pour la mort du lépreux? Sondages archéologiques du cimetière de Saint-Nicolas de la Chesnaie, Bayeux, AN, 47 (1997), pp. 69–90 and 'Chronique des fouilles médiévales', Archéologie médiévale, 24 (1994), pp. 465–7 for Sées. For England see R. Gilchrist, Contemplation and Action: the Other Monasticism, The Archaeology of Medieval Britain (London, 1995), pp. 8–61; M. Satchell, 'The Emergence of Leper Houses in Medieval England, 1100–1250' (D.Phil. thesis, University of Oxford, 1998). Carole Rawcliffe has recently published a survey of leprosy in England, Leprosy in Medieval England (Woodbridge, 2006), though its appearance was too late to respond to in this publication.
[45] For Normandy see K. A. Taglia, '"On Account of Scandal ...": Priests, their Children, and the Ecclesiastical Demand for Celibacy', Florilegium, 14 (1995–96), pp. 57–70 and A. L. Barstow, Married Priests and the Reforming Papacy: the Eleventh-Century Debates. Texts and Studies in Religion 12 (New York and Toronto, 1982). For the wider context see M. Boelens, Die Klerikerehe in der Gesetzgebung der Kirche unter besonderer Berücksichtigung der Strafe: eine rechtsgeschichtliche Untersuchung von den Anfängen der Kirche bis zum Jahre 1139 (Paderborn, 1968); C. N. L. Brooke, 'Gregorian Reform in Action: Clerical Marriage in England 1050–1200', Cambridge Historical Journal, 12 (1956), pp. 1–21 and M. Dortel-Claudot, 'Le prêtre et le mariage: evolution de la législation canonique dès origines aux XIIe siècle', L'année canonique, 17 (1973), pp. 319–44. For earlier periods see D. Elliott, Spiritual Marriage: Sexual Abstinence in Medieval Wedlock (Princeton, 1993), pp. 83–93 and S. Wemple, Women in Frankish Society: Marriage and the Cloister 500–900 (Philadelphia, 1985), pp. 127–36 and 142–8. For an overview see J. Brundage, Law, Sex and Christian Society in Medieval Europe (Chicago and London, 1987).
[46] See M. A. Kelleher, '"Like Man and Wife": Clerics' Concubines in the Diocese of Barcelona', JMH, 28 (2002), p. 350.

Sources

The ducal centre of Caen is still dominated today by the abbeys of La Trinité and St-Etienne.[47] Their churches respectively stand on the east and west sides of the town forming a visual reminder of ducal power and piety as well as the importance of Benedictine monasticism. The centrality of Benedictine monasticism is again reflected in the surviving architecture at Jumièges with its impressive and austere Romanesque west front.[48] In contrast, the thirteenth-century Cistercian foundation of Fontaine-Guérard can be read as an attempt by a community of women to validate their Cistercian credentials at a time when their place within the order was by no means certain. The architecture at this isolated and tranquil place is simple, yet elegant, reflecting Cistercian traditions of spirituality.[49] These examples are indicative of the diversity that existed within Norman religious communities: some were situated within or very close to major urban centres whilst others were literally in the wilderness.

Such magnificent architecture inspired contemporaries and continues to inspire historians nine hundred years later: it is crucial to our understanding of the use of space.[50] We are fortunate that despite the iconoclasm of the French Wars of Religion, the French Revolution and damage caused during the allied landings in 1944, medieval architecture from many monastic sites in Normandy survives.[51] Site visits allow us to understand the architecture of various religious communities in its landscape setting. When combined with published studies which examine iconography and building form, we can see how the influence of a patron and the needs of the community interacted. For example, the east range of the cloister at Le Trésor, a house for Cistercian nuns, contains star-shaped abaci in the Rayonnant fashion, the first such instance of this form of decoration in Normandy. Lindy Grant has argued that this embellishment illustrates a desire on the part of the Capetian patrons, Louis IX (1226–70) and Blanche of Castile (d.1252) to make the buildings appear less Norman and more French.[52] Some sites have, of course,

---

[47]   M. Baylé, *La Trinité de Caen. Sa place dans l'histoire de l'architecture et du décor roman*, Bibliothèque de la Société Française d'Archéologie 10 (Paris, 1979) and L. Grant, 'Caen: abbatiale Saint-Étienne' *L'architecture normande*, vol. 2, 156–8.
[48]   M. Baylé, 'Jumièges: abbatiale Notre-Dame', *L'architecture normande*, vol. 2, pp. 32–6. See also *Jumièges: congrès scientifique du XIIIᵉ centenaire*, 2 vols (Rouen, 1955).
[49]   M. Aubert, *L'architecture cistercienne en France*, 2 vols, 2nd edn (Paris, 1947), vol. 2, pp. 177, 197–200 and J. Fournée, *Abbaye de Fontaine-Guérard*, Abbayes et prieurés de Normandie 19 (Rouen, 1979)
[50]   Dr Margery Chibnall records that it was on a visit to the abbey church of St-Etienne in 1938 that she realised she must 'one day work on the men who could build like that', M. Chibnall, *The Debate on the Norman Conquest*, Issues in Historiography (Manchester, 1999), p. vii.
[51]   See P. A. Methuen, *Normandy Diary* (London, 1952) for damage caused to monuments by the 21st Army Group in 1944–5.
[52]   L. Grant, *Architecture and Society in Normandy, 1120–1270* (New Haven and London, 2005), pp. 144, 207–8.

completely disappeared from the architectural and archaeological record, such as Bondeville, and for their physical appearance we are reliant on surviving plans and drawings; though caution must be exercised in their interpretation as these depictions may be schematic.[53]

By far the most informative of the documentary sources are the visitation records of Archbishop Eudes of Rouen (1248–75) and Abbot Stephen of Lexington (1229–43), recording the visits each made to the monastic houses in their care.[54] Canon twelve of the Fourth Lateran Council in 1215 reiterated the duties of bishops and archbishops to ensure the correct practice of monasticism and supervise the secular clergy within their diocese.[55] As a result, these registers contain details relating to the incorrect observances of the monastic rules discovered after a process that involved questioning each monk or nun in the house.[56] Care is needed when reading visitation records which are necessarily one-sided documents: we do not have any indications of the responses of the monks, nuns and priests Eudes and Stephen visited. Information may not have been provided by individuals with the best of motives and some examples reveal community tensions. Although registers are lists of the 'wrongs' found during inspection visits and often contain salacious details, they do provide a great deal of material concerning the monastic buildings, the use of their space by monks, nuns and their personnel, and the monasteries' relations with the lay community.

Eudes's register records visits from 1248–69 to around twenty Augustinian communities; ninety-five Benedictine houses and five of the smaller, later Cistercian nunneries in the province of Rouen whose boundaries closely coincided with those of medieval Normandy. In addition he also inspected fourteen leper houses and hospitals and the parish clergy within the province. Eudes's register is one of the earliest and most comprehensive examples of archbishops' visitation records that survive from the Middle Ages and it has been published in the original Latin and also in an English translation.[57] Stephen of Lexington's

---

53   Bondeville was located on the outskirts of Rouen in what is now an industrial suburb of the city.

54   Eudes Rigaud was born around 1210 to a minor noble family in the Île-de-France. He entered the Franciscan order by 1236 before becoming archbishop of Rouen in 1248. He died on 2 July 1276. Adam Davis has recently published a detailed study of Eudes Rigaud's career, including his activities as head of the Franciscans at the University of Paris: A. Davis, *The Holy Bureaucrat: Eudes Rigaud and Religious Reform in Thirteenth-Century Normandy* (Ithaca and London, 2006). Although Davis discusses evidence from the register, he sets it in the context of Eudes's reform of the Norman Church, rather than a spatial one. Stephen came from a noble English family and entered the Cistercian abbey of Quarr on the Isle of Wight in 1221. He became abbot of Savigny in 1229 and his tenure in that post came to an end when he was appointed abbot of Clairvaux in 1243. Stephen died 1260.

55   *Decrees*, p. 241.

56   For a detailed discussion of the process of visitations and the problems associated with these sources, see C. R. Cheney, *Episcopal Visitation of Monasteries in the Thirteenth Century*, 2nd edn (Manchester, 1983) and N. Coulet, *Les visites pastorales*, Typologie des Sources du Moyen Âge Occidental 23 (Turnhout, 1977), pp. 28–33 and 51–9.

57   Bonnin and *Register*. The document is in the Bibliothèque nationale, Latin MS. 1245 and has been discussed most recently by Davis, *Holy Bureaucrat*. See also P. Johnson,

Registrum epistolarum contains information from the 1230s regarding the Savignac congregation of Cistercian houses, including houses of monks and nuns.[58] This register encompasses a much shorter time span than Eudes's, but still contains much valuable information about the use of space.[59]

For a fuller picture of monasticism, visitation records are best read in conjunction with the various monastic rules followed in the Middle Ages. Rules map out the expectation of spatial practice within monasteries, and thus contrast with the daily practices observed in Norman religious houses as seen by the abbot and bishop visitors. As well as the more general rules of St Benedict and St Augustine and some of the early constitutions of the Cistercian order, Lanfranc's constitutions for the cathedral priory of Christ Church Canterbury survive.[60] Although Christ Church was an English community, Lanfranc had spent many years in Normandy as prior of Bec and abbot of St-Etienne in Caen and thus probably imported some Norman practices to England which may be buried in his monastic guidance. Statutes also survive from two of the Norman hospitals and leper houses for our period – Lisieux and Vernon – with comparative material from the hôtel-Dieu at Pontoise.[61] As these institutions were not generally affiliated to a particular religious order nor followed a standard rule, the survival of several of these sources is very important for understanding their workings. The statutes not only tell us about the internal organisation of the hospitals and leper houses and the liturgical practices followed by the professed religious who staffed them, but also the restrictions placed on the inhabitants' movements in and around the surrounding area.

Information concerning the problems that professed religious encountered in their relationship with the laity, as well as about individual holy men and women, may be gleaned from the letter collections that survive. Most important are the episcopal collections of Lanfranc (1070–89) and Anselm (1093–1109), archbishops of Canterbury, both of whom were monks at the Norman abbey of Bec at one time, and Arnulf, bishop of Lisieux (d.1184).[62]

Equal in Monastic Profession: Religious Women in Medieval France, Women in Culture and Society (Chicago and London, 1991).

[58] *Registrum epistolarum*. I am grateful to Neil Wright and Laura Napran for help in translating passages from this source. Any errors remain my own.

[59] Fr Chrysogonus Waddell has briefly considered some of the visitation returns in an article on the daily life of Cistercian nuns, but otherwise the document seems to have been little studied from the point of view of religious women's experiences. C. Waddell, 'One Day in the Life of the Savigniac Nun: Jehanne de Deniscourt', *Cistercian Studies Quarterly*, 26 (1991), pp. 135–51. For monks and lay brothers, see Williams, *Cistercians in the Early Middle Ages* and B. Noell, 'Expectation and Unrest Among Cistercian Lay Brothers in the Twelfth and Thirteenth Centuries', *JMH* (2006), 253–74.

[60] *Rule*; *The Rule of St Augustine*, ed. T. J. van Bavel and trans. R. Canning, Cistercian Studies 138 (Kalamazoo, 1996); *Narrative and Legislative Texts from Early Cîteaux*, ed. C. Waddell, Studia et Documenta 9 (Cîteaux, 1999) and *Monastic Constitutions*.

[61] *Statuts*, pp. 203–5 for Lisieux, pp. 151–79 for Vernon and pp. 128–50 for Pontoise.

[62] *The Letters of Lanfranc Archbishop of Canterbury*, ed. and trans. H. Clover and M. Gibson, OMT (Oxford, 1979); for Anselm, see Schmitt and Fröhlich; for Arnulf, see Barlow and Schriber.

In common with other sources, the information conveyed by letters is limited in its scope. Letters more commonly elucidate the lives of the aristocracy and those who were literate in Latin to a high degree, or who at least had access to someone who could interpret for them.[63] Medieval letters were, on the whole, 'self-conscious, quasi-public literary documents' and were often written with 'an eye to future collection and publication'.[64] Although epistolary sources cannot be considered private in the same way personal letters are in modern society, letter collections do reveal interaction on an individual level and to some extent help us to get beyond the prescriptions of normative sources like monastic rules and conciliar legislation.

The surviving *miracula* from Normandy give us a valuable insight into how the laity might use sacred spaces, particularly non-nobles. These documents are reports of miracles which happened after the intercession of a saint. As the reports were collected by monks and clerics associated with a particular saint's shrine and were important in attracting pilgrims and wealth to churches, there is always a danger that the authors may have exaggerated the saint's efficacy.[65] Recent historians, however, have sought to underline the importance of *miracula* as a source for medieval life.[66] The miracles I consider come from various Norman abbeys and churches, including the abbeys St-Wandrille and St-Pierre-sur-Dives as well as the cathedral church of Coutances.[67] In addition, we have a remarkable and exciting source in the form of a letter written in 1107 by Marsilia, abbess of St-Amand in Rouen to the abbot of St-Amand-d'Elnone in Flanders, detailing a miracle that she wished to be added to the corpus of miracles effected by St Amand, which was kept in Flanders.[68] What is especially interesting in the context of this study, is the amount of detail devoted to the space where these miracles took place.

Lastly, chronicles also provide important evidence regarding the use of sacred space by laity and religious. Several chronicles, mostly written by monks, survive from Normandy which inevitably show the secular world

[63] E. Bos, 'Gender and Religious Guidance in the Twelfth Century' (Ph.D. thesis, University of Cambridge, 1999) p. 10.
[64] G. Constable, *Letters and Letter Collections*, Typologie des Sources du Moyen Âge Occidental 17 (Turnhout, 1976), p. 11.
[65] K. Quirk, 'Men, Women and Miracles in Normandy, 1050–1150', *Medieval Memories*, ed. van Houts, p. 53.
[66] For example, B. Ward, *Miracles and the Medieval Mind Theory Record and Event 1000–1215*, revised edn (Aldershot, 1987) and for France, P.-A. Sigal, *L'homme et le miracle dans la France médiévale (XIIe et XIIIe siècles)* (Paris, 1985). See also Quirk, 'Men, Women and Miracles in Normandy'.
[67] *Inventio et miracula sancti Vulfranni*, ed. Dom. J. Laporte, Mélanges publiés par la Société de l'Histoire de Normandie 14 (Rouen, 1938), pp. 9–87; *Miracula sancti Vulfranni episcopi*, AA SS, Martii, III, pp. 150–61 and *Miracula e. Constantiensis*. I am grateful to Elisabeth van Houts and Laura Napran for assistance in translating the miracle stories. All errors remain my own.
[68] *Historia mulieris suspensae ad vitam revocatae descripta a Marsilia abbatissa Rotomagensi ...*, AA SS, Febr., I, pp. 902–3, printed in Platelle and trans. in *Normans in Europe*, pp. 80–4.

from a monastic perspective.[69] Although chronicles purport to record what happened, they were not necessarily written by eyewitnesses to the events that they narrate. Stories were often recorded from a succession of oral witnesses or taken from other chronicles. The most important of the sources is Orderic Vitalis's monumental *Ecclesiastical History* (c.1110–41).[70] Orderic Vitalis was a monk of St-Évroul of mixed English and French parentage who provides a wealth of detail about the religious life, not only at his own monastery, but also in other communities in Normandy and England.[71] By virtue of his position as a cloistered monk, his information regarding the use of sacred space outside his own community is largely incidental to the main events of his narrative; however, when the needs of the laity and professed religious impinged directly on St-Évroul and those houses with which St-Évroul had connections, he makes due reference to them. There are other chronicles from Normandy, for example, *Gesta Normannorum ducum* of William of Jumièges (c.1050s–70)[72] with its interpolations by Orderic Vitalis (c.1110) and Robert of Torigni (c.1139), *Gesta Guillelmi* of William of Poitiers (c.1077),[73] and the chronicle of Robert of Torigni (c.1140–86),[74] but these are not as detailed or as intimate in their treatment of the religious life as Orderic's *Ecclesiastical History*.

The value of the Norman evidence and its importance in contributing to our knowledge of the use of sacred space by lay and religious groups lies not so much in its quantity, but in its variety and the exceptional quality of sources like Orderic's *Ecclesiastical History*, Archbishop Eudes Rigaud's register and

---

[69]   Chronicles as sources and the problems they pose to the historian are discussed in detail in E. van Houts, *Local and Regional Chronicles*, Typologie des Sources de Moyen Âge Occidental 74 (Turnhout, 1995), especially pp. 57–9. See also P. Skinner, *Women in Medieval Italian Society 500–1200*, Women and Men in History (Harlow, 2001), pp. 8–9. With regard to the Norman chronicles, specifically in the context of the Battle of Hastings, see Chibnall, *Debate on the Norman Conquest*, pp. 9–27.

[70]   OV, 6 vols.

[71]   Orderic Vitalis was born near Shrewsbury in 1075. He was sent to the monastery of St-Évroul as an oblate aged ten. He began the *Ecclesiastical History* at the command of his abbot, essentially as a history of the monastery, but it expanded to become a chronicle of Anglo-Norman society in the eleventh and early twelfth centuries up to 1141. Additional biographical information regarding Orderic can be found in the introduction to OV, vol. 1.

[72]   Little is known about William of Jumièges. He was probably born around the year 1000 as he was an eyewitness to some of the events of Duke Richard III's reign. He died after 1070: GND, vol. 1, pp. xii–xxiv.

[73]   William of Poitiers, *Gesta Guillelmi*, ed. and trans. R. C. H. Davis and M. Chibnall, OMT (Oxford, 1988). All that is known about William (d. after 1087) comes from the pages of Orderic Vitalis. William was a Norman by birth, from Préaux. He initially trained as a knight before pursuing a career in the Church and training at the schools in Poitiers. He served as chaplain to William the Conqueror and his sister became abbess of St-Léger: *Gesta Guillelmi*, pp. xv–xix and see also OV, vol. 2, pp. 78–9, 184–5 and 258–61.

[74]   Robert of Torigni, *Chronicon*, in *Chronicles*, ed. R. Howlett, RS 82, 4 vols (London, 1885), vol. 4. Robert was born at Torigini-sur-Vire. He entered the abbey of Bec in 1128 and was elected prior probably in 1149. In 1154 he became abbot of Mont-St-Michel and died in June 1186: GND, vol. 1, p. lxxvii.

the surviving architecture. This study adds substantially to existing scholar-ship in that it considers both men and women from a gendered perspective and focuses on the interaction of the two main groups in medieval society. An interdisciplinary and theoretically informed approach to the use of these sources enables us to examine the relationship between religious and the laity through the practices enacted in their quotidian spatial environments.

1

Display

Display of religious sentiment, wealth and affiliation, articulated through actions, symbols, architecture and ritual, was a very important part of medieval life, as anthropologically informed studies make clear.[1] Display manifests itself in several ways in relation to the construction of space as well as its use and the proper behaviour expected within it. It is also connected to symbolism and what these symbols meant to different groups of people and in different circumstances. In other words, display demonstrates what an individual or community thinks is important and what it wants others to see. Topography and external architecture were essential in showing links to a monastic order or the influence of secular founders. In terms of the religious life and the use of space, we begin to see the ways in which members of a religious order protected their vocation by clearly demarcating an area as dedicated to God, whilst discharging their duties to the laity. Similarly, leper houses and hospitals were concerned with the correct locations for their houses and these concerns go beyond the merely functional in terms of water supply and other necessities. Within communities, display was an essential part of community life through practices laid down in the monastic rule, notably chapter and aspects of the liturgy, for example, processions both within the church and around the monastic precinct. Processions were also important in parish and cathedral life. Correct dress was also a crucial factor in display, whether of the monastic vocation, priesthood or leper. Renunciation of this dress entailed the breaking of vows and ultimately apostasy. It is clear from the surviving evidence that religious display was important to the laity, monastics and parish clergy and that it was essential in building networks and relationships between these groups.

---

[1] For example, J. H. Arnold, *Belief and Unbelief in Medieval Europe* (London, 2005) especially pp. 15–20; T. Asad, 'On Ritual and Discipline in Medieval Christian Monasticism', *Economy and Society*, 16 (1987), pp. 159–203; C. W. Bynum, *Fragmentation and Redemption: Essays in Gender and the Human Body in Medieval Religion* (New York, 1991) which use and critique the work of, among others, Victor Turner and Clifford Geertz.

Topography

Religious houses, hospitals and leper houses were located in a variety of land-scapes and it is hard to generalise as to set locations for the various different orders.[2] Normandy is no exception; both male and female monastic houses were found in towns, on the edges of towns, or in primarily rural locations. For some of the Merovingian and Carolingian foundations, their pre-Norman history may have played a significant factor in their topographical setting, for example, Jumièges in the Seine valley.[3] This house had Merovingian antecedents and its location directly referred back to earlier traditions of monasticism. The Cistercians, as it is well known, preferred more isolated settings for their houses as is discussed below; however, L'abbaye Blanche, which was originally a Savignac house, was located just outside the town of Mortain.[4] The nature of an order's vocation also affected the setting of a community. Many Augustinian houses with their emphasis on parochial ministry were located close to towns, for example St-Lô, as were some hospitals, such as La Madeleine, in Rouen, the statutes of which were loosely based on the Augustinian rule.[5] In contrast, leper houses were generally situated outside settlements. With regard to monastic houses, instead of seeking to show connections between communities of particular orders, we shall instead consider several individual houses and what we may learn from them. The lack of specific information for individual hospitals and leper houses means that these will be discussed more generally.

Most of the monastic houses associated with urban centres were Benedictine and of an earlier foundation date. Communities situated within the original town walls were rare, with St-Amand in Rouen being a notable exception, located in the north-east angle of the original city boundary close to the *porte du Robec* with the city wall forming the east wall of the nunnery cloister.[6] Interestingly, this nunnery was a parallel foundation with La-Trinité-du-Mont (later Mont-Ste-Catherine), a male abbey, which was founded outside the walls of the city.[7] The other major community in Rouen that was also a Merovingian foundation, St-Ouen, was located just outside the original Gallo-Roman enclosure, though by the thirteenth century it was included within the new town walls built after the loss of Normandy in 1204 by King John

---

[2] See T. Pestell, *Landscapes of Monastic Foundation: the Establishment of Religious Houses in East Anglia, c.650–1200*, Anglo-Saxon Studies 5 (Woodbridge, 2004), pp. 192–217.
[3] At the first mention to each monastic house, leper house or hospital, reference is made to the appropriate appendix where information regarding the location, order and founder of the house may be found along with sources used in this book. Appendix A, no. 42.
[4] Appendix B, no. 15 and appendix A, no. 92.
[5] Appendix A, no. 81 and appendix C, no. 23.
[6] Appendix B, no. 18.
[7] Appendix A, no. 68.

(1199–1216).[8] Another community of nuns, St-Sauveur in Évreux, was also originally founded within the town walls – its original location was on the *rue St Nicolas* about twenty metres from the junction with the *rue de la Petite-Cité*. After the abbey's destruction by fire in 1194, during Philip Augustus's capture of the town, the nunnery was rebuilt outside the walls on land given by the cathedral near a branch of the river Iton.[9] Despite these urban examples, it was more common to find monastic communities situated outside town walls in more suburban locations. A certain degree of separation from the world was required in the practice of monasticism, so even houses with urban character-istics would be situated away from the centre of the settlement, for example St-Martin-de-Sées.[10]

It would be wrong to assume that just because some urban monastic houses were situated on the edge of towns, they were considered unimportant. If St-Amand in Rouen could be refounded in a location that had great significance for the community drawn from its Merovingian past, then the topographical setting of communities like St-Etienne and La Trinité in Caen was also deliberately planned to reflect the founders' intentions.[11] Duke William and his duchess, Matilda, were responsible for theses two Benedictine foundations. Caen was a relatively new urban centre and one that William hoped would rival the established principal city in Normandy of Rouen. The nunnery is situated at the summit of a hill over the confluence of the rivers Orne and Odon, just to the east of the city walls. St-Etienne was built on the opposite side of the town, to the west of the walls; and the castle, a symbol of temporal ducal power, was roughly equidistant between the two religious houses, though closer to the nunnery on higher ground. For travellers approaching from either direction, the first building of significance they would see would be a grand Benedictine abbey standing as a testament to the reciprocal support of the ducal house and the Church. Piety was undoubtedly a factor in the foundation of these communities as the gifts of both William and Matilda attest, but the desire to encourage urban growth creating what Laurence Jean-Marie has termed 'poles of attraction' was strong. The foundation of abbeys within two distinct neighbourhoods spurred on the economic development within them and thus contributed to the wealth of the city and the prestige of the ducal house.[12] The suburbs in which the two abbeys were situated became known in the course of the twelfth century as the *bourg l'abbé* and the *bourg l'abbesse*, which along with a third area, the *bourg le roi* gives a rough indication of where revenues generated in these areas went. A charter of William in favour of St-Etienne, dated to between 1081 and 1082, in which he granted the same privileges to St-Etienne as his own bourg illustrates this.[13] Other important

---

8   F. Neveux, 'L'urbanisme au moyen âge dans quelques villes de Normandie', *L'architecture normande*, vol. 1, p. 272, fig. 1. Appendix A, no. 70.

9   Appendix B, no. 10.

10   Appendix A, no. 93; Neveux, 'L'urbanisme au moyen âge dans quelques villes de Normandie', p. 280, fig. 6.

11   Appendix A, no. 21 and appendix B, no. 5.

12   Jean-Marie, *Caen aux XIe et XIIe siècles*, pp. 186–8.

13   *Regesta regum*, no. 50.

eleventh-century foundations, such as the nunnery of Montivilliers, also acted as magnets for urban growth through its involvement in local industries like cloth and leather.[14] In addition Montivilliers had extensive rights of taxation and tolls in the port of Harfleur, granted by Duke Robert the Magnificent, and situated close to the community and so played an important part in local commercial development.[15]

Monastic communities were also found in more isolated and rural settings. The majority of Norman nunneries were situated in a predominantly rural environment, including all the houses affiliated to Fontevraud – Acquigny, Chaise-Dieu-du-Theil, Clairruissel and Fumechon and most of the Cistercian houses.[16] Several Premonstratensian houses began life as small groups of hermits living in forests or other wilderness settings, before being brought together in more formal communities, for example, Belle-Étoile, Blancheland and L'Île-Dieu.[17] Many of the Benedictine communities for both men and women were also located in the countryside; however, the choice of site was vitally important as the *Life of Herluin* makes plain. If a house was initially built in the wrong location, then problems with water supply, health and construction of buildings would follow. After Herluin had initially set up his community at Bonneville, he received a vision instructing him to reject the original site 'which was totally lacking in suitable advantages' and move to Bec.[18] Gilbert Crispin described Bec as being situated 'in the woodland of Brionne, within a deep valley hemmed in on this side and that by forested hills. There were only three houses ... and very little ground that was habitable', though he also noted that the site provided 'every due convenience for people's use'.[19] The importance of location is underlined by the lengths Herluin underwent to persuade his neighbours to sell or donate land to the abbey in order that it would have sufficient space and resources to grow and develop.[20] The abbey possibly moved to a third site during Lanfranc's tenure as prior though this relocation probably owed a great deal to the increase in the size of the community following Lanfranc's arrival as Gilbert notes that

---

14 Appendix B, no. 14.
15 *Regesta regum*, no. 212. See also E. Hall and J. Sweeney, 'The *Licentia de Nam* of the Abbess of Montivilliers and the Origins of the Port of Harfleur', *Bulletin of the Institute of Historical Research*, 52 (1979), p. 5. Hall and Sweeney point out that Harfleur was a significant port for the wine trade and whaling from the early eleventh century.
16 Appendix B, nos 1, 7, 8, 12. The other rural nunneries were Almenèches, Bival, Bondeville, La Caine, Cordillon, Fontaine-Guérard, Moutons, St-Aubin, St-Léger-des-Préaux, St-Michel-du-Bosc, St-Saëns, Le Trésor, Villarceaux, Villers-Canivet and Vignats: see appendix B.
17 Appendix A, nos 13, 16, 40. See also Mondaye: appendix A, no. 51.
18 Appendix A, no. 12; Gilbert Crispin, *Vita Herluini* in *The Works of Gilbert Crispin, Abbot of Westminster*, ed. A. Sapir Abulafia and G. R. Evans, Auctores Britannici Medii Aevi 8 (London, 1986), p. 193 and trans. S. N. Vaughn, 'The Life of Lord Herluin, Abbot of Bec by Gilbert Crispin', Vaughn, *Abbey of Bec and the Anglo-Norman State*, p. 73. Other Norman houses moved site, including the Cistercian abbey of Val-Richer: appendix A, no. 101.
19 Gilbert Crispin, *Vita Herluini*, p. 193 and trans. Vaughn, 'Life of Herluin', p. 73.
20 Gilbert Crispin, *Vita Herluini*, p. 194 and trans. Vaughn, 'Life of Herluin', p. 74.

'the size of the dwelling could not contain the multitude of brothers who were united there and ... the place was hazardous to the health of the inmates'.[21] The case of the abbey of Bec demonstrates a fine line between the need for an isolated and suitably poor setting in order to follow the style of monasticism Herluin wished and too much asceticism being detrimental to the health and survival of an incipient community.

Above all, it is the Cistercian order that is associated with isolated locations. In contrast to the large Benedictine abbeys associated with urban centres, the thirteenth-century Cistercian foundation of Fontaine-Guérard is found in the peace and tranquillity of the Andelle valley, built against a wooded hillside.[22] This house was founded in the late twelfth century at a time when the order was at best ambivalent to the reception of women. The nuns may have sought ways in which to strengthen their Cistercian credentials to aid inclusion in the order through the adoption of an isolated setting and simple, but elegant architecture. The situation of other Cistercian houses, for example Coyroux, supports this contention.[23] This is not to say that Cistercian houses lacked powerful patrons or had little effect on the landscapes they inhabited. Fontaine-Guérard may be architecturally understated, but in terms of its monastic affiliation, it is all the more effective for it. Certainly, by 1216, the Cistercians had stipulated that a nunnery must be at least six leagues from a male abbey and ten from another nunnery, indicating that new foundations should seek isolated locations.[24] Cistercian monks were certainly aware of the importance of creating the right impression as Lindy Grant has demonstrated for Bonport, founded by King Richard I (1189–99). This abbey is sited in a slight bow beside the Seine and the architecture is so designed that anyone approaching from the east, for example, from Richard's political rival, France, would see the chevet of the church and then sail round the cloister to the north, a clear display of Angevin patronage within a traditional Cistercian landscape setting.[25]

As we have seen with Bec, there was a fine line between monastic ideals of poverty and survival in the foundation of new sites influenced by reform ideals. Many scholars have commented on the significance of isolated sites and ascetic locations, particularly in relation to nuns, though similar concerns affected the choice of sites for male houses as we have noted above. In an English context, Gilchrist suggests that these settings meant that the women concerned were

[21] Gilbert Crispin, *Vita Herluini*, p. 199 and trans. Vaughn, 'Life of Herluin', p. 77.
[22] Appendix B, no. 11.
[23] Coyroux was founded by Stephen of Obazine in 1142 near the male house from which he took his name, in an 'unattractive, naturally isolated wilderness' where the nuns were made totally dependent on the male community: B. Barrière, 'The Cistercian Convent of Coyroux in the Twelfth and Thirteenth Centuries', *Gesta*, 31 (1992), p. 76
[24] According to D. H. Williams, 'Cistercian Nunneries in Medieval Wales', *Cîteaux*, 26 (1975), p. 155, this was laid down by the general chapter, but I have been unable to locate it in the *Statuta*. Williams gives no source reference in his notes.
[25] Appendix A, no. 17. Grant, *Architecture and Society*, p. 115.

seeking an eremitic vocation.[26] In contrast, for France, Johnson has argued that such locations could have a very negative affect on the nuns' vocations as a 'bleak and isolated institutional setting was particularly destructive for nuns' religious resolve to adhere to their vows of chastity'.[27] Leaving aside the matter of chastity for the time being, we must be wary of making too broad a generalisation based on incomplete evidence regarding the motivation of both monks, nuns, and the founders of their communities in choosing particular locations. Gilchrist notes that whereas male houses had the resources and opportunity to reshape the landscape, communities of women were often unable to do this.[28] Just as there were poor nunneries, there were also poor monasteries – as Gilchrist notes, English nunneries were built on a scale comparable to the smaller Augustinian male houses – and the choice of landscape was equally as important to such men as it may have been to women.[29] Herluin worked tirelessly to ensure his community had the necessary means to survive at his chosen site, to the extent that fundraising forced him to spend a great deal of time outside the cloister.[30]

Hospitals and leper houses differed slightly in their topographical location. Biblical precepts required that lepers should dwell outside the camp, but the communities set up for their care were not hidden away.[31] Although they were often located outside settlement walls, they were still close to main lines of communication: for example, Ste-Madeleine in St-Lô was located on the old Roman road between Coutances and Bayeux.[32] The hospital of St-Jean Baptiste in Falaise was located at the gates to the town.[33] Leper houses at Bayeux, Isigny-sur-Mer, Mandeville, Putot-en-Bessin and Tour-en-Bessin could all be found on the Carentan to Lisieux road.[34] In addition, many houses, although outside the walls, were still very close to towns or within suburbs, for example, the leper house of Beaulieu, the hospital of St-Thomas and the hôtel-Dieu in Caen.[35] The leper houses at Avranches, Bayeux and Lisieux were similarly located close to the town walls.[36] Both Salle-aux-Puelles and Mont-aux-Malades at Rouen were located in the suburbs.[37] In addition to their

---

26 Gilchrist, *Gender and Material Culture*, p. 91.
27 Johnson, *Equal in Monastic Profession*, p. 128. The problems presented by the monastic vow of chastity are discussed below.
28 Gilchrist, *Gender and Material Culture*, p. 91.
29 Gilchrist, *Gender and Material Culture*, p. 45.
30 Milo Crispin, *Vita beati Lanfranci*, PL, vol. 150, col. 31 and trans. S. Vaughn, 'The Life of Lanfranc', Vaughn, *Abbey of Bec and the Anglo-Norman State*, p. 89.
31 Leviticus, 13:36 'He shall live alone and his dwelling shall be outside the camp' (New Revised Standard Version, Oxford, 1995).
32 Appendix C, no. 26; D. Jeanne, 'Les lépreux et les léproseries en Normandie moyenne et occidentale au moyen âge orientations des recherches', *Lèpre et lépreux en Normandie, Cahiers Léopold Delisle*, 46 (1997), p. 33.
33 Appendix C, no. 11.
34 Appendix C, nos 14, 16, 22, 27; Jeanne, 'Les lépreux et les léproseries en Normandie', p. 33.
35 Appendix C, nos 7, 8, 6.
36 Appendix C, nos 1, 2, 15.
37 Appendix C, nos 25, 24.

prominence in terms of proximity to settlements, many were located near bridges and rivers: St-Blaise and Ste-Clair at Lisieux was near the Touques and the hôtel-Dieu at Caen was on the banks of the Orne.[38] In this respect, the geographical location of leper houses and some hospitals mirrors the situation in England where Roberta Gilchrist has argued they 'were situated in order to frame medieval towns', as in Norwich, York and London.[39]

It seems, then, as if there was a contradiction between the desire to separate lepers in accordance with biblical precepts and the prominent landscape setting of leper houses. The conventional historiographical consensus is that leper houses were situated on the margins of settlements and downwind to minimise contagion.[40] This view has been challenged recently by François-Olivier Touati and Max Satchell on the grounds that it is predicated on a modern understanding of the transmission of disease as an external process and that it is thus anachronistic.[41] In the Middle Ages, disease was seen as the result of an internal imbalance of the four humours, so external factors like diet or contact with the sick and thus the siting of leper houses and hospitals in this respect were less important.[42] There were certainly measures put in place, articulated through surviving statutes, that sought to minimise contact between the sick and the healthy. Therefore, medieval notions of external, or indeed spiritual, contagion cannot be discounted completely. The topographical setting of leper houses and hospitals is explained by several other factors. Gilchrist argues that the liminality of leper houses and hospitals was used to control and observe groups that were stigmatised by medieval society, like the poor, the aged and the infirm. Thus in her argument the siting of hospitals can be explained by a desire to display stigmatised bodies.[43] Another argument, put forward by Peyroux, holds that the prominent location of many of these establishments near towns facilitated the collection of alms.[44] Hospitals and leper houses situated on major lines of communication were a very visible manifestation of charity. Not only could founders display their munificence to a wide audience, the visibility of these institutions also pricked the consciences

[38]   *Statuts*, p. 203.
[39]   R. Gilchrist, 'Medieval Bodies in the Material World: Gender Stigma and the Body', *Framing Medieval Bodies*, ed. Kay and Rubin, p. 47.
[40]   For example, Bériac, *Des lépreux aux cagots*, and *Histoire des lépreux au moyen âge*; R. I. Moore, *The Formation of a Persecuting Society: Power and Deviance in Western Europe* (Oxford, 1987), pp. 45–60 and C. Peyroux, 'The Leper's Kiss', *Monks and Nuns, Saints and Outcasts: Religion in Medieval Society*, ed. S. Farmer and B. H. Rosenwein (Ithaca and London, 2000), pp. 172–88.
[41]   Touati, *Maladie et société au moyen âge*; Satchell, 'Emergence of Leper Houses'. See also N. Bériou and F.-O. Touati, *Voluntate dei leprosus: les lépreux entre conversion et exclusion aux XIIe et XIIIe siècles*, Testi, Studi, Strumenti 4 (Spoleto, 1991), especially pp. 6–19. See also Rawcliffe, *Leprosy in Medieval England*, pp. 274–84.
[42]   Touati, *Maladie et société*, pp. 139–51 and Satchell, 'Emergence of Leper Houses', pp. 224 and 229–30.
[43]   Gilchrist, 'Medieval Bodies in the Material World', p. 49 and also 'Christian Bodies and Souls: the Archaeology of Life and Death in Later Medieval Hospitals', ed. S. Bassett, *Death in Towns: Urban Response to the Dying and the Dead, 100–1600* (London, and New York, 1992), p. 115.
[44]   Peyroux, 'Leper's Kiss', p. 175.

of passers-by.[45] In return, the lepers and the sick already suffering on earth for their sins prayed for their benefactors. Carole Rawcliffe has observed that although there were practical reasons for locating leper houses near fords and bridges, for example, the ease of drainage and the provision of water, 'the analogy with the soul's passage from earth to heaven was unmistakable'.[46] The sick, then, existed on multiple thresholds. Lepers, due to the nature of their illness, occupied an ambivalent space somewhere between life and death and thus between this world and the next. In addition, they were a very visible manifestation of the divide between the included (the healthy) and the excluded (the sick) in medieval society.

The landscape settings of monastic houses, hospitals and leper houses were not accidental. In common with architecture and the liturgical practices, topography had meanings that displayed various concepts to a wider audience. These concepts were not mutually exclusive and a community could be a symbol of many different aims. Aside from general considerations of piety, founders and communities could make use of the landscape in order to demonstrate prestige, wealth and affiliation with a particular order. Urban communities, like the abbeys in Caen and Montivilliers, demonstrated the power of the ducal house, whilst Fontaine-Guérard illustrated the Cistercian ideals of solitude and simplicity. Leper houses and hospitals, situated in the main at thresholds and in marginal locations reflected the marginal place of those cared for within their walls. Whatever the affiliation of vocation of a community, the number of religious houses within the Norman landscape was a visible reminder of the presence of God.

Architecture

Architecture was certainly the most visible way a religious community physically displayed a collective identity to the wider world. Monasteries followed a similar plan as we shall discuss below and their buildings, were very much part of the landscape.[47] I do not propose to discuss the development of Romanesque and Gothic architecture here, as it has been discussed fully elsewhere.[48] Instead, I shall consider some specific examples in order to demonstrate the different ideas and concepts that the architecture of religious communities might display to a wider community, for example, significant events in a

---

[45]   Gilchrist, 'Medieval Bodies in the Material World', p. 49.

[46]   C. Rawcliffe, 'Learning to Love the Leper: Aspects of Institutional Charity in Anglo-Norman England', ANS, 23 (2001), p. 241. The hospital of St John at Canterbury was located near the River Stour, which flushed the latrines. See also the discussion on St Nicholas Harbledown below and Rawcliffe, Leprosy in Medieval England, pp. 307–15.

[47]   See chapter three below and the section on topography above.

[48]   See for example, Grant, Architecture and Society; M. Baylé, 'L'architecture romane en Normandie', L'architecture normande, vol. 1, pp. 13–35 and A. Erlande-Brandernburg, 'L'architecture gothique en Normandie', L'architecture normande, vol. 1, pp. 127–36.

community's history; connections with secular powers; the presence of relics; penance and affiliation with a particular religious order.

We have already seen in the section on topography how the early history of a monastic house could affect its topographical setting. For houses refounded after the Viking raids, architecture was influenced in a similar manner, as can be seen at Jumièges. The abbey of Jumièges was one of the earliest monasteries in the duchy of Normandy and was originally founded in the seventh century by St Philibert assisted by Queen Bathilde, the wife of Clovis II.[49] After the site was abandoned in 885, following the monastery's destruction by the Vikings in 841, the community was re-established by William Longsword. He brought monks from St-Cyprien in Poitiers to Normandy who repaired the church of St-Pierre.[50] The monastery grew in importance following the arrival in 1017 of Abbot Thierry who was a disciple of William of Volpiano, the leading figure of the revival of Benedictine monasticism in Normandy.[51] Although architecture in the form of parts of the church of St-Pierre dates from the early ninth century, the increase in the number of monks meant the community had outgrown this small church. The abbatial church of Notre-Dame was begun in the mid-eleventh century under Abbot Robert Champart (c.1037–45), replacing the remains of earlier structures.[52] This new church is interesting as it simultaneously looks back towards the earlier history of the abbey whilst including new features that were just beginning to make an appearance in the region. The two towers at the west end flank a Carolingian style west-work with a gallery above the porch. These towers are possibly restorations of the two structures ransomed by a priest called Clement after Rodulf Torta destroyed the reconstructed community after the death of William Longsword.[53] In contrast, the church has an early example of an ambulatory in Normandy. It is possible that the archaic elements were copied from the Carolingian church Notre-Dame replaced. The monks did not want to lose sight of their history completely. By mixing earlier styles with new designs their link with the past was maintained while reflecting the wealth and status of the re-established and reformed community.[54] The element of architectural display firmly located Jumièges within a long-standing tradition of European Benedictine monasticism as well as reflecting the vibrancy of the Church in ducal Normandy.

[49]   J. Le Maho, *Jumièges Abbey* (Paris, 2001), p. 4. See also *GND*, vol. 1, pp. 18–19.

[50]   *GND*, vol. 1, pp. 84–7.

[51]   Rodulfus Glaber, *Vita domni Willelmi abbatis* in *Historiarum Libri quinque et Vita domni Willelmi abbatis*, ed. N. Bulst and trans. J. France and P. Reynolds, OMT (Oxford, 1989), pp. 270–3. See also V. Gazeau, 'Guillaume de Volpiano et le monachisme normand', *Normandie vers l'an mil*, ed. F. de Beaurepaire and J.-P. Chaline (Rouen, 2000), pp. 132–6.

[52]   The church of Notre-Dame was dedicated in 1067 by Archbishop Maurillius of Rouen aided by Bishops John of Avranches, Geoffrey of Coutances, Hugh of Lisieux and Baldwin of Évreux: *GND*, vol. 2, pp. 172–3. Robert later became bishop of London and then archbishop of Canterbury in c.1050.

[53]   *GND*, vol. 1, pp. 108–11. Rodulf Torta was King Louis IV's governor in Normandy after the death of William Longsword.

[54]   Grant, *Architecture and Society*, pp. 52–4.

Fécamp was similar to Jumièges in some respects: it too was originally founded in the seventh century, destroyed by the Vikings and restored by William Longsword.[55] The ducal refoundation, originally a secular college, was the first monastic community to be reformed by William of Volpiano who became its abbot. Fécamp also differed in one other crucial respect, as the secular college was refounded in the grounds of the ducal palace. The early history of the reformed abbey was closely bound up with the ducal house and both the early dukes Richard I and Richard II were buried there.[56] Nothing, however, survives of this early church and the structures that do remain are illustrative of different aspects of display: the importance of relics and influence of a powerful superior. With the foundation of William the Conqueror and Matilda's abbeys in Caen and the conquest of England, ducal interest in Fécamp declined. Instead of focusing on the church as a ducal mausoleum, the monks sought to develop their abbey as a pilgrimage centre for the relic of the Holy Blood, which they claimed to have. Under Abbot William of Rots (1082–1108), the church was rebuilt in Romanesque fashion containing an ambulatory with radiating chapels and a nave of 'unusually long' dimensions.[57] According to the Fécamp miracula the rebuilding was necessary due to the number of pilgrims wanting to visit.[58] Space was needed to accommodate a large number of lay people within a monastic church without disturbing the monastic routine. A long nave allowed more people to attend mass and provide space in which to lay out the sick.[59] The ambulatory enabled pilgrims to circulate freely around the east end of the church without them having to walk through the monk's choir, a practice that Archbishop Eudes Rigaud later condemned at some Norman houses.[60] This early church was largely destroyed by fire in 1168. The subsequent grand rebuilding owed much to the abbot, Henry de Sully, who was a nephew of the brothers King Stephen and Henry of Blois, bishop of Winchester. Abbot Henry had come to terms with the Angevin King Henry II's position as duke of Normandy and his church was designed both as a pilgrimage centre and as a reflection of Fécamp's links with the ducal house. These links had been reinforced in 1162 when Henry II gathered up the remains of his predecessors Richard I and Richard II and placed them in an elaborate stone tomb carved with episodes from the life of Christ.[61] Henry II needed to cement his position as duke of Normandy and

---

55   Appendix A, no. 33.
56   This is discussed further in chapter four.
57   Grant, Architecture and Society, pp. 75–6.
58   A. Sauvage, 'Des miracles advenus en l'église de Fécamp', Mélanges de la Société de l'histoire de Normandie, 2e série 2 (Rouen, 1893), p. 33.
59   This practice is discussed in more detail in chapter two.
60   See chapter two.
61   Robert of Torigny, Chronicon, pp. 212–13 and Wace, Roman de Rou, trans. G. Burgess with the text of A. J. Holden and notes by G. Burgess and E. van Houts (St Helier, Jersey, 2002), pp. 152–3, lines 2241–6. For a description of the sarcophagus and discussion of the dating, see S. E. Jones 'The Twelfth-Century Reliefs from Fécamp: New Evidence for their Dating and Original Purpose', Journal of the British Archaeological Association, 138 (1985), pp. 79–88. This episode is recounted in a vernacular poem written in the first third of the thirteenth century.

through the reverent reburial of the previous dukes behind the high altar, he boosted Fécamp's place as one of the leading ducal monastic houses.[62] Further impetus to the rebuilding, which included elements of Abbot Suger's design of St-Denis, was given by the rediscovery of the Holy Blood, but it is interesting to note that the monks retained some of the original Romanesque features, notably in retention of the ambulatory, radiating chapels and part of the choir.[63] The influence of their superior renewed links with the ducal house and the presence of a relic added to the community's prestige. This prestige possibly contributed to the community's desire to incorporate some of the architectural innovations from Paris, but, like Jumièges, the monks also needed to maintain links with their past.

The need to atone for sin led to building or rebuilding programmes within the Norman Church. Tradition has it that Duke William and Duchess Matilda founded their abbeys in Caen in part as penance for a consanguineous marriage.[64] Henry II famously had to do penance following the murder of Thomas Becket in 1170. Although he undertook public penance in Canterbury as part of his reconciliation with the Church, aspects of his ecclesiastical patronage also reflected his need for atonement. One of Henry's acts was the building of a new chapel and priory for the leper house at Mont-aux-Malades in Rouen. This house had been founded for Augustinian canons and took in lepers from the parishes in Rouen. The chapel was originally dedicated to St-Jacques, but following the murder of Thomas, Henry II built a new priory and church on the site dedicated to the martyred archbishop. Unfortunately, the chapel has been much altered since the late twelfth century, but it was a fairly simple design with a flat east end, suitable for a community of lepers that did not anticipate an influx of lay people.[65] The reason for the building of the church was remembered through its dedication to the victim of a vicious crime and the king's penance would live on in the collective memory of the community. Such a public demonstration of remorse also reinforced the fact that not even the most powerful of rulers could evade the rules of the Church. The king, like his subjects, was subject to the law of God and as such must atone for his misdeeds. Indeed it may be argued that because the king was so powerful, the penance undertaken must be commensurately greater.

So far we have considered male houses and a leper house. Female monastic communities also used architectural display to reinforce congregational links and connections to founders. The position of women in the Cistercian order was an ambiguous one and has exercised scholars for many years. Norman Cistercian nunneries were in a different position to much of the rest of France as the region had its own reformed order, that of Savigny founded by Vitalis.[66] The Savignac order had no qualms about accepting women. L'abbaye

62 Jones, 'Twelfth-Century Reliefs from Fécamp', p. 82.
63 Grant, *Architecture and Society*, p. 78.
64 Milo Crispin, *Vita beati Lanfranci*, cols 35–6 and trans. Vaughn, 'Life of Lanfranc', p. 92.
65 See chapter three.
66 Appendix A, no. 92.

Blanche in Mortain was founded by William, count of Mortain, for Vitalis's sister Adeline who became the first abbess, and other foundations – Bival, Bondeville, Villers-Canivet – followed.[67] Four houses, Fontaine-Guérard, Le Trésor, St-Aubin and St-Saëns, were Cistercian from their foundation, with the latter founded from Bival.[68] There has been much debate as to the existence of a Cistercian architectural plan for churches and monastic buildings and it is tempting to try and set the Norman houses within that debate; but architecture, as we have seen above, is not generally reflective of one single factor. The Savignac and Cistercian nunneries on the whole do seem to have had less complex church plans than those of their Benedictine sisters. Constance Berman has argued that among the many factors that might have influenced Cistercian architecture, including climate, available building materials and style, poverty may be the primary reason for the austere churches constructed in the south of France, but as she points out, wealthy communities, male and female, could build and keep austere churches.[69]

Little architecture survives from the Savignac houses, with the exception of Mortain, though we know that Mortain and Villers-Canivet both had cruciform churches with flat east ends that were typical of the Cistercian order. The community at Mortain had actually moved location to the outskirts of the town after its incorporation into the Cistercian order and it is possible that the nuns adopted a simpler style of architecture to reflect their new position within a larger order. Bondeville, in contrast was rebuilt in the thirteenth and fourteenth centuries, and if the drawings in the Gagnières collection are accurate, in a much more elaborate style: the east end terminated in an apse.[70] The houses initially founded as Cistercian also exhibited simple church plans as is shown in surviving architecture from Fontaine-Guérard and Le Trésor. These houses were founded in the late twelfth and early thirteenth centuries respectively, at a time when the Church was becoming increasingly hostile to any specific expression of female spirituality and the Cistercians themselves were suspicious of nuns.[71] It is interesting to note that these nunneries had powerful founders and patrons: Robert III, earl of Leicester, and his wife Petronilla of Grandmesnil in the case of Fontaine-Guérard and King Louis IX of France and his mother Blanche of Castille for Le Trésor. When considered alongside its geographical location deep in the countryside, the church and topography of Fontaine-Guérard can be seen as conscious attempts on the part of the community to identify strongly with Cistercian traditions. The nuns may have sought ways in which to strengthen their ascetic credentials to aid inclusion within the Cistercian order, but the quality and elegance of the architecture also reflects the influence of their secular aristocratic founders. A simple church plan might be desirable, but this did not equate to poor

---

67   Appendix B, nos 3, 4, 26.
68   Appendix B, nos 11, 19, 22, 23.
69   Berman, *Cistercian Evolution*, pp. 24, 29.
70   Appendix B, no. 4.
71   See for example, S. Thompson, 'The Problem of Cistercian Nuns in the Twelfth and Early Thirteenth Centuries', *Medieval Women*, ed. D. Baker, Studies in Church History subsidia 1 (Oxford, 1978), pp. 227–52.

architecture and design. The same is true at Le Trésor where Louis IX and Blanche of Castille were great benefactors. The Capetian styles evident in the architecture of the house, for example the star-shaped abaci in the east range of the cloister, may well have been an expression of a desire to extend their influence in Normandy.[72]

The architecture of Norman religious foundations displayed many ideas of affiliation, patronage, penance and history to a wider world. How far these ideas were understood by ordinary people in the Middle Ages is debateable.[73] The number of people who had access to the cloister of Le Trésor and who could view the star-shaped abaci was few, but someone, whether architect, patron or abbess, made a deliberate decision to incorporate the motif in the decorative scheme of the nunnery. Features that referred back to the earlier history of a community were presumably understood by that community and maintained in oral and possibly written traditions. Any visitors to the abbey may have had the importance of elements like the west towers at Jumièges explained to them: Lanfranc's monastic constitutions certainly make provision for visitors to be shown the monastic buildings.[74] Architecture related to penance, as in the rebuilding of the chapel at Mont-aux-Malades, may have found a deeper resonance within the lay community of Normandy, especially as the murder of Thomas Becket had international implications and was well known throughout most of western Europe. Architecture displayed many meanings, but some were designed to be seen by the few and some by the many.

Clothing

Display of monastic affiliation, secular patronage or religious vocation was not limited to static buildings or topographical location. One of the most important, visible and portable means of display for those with a monastic or priestly vocation was through their clothing. The monastic habit and priest's garments were symbolic of their calling and rendered their wearers immediately identifiable to the laity. Clothing, especially that worn by monks and nuns, was the outer sign of their profession. Lepers were also sometimes distinguished by clothing, as surviving statutes make plain. Archbishop Eudes and Abbot Stephen had much to say on the subject of clothing regulations, but interestingly it was nuns and priests that were deemed most negligent in

---

[72] Grant, *Architecture and Society*, pp. 207–8. In architecture an abacus is uppermost part of the capital.

[73] Arnold, *Belief and Unbelief*, p. 54.

[74] *Monastic Constitutions*, pp. 130–3. One of the duties of the guestmaster is 'to show the buildings to those who wish to see them, taking care that the community is not then sitting in the cloister'.

this respect.[75] There were differences in the dress for monastics, lepers and priests and these shall be dealt with in turn.

The habit and short hairstyle of monks, nuns and priests were the outward signs of renunciation of self, class and sexuality. As such, these symbols associated a group of men and women with a particular place, in this case the cloister and parish church. As Robert Bartlett has stated, 'the treatment of hair ... is a pre-eminently socially visible act'.[76] Consequently, the way different groups of people cut or styled their hair was important in group identification, whether secular or religious.[77] The heads of monks and priests were uncovered through their distinctive haircut, the tonsure. According to canon sixteen of the Fourth Lateran Council, priests were to have a 'suitable crown and tonsure'.[78] In other words, the shaved part of the head should be of a suitable size and the hair not too long. Archbishop Eudes criticised Master Auger of the Évreux cathedral chapter for the shape of his tonsure and its very small *corona* or crown.[79] For monks and priests, this hairstyle was symbolic of Christ's crown of thorns and was a public sign of their service to God.[80] In contrast, the Cistercian lay brothers exhibited their specific vocation by growing beards, which were not to be more than two fingers in length.[81] The *conversi*, although part of a religious order, were still laymen in status and thus were not tonsured.

For nuns, cutting their hair was a very real sign of their renunciation. In Norman and Anglo-Norman society long hair was regarded as an expression of femininity, especially in the eyes of churchmen. It was also a sign of virginity, as when a woman married she bound her hair. For nuns to cut their hair distinguished them from women with a different gendered identity. They were not available for marriage, so long flowing hair was unsuitable, nor were they married to earthly husbands. Short hair was thus a means of indicating their different status, as well as expressing humility and appropriately modest behaviour. Criticism of nuns' hairstyles centred on what the ecclesiastical visitors deemed to be inappropriate. Archbishop Eudes castigated the nuns of Villarceaux for their long hair 'arrayed in vain curls'.[82] At Montivilliers, the nuns were not to grow their hair.[83] By adorning their tresses or letting them

---

75   For an account of clothing infringements in Eudes's register see S. M. Carroll-Clark, 'Bad Habits: Clothing and Textile References in the Register of Eudes Rigaud, Archbishop of Rouen', *Medieval Clothing and Textiles*, 1, ed R. Netherton and G. R. Owen-Crocker (Woodbridge, 2005), pp. 81–103. This article approaches the register in relation to monastic reform.

76   R. Bartlett, 'Symbolic Meanings of Hair in the Middle Ages', *Transactions of the Royal Historical Society*, 6th series 4 (1994), p. 43.

77   P. Stafford, 'The Meanings of Hair in the Anglo-Norman World: Masculinity, Reform and National Identity', *Saints, Scholars and Politicians: Gender as a Tool in Medieval Studies*, ed. M. van Dijk and R. Nip (Turnhout, 2005), pp. 153–71.

78   *Decrees*, p. 243.

79   Bonnin, p. 72 and *Register*, p. 81.

30   Bartlett, 'Symbolic Meanings of Hair', p. 58.

81   Williams, *Cistercians in the Early Middle Ages*, p. 80.

82   Appendix B, no. 25. Bonnin, p. 44 and *Register*, p. 50.

83   Bonnin, p. 564 and *Register*, p. 647.

grow, the nuns exhibited an interest in worldly appearance that was unacceptable to the archbishop. In addition, if their hair was too long it would protrude beyond the bottom of their veils and wimples, making it visible.

The main difference in habits of monks and nuns was that nuns had their heads entirely covered by wimples and veils, whereas monks' heads were exposed, both by being uncovered and through their tonsure. The nun's habit was an extension of religious space. In contrast, the public exposure of the monk's head through the tonsure, especially if he was also a priest engaged in parish duties, showed his availability as a conduit for the sacraments.[84] The cloister as a means of enclosure was symbolically represented by the nun's habit. This garment enclosed her body and helped to keep it a suitably chaste vessel, as befitted a bride of Christ. Veils and wimples covered the greater part of nuns' heads showing only their face. In this way nuns were hidden from the eyes of the public. If they had to leave their convent, then they were fully enclosed in their habit, which was in effect a portable cloister. The wimple limited their view of the outside world. Dress codes were a way of controlling access in relation to oneself and to the outside world. As Barbara Hanawalt notes, even laywomen wore veils, hoods or caps when venturing out of the home, which allowed them to walk in 'the privacy of their own space'.[85]

The importance of monastic clothing as an outward sign of profession was underlined by theologians like Lanfranc and Anselm in their capacity as archbishops of Canterbury after they had left their cloisters at Caen and Bec. Both archbishops believed that for a woman to don a veil was a tacit profession of a vocation.[86] These attitudes led to difficulties for some English noblewomen who had fled to nunneries to escape the Normans in the aftermath of the Conquest. Lanfranc, citing William the Conqueror's approval, eventually decided that if it could be proved that a woman had donned a veil for her own protection rather than through a vocation she could leave the nunnery. He did, however, make the point that 'nuns who have made profession that they will keep a rule or who, although not yet professed have been presented at the altar, are to be enjoined, exhorted and obliged to keep the rule in their manner of life'.[87] Lanfranc's successor, Anselm, also adopted this attitude as can been seen from one of his letters to Gunhilda, the daughter of King Harold (1066), who had stayed at the abbey of Wilton, but later left probably in order to marry first Count Alan the Red then, when he died before they could marry, his brother, Count Alan the Black. This union, had it happened, would have posed a great danger to William Rufus's throne in the eyes of Anselm:

> Even though you were not consecrated by the bishop and did not read your
> vows in his presence, nevertheless these vows were evident and cannot be

---

[84]   Gilchrist, *Gender and Material Culture*, p. 18.
[85]   Hanawalt, 'At the Margin of Women's Space', p. 8.
[86]   Neither Lanfranc nor Anselm seems to have had a similar insistence that monks were similarly tacitly professed: i.e. by virtue of adopting the habit rather than making a verbal profession.
[87]   *Letters of Lanfranc*, no. 53, pp. 166–7.

denied since you wore the habit of your holy intention, both in public and in private, and through this you affirmed to everyone who saw you that you were dedicated to God no less than if you had read out your vows.[88]

Vaughn has speculated that Archbishop Anselm was acting in King William's interests by seeking to prevent this marriage, and his position is entirely consistent with his earlier ruling, later reversed, that Edith-Matilda (d.1118), daughter of King Malcolm III of Scotland (1058–93), was a nun and thus unable to marry Alan the Red.[89] The views expressed in Anselm's letter to Gunhilda contrast with his advice to Countess Matilda of Tuscany, who had not made a monastic profession tacitly or otherwise. He advised her to keep a veil handy so that when she was in danger she could pop it on her head.[90] Presumably the sanctity and respect in which nuns should be held according to Anselm, would prove protection enough from Matilda's enemies. For the archbishop, the difference seems to lie in a woman's intention. Anselm was trying to persuade Gunhilda to return to the monastic life fully, whereas he had no doubt as to Countess Matilda's strong spirituality, despite her status as a laywoman, stemming from her material support for Pope Gregory VII (1073–85) during the investiture contest.

The monastic habit was also symbolic of a communal way of life. The renunciation of self was emphasised by the uniformity of clothing amongst the community. Simple and unadorned habits were also reflective of the vow of poverty. The Benedictine rule states that the monks were 'not to make an issue of the colour and coarseness' of their clothes, but were to use what was available locally.[91] The importance of this communality was underlined during Abbot Stephen's first visit to Mortain when he listed the nuns' clothing specifications. Each nun was to have two mantles which might be trimmed with fur but should not be overly delicate, four tunics, four wimples, six veils, three pairs of shoes, three pairs of stockings, night slippers, day sandals, two scapulars 'without capuces according to our universal rule and customs' and if the weather was hot, they might ask for a fifth robe of lighter material.[92]

---

88   Schmitt, vol. 4, no. 168, pp. 43–6 and Fröhlich, vol. 2, no. 168, p. 66. See also Bos, 'Gender and Religious Guidance', pp. 43, note 72 and 222–9

89   S. Vaughn, *St Anselm and the Handmaidens of God: A Study of Anselm's Correspondence with Women*, Utrecht Studies in Medieval Literacy (Turnhout, 2002), pp. 184–98, 185. Anselm reversed his decision on Edith-Matilda allowing Henry I to marry her. He attracted a great deal of criticism for this apparent about-turn, even though the reason for his change of heart lay in the fact that Edith-Matilda had been forced to wear the veil and Gunhilda had not, and his biographer, Eadmer, sought to justify it: *Eadmeri historia novorum in Anglia et opuscula duo de vita sancti Anselmi et quibusdam miraculis ejus*, ed. M. Rule, RS 81 (London, 1884), pp. 121–3 and trans. G. Bosanquet, *Eadmer's History of Recent Events in England* (London, 1964), pp. 126–8.

90   Schmitt, vol. 4, no. 325 p. 257 and Fröhlich, vol. 3, no. 325, p. 39. See also Bos, 'Gender and religious guidance', p. 158.

91   *Rule*, ch. 55, pp. 253–4.

92   'duo scapularia sine caputiis, secundum quod se habet monialium ordinis nostri universalis consuetudo'; *Registrum epistolarum*, p. 236. A mantle was a loose outer garment or cloak and the scapular was a specifically monastic garment that hung loosely in front and behind, see Piponnier and Mane, *Dress in the Middle Ages*, pp. 166–7. The

Uniformity did depend on a community having sufficient financial resources to dress its members in the appropriate habit. Some houses were unable to do this. For example, at Ste-Marguerite-en-Gouffern, Archbishop Eudes recorded that the nuns did not wear the same habit due to poverty.[93] Lack of money had an effect, considered negative by the archbishop, on the nuns' experience of their vocation. A more common infringement, found in male houses as well, was the desire to express individuality and perhaps secular wealth through styles that were deemed to be too elaborate. The monks at Montaure had cloaks trimmed with fox fur; the community at Pré used cat and fox skin and those at Ste-Gauberge wore barracan (goatskin).[94] At Beaumont-en-Auge, the archbishop found it necessary to state that any riding capes possessed by individuals should be held in common and, at Cherbourg, two of the canons had bought capes that they were unwilling to share with the rest of the community.[95] On his first visit to St-Amand, Eudes recorded that the nuns had chemises and wore cloaks of rabbit skin, which were deemed to be too luxurious.[96] The problem was more severe at Villarceaux, and Eudes found it necessary to decree that 'no more saffron should be placed on veils, that the hair be not arrayed in vain curls, nor shall silver or metalled belts, or the skins of divers and wild animals be worn, nor shall the hair be allowed to grow below the ears'.[97] Neglect of the rules regarding clothing in this manner indicated too worldly a concern with outward appearance.[98] For monks and nuns, proper observance of such rules avoided shame and focused their attention on more spiritual concerns.

Irregularities in monastic dress were associated with other lapses in observance. Lawrence, a priest associated with Mont-Ste-Catherine in Rouen, who was staying at Pavilly, was accused of lapses in the observance of chastity and of buying a secular garment.[99] Joan Martel, who was a professed nun at St-Saëns, was described as 'rebellious and disobedient ... [she] quarrelled with the prioress; she rode out on horseback to see her relatives, clad in a sleeved gown made of dark material; she had her own messenger whom she sent often to her relatives'.[100] It is worth underlining here that Joan was wearing a sleeved gown. The reason why this garment so angered Eudes was that instead

---

references to capuces meant that the scapulars did not have hoods attached. Stephen does not seem to have listed the monks' allocation of clothing. Communality was also emphasised in the Augustinian rule: *Rule of Saint Augustine*, ed. van Bavel and trans. Canning, p. 33.

[93]   Appendix B, no. 20. Bonnin, p. 83 and *Register*, p. 94.
[94]   Appendix A, nos 52, 66, 76; Bonnin, pp. 74, 34–5, 233 and *Register*, pp. 84, 39, 257.
[95]   Appendix A, nos 10, 24; Bonnin, pp. 60, 201 and *Register*, pp. 67, 217.
[96]   Bonnin, p. 16 and *Register*, p. 19. It is interesting to note that while Eudes mentions the use of hare, cat and fox fur, he only banned rabbit. It is possible that he meant for the ban on rabbit fur to stand as a general prohibition on all animal skins.
[97]   Bonnin, p. 44 and *Register*, p. 50.
[98]   'Do not attract attention by the way you dress. Endeavour to impress by your manner of life, not by the clothes you wear': *Rule of Saint Augustine*, ed. van Banvel and trans. Canning, p. 29.
[99]   Appendix A, no. 63 for Pavilly; Bonnin, p. 168 and *Register*, p. 184.
[100] Bonnin, p. 338 and *Register*, p. 383.

of being attached to the main body of the gown as was the case with the habit, the sleeves were detachable and were thus the antithesis of monastic dress, designed as an outward symbol of renunciation.[101] Although it is not clear whether or not Joan renounced her vocation, her behaviour is not far from outright apostasy, as indeed was that of Brother Thomas of St-Michel at Veronnet, whom Eudes described thus:

> Brother Thomas is a man of property and had gold rings. He used to go about at night clad in a cuirass without his monk's habit. He has wounded many at night, both lay and cleric and has himself been wounded and had had the tip of his finger cut off.[102]

A clear sign of the rejection of the religious life was the abandonment of the habit: the wearing of secular clothes was equated with the presumption of apostasy. Neglect of the monastic clothing regulations was just as much a rejection of the cloister as physically leaving it. This connection is made explicit in the case of Agnes of Merla, a nun at L'abbaye Blanche in Mortain, who left after thirty years as a Cistercian. According to letters included in Stephen of Lexington's visitation records, she fled by night, abandoning her habit and returning to 'debauchery' (vomitus), in other words, a secular and sexually active life.[103] She was duly declared excommunicate by the ecclesiastical authorities, though both Stephen and the community continued to hope that she might return.[104]

Dress was also used as a means of distinguishing different groups of people within the monastic community. Early Cistercian statutes underline the difference in status between choir monks and conversi as reflected in their dress and appearance. We have already noted their beards, but the twelfth-century usages also give details of their garments. The conversi were to be supplied with a cloak, tunics, sandals, shoes and a hood covering the shoulders and

---

[101] Sleeves could be presented to knights in tournaments by ladies, as tokens. In *The Story of the Grail (Perceval)* by Chrétien de Troyes, Tiebaut has an adult-sized sleeve made for his younger daughter, the Maiden with the Little Sleeves, so she can present it to Gawain as a token of her affection. The girl was afraid that if she sent one of her own sleeves, the knight would not think much of it as it was so small: Chrétien de Troyes, *Arthurian Romances*, trans. W. Kibler (Harmondsworth, 1991), p. 448. See also D. O. Hughes, 'Regulating Women's Fashions', *A History of Women in the West vol. 2: Silences of the Middle Ages*, ed. C. Klapisch-Zuber (Cambridge, MA and London, 1992), p. 141.

[102] Appendix A, no. 102; Bonnin, p. 109 and *Register*, p. 124.

[103] *Registrum epistolarum*, p. 246. Laura Napran, in personal communication, has suggested that this might be a case of abduction or elopement. Chrysogonus Waddell erroneously states that Agnes returned to Mortain to live as a secular, 'One day in the Life of the Savignac Nun', p. 149.

[104] For what might be expected of Agnes if she returned to the cloister, see Abbot Stephen's letter to the prior of Villers-Canivet in which he lays down the penances required from a fugitive monk before he can be readmitted to the community; *Registrum epistolarum*, pp. 296–8. The fugitive was presumably one of the brothers tasked with providing practical and spiritual assistance to the nuns. See the section on male staff below. Apostasy will be discussed below with regard to excommunication and penance.

chest only, as opposed to the choir monks' cowls. Blacksmiths were to have smocks described as 'black and rounded', presumably made from leather, to protect their other garments when working.[105] The difference in clothing lay in the contrast between the choir monks, whose main task was the performance of the divine office, and the *conversi* who acted as manual labourers in the communities' granges and workshops. *Conversi* therefore spent most of their time outdoors and so were allotted four tunics so they might have an extra one for warmth.[106]

There does not appear to have been an attempt by the Church to enforce a strict dress code on lepers in a similar way to that of priests and members of monastic communities.[107] It seems that regulation was left to individual communities or localities and reflects the communal nature of life in a leper house rather than a desire to stigmatise, at least initially. That some lepers living in community had to observe regulations regarding their clothes reflects the idea that leper houses were religious spaces with the disease itself viewed as almost being a vocation. According to the statutes of the leper house of Lisieux, lepers could only leave the community if they were properly attired in a closed cape or other reasonable clothes.[108] As we shall see below, there are some similarities here with the dress prescribed for priests. Lepers, both male and female, were an order of people who, whilst not lay, were not fully professed monastics either. It is possible that as attitudes towards those with leprosy switched from charity to fear, not only did clothing reinforce an idea of a communal life, but also marked out a particular group as lepers. Although clothes in this instance could act as markers of stigma, they also might offer some degree of protection to the lepers. As the statutes discussed below show, reasonable clothing was a prerequisite for lepers temporarily leaving their communities.[109] If they were then attacked, presumably some action could be taken against their assailants, as the lepers would have been clearly identified as members of a community and subject to ecclesiastical discipline.

The secular clergy, with the exception of those in collegiate churches like Les Andelys, were in a markedly different situation to monks and nuns as they did not live in community with other priests but in parishes with their parishioners; however, certain standards of behaviour were expected of them by the ecclesiastical authorities. The importance of gender is relevant here, as parish priests interacted with the laity to a greater degree than did monks. The issue of clerical celibacy will be discussed below, but some of the problems encountered in trying to enforce correct behaviour, especially with regard to dress, lie in the contradiction of celibate males living within the lay commu-

[105] *Cistercian Lay Brothers' Twelfth-Century Usages with Related Texts*, ed. C. Waddell, Studia et documenta 10 (Brecht, 2000), pp. 73–4 and trans. p. 189.
[106] *Twelfth-Century Statutes*, 1157, no. 69, p. 69.
[107] Piponnier and Maine, *Dress in the Middle Ages*, p. 136; Rawcliffe, *Leprosy in Medieval England*, pp. 265–6.
[108] *Statuts*, p. 203. See also the diocesan statutes from Coutances c.1300, Mansi, col. 25, col. 30.
[109] See chapter three on enclosure.

nity.[110] The rules regarding clerical dress were not as clear cut as those for professed religious. The councils of Lateran II (1139) and Lateran IV (1215), along with other regional councils laid down guidelines that priests were to follow. According to canon four of the Second Lateran Council, bishops and clergy were to 'take pains to be pleasing to God and to humans in both their interior and exterior comportment'. They were not to give offence to the laity, for whom they were an example, 'by the excess, cut or colour of their clothes, not with regard to the tonsure, but rather, as is fitting for them, let them exhibit holiness': the penalty for disobeying was to be deprived of their benefice.[111] Canon sixteen of Lateran IV was more prescriptive: priests 'outer garments should be closed and neither too short nor too long'. Ornamentation was frowned upon, including red or green cloths; 'long sleeves or shoes with embroidery or pointed toes ... buckles or belts ornamented with gold or silver'; and harnesses for horses.[112] This canon was reinforced by leading theologians, such as Thomas of Chobham who reminded the clergy that they should 'live according to the requirements of canon law' and thus were prohibited from wearing 'green or red cloth, long-sleeved cloaks or gloves, laced shoes and things like this'.[113] After all, good behaviour for a priest referred to 'not only his manner of life but also his style of dress'.[114] They may not have been living in community, but parish priests were still an order apart from the laity: their vocation entailed a renunciation of secular ways and their lives were a living example to the laity in their care.

Synodal statutes present a different picture to the problems Archbishop Eudes Rigaud found in his visitation of priests in the archdiocese of Rouen. The main problem he encountered was the reluctance of some priests to wear their gown, a seemly and modest garment. The priests of the deaneries of Longueville and Aumale were required to obtain closed gowns.[115] Immodest dress led to inappropriate behaviour, a connection made explicit in the archbishop's sermons.[116] Matthew, the priest at Vieux-Rouen, wore a sword and clothes described as 'unseemly'; he was also guilty of sexual incontinence in that 'although he was disciplined by the archdeacon in the manner of one woman he has not ceased to carry on with others'.[117] The priests at Royville

---

[110] See chapter two for a full discussion of clerical celibacy. For a brief consideration of priests' clothing in thirteenth-century Normandy, see Davis, *Holy Bureaucrat*, pp. 112–14.

[111] *Decrees*, p. 197.

[112] *Decrees*, p. 243. See also T. M. Izbicki, 'Forbidden Colors in the Regulation of Clerical Dress from the Fourth Lateran Council (1215) to the Time of Nicholas of Cusa (d. 1464)', *Medieval Clothing and Textiles*, ed. Netherton and Owen-Crocker, pp. 105–14.

[113] Thomas of Chobham, *Summa confessorum*, ed. F. Broomfield, Analecta Mediaevalia Namurcensia 25 (Louvain and Paris, 1968), p. 83 and translated in *Pastors and the Care of Souls in Medieval England*, ed. J. Shinners and W. J. Dohar (Notre Dame, IN, 1998), p. 8.

[114] Thomas of Chobham, *Summa confessorum*, p. 83; *Pastors and the Care of Souls*, ed. Shinners and Dohar, p. 8.

[115] Bonnin, pp. 17, 18–19 and *Register*, pp. 21, 23.

[116] Davis, *Holy Bureaucrat*, pp. 112–13.

[117] Bonnin, p. 20 and *Register*, p. 24.

and St-Aignan likewise wore inappropriate garments and were considered to be lax in their observance of celibacy.[118] In contrast, the priest at Baudribosc was interested in pursuing the more martial aspects of secular life. According to Eudes, he wore 'unseemly clothing, conducts himself like a soldier and is in the habit of taking charge of the lances at tournaments'.[119] Jousts and tournaments had previously been prohibited in canon fourteen of Lateran II on the grounds that they 'often result in human deaths and danger to souls'.[120] Clerics, we have noted, were not to bear swords, nor were they to be involved in any judicial or other process which entailed the shedding of blood, so participation in tournaments, which was not even officially sanctioned for the laity, was a serious matter.[121] Not only did they renounce violence, but also, as Megan McLaughlin highlights, other practices regarded as masculine like the creation of wealth and of course, the fathering of children.[122] There is a tension here between the priests' position as ordained celibates who were channels for the delivery of the sacraments, and their masculinity. Some clearly struggled with their own perception of themselves as active and virile men, and the Church's expectation that they should be sober and moderate in all things, in effect to live a semi-monastic life. By adopting secular garb, they could display their masculinity and reassert the qualities that medieval society saw as male.

Chapter

Central to display within the monastery was the chapter house, one of the most important and sacred spaces within the precinct.[123] This room was the setting for a number of functions connected to visual display of monastic practices within the community: it was the site of communal prayer; the place where extracts from the rule were read; a forum for the discussion of general and administrative matters, and the place where important guests, both lay and religious, were received. Significantly, the chapter house was also a burial place for important members of the community and thus a site for the commemoration of the dead. This room was, in addition, the scene of punishment of those who offended against the rule.[124] The chapter house was

---

[118] Bonnin, pp. 26 and 29 and *Register*, pp. 30, 33.
[119] 'Defert habitum inhonestum et gerit se tanquam armiger et solet ministrare lanceas ad bohordamentu': Bonnin, p. 28 and *Register*, p. 32.
[120] *Decrees*, p. 200.
[121] Canon eighteen, Lateran IV, *Decrees*, p. 244.
[122] M. McLaughlin, 'Secular and Spiritual Fatherhood in the Eleventh Century', *Conflicted Identities and Multiple Masculinities*, ed. Murray p. 27.
[123] Megan Cassidy-Welch in her discussion of thirteenth-century Cistercian houses in Yorkshire quotes Héliand of Froidmont's belief that the chapter house was the 'holiest and most sacred part of the monastery': *Monastic Spaces and their Meanings*, p. 105. See also Gilchrist, *Norwich Cathedral Close*, p. 109.
[124] Cassidy-Welch, *Monastic Spaces and their Meanings*, p. 106.

thus a space that reinforced the idea of community. The practices enacted in it connected the monks of the present community with each other and the wider community, both dead and alive.[125]

The importance of the chapter house was displayed to the community and world beyond through its architecture. Surviving examples of chapter houses from Normandy show a high degree of architectural elaboration. Although their location was generally fixed in the east range of the cloister, there was no common plan for chapter houses in Normandy.[126] The chapter house at Mortain dates to the first half of the twelfth century. The room itself opened onto the cloister through two Romanesque arches resting on a central pillar and was divided into two by a central row of five pillars on which rested groin vaults. The entrance was mirrored by two windows in the east wall.[127] The abbey of Fontaine-Guérard, another Cistercian house, also had an elaborate chapter house dating from the thirteenth century. Here, the entrance from the cloister comprises three moulded arches, again mirrored by a triple-arched window in the east wall. The room is divided into three aisles, the ceiling is vaulted and the four supporting columns are ornamented with foliated capitals. In addition, one of the roof bosses depicts an owl, probably chosen to signify the wisdom that should guide the nuns' discussions.[128] Male houses also had elaborate chapter houses. At Hambye for example, the chapter house dates from the beginning of the thirteenth century. The building terminates in a polygonal chevet lit by three windows and is divided into two aisles which open onto the cloister through two large arches.[129] No matter to which order a particular house was affiliated, the internal seating arrangements were the same. As at Fontaine-Guérard, a stone bench or benches, depending on the size of the community, ran around the walls of the interior. The east side of the chapter house that faced the cloister was generally reserved for the head of the community. As we shall see, this arrangement facilitated the witnessing and participation in the ceremonies performed in the chapter house.

Scholars have speculated at length on why chapter houses had such elaborate entrances. The conventional explanation is that the large openings allowed people outside the room to see and hear what was going on in the room at times when there was insufficient space to accommodate everyone. Stein-Kecks has argued that this was not the case, citing evidence from the

---

[125] Cassidy-Welch, *Monastic Spaces and their Meanings*, p. 132.

[126] Due to its east-range location, Gilchrist has described the chapter houses as one of the most inaccessible part of the monastery to outsiders: *Gender and Material Culture*, p. 166.

[127] B. Beck, 'Recherches sur les salles capitulaires en Normandie et notamment dans les diocèses d'Avranches, Bayeux et Coutances', *BSAN*, 58 (1965–66), p. 30.

[128] Beck, 'Recherches sur les salles capitulaires', p. 88; Fournée, *Abbaye de Fontaine-Guérard*, pp. 34–5.

[129] Appendix A, no. 38. Beck points out that the interior plan is similar to those found at the Premonstratensian houses of Ardenne and La Lucerne and the Cistercian abbey of Mortain: Beck, 'Recherches sur les salles capitulaires', p. 36; appendix A, nos 2, 49 and appendix B, no. 15.

Cistercian usages and Cluny to support his position.[130] In Cistercian houses the *conversi* had their own chapter once a week in the west range of the cloister that housed their quarters. This meeting took place at the same time as the monks' chapter and so there was no need for them to congregate in the east range. If a general sermon was preached to the entire community then the *conversi* joined the monks in their chapter house. At Cluny, an architectural reason may be found for the decoration of chapter house entrances in the link between the chapter house and St Mary's chapel. Thus, the chapter house had a dual function, acting not only as a meeting place in which to hear the rule or do penance, but also as an 'entrance hall' for the chapel, highlighting the particularly sacred nature of the space.[131] This dual function is further underlined in the iconography that survives from examples in Normandy. For example, sculpture at the entrance to the chapter house at St-Georges-de-Boscherville shows St Benedict or an abbot and figures representing life and death holding ribbons with extracts of the rule on them. One of the capitals inside the room shows two monks stripped to the waist being beaten.[132]

Daily chapter was held under the guidance of the superior or their appointed deputy and Eudes castigated several religious for not attending regularly.[133] He criticised other houses for not holding chapter at all, for example at Notre-Dame at Chaumont and Gasny.[134] Occasionally there was a good reason for such a lapse in observance as at Pré, where a lack of monks and the presence of workmen made it impossible for the community to hold chapter everyday.[135] In contrast, chapter was not held at Noyon-sur-Andelle because the chapter house 'had been closed for many days being used for storing wines and other inappropriate uses': Eudes ordered its immediate reopening and employment for proper use.[136] Clerics within cathedrals also held chapter on a regular basis, though at Lisieux the bishop and canons met in the vestry as they had no space that could be used specifically as a chapter house.[137] The archbishop was not just being pedantic in his insistence of the proper observance of monastic and cathedral chapter: it was designed to reinforce the common purpose of the community's monastic vocation, its identification with a particular order and the wider monastic world. Chapter therefore had to be held in a place large enough to admit the entire community and which was properly laid out, so that all might hear and bear witness to the maintenance of order

---

[130] H. Stein-Kecks, '*Clastrum* and *Capitulum*: Some Remarks on the Façade and Interior of the Chapter House', *Der mittelalterliche Kreuzgang–the Medieval Cloister–le Cloître au moyen âge. Architektur, Function und Programm*, ed. P. K. Klein (Regensburg, 2004), p. 162.

[131] Stein-Kecks, '*Clastrum* and *Capitulum*', p. 167.

[132] Appendix A, no. 77. Beck, 'Recherches sur les salles capitulaires', p. 108 and K. A. Morrison, 'The Figural Capitals of the Chapterhouse of Saint-Georges-de-Boscherville', *Medieval Art, Architecture and Archaeology at Rouen*, ed. J. Stratford, British Archaeological Association Conference Transactions 12 (Leeds, 1993), p. 46.

[133] Bonnin, pp. 296, 410, 431 and *Register*, pp. 334, 467, 490.

[134] Appendix A, nos 23, 35; Bonnin, pp. 41, 45 and *Register*, pp. 46, 51.

[135] Bonnin, pp. 34–5 and *Register*, p. 39.

[136] Appendix A, no. 61; Bonnin, p. 426 and *Register*, p. 486.

[137] Bonnin, pp. 296–7 and *Register*, p. 336.

within the community through the reading of the rule and performance of penance. One can imagine that the canons of Lisieux were rather cramped in the vestry. Such a space would also be hardly adequate for the reception of important visitors, including the archbishop, to whom it would be essential to display good order.

One of the primary ways in which the idea of community was reinforced was through the confession or accusation of faults before the assembled monks or nuns. The obligations of the monastic life were reiterated in the reading of the rule and dealing with faults was a way of binding the community closer together. Megan Cassidy-Welch has discussed in detail the procedure adopted in Cistercian houses in Yorkshire that followed the *Ecclesiastica Officia* and it seems likely that similar practices were followed in Cistercian houses in Normandy. The procedure began with the naming of the accused and a short statement of the sin committed. The accused was then questioned by the superior before confessing and receiving his penalty. This practice differed from private confession in one very important respect: confession in chapter, in front of the assembled monks or nuns, involved transgressions against the common life; private confession involved private thoughts.[138] To this end monks and nuns were to accuse one another of any offences against the rule and lapses in observance. They were not to do so harshly: Archbishop Eudes was unimpressed with the Benedictine monks of St-Wandrille who only accused each other for 'insulting gestures, quarrelling and affronts'.[139] In other words, the monks were not pointing out lapses in observance in order that their brothers might become better monks, but were only picking up on offences directed at themselves as individuals: clearly all were at fault here.

Punishment was also public and was determined by the gravity of an individual's actions or omissions.[140] By being administered in front of the whole community, punishment served a dual purpose: it acted as a deterrent and humiliated the transgressor. Stephen of Lexington reserved some faults for correction by the abbot of Savigny, the head of the congregation, and monks deemed guilty were to go to the monastery on foot to confess their faults at the mother house.[141] Monasticism required the renunciation of self and individual will. Sins against the common life were a failure in this respect. Eudes recorded several different penalties ranging from fasts and corporal punishment to temporary or permanent removal from the community and excommunication. Superiors, although they conducted chapters, were not immune from punishment if they transgressed as Eudes's register shows. Penalties varied depending on the severity of the offence and the willingness of the individual to reform. Comtesse, the prioress of the troublesome nunnery of Bondeville, was sentenced to one discipline in chapter for allowing her

---

138 *Les ecclesiastica officia Cisterciens du XIIe siècle*, ed. D. Choisselet and P. Vernet, La documentation cistercienne 22 (Reiningue, 1989), ch. 70, pp. 202–9 and Cassidy-Welch, *Monastic Spaces and their Meanings*, p. 116.

139 Appendix A, no. 90; Bonnin, p. 171 and *Register*, p. 189.

140 Individuals were deemed to be in either 'levi culpa' or 'gravi culpa' – light or grave fault.

141 *Registrum epistolarum*, p. 197.

nuns to use the convent seal.[142] In contrast, the prior of St-Laurent-en-Lyons who had not sent a companion to the canon living on his own, despite being ordered to by Eudes in 1254/5, was to sing the seven penitential psalms and the litany in recompense, as well as to receive scourgings in Lent.[143] The prior's crime was serious, as the monastic life by its very nature was a communal one. By failing to send a companion to the canon in his dependent priory, he was forcing him to live outside the community. The monastic vocation had to be pursued in community and so a singular monk, canon or nun was an impossibility.[144] The severity of the prior's punishment was thus fitting.

Sister Lucy of Crèvecour, although not a superior, was clearly a senior, and her position in a disputed abbatial election at La Trinité deserves discussion here.[145] The circumstances of the election are vague. The original choice was a certain Beatrice, but her election was not accepted by the bishop of Bayeux who appointed Lucy instead. Beatrice appealed to Eudes in his capacity as metropolitan but he declared both elections void, appointing instead a third woman, Jeanne du Châtel from St-Sauveur in Évreux, as abbess. She, however, did not accept the office. Eventually the parties concerned appealed to Rome: the pope seems to have ruled in favour of Beatrice who was elected by the community in the first place: she is mentioned as abbess in 1270.[146] Lucy was declared excommunicate by Eudes, but her sentence seems more to do with her appropriation of abbey goods than her election. In 1267/8, she appeared before the archbishop and was granted absolution. By way of penance, she was to accept three disciplines in chapter, to repeat three psalters, to fast for two Fridays on bread and water, and to fast every Friday for a year on common food as well as to return the goods she had taken.[147] Although the sentence of excommunication was then lifted, Lucy was still not fully part of the community, marked by a sentence of corporal punishment to be administered in front of the community, and different food. In addition, her penance consisted of a private element, the recitation of the psalter, in which she would have time to reflect on her misdeeds.

Among the wider monastic community, often the faults discovered by Eudes related to a breakdown in community life, which is discussed in more detail below.[148] For example, at Bival, Eudes ordered that the perpetrators of the discord and quarrels were to be 'brought forth in a cart' in a public

---

[142]   That is, corporal punishment. The convent seal was the means by which the community confirmed transactions, etc. By allowing the nuns to use the convent seal, Comtesse was guilty of allowing them to conduct business without the knowledge of either herself or the chapter. Bonnin, p. 348 and *Register*, p. 396.

[143]   Appendix A, no. 80. Bonnin, p. 206 and *Register*, p. 224. Eudes had visited previously in 1252. The seven penitential psalms are 6, 32, 38, 51, 102, 130 and 143.

[144]   See the statutes of Pope Gregory IX amongst others that prohibit monks residing alone: *Register*, p. 738.

[145]   Disputed or irregular elections were not uncommon. Other examples exist from Normandy. See *Twelfth-Century Statutes*, 1190, no. 54, p. 209 for an irregular election at Le Valasse presided over by the abbot of Mortemer. Appendix A, no. 99.

[146]   GC, vol. 11, cols 1433–4.

[147]   Bonnin, pp. 591–2 and *Register*, p. 681.

[148]   See chapter three.

display of their disgrace.[149] Brother Richard of Vernon, a member of the Augustinian priory of Sausseuse, had been rebellious and disobedient and was ordered to eat at the bench in the refectory, rather than at his usual place with the community, until he had made satisfaction for his behaviour.[150] A more extreme penalty was meted out to Brother Julian at Beaulieu who was sentenced to three disciplines in chapter in the presence of the community and to eat three times at the floor of the refectory rather than at table in order of seniority.[151] Discord was the antithesis of living in charity and those guilty of such behaviour put themselves outside the community spiritually. Through the awarding of suitable penances, their spiritual dislocation was made physical in their removal from their place in the community order, for example, eating at a different place in the refectory, and their transgressions were thus displayed to the entire community.

As is the case of Lucy of Crèvecour, the most serious offences resulted in excommunication in which an individual was cast out not only from the monastic community but from the Church and its sacraments as well: this could be temporary, until a sinner repented, or permanent.[152] We have already noted that Agnes of Mortain was declared excommunicate after she abandoned the abbey of Mortain.[153] Monastic excommunication was the ultimate punishment of an individual monk or nun deemed to be in grave fault. The Benedictine rule states that any individual at fault should, 'according to our Lord's command be secretly admonished once and a second time by his seniors. If he do not amend, let him be reproved publicly before all. If even then he do not correct himself, let him undergo excommunication'.[154] Such permanent exclusion was rare, but it did happen. Abbot Thierry of St-Évroul had cause to expel a monk called Romanus, who despite several admonitions continued to steal, as he was unable to reform.[155] Other monastics in grave fault, after exposure of their sins in chapter, were incarcerated in monastery prisons: for example, Caleboche and another monk of Mont-Ste-Catherine in Rouen who were imprisoned for singing 'dissolute songs'. Eudes ruled that they were to be subject to flagellation, presumably in chapter, and fasting.[156] John

---

[149] 'In una quadriga adduci': Bonnin, p. 229 and *Register*, p. 252.

[150] Appendix A, no. 91; Bonnin, p. 190 and *Register*, p. 203. One of the more common punishments was for monks or nuns to be temporarily demoted from their place in the community in order of seniority.

[151] Appendix A, no. 9; Bonnin, p. 363 and *Register*, p. 414.

[152] I discuss excommunication in 'Exclusion as Exile: Spiritual Punishment and Physical Illness', *Exile in the Middle Ages*, ed. L. Napran and E. van Houts, International Medieval Research 13 (Turnhout, 2004), pp. 146–55. I am grateful to Simon Forde for permission to reuse material from that article here. For excommunication in a secular context see L. Napran, 'Marriage and Excommunication: the Comital House of Flanders' in the same volume, pp. 69–80.

[153] See the section on clothing above.

[154] *Rule*, ch. 23, p. 156. See also ch. 28. For a discussion of the Rule in this context, see F. Donald Logan, *Runaway Religious in Medieval England c. 1240–1540*, Cambridge Studies in Medieval Life and Thought, 4th series 32 (Cambridge, 1996), pp. 147–50.

[155] Appendix A, no. 74: OV, vol. 2, p. 43.

[156] 'Dissolute cantant': Bonnin, p. 103 and *Register*, p. 118.

Gaul of Ouville had left his monastery so often that the prior was 'to prepare for him a place in some remote part of the house' and if he were to leave he was to be permanently expelled from the order.[157] Whereas in the case of Caleboche and his friend their removal from community life was temporary, for John his spatial separation was permanent as he was sentenced to live the rest of his life on the margins of his former home. His only choice was to remain in isolation or risk damnation by becoming apostate. By removing miscreants from communal life but by keeping them within the precinct, the Church still held these people under monastic discipline.[158] They also served as a warning to the rest of the community. Prisons were considered to be an integral space in the monastery. Lanfranc of Canterbury made provision to hold rebel monks at the cathedral priory of Christ Church, and Montivilliers had a prison within the precincts of the monastery.[159]

If ties with the wider monastic community were cemented through the reading of the rule and the enforcing of its statutes in chapter, then visual reminders of the dead served to connect the present community with those promoted to eternal glory. At Orderic Vitalis's monastery of St-Évroul, several abbots – Osbern (d.1066), Mainer, Roger of Le Sap (d.1126) and Warin (d.1137) – were all buried in the chapter house before Orderic completed his chronicle.[160] As we shall see below, these spiritual fathers were joined in death by members of the lay founders' families.[161] At Jumièges, a whole group of tombs indicated by enamelled terracotta floor tiles and dedicated to abbots, but now lost, were recorded in the Gaignières collection. The abbots were William I (d.1037), Ours (d.1127), William II (d.1142), Ustacius I (d.1155), Peter I (d.1166), Roger I (d.1176), Roger II (d.1190), Roger III (died between 1190 and 1198), Richard de la Mare (d.1198) and Alexander (d.123?). Their memorials all date from the thirteenth century and are very similar in design. All except one, which shows the abbot dressed in his monk's habit, depict the abbot dressed in priestly robes.[162] The Jumièges tombs reveal a definite attempt to honour past abbots and may link with a continuation of the monastery's annals written at this time.[163] Several abbesses of La Trinité in Caen were also buried in their chapter house and their tombs depict either a nun in habit and veil holding a book or a crosier and a book, or, in the case of Julienne de St-Céneri just a crosier and inscription. The burial of heads of house in chapter houses was common practice across Europe. Their memory was reinforced in

[157] Appendix A, no. 62; Bonnin, p. 54 and *Register*, p. 59
[158] See V. Flint, 'Spaces and Discipline in early Medieval Europe', *Medieval Practices of Space*, ed. Hanawalt and Kobialka, pp. 149–66 for another consideration of the use of space in punishment.
[159] *Monastic Constitutions*, pp. 152–3. Appendix B, no. 14.
[160] OV, vol. 4, pp. 338–9; vol. 2, pp. 134–5; vol. 6, pp. 326–7, 486–7.
[161] See chapter four.
[162] J. Adhémar, 'Les tombeaux de la collection Gaignières', *Gazette des Beaux-Arts*, 84 (1974), pp. 45–6.
[163] I am grateful to Alison Alexander, who is currently pursuing doctoral research with Dr Elisabeth van Houts into Norman monastic annals, for drawing this continuation to my attention.

the office for the commemoration of the dead recited in the chapter house and thus their tombs provided a visual link between the monastic living of this world and the dead of the next.

The chapter house and the activities that took place within it were at the centre of monastic life. If the church was where the spiritual side of the vocation was expressed and in essence, the very reason for being a monk or nun, chapter dealt with the daily business of living in community and the outside world. Through the exhibition of penance and punishment and the visible display of the dead, links were formed and individuals moulded into a community living, at least in theory, with one purpose in mind: devotion to and love of God, as expressed through the monastic rule.

The laity and display: public penance

Religious and the secular clergy did not have a monopoly on displaying devotion or penitential practice. Lay people in Normandy also took part in public penance and pilgrimage, atoning for their sins and seeking spiritual aid. Lay pilgrimage and use of monastic space will be examined in detail below, but here we shall consider which spaces were considered important for the expiation of sin.[164] The practice of penance has been examined in great detail by historians.[165] The historiography of this subject has centred around developments within the Church leading to statutes requiring that all Christians should make an annual confession, and a supposed shift from the external performance of penance to individual contrition; but as Hamilton has highlighted, the problems posed by trying to enforce a strict separation of public and private in other areas of medieval life are just as apparent in a discussion of penance.[166] I do not propose to consider in detail canonical developments, but it is worth discussing some of the practices that Eudes Rigaud imposed on the laity and some parish priests within the diocese of Rouen.

By the thirteenth century, the archbishop of Rouen was involved in the administration of secular justice in Normandy and the kingdom of France. He was also the supreme judge in the ecclesiastical courts of his province. The ecclesiastical courts dealt with cases involving the clergy and other people under the Church's jurisdiction, including professed religious, lay brothers and sisters and sometimes widows and crusaders. As Davis has shown, it was largely

---

164   See chapter two for lay pilgrimage.
165   For the early Middle Ages see S. Hamilton, *The Practice of Penance 900–1050*, Studies in History, new series (Woodbridge, 2001). The later period has been studied by Mary Mansfield, particularly the development of public penance. She discussed fully the expulsion of the penitents from the church on Ash Wednesday and their readmittance to the community of the faithful on Maundy Thursday as well as the liturgies and rites associated with this: M. C. Mansfield, *The Humiliation of Sinners: Public Penance in Thirteenth-Century France* (Ithaca and London, 1995). For Ash Wednesday and Maundy Thursday see Mansfield, *Humiliation of Sinners*, pp. 159–247.
166   Hamilton, *Practice of Penance*, pp. 7, 9.

a matter of custom as to what cases came to which court, customs that in Normandy were written down c.1200.[167] It is the cases that came before the ecclesiastical court or that people submitted to the archbishop for arbitration that concern us here. These cases involve offences against church property and clergy, which entailed an automatic sentence of excommunication that could only be lifted through the imposition of a suitable penance and the payment of a fine. The penances Archbishop Eudes imposed were designed not only to expiate sin and restore the sinner to a state of grace, but also to ensure justice was done. These crimes were not secret sins of the heart, but actions that had caused trouble within the local village or town requiring mediation, or violent actions against the Church.

The case of Walter Charue and the commune of Gamaches illustrates how penance was used both as a spiritual and judicial punishment. Walter and the commune were guilty of attacking the archiepiscopal manor at Aliermont, following the death of Eudes's predecessor, Clement, in the process killing a man and looting a church. The archbishop instructed the perpetrators first to make financial restitution, to himself; to the woman whose son was killed; to the priest at St-Aubin for damage caused to his church; to a certain Nicolas for personal injury; and to a general fund for complaints yet to be investigated.[168] Walter Charue, the accused, along with eleven 'prominent men, leaders in their community', were to make twelve processions within eight months. Further humiliation was to follow as the twelve men were to process barefoot and bareheaded in shirt and trunk-hose, whilst Walter was to wear his linen drawers and a hair shirt. Each man was to carry a wand with which he would be beaten by priests at the conclusion of the procession. The group was to process to the cathedrals of Rouen, Évreux, Lisieux, Beauvais, Amiens, Dreux and Gamaches, three times to the church at Aliermont and once to the churches of St-Aubin and St-Vaast. The people at each of these locations were to be informed of the offences for which Walter and his companions were doing penance.[169] Display was two-fold in this instance. Walter and the community leaders were performing a very public act of penance for a crime committed by Walter himself and other members of the commune so they would be reconciled with the Church; Eudes was displaying his power and authority as archbishop. Restitution was thus made to God and the people.

The penance imposed on Walter and his companions encompassed a relatively short time span; that which was imposed on Girard of Montiavoul, Roger of Montiavoul and Peter of Essarts was of ten years' duration. Their offence was also a crime against the Church, namely the murder of a lay

---

[167] Davis, Holy Bureaucrat, p. 131. The customs have been published as Coutumiers de Normandie, I: Le très ancien coutumier de Normandie, ed. E.-J. Tardif, Société de l'Histoire de Normandie (Rouen, 1881). For Eudes Rigaud as an administrator of justice see Davis, Holy Bureaucrat, pp. 130–43. For the secular administration of Normandy see J. R. Strayer, The Administration of Normandy under Saint Louis (Cambridge, MA, 1932).

[168] Nicolas is unidentified, but it is highly likely that he lived or worked on the manor.

[169] Bonnin, p. 24 and Register, pp. 28–9. See also Mansfield, Humiliation of Sinners, pp. 126–7 and Davis, Holy Bureaucrat, pp. 139–40.

brother of Marcheroux. There are similarities with the previous case in that the three men were expected to perform penitential pilgrimages 'clad only in trunk-hose', carrying rods and in addition they were to wear halters round their necks. The first procession was to be to the church of the place in which the murder was committed, where they were to be whipped by the priests and publicly admit their offence. They were to do the same at Gisors the following Easter, Chaumont two weeks after Easter and Frênes the following Sunday. In addition, the three men were to fast every Friday for ten years and to visit Santiago di Compostella before the feast of John the Baptist (24 June).[170] The public penitential pilgrimages imposed on these men ensured that their guilt was acknowledged by the people and it marked them out for some time to come. Even after the memory of the spectacle they presented had died down, people might still wish to know why they fasted on Fridays. In contrast to the previous example where the community leaders appear to have been collectively responsible for the actions of the commune, the three men here were the known murderers.

Eudes's register contains many more examples of penance enjoined on parties for various reasons. As Mary Mansfield has discussed, penance was a useful tool in restoring the peace. Eudes was chosen as an arbiter in a dispute between William of Sauqueville and Thomas the Miller, in which Thomas was alleged to have killed William's brother Gilbert. Eudes seemed to think that Thomas was not guilty of any malicious action but enjoined penance on him anyway, to settle the dispute and restore normal relations within the locality.[171] Here it would seem that Eudes's reputation for fairness was preferred to the secular justice, which could hand down sentences of bodily mutilation and execution.[172] For whatever reason – a lack of evidence to take before the secular courts or the issuing of counter accusations – the parties concerned agreed to arbitration by the archbishop.[173] Other penances involved priests undertaking pilgrimages in recompense for concubinage, often to Rome to seek absolution from the pope and other authorities: for example, Florent, priest of Limay, who was to visit the portals of SS Peter and Paul before the octave of the Epiphany and bring a letter from the papal penitentiary as proof.[174] Clerical celibacy was a serious issue in the ecclesiastical courts and thus the guilty had to travel further afield in order to seek absolution. Whereas in the other examples we have looked at, the perpetrators of crimes against the Church travelled to the scenes of their crime in order to perform penance, or to cathedrals to acknowledge their transgression against archiepiscopal authority, concubinary priests, whose sin was primarily against God,

170 Bonnin, p. 362 and *Register*, p. 413.
171 Bonnin, p. 507 and *Register*, p. 577. Mansfield, *Humiliation of Sinners*, pp. 111–12.
172 Davis, *Holy Bureaucrat*, pp. 136, 141.
173 This is an interesting case and it is not entirely clear how Eudes became involved. As Adam Davis has pointed out in personal communication, there were no obvious grounds for transferring the case to the ecclesiastical courts. He also considers it likely that as the case could not be resolved satisfactorily both sides submitted to arbitration, and that arbiter just happened to be the archbishop.
174 Bonnin, pp. 325–6 and *Register*, p. 372.

therefore had to travel to the seat of God's representative on earth, Rome. Of course, all sins were sins against God in some respect, hence the emphasis on visiting churches in penitential pilgrimages to seek forgiveness, but in these cases, the processions had the effect of memorialising the place and nature of the crime, fixing it in the minds of the people and hopefully acting as a deterrent. Concubinary priests were not committing a sin against a particular place, hence their need to travel to Rome.

The importance of gender is hard to determine in the examples of penance we have discussed above, both in the monastic and lay context. Certainly, concubinary priests were a specific example of how conflicts of gendered identity could impact on an individual's spiritual life but this is discussed in more detail below. Within the monastery the penances enjoined on individuals reflected their place within the monastic community, thus superiors were punished more harshly than subordinates. In the case of the severe public penances imposed by Eudes in his capacity as judge in the ecclesiastical court on members of the laity in Normandy, all our examples concern men. These men were in positions of authority or had sufficient status to make them well-known figures within the community. The imposition of a harsh penance thus impacted on that status through the removal of dignity and further humiliations. Again, this is perhaps indicative of more severe penalties inflicted on people who should be setting an example. We can only speculate why similarly public penances were not imposed on women. Perhaps it was deemed unseemly to expose women in this way. A fuller study of the gendered implications of penance is needed.

Liturgical display

At the centre of organised medieval religion was liturgical practice, particularly the celebration of the mass. The divine office marked the hours of the day and regulated the behaviour of those bound to it. The bells that called monks and nuns to prayer also provided a way of marking the passage of time for the laity who lived near by. The divine office was work in the service of God and so everything had to be performed correctly. Elaborate rituals developed around certain feast days, and processions were as much a part of monastic life as they were in the practice of religion outside it. In this section we shall consider the performance of services and the importance of processions in turn.

The various offices that made up the daily round of prayer – Matins, Lauds, Prime, Terce, Sext, None, Vespers and Compline – along with a daily mass, displayed the purpose of the contemplative vocation to the wider world. Although the services took place in an enclosed community at set times during the day and night, visitors from outside would sometimes attend and, if the church was shared with the local parish, at least one mass a day would be open to the laity. Consequently, ecclesiastical visitors like Abbot Stephen and Archbishop Eudes were anxious to ensure correct practices were followed in terms of liturgy, clothing and vessels.

We have discussed the importance of clothing as a marker of identification with a particular group or vocation. Clothing was also vitally important for the liturgy: a priest and his deacon had to be suitably attired. At times during his visits Eudes celebrated mass, and at Bourg-Achard he did this in his pontificals – his archiepiscopal robes rather than his friar's habit – and preached to the canons and parishioners gathered in the church.[175] By wearing his pontificals, Eudes was demonstrating his authority and status as archbishop, the leading cleric in the province, as opposed to his vocation as a Franciscan friar. The lack of appropriate liturgical clothing in monasteries and parish churches was a serious matter and the archbishop commented on it, but this is discussed below.[176] More important in the context of display was the proper location and housing of relics and the blessed sacrament, namely the consecrated host. Attitudes towards the host and liturgical practice changed throughout the Middle Ages. As Michal Kobialka has shown, devotion to the body of Christ in the sacrament appeared in western churches from the early twelfth century onwards.[177] New ritual practices accompanied this devotion like the burning of a perpetual light in front of the sacrament and the introduction of the elevation of the host during the mass. The Fourth Lateran Council of 1215 decreed that the Eucharist was to be kept locked away, presumably in an aumbry safe or similar receptacle.[178] Eudes was most concerned to find that this was not the case in some of the houses he visited. The candle that was to burn before the blessed sacrament at St-Wandrille was no longer alight and, on a later visit, the monks were instructed to place the sacrament on the altar in a precious repository.[179] The sacrament was placed in a window at Sacey, which meant that the monks had to turn their backs on it during the monastic offices; Eudes instructed them to place it 'honourably upon the altar, in some tabernacle or pyx'.[180] The proper veneration of the sacrament was important not because it represented the body of Christ, but because, according to the doctrine of transubstantiation, it was the body of Christ and therefore must be treated with the utmost reverence. This point was made explicitly by Eudes at St-Ouen in Rouen where he found that the sacrament which should be 'kept with all diligence and treated with reverence and honour according to the canons [of the church councils] was kept in dirty cloths'.[181] Interestingly, the archbishop does not criticise the nunneries for such lapses.

---

175 Appendix A, no. 18; Bonnin, p. 622 and *Register*, p. 716.

176 See chapter three for the use of liturgical space.

177 M. Kobialka, *This is My Body: Representational Practices in the Early Middle Ages* (Ann Arbor, 1999), p. 158.

178 Canon twenty: *Decrees*, p. 244.

179 Bonnin, pp. 134, 637 and *Register*, pp. 152, 733.

180 Appendix A, no. 71; Bonnin, p. 246 and *Register*, p. 274. This issue is also discussed by Davis, *Holy Bureaucrat*, p. 88.

181 Bonnin, pp. 56–7 and *Register*, p. 62. See also canon nineteen of Lateran IV, which stated that church vessels, linen and vestments should be clean and suitable, *Decrees*, p. 244.

The blessed sacrament as the body of Christ may be considered a relic. Relics of course had to be treated with due reverence and displayed in an appropriate manner. They were also many and various. La Trinité in Caen, for example, claimed possession of the hair and beard of St Peter, fingers of St Nicholas, some of Mary Magdelene's hair and the body of one of the Holy Innocents; St-Etienne in the same city had relics of the martyr St Stephen.[182] Relics were not only important due to their sanctity, but also because they drew the faithful into religious communities as we will see later;[183] however, Eudes noticed that in one community in particular, the chapter of St-Mellon in Pontoise, the reliquaries of St Mellon and other saints had rotted away. Decay had reached such an advanced state that the reliquaries crumbled when touched.[184] The archbishop does not explain how or why the deterioration occurred. Clearly, this would present problems when the faithful came to seek the intercession of the saint. Questions might be raised as to why the saints had allowed such a thing to happen. The uncertainty about the moral state of the priests serving the church which might result would have a disastrous effect on the reputation of the community.

In the positioning of the sacrament and relics, space was paramount. Both objects had to be clearly visible and placed where they might be kept in good condition and treated with due reverence. Nothing was more important in the monastery than God. People became monks and nuns in theory because they wanted to live closer to God. The physical incarnation of God in Christ's body re-enacted in the Eucharist and displayed on the altar, was at the centre of monastic devotion.

Processions were an important part of liturgical practice both inside and outside the monastery. We have noted already their role in the performance of lay penance. Processions were also an important part of pilgrimage as we shall see below.[185] Professed religious, secular clergy and the laity participated in processions to mark specific days in the liturgical calendar such as Palm Sunday and other major feasts. These processions therefore presented an opportunity for different groups of people to mingle. The monks of Fécamp's Palm Sunday procession encompassed the entire precinct, stopping at the gates of the ducal castle on the return to the church.[186] Processions also took place weekly on Sundays. Archbishop Eudes noted that at St-Martin in Pontoise, women and laymen entered the cloister on Sundays marching in procession, presumably before or after mass.[187] Eudes disapproved and banned further displays of this kind. We do not know why or what form this exercise took, but it seems to have been a customary practice for the people in this locality, cementing links between the secular parish and monastic community. Certainly, as we shall see below, Eudes was very keen to keep women out

182   Fauroux, nos 29–30.
183   See chapter two for pilgrimage.
184   Bonnin, p. 316 and *Register*, p. 360.
185   See chapter two.
186   *The Ordinal of the Abbey of the Holy Trinity Fécamp*, ed. D. Chadd, Henry Bradshaw Society 3, 2 vols (Woodbridge, 1999), vol. 1, p. 214.
187   Appendix A, no. 65; Bonnin, p. 41 and *Register*, p. 46.

of male monastic cloisters, but his insistence on a greater separation of lay and monastic people is reflective of trends that sought a sharper division of the people from the clergy. Lay folk caused problems at the nuns' abbey of Montivilliers, though here it was the nuns themselves who were penalised and their processions stopped. The nuns shared part of their abbey church, the north aisle of the nave, with the parish of St-Sauveur. The nuns' processions through their own church may have brought them into contact with the parishioners. Nothing concrete that would have brought the nuns into disrepute was reported and the archbishop's actions seem to have been a pre-emptive measure designed to prevent scandal. Eudes ruled that the prayers and antiphons sung during the procession must instead be sung by the nuns standing in the choir.[188] This changed a liturgical practice from movement through space to a static service, limiting the ways in which the nuns could worship and possibly changing the meaning of their prayers, which would have been sung at particular locations in their procession. An earlier prohibition had been placed on the nuns of St-Amand in Rouen. A papal bull of Innocent IV, dated December 1244, banned these nuns from holding processions unless they had ecclesiastical permission. This document laid down other restrictions which included celebrating the office with the church doors closed, in a low voice and without sounding bells.[189] St-Amand was situated within the ancient city walls in Rouen, in close proximity to the male house of St-Ouen to the north and not far from the cathedral, which was to the south of the abbey. The church authorities may have wanted the community to appear as unobtrusive as possible given its proximity to the cathedral church and monastery. Penelope Johnson argues that the late twelfth and thirteenth centuries saw the Church try and limit nuns' involvement in extra-claustral processions, specifically the Rogation day processions.[190] The prohibitions placed on St-Amand are a consequence of hardening attitudes. Abbot Stephen, for example, objected to the nuns at Mortain allowing the clerics of the church of St-Firmatus to enter their choir and to the nuns leaving their church in the direction of Bayeux when processing.[191] The separation of lay and monastic, especially female monastics who, by virtue of their sex, could not become priests and thus had no reason to mingle with laity, had to be maintained.

188 Bonnin, p. 472 and *Register*, pp. 538–9.
189 Printed in Dom. Pommeraye, *Histoire de l'abbaye de Saint-Amand* (Rouen, 1662, following *Histoire de l'abbaye royale de Saint-Ouen*), pp. 93–4 and M.-J. Le Cacheux, 'Histoire de l'abbaye de Saint-Amand-de-Rouen des origines à la fin du XVIe siècle', *BSAN*, 44 (1937), pp. 254–8. The bull is also listed in *Regesta ponitificum Romanorum 1198–1304*, ed. A. Potthast, 2 vols (Berlin, 1875), vol. 2, p. 955. The bull is discussed in Johnson, *Equal in Monastic Profession*, p. 141, where she gives the date as 3 June 1244, following Le Cacheux, 'Histoire de l'abbaye de Saint-Amand', p. 44 and pp. 254–8. Le Cacheux lists this document as a bull of Celestine III of 1191 preserved in a *vidimus* of 1355. There is no reference to any such document in Potthast.
190 Johnson, *Equal in Monastic Profession*, pp. 140–1. Rogation days were the three days preceding Ascension Day, which occurred forty days after Easter.
191 *Registrum epistolarum*, p. 241.

Within the cloister, there were times when processions were allowed, notably at the burial of important members of the community and founding family. Display is again paramount both in the honouring of the deceased and through collective mourning and thanksgiving. The need for processional spaces affected the architecture of the church. At La Trinité, in Caen, the move from a rectangular chevet to an ambulatory was designed to accommodate processions and facilitate better movement through the church.[192] A very good example of how architecture was designed to encompass processions is the provision made for the burial of Bishop Hugh of Lisieux in the nuns' church at the abbey of St-Désir in Lisieux.[193] Archaeological excavation, carried out shortly after the Second World War, revealed the remains of an ornamental Romanesque pavement situated within a primitive church dating from the eleventh century comprising a single nave and an apse. It is possible that the structure was designed to be included in a larger building as the community became more established.[194] Deshayes argues that the date of the pavement coincides with the death of Bishop Hugh in 1077. We know from Orderic Vitalis that work on the nuns' church was fairly advanced because Hugh was buried in the choir, possibly the structure outlined above, with his tomb bordered by two openings in the side walls.[195] Deshayes argues that the pavement assumed a liturgical function. It was composed of three parallel routes forming a symbolic access towards Hugh's tomb and the altar beyond. The pavement could therefore have been designed as a means of facilitating liturgical processions and movement through and towards the most sacred spaces of the church, namely the choir and sanctuary. Certainly funerals of important benefactors were grand occasions within the life of a community, as can be seen from the burial of William the Conqueror at St-Etienne in Caen at which Orderic tells us a great many lay people were present.[196] It is possible that similar practices were followed at La Trinité, where the founder, Duchess Matilda, was buried in the choir in 1083. Display associated with burial will be discussed below, but in the example of the pavement at St-Désir, we can see how liturgical practices and the need to display the tomb of the abbey's founder determined the church plan and use of space.

---

[192] For details regarding architectural changes to the east end of the church see M. Baylé, 'La Trinité de Caen', *Congrès archéologique de France*, (1978), p. 36.

[193] Appendix B, no. 13.

[194] J. Deshayes, 'Le pavement roman de l'ancienne abbatiale Notre-Dame-du-Pré à Saint-Désir de Lisieux et le problème de la sépulture de l'évêque Hughes d'Eu', *Chapitre et cathédrals en Normandie*, ed. S. Lemagner et al., Annales de Normandie Série des congrès des Sociétés Historiques et Archéologiques de Normandie 2 (Caen, 1997), p. 472.

[195] Deshayes, 'Le pavement roman', p. 475 and OV, vol. 3, pp. 16–19.

[196] See below chapter four.

Conclusion

Display was an essential and multifaceted part of religious life in Normandy that worked to the benefit of the laity, secular clergy and professed religious. Monastic buildings demonstrated an affiliation with a particular order and so attracted donations from supporters of that order. Likewise, abbeys founded by wealthy patrons, for example La Trinité and St-Etienne in Caen, exhibited through their architecture and community the benefactor's position and influence in secular society, as well as attracting further donations from individuals who wished to be associated with such an establishment. Display also operated on an individual scale. Monks and nuns were supposed to adopt certain clothing on entering the religious life, and by conforming to or rejecting the habit, they demonstrated their commitment to their vocation and the surrendering or otherwise of their individual will. Lepers' and priests' clothing also marked them as groups apart from society. Unlike monastics and lepers though, priests lived outside cloister walls within the secular world and so their clothing served to remind everyone of their status. Display was also a way of forming communities through common practices notably in the chapter houses of monasteries where links between individual monks and nuns and their wider order were forged: this included the practice of penance. For the laity, public penance served to fix crimes and sins in the memory and serve as a very visible deterrent as well as displaying ecclesiastical power. Display not only marked areas set aside for God through particular architecture and ground plans, but also acted as a magnet for the laity to come to these places for worship, healing, work and hospitality, and it is to the reception and intrusion of the laity into sacred spaces that we now turn.

2

Reception and Intrusion

In this chapter I examine the theme of intrusion by the laity into sacred space and the methods used to accommodate it. It would be wrong to talk of intrusion purely as the incorrect use of space. Attitudes towards a lay presence in religious spaces varied according to context, and, accordingly, could be welcomed or discouraged. Reception and intrusion can, however, be seen as a direct result of display and are revealed most obviously in normative texts and *miracula*.[1] The services provided by monastic houses for lay people led to ingress by the laity into both nuns' and monks' cloisters. The laity came into monastic houses seeking hospitality, charity, schooling for their children and a place for retirement. Churches and monasteries also provided access to shrines and relics for pilgrims, which resulted in lay people trespassing into areas reserved for the monks, nuns and clergy. The problem of intrusion is particularly acute in a discussion of clerical celibacy, as revealed in Bishop Arnulf of Lisieux's letters and Archbishop Eudes Rigaud's register. Parish priests interacted with the laity to a greater extent than their monastic counterparts. Problems of gender are apparent, both in terms of the intrusion of wives and concubines into a male sacred space, and in the identity of priests as celibate males in a secular society. There was a very real tension between a strict interpretation of the rule favoured by the Church hierarchy and the need to deal with more practical day-to-day matters.

The laity in the cloister: temporal reasons

The presence of the laity in monastic cloisters and cathedral precincts can be explained by two factors: the practical services that religious houses provided and the sacral functions that they performed for the laity. In the first group fall the themes of hospitality, including provision for old age, charity, education and work. In the second group the power of the saints as manifested through the maintenance of holy places, and church services are considered. The attitude of the Church to interaction in these various forms differed according to circumstances.

---

[1]   The theme of display is considered in chapter one.

Religious houses in medieval society had a duty of hospitality, which was considered a necessary part of the monastic vocation in the rule of St Benedict. Chapter fifty-three of the rule prescribed that all guests should be shown charity and received 'as Christ' who would say 'I was a guest and you took me in'.[2] St Benedict laid down how a guest was to be received with great precision. The guest was to be met by the abbot and the brethren and then they would pray together. After prayer, the guest was to be given the kiss of peace. Benedict underlined the humility with which guests were to be received as befitting the reception of Christ in the form of a stranger. After the guest's reception, he should be 'led to prayer' presumably so he could undertake private prayer in the church, before sitting down to hear the law of God and eating with the head of the community or someone appointed by him. The reception of the guest was completed by the washing of his feet. The procedure laid down in the rule marks the movement of the guest from the secular space of the world outside the monastery to the sacred space of the enclosure. Temporarily the guest became an associate member of the community though still separate, both in terms of mental and physical space. Guests ate at the abbot's table, not with the community as a whole.[3] This separation was underlined by the provision of a separate kitchen so 'that guests who turn up at unexpected hours – and a monastery is never short of them – may not disturb the brethren'.[4] Only monks so authorised were allowed to associate or to speak with guests: should a brother come across a guest he was to ask for a blessing and explain he was otherwise not allowed to speak.[5]

By the period under consideration here, the rule had been modified by some commentators. Lanfranc, for example, stated that the abbot was to eat in the refectory with the community in order to maintain discipline.[6] Visiting clerks might be granted permission to eat at the abbot's table in the refectory, but other guests ate in the accommodation set aside for them separate from the monks.[7] The guest master was the intermediary between the monks in the cloister and the guests. He was to ensure that no one entered the cloister wearing riding boots or spurs, barefoot, or in their underwear. Lanfranc makes it clear that guests were not allowed to wander around the cloister at will: should they wish to see the buildings of the monastery, then the guest master might give them a guided tour, but was to ensure that the community was not sitting in the cloister.[8] As guests according to Lanfranc's constitutions ate separately, the guest master was to ensure that the guest house was adequately stocked and to fetch comestibles from the cellarer.[9] These statutes

---

2   *Rule*, ch. 53, pp. 246, 248 and Matthew 25:35. As the rule of St Benedict was written by a man for men, the male pronoun is used throughout in the translation here.
3   *Rule*, ch. 56, p. 257.
4   *Rule*, ch. 53, pp. 247–8.
5   *Rule*, ch. 53, pp. 247–8.
6   *Monastic Constitutions*, pp. 108–13 and *passim*.
7   *Monastic Constitutions*, pp. 130–1.
8   *Monastic Constitutions*, pp. 132–3. The community would sit in the cloister for private prayer and reading.
9   *Monastic Constitutions*, pp. 130–1.

again underline the separateness of the cloistered religious and their guests. The exact mechanics of hospitality differed from house to house, but in all communities the tension between the presence of lay visitors and the need to continue the daily round of monastic life was present. As Julie Kerr has indicated: hospitality 'could upset the quietude of the cloister, distract the brethren from their spiritual duties, or encourage lax behaviour such as casual conversation and a more luxurious diet'.[10]

Unfortunately, little information exists as to the exact nature of the hospitality required by guests at Norman monastic houses and, in particular, as to where the guests were housed. At Jumièges, a large twelfth-century vaulted hall in the west range of the cloister served as the guest house.[11] The engravings collected in *Monasticon Gallicanum* show great variation in the siting of guest accommodation, but only in houses of monks. These engravings have to be treated with caution as they date from the seventeenth century, after many of the medieval buildings had been replaced with more modern ones, and are executed in a very stylised manner. It is possible, though by no means certain, that the buildings labelled on the plans correspond to the medieval location of certain areas. According to these engravings, sometimes the guest house was located in the west range as at St-Vigor near Bayeux or Bernay.[12] The guest house in other Norman houses was situated away from the cloister as at Conches.[13] It is therefore difficult to draw any firm conclusions as to where guests on the whole were located. As monastic houses differentiated between guests in terms of social and religious status, different areas were set aside respectively in the precinct or cloister and so the lodgings for guests varied from house to house.[14]

Additional information as to the location of guest accommodation is found in the written sources. In his register of visitations, Archbishop Eudes mentions a number of places where guests were housed and fed. Some communities did have specific areas set aside for the reception of guests, which Eudes refers to as 'guest houses' (*hospitalia*).[15] At Bourg-Achard, guests were received in a 'farmhouse behind the gardens'.[16] Communities of nuns also made provision for guests: for example, Bondeville had a guest house, but it was situated too close to the community and would thus have disturbed the peace of the cloister.[17] Within communities of Augustinian canons, communities charged with pastoral work in the parishes, guests were received in the canons'

[10] J. Kerr, 'Monastic Hospitality: the Benedictines in England, c.1070–1245', ANS, 23 (2000, 2001), p. 97.
[11] Appendix A, no. 42.
[12] Appendix A, nos 89, 14.
[13] Appendix A, no. 25.
[14] Julie Kerr has noted similar problems in her work on the Benedictines in England. She suggests that male and female guests were simultaneously lodged in various places including the west range of the cloister. J. Kerr, 'Monastic Hospitality: the Benedictines in England c.1070–1245', (Ph.D. thesis, University of St Andrews, 2000), p. 66.
[15] For example, St-Pierre-sur-Dives, Bonnin, p. 77 and *Register*, p. 87.
[16] Bonnin, p. 514 and *Register*, p. 587.
[17] Bonnin, p. 615 and *Register*, p. 708.

houses.[18] Comparative material from England exists that indicates that guest provision could be quite spacious. At St Albans, Abbot Geoffrey (1119–46) built a large and noble hall for the reception of guests with the queen's chamber adjacent to it – the queen being the only woman permitted to stay in the monastery.[19] Within Normandy we can speculate that, at a number of religious houses, specific areas were set aside for the reception of guests. These areas would have been located away from the main claustral areas used by the community, namely the church, chapter house, refectory and dormitory, and so were probably located either in the west range of the cloister or in the precinct, as at Bourg-Achard.

More information exists as to the reception of guests by monastic houses and the ecclesiastical authorities' response to the practice of hospitality. It is clear from the pages of Archbishop Eudes's and Abbot Stephen's visitation records that not everyone was welcome at all houses. These prescriptions were largely based on gender. At Villers-Canivet, Stephen prohibited noblewomen or their maidservants from spending the night in the abbey.[20] Although they might visit in the daytime, Stephen considered it unacceptable for secular women, who might be wives and mothers, to spend the night in a community of virgins and other celibate women. This prohibition presumably extended to men as well: at Mortain, the other Norman nunnery in Stephen's care, they were to remain outside the cloister when their women came to visit.[21] Eudes forbade women to dine at the male communities of Bures, Longueil, Alençon, Bourg-Achard, Gasny, Sigy and Beuvron.[22] In comparison, in England women were also prohibited from spending the night in the confines of Benedictine abbeys like York.[23]

The Cistercian order took a particularly strict line regarding the presence of women guests. The earliest surviving *capitula* from the first half of the twelfth century state that women were not allowed to come inside the monastery gate, nor were they to be lodged within the enclosure.[24] Later statutes laid down harsh penalties for abbots and communities who allowed women into their monasteries. In a statute of 1193, abbots were to be deposed from office and any monk who aided women to enter the cloister without the abbot's permission was to be transferred to another house.[25] In 1197, punishment was extended to the whole community as the general chapter forbade the celebration of the conventual mass for a three-day period.[26] These earlier statutes are echoed in Abbot Stephen of Lexington's instructions to Cistercian monks in Normandy

18   For example at Graville: Bonnin, p. 266 and *Register*, p. 298.
19   Kerr, 'Monastic Hospitality', thesis, pp. 66 and 101.
20   *Registrum epistolarum*, p. 242.
21   *Registrum epistolarum*, p. 239.
22   Appendix A, nos 1, 20, 47, 35, 94, 15; Bonnin, pp. 208, 209, 373, 281, 390, 441, 459 and *Register*, pp. 228, 230, 422, 316, 444, 512, 523.
23   Kerr, 'Monastic Hospitality', thesis, p. 101 and note 127.
24   *Narrative and Legislative Texts from Early Cîteaux*, p. 411.
25   *Twelfth-century Statutes*, 1193, no. 11, p. 261.
26   *Twelfth-century Statutes*, 1197 no. 6, pp. 381–2. See also Williams, *Cistercians in the Early Middle Ages*, p. 132.

that they should only speak with women at the door to the monastery rarely and briefly, whilst chaperoned by someone of good moral standing, so avoiding the need for women to come in at all.[27] Problems were not confined to Normandy, as similar examples from England and France demonstrate. The prior and cellarer of the Cistercian abbey of Beaulieu in Hampshire were dismissed for allowing the queen to stay at the house for almost three weeks following its dedication in 1246, even though Prince Edward's illness dictated that she should remain.[28] Ingeborg of Denmark, King Philip Augustus's second wife, spent two nights in the infirmary at Pontigny in 1205, which caused the Cistercian general chapter to declare that such actions were against the *forma* of the order.[29] The injunctions against the presence of women in male houses were based on the sexual threat that women posed to the celibate monks. In order to ensure the maintenance of chastity, it was necessary to prohibit the presence of women within the monastic precincts: they were seen as a source of pollution and were thus a danger to the sacred space of the monastery and the bodily sacred space of the monks themselves. These injunctions give some indication of the nature of the tension arising from the duty to provide hospitality and the need to maintain the integrity of the cloister.

There is no doubt that hospitality could prove to be extremely burdensome to a community and an abuse of monastic space. Just how great a burden these visits could be is demonstrated by the case of Mabel of Bellême and the monastery of St-Évroul. Orderic Vitalis complained that Mabel hated the monks due to the long feud between her family of Bellême and the founders of the monastery, the Giroie. As a result she looked for ways to injure the monks surreptitiously. She could not act openly since her husband, Roger of Montgomery supported the community. Consequently she acted against the monks by abusing their hospitality and descending on them with a large retinue of knights, thus reducing the sacred nature of the monastery.[30] After the foundation of the women's community at St-Léger-des-Préaux, Humphrey of Vieilles's sons, Roger de Beaumont and Robert, *dapifer*, brought Duke William to the abbey with a great company of warriors.[31] These warriors would have required food and drink for themselves and their horses, all at the expense of the community.

The financial burden placed on communities by the provision of hospitality was recognised by Abbot Stephen and Archbishop Eudes. Stephen calculated that Savigny used as much bread daily in the guest house as was consumed by twenty monks in the refectory.[32] At St-Martin-de-Pontoise, Eudes forbade

---

27   *Registrum epistolarum*, pp. 214 and 221.
28   W. H. St J. Hope and H. Brakspear, 'The Cistercian Abbey of Beaulieu in the County of Southampton', *Archaeological Journal*, 63 (1906), p. 137.
29   *Statuta*, vol. 1, 1205, no. 10, pp. 308–9 and Kerr, 'Monastic Hospitality', thesis, p. 101 and note 127.
30   OV, vol. 2, pp. 54–5.
31   Appendix B, no. 17. *Regesta regum*, no. 217.
32   *Registrum epistolarum*, pp. 227–8. See also D. H. Williams, 'Layfolk within Cistercian Precincts', *Monastic Studies II: the Continuity of Tradition*, ed. J. Loades (Bangor, 1991), pp. 87–118.

the abbot to receive anyone as a monk or guest without his permission: an exception was made if the guest was of the household of the king or 'such a one to whom hospitality could not be denied without violating the spirit of hospitality'.[33] At the Cistercian nunnery of Bival, the admission of lay people was restricted to those 'whom it would be a scandal to keep out' and no guests were received at Notre-Dame-de-Chaumont, a male community, because of its poverty.[34] The people to whom it would be a scandal to deny hospitality were benefactors of the house or those of very high social status. It was generally accepted in medieval society that royalty or patrons could find hospitality at monastic houses and this is reflected in the literature of the period, illustrated by a passage from one of Marie de France's *Lais*. In *La Fresne*, the male protagonist 'hit upon a scheme: he would become a benefactor of the abbey, give it so much land that it would be enriched forever; he'd thus establish a patron's right to live there'.[35] A practical example exists from Normandy in which Roger Balfour granted various lands to St-Etienne in Caen in return for reception into the confraternity of the abbey and the right to stay there for one night, four times a year. The abbey prudently stipulated that Roger should not visit with a large retinue.[36] Monastic houses then, had to make an effort to provide hospitality in keeping with the precepts of the rule, unless their poverty – and this afflicted male and female communities alike – was such that this duty would place an intolerable burden on their financial resources.

Whilst some Norman houses struggled through poverty to provide for their guests, others were just plain neglectful. At several houses Archbishop Eudes commented that guests were not well received. At St-Laurent-en-Lyons a canon was to be appointed specifically to deal with the needs of the community's guests.[37] At St-Pierre-sur-Dives, which had a guest house, the guests were not well looked after because the community had given part of the building to a certain layman. Eudes instructed the abbot to appoint one of the monks to look after the guests more honourably within three days and to use his own funds if there was a deficit in the financial provision for hospitality.[38] At Bourg-Achard any visitors would have endured an uncomfortable night as the buildings of the monastery were badly roofed and uninhabitable in many places, especially the farmhouse that served as the guest quarters.[39]

So far we have considered the nature of the guests received and the financial problems linked to the provision of monastic hospitality. As well as these material problems, hospitality also affected the spiritual life of the monastery. We have already noted that an influx of visitors could cause disturbance to the smooth running of the community and this disturbance can be seen

33 Bonnin, p. 241 and *Register*, p. 267.
34 Bonnin, pp. 117, 529 and *Register*, pp. 131, 604.
35 Marie de France, *Lais*, ed. A. Ewert, with an introduction and bibliography by G. S. Burgess, French Texts (London, 1995), p. 41 and *The Lais of Marie de France*, trans. R. Hanning and J. Ferrante (Durham, NC, 1978), p. 80.
36 Cited in Potts, *Monastic Revival*, p. 48.
37 Bonnin, p. 66 and *Register*, p. 75.
38 Appendix A, no. 84; Bonnin, p. 77 and *Register*, p. 87.
39 Bonnin, p. 514 and *Register*, p. 587.

throughout the period under consideration. Before Herluin founded Bec in c.1030 and became a monk, he travelled around various houses searching for the best place to fulfil his vocation. In his *Life* of Herluin, written between 1109 and 1117, Gilbert Crispin reports on the problems Herluin encountered in finding a suitable place. One Christmas Day he visited a monastery of greater reputation than others he had previously seen. After the festive procession, Herluin saw everywhere 'monks laughing at laymen with unfitting condescension' and two monks came to blows.[40] No doubt the presence of a large number of lay persons might encourage the monks to act in an unseemly fashion and contrary to their spiritual vocation. Archbishop Eudes also recorded instances of disturbance to the spiritual side of monasticism in the thirteenth century. At St-Wandrille, certain monks were in the habit of dining with guests until such a late hour that they could not attend Compline.[41] Abbot Robert of Jumièges was reprimanded and told that he should refrain from his habit of sitting up late with certain guests, 'telling jokes and drinking'.[42] Alas, the archbishop does not give us any examples of the venerable abbot's jokes. What Herluin found so shocking, and what Eudes objected to, was the behaviour of the monks in the presence of lay people. It was unacceptable for persons vowed to God, and who should thus be setting an example of Christian piety, to act in an unmonastic way before their guests: their vocation was paramount. Part of Eudes's insistence on there being a monk in charge of the guest quarters at some houses was so that the rest of the community could follow the monastic day with a minimum of interruption. Guests had needs to be seen to, but not at the expense of the monastic office. If the duty of hospitality lay in the reception of Christ as a stranger, then the quality of the space into which the guest was received should reflect this fact. The monastery was a sacred space, sanctified by the activities of the people within the community. The reception of Christ as a stranger further sanctified the space and so the community and its guests should act accordingly.

In addition to the reception of temporary guests, religious communities also took in lodgers on a more permanent basis in their retirement. An individual wishing to retire to a monastery or hospital would give a grant of land or property in return for subsistence during the remainder of their lifetime.[43] This course of action seems to have been popular at the Cistercian nunneries in Abbot Stephen's care. As a consequence he found it necessary to state that seculars – he does not specify whether these individuals were men or women – could be received to live in the outer court with his permission, but were absolutely forbidden to intrude further into the nuns' space and live in the cloister.[44] A donor to Bondeville, a certain Robert, placed a condition on

---

[40]   Gilbert Crispin, *Vita Herluini*, p. 191 and trans. Vaughn, 'Life of Lord Herluin', p. 72. See also *GND*, vol. 2, pp. 60–5.

[41]   Bonnin, p. 325 and *Register*, p. 371.

[42]   Bonnin, p. 585 and *Register*, p. 674.

[43]   See B. Harvey, *Living and Dying in England 1100–1540: the Monastic Experience* (Oxford, 1993), pp. 192–8.

[44]   *Registrum epistolarum*, p. 235. Waddell, 'One Day in the Life of the Savigniac Nun', p. 145.

his gift that 'my Genevieve be able to have one room in the aforementioned house in which she can remain the rest of her life'.[45] We do not know who this woman was nor whether she took vows, only that she and Robert deemed Bondeville a fit place for her retirement. It is not precisely clear why people chose to retire to religious houses. Shulamith Shahar has suggested that old nobles retired to monasteries because they may have felt weary and were conscious that their status in society was diminished.[46] The benefit to the community was the initial grant. The reverse side of the deal was that in times of financial necessity, there was an extra person to cater for. In addition, a lay person who was living within the precincts of the monastery, but not actually under obedience, was essentially unregulated by the rule. They could come and go as they pleased and introduced an element of disturbance to the life of the community.

The presence of people seeking a comfortable retirement in hospitals or leper houses raises a different question: what was the purpose of such institutions?[47] Prior to the last quarter of the twelfth century, leper houses and hospitals operated in a more informal manner than other religious houses. After the Third Lateran Council of 1179, the idea of these institutions as *loci religiosi*, sacred places, became much more marked. Canon twenty-three of the council decreed that all lepers living in a community should have for their own usage a church, cemetery and priest, thus making these establishments spiritually autonomous from the local parish.[48] The statute is quite clear that lepers were to have their own provision for their own needs. The problem of healthy people entering a hospital or a leper house because they perceived it as being a suitable place for their retirement was tackled in the provincial councils of the early thirteenth century. The councils of Paris (1212) and of Rouen (1214) dealt with the reform of staff serving in hospitals, placing a firm emphasis on caring for the sick as a religious vocation.[49] The Rouen council issued a statement that the staff serving in hospitals and leper houses were to take the three vows of poverty, chastity and obedience and that they had to wear the religious habit. Staff members were to be reduced so that there were no more than was strictly necessary. In other words, those healthy persons who entered such an establishment were there to care for the sick and administer the revenues of the house accordingly. People who wished to be maintained

---

45 Johnson, *Equal in Monastic Profession*, pp. 179–80 and note 43 citing an unpublished charter dated to 1281. Robert became a monk, presumably a lay brother, at the priory in 1290.

46 S. Shahar, *Growing Old in the Middle Ages* (London and New York, 1997), pp. 121–5.

47 The questions raised by the presence of different groups of lay people in hospitals and leper houses has briefly been discussed by F.-O. Touati in 'Les groups de laics dans les hôpitaux et les leprosaries au moyen âge', *Les mouvances laïques des orders religieux*, pp. 137–62. See also Rawcliffe, *Leprosy in Medieval England*, pp. 297–9.

48 *Decrees*, pp. 222–3. The implications of Lateran III for lepers are discussed in J. Avril, 'Le III concile de Latran et les communautés des lépreux', *Revue Mabillon*, 60 (1981) pp. 21–76.

49 For Paris (1212), see Mansi, vol. 22, cols 835–6 and for Rouen (1214), see Mansi, vol. 22, col. 913.

at the expense of the hospital but without taking on religious obligations were to be excluded.

That healthy people were found in hospitals and leper houses to the detriment of the sick can be seen in the pages of Archbishop Eudes's register. During a visit to Salle-aux-Puelles in 1265/6, Eudes encountered one Isabelle of Avenes, a healthy woman living in a community of leprous sisters. Eudes was angered by her presence on two accounts: first she was a healthy woman living in a place she had no right to be, and second she had infringed the vow of chastity that the sisters were obliged to take by giving birth to a child. The sin was compounded by the fact that the father of her child was the chaplain at another leper house.[50] Obligations towards the sick were not taken seriously by the various brothers and sisters at other hospitals in Normandy. Eudes noted that at the hôtel-Dieu in Gournay, one of the sisters was 'destroying and even pilfering the goods of the house' as was Brother John of La Madeleine in Rouen.[51] Incompetence or fraud in financial affairs continued at Gournay where, in 1261, the archbishop recorded that the sick poor received little from the goods of the house.[52] It seems that the staff had little interest in the management of the hospital for the benefit of the sick poor and were interested mainly in their own comfort. Their actions were a form of lay intrusion into sacred space by subverting the purpose of the foundation. Healthy people who had a vocation to tend the sick poor and entered hospitals and leper houses as brothers and sisters for that reason were welcomed. Those people who wished for a comfortable place to live, entered in contravention of numerous statutes and were responsible for a reduction in the sacral nature of the space devoted to the service of God through the service of the poor.

Throughout the period 1050–1300 there was a conflict between the duties to provide hospitality; the financial needs of the communities concerned, especially in the case of nunneries and hospitals; and the need to maintain the enclosure as a sacred space set aside for the worship of God. This conflict had to be negotiated and accommodated as hospitality was for religious communities a sacred and cultural duty. There was great variation between houses as to guests received and where they were housed, both between orders and within houses of the same affiliation. There were, however, limits placed on monastic hospitality based on gender and social status and therefore very few communities operated an open house policy towards guests. At Cistercian houses, every effort was made to prevent any lay person staying with the community overnight. Men were prohibited from entering the precincts of women's houses and women were banned from houses of monks. Benedictine houses had greater leeway to admit guests, though they generally had to be of good standing, presumably patrons. This accommodation extended to some women who wished to visit male houses. Casual visits were discouraged in all religious communities. Those houses that experienced financial difficulties

---

[50]   Bonnin, p. 538 and *Register*, pp. 614–15. See also Bériac, *Histoire des lépreux au moyen âge*, p. 239.
[51]   Appendix C, no. 12; Bonnin, pp. 283, 563 and *Register*, pp. 319, 645.
[52]   Bonnin, p. 413 and *Register*, p. 471.

were prohibited from accepting guests at all, due to the burden this placed on the communities' resources.

The duty of hospitality introduced an element of disturbance into the day-to-day life of the monastery. Guests had needs that must be met and which could lead to a diminution in the quality of the sacred space of the monastery; they could also, as we have seen, encourage monks and nuns to behave in an unseemly fashion. The presence of guests in hospitals and leper houses, other than pilgrims or the sick poor, constituted a serious subversion of the purpose of these institutions. Providing a space within the precincts of such communities for healthy persons resulted in a decrease in the finances set aside for the care of the sick poor, thus negating the sacred quality of the space. Some communities did allow older people to retire and live within their precincts, though rules were put in place to prevent them intruding unduly into the life of the community. In contrast to the provision of more temporary hospitality, monasteries benefited from such arrangements due to the provision of land or monetary donations to support the retired person.

Connected with the monastic duty of hospitality was the need to care for the sick and poor. Just as hospitality involved the reception of Christ as a stranger, ministry to the poor allowed the adoration of Christ in the poor. This was both formalised in the liturgy and enacted through the distribution of alms. The reception of the poor and distribution of charity present several problems in the context of lay people coming into monastic precincts: notably to whom were alms given; where were alms given and were there any regulations in place to ensure the efficient distribution of alms? Those who received alms from Norman religious houses were a very diverse group including lepers, scholars and uncategorised poor. Practices differed from house to house and order to order, but it was clear from the records of both Archbishop Eudes Rigaud and Abbot Stephen of Lexington, that monastic charity was viewed as an essential part of the vocation. Charity was both practical in terms of alleviating poverty and symbolic in the adoration of the poor.[53]

In keeping with Christ's example of servant leadership at the Last Supper, the poor played a significant part in the Maundy Thursday liturgy. Lanfranc gives a very detailed description of the rituals in the monastic constitutions. The poor men were led into the cloister by the cellarer and almoner and had their feet washed. Following this, the abbot and community genuflected before the poor in order to adore Christ before washing the feet of the poor and kissing them on the mouth and eyes. In addition, each man was given

---

[53]   There is a great deal of debate about the efficacy of monastic charity in alleviating poverty, particularly in regard to the dissolution of the monasteries in England and Wales. See Harvey, *Living and Dying in England* and M. Mollat, *The Poor in the Middle Ages: an Essay in Social History* (New Haven and London, 1986). For the effects of the dissolution see N. Rushton, 'Monastic Charitable Provision in Tudor England: Quantifying and Qualifying Poor Relief in the Early Sixteenth Century', *Continuity and Change*, 16 (2001), pp. 9–44. It is not my purpose to try and analyse statistically or otherwise the amount of alms dispensed by Norman religious houses, but to try and address some of the spatial problems raised.

drinks and two pence.[54] Acts similar to this would have been performed in religious houses in Normandy. Pious lay people also adopted this practice. Queen Margaret of Scotland (c.1046–93), wife of Malcolm III, was known for her charity in keeping twenty-four poor persons whom she fed and clothed.[55] Their daughter, Edith-Matilda, wife of King Henry I, brought lepers into her apartments to wash their feet and kiss them.[56] King Henry III of England (1207–72) and his counterpart in France, Louis IX, were also renowned for their charity and they committed huge resources to alms-giving and feeding the poor.[57]

Whereas the Maundy rites were highly ritualised, charity was also given on a more practical level at frequent intervals during the week. In Benedictine houses, the almoner was in charge of the collection and distribution of alms, whereas in Cistercian houses it was the porter's job. Alms were also dispensed by houses of canons and hospitals and leper houses. There were no hard and fast rules about when, where and to whom alms should be distributed and practices differed from house to house, though it is clear the poor should be the main beneficiaries. The abbot of Barbery, in the diocese of Bayeux, was censured by the Cisterican general chapter in 1200 for providing money to Archbishop Gautier of Rouen's (1184–1207) servants to buy shoes, who presumably could call upon the prelate to provide for their needs.[58] Provision for charity was made by founders and benefactors of various communities. For example, Duke William and Duchess Matilda assigned portions of the patrimony of the abbey of La Trinité in Caen to the almonry as well as establishing a church dedicated to St Giles for the burial of the poor, which was to be carried out in the presence of the almoner and the four canons who served the abbey.[59] William de Vatteville and his wife granted the church and tithes of Croixmare to the abbey of Jumièges to feed the poor.[60] It is clear also from the pages of Eudes Rigaud's register that houses maintained an income for alms-giving, as well as collecting leftovers in the refectory. One of the major faults the archbishop discovered was communities that diminished the supply of alms. The monks of St-Ouen in Rouen were admonished to give more liberally to the poor, and at St-Georges-de-Boscherville the monks were reminded not to carry anything away from the refectory or to give away food, but that all remnants were to be devoted to alms.[61] Poverty was one reason why a community might reduce its alms supply. At Liancourt, which Eudes

---

54   *Monastic Constitutions*, pp. 48–53.
55   William of Malmesbury, *Gesta regum Anglorum*, ed. and trans. R. A. B. Mynors, R. M. Thomson and M. Winterbottom, OMT, 2 vols (Oxford, 1998), vol. 1, pp. 554–5.
56   L. L. Huneycutt, *Matilda of Scotland: a Study in Medieval Queenship* (Woodbridge, 2003), p. 104. Peyroux, 'Leper's Kiss', p. 183.
57   S. Dixon-Smith, 'The Image and Reality of Alms-giving in the Great Halls of Henry III', *Journal of the British Archaeological Association*, 152 (1999), pp. 79–96. See appendix C, no. 28 for the funds that Louis committed to the building of the hospital in Vernon.
58   Appendix A, no. 7 and *Twelfth-century Statutes*, 1200, no. 52, p. 472.
59   *Regesta regum*, no. 62 dated 1066 x 1083.
60   *Regesta regum*, no. 163 dated 25 December 1083 x 25 December 1084.
61   Bonnin, pp. 57, 134 and *Register*, pp. 63, 151.

found to be 'in a miserable spiritual and temporal condition', the community offered neither hospitality nor alms.[62] At the nunnery of St-Amand in Rouen, Eudes forbade the nuns to appoint an almoness or to give away alms without consent.[63] In part this may have been to alleviate poverty, but also served as a reminder that independent action of this sort was unsuitable for those who had taken monastic vows of obedience.

The people to whom alms were given also varied from house to house. Whereas some communities, for example, Cerisy, maintained a daily general distribution of alms to everyone who came,[64] other houses seem to have operated a rota system. At Conches, alms were given four times a week to all comers, twice a week to clerical scholars and once a week to lepers.[65] It is not clear whether or not these groups overlapped on certain days, or whether alms were distributed to different groups each day. The latter was the case at Eu: clerics received alms on Monday, Wednesday and Friday; other poor people on Tuesday, Thursday and Saturday; and on Sunday, those too ashamed, presumably, to come to the monastery, received alms at a hospice in town.[66] At Noyon-sur-Andelle, a general distribution of alms took place on Sundays, while on other days travellers were the beneficiaries and people who lived in the vicinity of the house, who received various dishes of food.[67] Sunday was also the day for a general distribution at Neufmarché, while other days were reserved for 'distressed persons' though Eudes is not specific as to whom they might be.[68] At Montivilliers, alms were given three times a week and in addition the abbess was obliged to feed thirteen poor people a day by a custom introduced by a former abbess called Alice.[69] As well as catering for its own leprous sisters, the community at Salle-aux-Puelles also gave alms to 'the poor lepers outside' the house and leftovers were given to a 'certain leprous woman at Moulineaux'.[70] The variety of people who benefited from alms given by Norman religious houses was therefore quite large, which raises questions about their accommodation within the monastic precincts.

The allocation of different groups to specific days of the week, as at Conches and other communities, would have had the practical effect of controlling the number of indigents seeking charity on particular days. In the case of communities that distributed alms to lepers, the necessary segregation between the healthy and sick could be maintained. Unfortunately, Eudes does not often specify where the distribution of alms took place. We have already noted that the Augustinian abbey of Eu maintained a hospice in the town where people too ashamed to beg openly could go and that people living close to Noyon-sur-Andelle received food. Certainly, Lanfranc thought it important

---

62 Appendix A, no. 45; Bonnin, p. 529 and *Register*, p. 604.
63 Bonnin, p. 285 and *Register*, p. 322.
64 Appendix A, no. 22; Bonnin, p. 260 and *Register*, p. 291.
65 Bonnin, p. 219 and *Register*, pp. 240–1.
66 Appendix A, no. 31; Bonnin, p. 229 and *Register*, p. 251.
67 Bonnin, p. 285 and *Register*, p. 321.
68 Appendix A, no. 59; Bonnin, p. 360 and *Register*, p. 410.
69 Bonnin, p. 431 and *Register*, p. 490.
70 Bonnin, pp. 101, 538 and *Register*, pp. 116, 615.

that the almoner at Christ Church Canterbury should make enquiries as to the number of sick in need of alms who were unable to come to the priory and visit them himself, with the precaution that all women should leave the house first.[71] In some communities then, charity was proactive and involved monks or canons leaving their cloisters to visit the sick.

In contrast, at St-Martin-la-Garenne alms were dispensed to 'all who came to the gate'.[72] This statement is somewhat ambiguous. Eudes could merely be referring to the precinct or inner court gate or he could mean an area specifically set aside for the distribution of alms. We know from English examples like St Augustine's, Canterbury, that some communities had almonry complexes that were outside their main precincts.[73] Westminster Abbey also had a purpose-built almonry to the west of the monastery.[74] That Norman houses also had purpose-built areas for the reception of the poor or the sick is shown by the evidence from the Cistercian and some Augustinian houses. Fourcarmont had a house for lepers next to the scriptorium, which was surrounded by a hedge; Montmorel also had an infirmary for lepers.[75] Lay infirmaries were also provided at St-André-en-Gouffern and at Bonport.[76] The abbey of Beaubec built an external infirmary by St-Lô near Rouen, thus preserving the quietude of the cloister.[77] The people received in these infirmaries seem to have been granted a more permanent residence than the poor who flocked to monastery gates for general distributions of alms. Stephen of Lexington had to remind the porters of the Savignac congregation 'to show themselves more merciful and humane towards the poor'.[78] This seemingly did not include women, who were to be fed only in times of famine: women with young children were to eat outside the gatehouse.[79] Even in the provision of alms to the poor, gender considerations came into play. This raises some very serious issues for the position of poor women in Norman society. If a significant proportion of religious houses were prohibited from giving practical help to women, and, at least by the thirteenth century, the nunneries were under restrictions in the provision of alms, then poor women must have suffered disproportionately to poor men.[80] Much more work needs to be done on the charitable provision of Norman religious houses for our period, but it is clear that the ecclesiastical authorities regarded alms giving as an essential service,

[71] *Monastic Constitutions*, p. 133.
[72] Appendix A, no. 83; Bonnin, p. 189 and *Register*, p. 202.
[73] Rushton, 'Monastic Charitable Provision', p. 30.
[74] Harvey, *Living and Dying in England*, p. 28.
[75] Appendix A, nos 34, 54. *Registrum epistolarum*, p. 214; Bonnin, pp. 83–4 and *Register*, pp. 95–6.
[76] Appendix A, no. 72 for St-André. *Registrum epistolarum*, p. 208 and Williams, *Cistercians in the Early Middle Ages*, pp. 119–20.
[77] Appendix A, no. 8; S. Deck, 'Le temporal de l'abbaye cistercienne de Beaubec I. Du XIIe a la fin du XIVe siècle', *AN*, 24 (1974), p. 134.
[78] *Registrum epistolarum*, p. 229 and Williams, *Cistercians in the Early Middle Ages*, p. 117.
[79] *Les ecclesiastica officia cisterciens*, chs 18 and 19, pp. 334–7. Williams, *Cistercians in the Early Middle Ages*, p. 117.
[80] Sharon Farmer points out that charity for women in Paris was insufficient to meet their needs, *Surviving Poverty*, p. 164.

and strove to make sure the professed religious within the region performed this part of their vocation properly.

One of the services that Norman religious houses provided for the laity was the education of children. Many of these children, especially in the early part of the period under consideration were oblates, that is to say, children who had been given to the monastery at a young age by their parents in order that they should make their full profession on reaching the age of majority. The eleventh-century *Monastic Constitutions* of Lanfranc, a former prior of Bec and archbishop of Canterbury, mention a school and master for the young boys.[81] Lanfranc's writings show how they were integrated into the community at all levels, through their participation in the divine office and *lectio divina*.[82] The boys also formed part of the processions that were conducted in order to meet visiting dignitaries.[83] At St-Évroul, in the late eleventh century, the boys were taught by Abbot Thierry (c.1048–c.1059) to excel in reading aloud, singing, writing and all other studies necessary for the servants of God.[84] Of course, part of the reforms of the eleventh and twelfth centuries was directed at eradicating the practice of child oblation. The Cistercians in particular regarded children as a disruptive presence and were concerned that individuals should only enter the order through their own free will.[85] The twelfth century also saw a rise in the secular schools and, coupled with the developments in canon law, the presence of children in religious communities began to decline.

By the thirteenth century, the presence of children in monasteries in Normandy was in contravention of conciliar legislation, particularly canon four of the council of Rouen (1231).[86] Monastic houses were not designed to be nurseries or schools in which to bring up children. Despite ecclesiastical prohibitions, some small children were still offered as oblates to communities or were sent to board there by their parents, thus ensuring their presence in religious houses. Most of our Norman examples come from Archbishop Eudes's register of visitations and they generally refer to girls in houses of nuns. The lack of references to boys boarding in male monasteries probably lies in the rise of the secular schools and song schools attached to cathedrals at this time, which girls, by virtue of their sex, were unable to attend.

---

81 *Monastic Constitutions*, pp. 170–5. It is interesting to note that the Benedictine nunnery of Santa Maria Latina in Palermo was founded with a girls' school attached: Skinner, *Women in Medieval Italian Society*, p. 178. For the presence and role of boys in communities of monks see S. Boynton, 'The Liturgical Role of Children in Monastic Customaries from the Central Middle Ages', *Studia Liturgica*, 28 (1998), pp. 194–209.

82 See, for example, *Monastic Constitutions*, pp. 6–7, 170–5.

83 *Monastic Constitutions*, pp. 106–7.

84 OV, vol. 2, pp. 20–1.

85 *Statuta*, vol. I, 1134, no. 78, p. 31 and 1175, no. 26, p. 84. For education more generally see S. Shahar, *Childhood in the Middle Ages* (London and New York, 1990), pp. 184–201. For oblation in an earlier period see M. de Jong, *In Samuel's Image: Child Oblations in the Early Medieval West*, Brill's Studies in Intellectual History 12 (Leiden, 1996).

86 'Pueri, vel puellae qui ibi solent nutriri et instrui, penitus repellantur'; Mansi, vol. 23, col. 214.

It is probable that at least some of the girls we find in Norman nunneries during the thirteenth century were being educated in the hope that they might later take the veil, but Eudes required the removal of children at a number of houses, for example, St-Sauveur, St-Aubin, Bondeville, St-Saëns, St-Amand and Villarceaux.[87] Some of the children were relatives of the nuns, normally nieces as it was common for girls to be sent to nunneries where their aunts had already taken the veil. Stephen was also wary of the presence of minors within monastic communities. He banned the reception of secular boys and girls within the cloister in the general statutes for Mortain. Girls could be received from the age of twelve onwards but could not be admitted as nuns until they were nineteen. In the intervening years they were to be cared for by a mature nun appointed for the task, to prevent nuns gathering small cliques around them.[88] At Villers-Canivet, the young girls below the age of nineteen were allotted their own place in the refectory at a 'lower table in front of the main table', until they entered the novitiate.[89] In this way, they were spatially removed from the main community. As they were still lay girls and thus might marry, it was inappropriate for them to have a place at table within the main community. Aside from this spatial reference it is not known where the children were housed. I speculate that they were accommodated in their own area, possibly outside the cloister due to their lay status, but within the precinct.[90] The outright prohibition on the reception of children, or limits on their age, were designed to keep out those who were incapable of making a solemn profession and to prevent the nuns becoming too attached to certain individuals. In this case one can see a conflict in the role model held up to medieval nuns to follow, namely the Blessed Virgin Mary. The nuns were supposed to emulate her virginity, but it is possible that they also identified with her role as a mother. This contradiction does not appear to have been a problem for monks. Identification with the Virgin's role as the mother of Christ may have been especially important for those nuns who had given birth to children themselves, some of whom may have been housed in monasteries. Again, by virtue of biological factors like the need to breast feed infants, the presence of the natural children of monks was more unlikely in male houses. The presence of children within a sacred context thus presented another source of potential conflict between the monastic ideal and what women particularly actually experienced.

---

[87] For example, Bonnin, pp. 220, 310, 410, 412, 486, 572 and *Register*, pp. 241, 353, 467, 471, 554, 658.

[88] *Registrum epistolarum*, p. 234. The problem of cliques and their detrimental effect on the common life will be discussed in due course. See chapter three on enclosure below.

[89] *Registrum epistolarum*, p. 242.

[90] The school at the nunnery of Essen in Germany, for example, was located in the west wing of the cloister: W. Bader, 'Eine Art Einleitung zur Geschichte des Essener Kanonissenstiftes', *Bonner Jahrbücher*, 167 (1967), p. 318. I am grateful to Miriam Shergold for this reference.

As well as lay sisters and brothers who carried out the bulk of the manual labour within the community, religious houses in Normandy also employed a number of servants to help with the day-to-day running of the business affairs of the monastery.[91] These servants differed from monastic lay brethren in a number of ways. They were paid for their work, they did not wear a habit and although they might take an oath of fidelity to the house and, particularly in the case of maids, chastity while in its service, their vows were not in any way religious or permanent.[92] Hospitals also employed servants. Whereas the nursing of the sick was carried out by those in religious vows, servants catered for the needs of other groups within hospitals, such as those seeking hospitality like travellers or pilgrims.[93] The presence of servants had its advantages. As these individuals were not professed to any religious order, they had more freedom to come and go as necessity dictated, as they were not bound by the restrictions surrounding enclosure. They also did not have to break from work to attend monastic services and thus ensured that the temporal aspects of monastery life ran smoothly.

Abbot Stephen and Archbishop Eudes sometimes saw the employment of servants as a problem. As noted above, lay monastery officials had more freedom than monks and nuns and their presence could also put further strain on a community's already stretched resources. Both Abbot Stephen and Archbishop Eudes ordered that the number of maidservants within nunneries should be restricted.[94] There were also restrictions placed on servants in male houses. The statutes of Pope Gregory IX stated that 'women shall not be admitted in person to any place for the service of monks'.[95] This ordinance implies that women were not to be employed as servants, but the pages of Archbishop Eudes's register show that several male monastic houses employed women in some kind of domestic service. Eudes was not altogether happy with their presence and generally instructed that they should be sent away. In relation to houses of women religious, Eudes's primary reason for sending maid-servants away was that they were deemed to be excessive in number. For male houses the problem rested on the sexual temptation that all women, regardless of position, presented to the monks. At Muzy, the monks were instructed to send away their maid who was probably a young woman, for Eudes added that if they were to receive another maid she should be older.[96] A young girl who lived at the priory of Ste-Radegonde, preparing meals for the prior and his companion Reginald, a monk of St-Pierre at Préaux, was likewise to be removed, while the monks of Heudreville were instructed to find maidservants

---

91 See P. Racinet 'Familiers et convers, l'entourage des prieurés bénédictines au moyen âge', *Les mouvances laïques des orders religieux*, pp. 19–34 and Berkhofer, *Day of Reckoning*, pp. 123–58.

92 *Registrum epistolarum*, p. 235. The specific problem of male staff in nunneries is discussed in chapter three.

93 *Statuts*, p. 155 and Gilchrist, *Contemplation and Action*, pp. 9–11.

94 *Registrum epistolarum*, p. 235; Bonnin, pp. 245–6 and *Register*, p. 334.

95 Bonnin, p. 646 and *Register*, p. 744.

96 Appendix A, no. 58; Bonnin, p. 70 and *Register*, p. 78.

who caused less suspicion, presumably older ones.[97] Although the statutes of Gregory IX prohibited the employment of women within male monastic houses, Eudes seems to have allowed some compromise in this respect.

The presence of lay servants also had a more negative effect on the lives of professed monastics.[98] As we have seen, Archbishop Eudes recognised that to eradicate the presence of servants within monasteries was either impractical or undesirable. Controls were put in place to ensure that servants did not distract from the primary work of monastics, that is to say devotion to God, or cause unnecessary disturbance. During a visit to St-Wandrille in 1251, Eudes noted that lay people were serving in the refectory, something that was contrary to monastic practice.[99] At Mont-Ste-Catherine in Rouen, more specific faults were found with the monastery staff. The monks complained that the staff of the monastery, abbot and bailiff came to the refectory every day through the cloister, seeking food and drink. The monk in charge of the refectory was under an obligation not just to provide them with food, but portions of meat.[100] In this case, it seems that the lay servants of the monastery were exercising undue control over aspects of the daily routine that did not fall under their remit, namely diet. In addition, the cloister was in theory out of bounds to all lay persons except in limited circumstances. In respect to the situation at Mont-Ste-Catherine, the archbishop considered that the monks had good reason to grumble.

In houses of nuns, Eudes was also concerned as to the effect that the presence of maidservants would have on community life. Here, he was not so much concerned with their presence in the cloister, but their relationships to individual nuns. At Almenèches, for example, the maidservants did not serve the whole community, but instead were presumably attached to individuals or small groups.[101] There were private maidservants as well as general ones at St-Léger.[102] It is possible that these women had been servants to the nuns before their mistresses had taken the veil. If this is the case, then their presence within an enclosed monastic community was an unacceptable reminder of secular status and rank. Worldly concerns thus transgressed the boundaries of the cloister and trespassed on a sacred space. Entrance into a monastery entailed a renunciation of the world and its ways and a narrowing of one's horizons to the cloister, thus enabling the professed religious to concentrate fully on their vocation. The presence of personal servants entailed a breach of the common life and a transgression of the sacred space both in terms of a lay person being in the cloister and in terms of the distraction of the professed monastic. For the nuns, the presence of personal servants may well have been a way of maintaining their identity and independence. We may speculate that it was hard for a woman used to high social status to surrender her will to that

[97] Appendix A, nos 85, 67, 39; Bonnin, pp. 208, 625 and *Register*, pp. 227, 720.
[98] The problems presented by nuns' and monks' relatives who worked in monasteries is discussed in chapter four.
[99] Bonnin, p. 111 and *Register*, p. 127.
[100] Bonnin, p. 346 and *Register*, p. 394.
[101] Appendix B, no. 2. Bonnin, p. 235 and *Register*, p. 260.
[102] Bonnin, p. 591 and *Register*, p. 680.

of the community, especially if she had no true vocation and her entrance to the monastery had been forced.

Lay servants were a necessary facet of the monastic household, freeing up monks and nuns from some of the temporal aspects of running the community and thus allowing them, in theory, to devote themselves fully to God. Their presence caused concern amongst the ecclesiastical visitors for a number of reasons. Their status as lay people compromised the enclosure rules and introduced a transient element and possible source of disturbance to the household. Young female servants in male communities were perceived as presenting a sexual threat to the chastity of the monks, while in nunneries, their relationships with individual nuns were an unwelcome reminder of secular status.

The laity in the cloister: sacral reasons

Buildings in sacred spaces, for example the abbatial churches, belonged to the communities of professed religious who built them, but in some aspects of reception and intrusion we find the Norman laity laying claim to these sacred spaces. Although monks and nuns lived apart from the laity and, as a rule, tried to keep them away from their cloisters, in two very important aspects ingress into cloisters and churches specifically was seen as legitimate: the laity wished to visit shrines and attend church services. This was the basis of a reciprocal arrangement between religious houses and the laity that ensured material support for the communities' vocation.

Some religious communities and cathedrals in Normandy attracted members of the laity on pilgrimages who were often seeking healing or fulfilling vows. Professed religious and cathedral clerics were perceived as having a particular role to play: not only was it their duty to pray for all people, but also to maintain shrines for the benefit of those in need and the greater glory of God. In turn, the financial and other offerings left by the laity at these shrines helped the communities fund themselves. The presence of pilgrims in religious houses and cathedrals could cause great disruption to the running of the community, but this seems to have been welcomed and accommodated to a greater extent by both the communities and the ecclesiastical authorities than the other forms of intrusion considered in this chapter. Pilgrimages in search of healing involved both men and women visiting various types of religious communities.

One miracle in particular gives us a very good indication as to the disruption just one pilgrim could cause within a religious community, and it is recounted in a remarkable letter from Marsilia (d.1108), abbess of St-Amand in Rouen, to Abbot Bovon (1107–21) of St-Amand-d'Elnone in Flanders, which can be dated to 1107. The miracle concerns an unnamed woman from Lisieux who was suffering from depression. Her depression and subsequent desire to commit suicide stemmed from a belief stirred up by gossipy neighbours that her husband did not love her. He brought her to the abbey of St-Amand in Rouen to prevent further suicide attempts and in the hope that such a course of action would have a beneficial effect on her mental health. While in the nuns' custody, she attempted to hang herself and appeared to succeed until being restored to life through the nuns' prayers to St Amand.

The use of space is very important in this miracle. Despite the fact that there was a house of female religious in Lisieux where the woman lived, she was brought to the abbey of St-Amand in Rouen, because the abbey's patron saint was believed to be particularly efficacious in the treatment of demoniacs.[103] Marsilia wrote that 'no diabolical strength' was able to resist the saint.[104] Once she arrived at the nunnery, the woman was taken into the church. Later in the story it becomes clear that a bed was made up for her 'beyond the choir' and 'before the altar on which St Amand had been accustomed to celebrate masses'.[105] The belief that St Amand had celebrated mass on this site must have been central to the nuns' decision to place her in front of the altar, where she remained for seven days and seven nights. Here, she was in the most sacred place in the monastery; the place most closely associated with the saint. This practice, referred to as incubation, is reflected in the early medieval *Life* of St Amand. During his pilgrimage to Rome, he wished to spend a night in prayer at St Peter's. He slept on the steps of the church and was gratified by a vision of the saint who ordered his immediate return to Gaul.[106] We know that Marsilia was acquainted with the saint's *Life* because in her letter to Abbot Bovon she asked him to include her miracle in the St Amand life and miracle collection kept at Elnone: it was this text and the association of the community with the saint that provided the authority to house the woman in the church.

In addition to locating the woman in the most sacred space of the monastery and at the heart of the nuns' liturgical space, the community provided her with a cadre of nuns to guard and watch over her. She was also counselled by a succession of learned men, both lay and religious. The presence of these men introduces another element of necessary intrusion into the nuns' church. Unless we are to gather from the text that the men stood in the nave of the church and bellowed their advice to the woman located before the altar, we must assume that the men too were granted access to the choir. The woman did not respond in a positive manner to her advisers and told them 'with adequately composed speech, that she was completely delivered to the infernal flames and sulphurous punishments, and while detained in this world she would experience that just part of these punishments, and she expected the remainder not long afterwards'.[107] Clearly, advice and the mere fact of

---

[103] A. Murray, *Suicide in the Middle Ages vol. 1: the Violent Against Themselves* (Oxford, 1998), pp. 326–7.

[104] Platelle, p. 105 and *Normans in Europe*, p. 81.

[105] Platelle, p. 105 and *Normans in Europe*, p. 82.

[106] *Vita Amandi*, AA SS, Febr. I, p. 860 and Platelle, p. 91. Incubation is also discussed by D. Gonthier and C. Le Bas 'Analyse socio-économique de quelques recueils de miracles dans la Normandie du XIe au XIIIe siècles', *AN*, 24 (1974), p. 33.

[107] Platelle, p. 105 and *Normans in Europe*, pp. 81–2.

spending time in the church was not going to cure this poor woman of her depression. The learned men then decreed that she should be blessed with holy water from a chalice and the following day have her demons exorcised by priests.[108]

Unfortunately, this decision proved to be the catalyst for a dramatic turn of events. The woman was completely unsettled by the thought of the treatment to come so decided to kill herself by hanging. She pretended to her guards that she wished to sleep and, as they were exhausted, that they should rest too. Once the nuns were asleep she pursued her intention to kill herself. Marsilia is not specific as to which part of the church the woman moved to, but it seems likely that she went into the nave. Assuming that the church of St-Amand in Rouen followed other female houses of a similar date and status in its architecture, it would have had a triforium gallery with a wall passage in the elevation of the nave.[109] If this were indeed the case, it would not have been too difficult for the unfortunate woman to gain access to the gallery where she hanged herself from one of the supporting columns with a noose made from her veil.[110] If she did move to the nave, the choice of space is significant. As well as being more convenient in terms of access to a high place from which to jump and break her neck, the nave was further removed from the most sacred part of the church, that most closely associated with the saint. In which case, the move from the choir to the nave emphasises how far the woman had turned from God in her desperation.

The nuns did not give up on their charge with her apparent death. Three of their number broke their enclosure and went out into the night to seek advice from the archdeacon who ordered that the body be removed from the church and be thrown in a pit. Unfortunately, we do not know where the archdeacon lived at this time. Possibly he lived near the cathedral in which case the nuns would not have had to venture very far. We can speculate that the archdeacon's horror of an occurrence of suicide in a sanctified space led him, as Marsilia tells us, to order the disposal of the body in a pit outside the city walls. The nuns for the moment ignored the archdeacon's directives and instead offered prayers to St Amand. His intervention revived the woman who then recovered enough to make her confession.[111]

We know from this letter the degree of care the nuns provided for a woman in genuine mental distress. What is particularly interesting is the extent to which they took her into their community; evidently the restoration of her mental health was very important to them. Earlier precedents from the *Life* of St Amand dictated that she be housed in the church rather than in some other space like the abbey guest house or infirmary. It is very significant that she was not provided with a bed within the nave, the space in a church

108 Platelle, p. 105 and *Normans in Europe*, p. 82.
109 M. Baylé, 'Caen: abbatiale de la Trinité (Abbaye-aux-Dames)', *L'architecture normande*, vol. 2, p. 51 and M. Baylé. 'Montivilliers: abbatiale Notre-Dame', *L'architecture normande*, vol. 2, p. 118.
110 Platelle, p. 105 and *Normans in Europe*, p. 82.
111 Platelle, p. 106 and *Normans in Europe*, p. 83.

associated with the laity, but beyond the nuns' choir in the sanctuary, a space generally reserved for the monastic community and possibly only the male chaplain. The woman was also provided with a team of nuns to care for her. This fact, combined with the actions of the nuns following the discovery of the woman's body, is indicative of a perception of their vocation that would prove to be very different from that of the late thirteenth-century ecclesiastical hierarchy. In the early twelfth century, the nuns believed it was their job to restore their patient to her right mind regardless of the fact that it meant bringing a lay person within the boundaries of their church and cloister and leaving the cloister themselves to seek advice.

In contrast to Marsilia's letter detailing an isolated individual, two other miracle collections from Normandy are excellent examples of how space was used during mass pilgrimages. These collections both relate to the miraculous power of the Blessed Virgin Mary and come from the cathedral church of Coutances and the Benedictine monastery for men at St-Pierre-sur-Dives.[112]

In the Coutances collection, the author, John of Coutances, gives several details relating to the interior disposition of the church in his retelling of the miracles. Although the exact plan of the eleventh-century cathedral at Coutances is unknown, it is probable that it was cruciform in shape, with a crossing tower.[113] From the miracles it is apparent that the church had four altars: the high altar above which was situated a crucifix; St John's altar in front of and to the left of the high altar; an altar dedicated to the Virgin in front of and to the right of the high altar; and the altar of St Nicholas.[114] I speculate that St John's altar and that dedicated to the Virgin were located in the transepts of the cathedral with the high altar located beyond the crossing tower in the choir. The miracle collection makes it plain that the laity were allowed access to all the altars in the church. A woman who had previously been unable to walk, regained the use of her feet after praying in the church. She ran through the canons' choir and made her way to the high altar on which she placed a candle she had brought with her in thanks to God and the Virgin. Not only did this woman enter the part of the cathedral reserved for the clergy, she did this while the clergy were present, as John of Coutances records that the clergy and people marvelled at the sight of the woman running.[115] Other miracles in this collection show that individuals spent nights in the church, echoing the treatment of the depressed woman from Lisieux at St-Amand in Rouen. For example, a blind woman came to the church with her husband and many other people at the feast of the Assumption and spent the night in front of the statue of the Virgin, located on her altar.[116] She was presumably allowed to get very close to the altar itself.

[112] *Miracula e. Constantiensis* and Haimon.
[113] For tentative reconstructions of the eleventh-century cathedral at Coutances see M. Baylé, 'Coutances: cathédrale Notre-Dame', *L'architecture normande* vol. 2, pp. 43–4 and J. Herschman 'The Eleventh-century Nave of the Cathedral of Coutances: a New Reconstruction', *Gesta*, 22 (1983), pp. 121–34.
[114] *Miracula e. Constantiensis*, pp. 380 and 383.
[115] *Miracula e. Constantiensis*, p. 369.
[116] *Miracula e. Constantiensis*, p. 372.

Another woman, by the name of Orielda, who was lame, spent two days before the cross, presumably the one on the high altar.[117] Again, a lay person was allowed into the most sacred part of the church in order to conduct a vigil and seek healing for her ailments.

The miracle collection from St-Pierre-sur-Dives differs from the Coutances collection in one very crucial respect: it records a mass pilgrimage to a community of monks during the rebuilding of their church in 1145, rather than a secular cathedral. Again, the author of this collection, Abbot Haimo of St-Pierre, gives us a great deal of detail regarding the use of space by the laity. Lay people came to the site as the monks had asked for donations of building materials which were then pulled to the site in wagons by the pilgrims, including men, women and children. In an echo of the construction of the cathedral at Chartres, they also brought their sick for healing.[118] The presence of the laity is significant in that it shows the level of piety of the Norman populace and the fact that the laity was laying claim to the sacred spaces of the region. The church at St-Pierre may have been built for a community of contemplative monks, but in addition to the stone and wood that formed the physical building, the church was also built through the participation of the laity and was sanctified by the miracles that happened to various lay individuals.

In one particular case, Haimo gives us a great deal of information regarding what happened when the sick arrived at the building site. Rohaise, the wife of Ralph of Caen, brought her lame daughter to St-Pierre to seek a cure. The girl was carried to the altar and cured before spending the night in the church.[119] Rohaise later returned with a deaf and dumb boy. As night fell, the wagon containing the sick people was brought to the church's forecourt and the ill and weak put into the warm church with candles lit all around them. As regards the boy, he was first put on display on the wagon outside the church where he pointed to an apparition of the Virgin Mary, seen only by him, in a niche in the abbey church's tower. After he had begun to speak, he was brought to the altar and then carried on the shoulders of several people in the crowd round the cloister and the church in a public display of his regained health.[120] This example underlines the extent to which lay people, including women and children, were accepted into male sacred space. Not only were they coming into the monks' part of the church, namely the choir and the high altar, they also entered the enclosure, by processing around the cloister. This intrusion is underlined by other miracles. A woman by the name of Emma, who was possibly in a coma, was given up for dead. She was placed in a bed in front of the cross in the church at St-Pierre, though we do not know exactly where in the church this was, for three days during which time

---

117 *Miracula e. Constantiensis*, p. 380.
118 Haimon, p. 115; also Hayes, *Body and Sacred Place*, *passim*. Work began on Chartres cathedral in 1020. The west front was erected in 1134. After the building was destroyed by fire, reconstruction began in 1194.
119 Haimon, p. 126.
120 Haimon, pp. 131–4.

she experienced visions. She recovered and was fit enough to return home.[121] A poor lame girl named Matilda, who was known to the family of Robert of Courcy as she was given alms by them every day, was cured on the way to the church. So successful was this cure that she was able to help the other women pulling the wagon with the sick. Out of gratitude she spent a further forty days in the church helping the sick and weak.[122]

It was important for medieval religious houses to ensure access to their relics both as sources of prestige and in terms of the miracles that might happen at shrines. The power of miracles to attract pilgrims is attested in a letter from Bishop Arnulf of Lisieux to Pope Alexander III in 1166, recounting a disturbing incident at the abbey of Grestain.[123] In an effort to effect a cure, 'so that they might be believed to work miracles and so invite with lies the frequent approach of secular persons', the Benedictine monks of Grestain killed a woman by repeatedly submerging her in icy water. The monks were certainly desirous of augmenting their revenues but their dubious motives negated any chance of a successful miracle occurring.[124]

Smaller monastic communities also attracted lay pilgrims who came to venerate the relics displayed in their churches. Although many of the people came to the monasteries with the best of intentions, women especially were regarded as a potential danger and their presence needed to be carefully regulated. As the miracle collections from Coutances and St-Pierre-sur-Dives show, the laity viewed these sites as crucial in seeking divine aid. The location of relics within a religious house could clearly cause conflict between the needs of the laity visiting the shrine and those of the monks or canons who lived and worked there. In Archbishop Eudes's visitation register, we see how access to the relics was regulated in order to minimise disruption to the monastic day. The conflict between the community and the laity centred on the problem that any shrine with relics was normally kept near the altar or in the choir of the church, the most sacred part of the church building and thus forbidden to the laity. At the Augustinian houses of Graville, Ouville and Eu, lay folk entered the choir of the canons' church to view relics and thus intruded into that part of the church reserved for the community.[125]

---

[121]   Haimon, pp. 129–31.

[122]   Haimon, pp. 127–9. A comparative case can be found in the miracles of Chartres where a man named William was cured of his hernia but remained in the church in honour of the Virgin and to look after the sick, Hayes, Body and Sacred Place, pp. 56–7 and Jean le Marchant, Les miracles de Notre-Dame de Chartres, ed. P. Kuntsmann, Publications Médiévales de l'Univerisité d'Ottawa, 1: Société Archéologique d'Eure-et-Loire, 26 (1973), pp. 134–5. For another Norman example of a pilgrim calling on the aid of a saint en route, see Introductio monachorum et miracula insigniora per Beatum Michaelem archangelum patrata in ecclesia quae dicitur Tumba in periculo maris situ, nomine ipsius Archangeli fabricata, ed. E. de Robillard de Beaurepaire, MSAN 2 (1877) pp. 888–90, for a woman who gave birth in the sea, protected by the saint, on the way back from Mont-St-Michel.

[123]   Appendix A, no. 37.

[124]   Barlow, no. 47, p. 83 and Schriber p. 108.

[125]   Appendix A, no. 36 for Graville; Bonnin, pp. 137, 385–6, 452 and Register, pp. 155, 438 and 516.

The laity did, however, need access to the relics. Lanfranc of Canterbury recognised this conflict in the eleventh century. In his *Monastic Constitutions* for Good Friday he stated that 'of any clerics or lay folk be there who wish to adore the cross, this shall be carried to them in another place more suitable for their worship', that is to say not the choir.[126] Eudes followed similar practices: he proposed that in all communities experiencing problems with the laity viewing relics, the relics should be placed outside the choir or chancel on a different altar, thus enabling the lay people to have access to the shrines without unduly disturbing the canons during the daily offices.[127] The canons found themselves in an ambiguous situation here. On the one hand they and Eudes were concerned that the laity should not intrude into parts of the house reserved for professed religious; on the other hand, the canons at Eu told the archbishop that they thought that great harm would be done if they did not open the entrances to the choir and chancel to allow access to the relics.[128] The canons feared that they might lose the support of their local lay community if such access was denied. It is also noteworthy that even in communities devoted to pastoral care, a degree of separation between laity and religious was essential.

The examples from the Norman *miracula* and the cases recorded in Archbishop Eudes's register discussed above reveal how the laity were accepted or deemed intrusive in sacred spaces to varying degrees. The miracles took place in two monasteries and a cathedral and involve a variety of people. These miracles also took place in very precise circumstances. The case recorded by Abbess Marsilia is exceptional by any standards; pilgrims came to Coutances at the feasts associated with the Virgin; and the rebuilding of the church at St-Pierre-sur-Dives was the motivation for the pilgrimage there. The laity who venerated the relics in the houses of canons discussed above, did so on a more day-to-day basis. The effects of ingress by the laity is greater in the case of the monasteries than the cathedral as religious communities were set apart from the world: the sacredness of this space depended on their separation from secular concerns. A cathedral was more open to the laity, being a secular foundation. Even here though, lay people entered areas that were usually reserved for the clergy. The laity did not only come into religious houses to visit shrines and relics, but also caused concern by attending church services and it is to these concerns I now turn.

For some of the laity in Normandy, their regular worship entailed going to a monastic house to hear the mass, as it was the nearest church they could use, or to attend services on special feast days. This again caused problems for the ecclesiastical authorities, the lay people and the communities concerned. If the community church was also shared with the parish then provision had to be made for the competing needs of two groups of people. Where the monas-

126 *Monastic Constitutions*, pp. 62–3. The word 'clerics' here refers to the secular clergy, namely those who were not part of a religious order.
127 Bonnin, pp. 137, 385–6, 452 and *Register*, pp. 155, 438, 516.
128 Bonnin, p. 452 and *Register*, p. 516.

tery did not share its church with a parish, then efforts were made to ensure that the laity remained in their allotted place within the nave. Just as in our consideration of the presence of relics as a cause of intrusion, and the laity's need to have some share in the sacred space of monasteries and churches, the issue of lay people coming to religious communities to hear church services also raises questions concerning the ownership of spaces.

In cases where a monastery church was shared with a parish, then both groups of people had an equal claim on the space; however, careful arrangements had to be made so cloistered communities did not come into unnecessary contact with the laity. At Montivilliers, the nuns shared their abbey church with the parish of St-Sauveur; the parish church was located in the northern aisle of the nave. To ensure that the nuns did not come into contact with the laity and so cause scandal, Archbishop Eudes banned their processions through the church and instructed them to sing the prayers and antiphons standing stationary in the choir.[129] The canons at Corneville also shared their church with the local parish. Eudes noted that the parishioners often came to the monastery 'to hear masses and the service or to strike the two bells which [they] possess in the tower'. Presumably these were the bells which the laity tolled in order to call others to the parish services. The canons also had bells in the tower, which they used to mark the hours of the divine office. Eudes instructed them to create a partition between the bells so the 'canons might sound their own bells more freely and be able to concentrate upon the divine cult with more quiet'.[130] There was also conflict between the parish and local religious community at Neufmarché. The parishioners complained that the mass was always celebrated in the monks' choir. If the monks' choir was screened off from the main body of the church, then the laity would not have been able to see or hear their mass properly and would also have to enter the monks' part of the church to receive communion. Eudes ordered the prior to build a special altar 'before the cross', presumably a cross situated between the nave and the choir, on which the parish priest could celebrate the daily mass.[131] In such a manner the parish did not then have to intrude on the liturgical space of the priory, nor did the priory cause the parishioners to be more separated from their right to hear mass than was necessary. Later on in his episcopate, Eudes instructed the prior to have the choir repaired and arranged so that the lay folk could not reach or see the monks, suggesting some sort of screen was put in place.[132]

Concerns regarding the use of monastic space by lay people entering monasteries to hear the services centre on problems of access, namely in to which parts of the cloister and precincts the laity were legitimately allowed. Archbishop Eudes's register contains a number of cases of the laity entering monastic space for liturgical reasons and from these examples we get a good idea of where they were allowed. Eudes's prescriptions centre around two

[129]   Bonnin, p. 472 and *Register*, pp. 538–9.
[130]   Appendix A, no. 27; Bonnin, p. 280 and *Register*, p. 315.
[131]   Bonnin, p. 282 and *Register*, p. 318.
[132]   Bonnin, p. 620 and *Register*, p. 713.

areas, the cloister and the choir. At Bourg-Achard, lay folk remained in the choir during the services and at Conches they, including women, entered the cloister and choir to hear masses.[133] At the Augustinian house in Cherbourg, women entered the church and proceeded 'even to the altar'. For Eudes this intrusion into the canons' area of the church was completely unacceptable and he ordered that the women were to be kept out entirely and the doors shut to prevent them coming in.[134] In other monastic houses, the laity only intruded into claustral areas on specific occasions. For example, at Notre-Dame-d'Ivry women entered the cloister and the choir for solemn masses and the annual feasts.[135] Eudes instructed the community to keep the laity out of the cloister at Notre-Dame-du-Pré outside Rouen, especially women 'who were in the habit of passing through the cloister on their way to the monastery church when memorial masses for their friends were being celebrated'; the women were to stay in the nave of the monastery church.[136] All these examples concern problems of access. It seems that, in the eyes of the archbishop, no proper provision was made at such houses to enable the laity to attend the services without encroaching on the claustral areas. This problem was recognised at Eu, where Eudes asked the canons to try and arrange another route for the laity to proceed to communion so they would not walk through the choir.[137] The cloister and the choir were part of the monastic enclosure and, as such, had to be protected from those who could disrupt the smooth running of the monastery: the laity. Monastic houses were designed as the perfect environment in which devotion of God was maintained through a combination of prayer, work and study. To enable concentration, these areas were shut off from the rest of the world. Unwelcome intrusion by the laity into areas like the cloister and the choir distracted professed religious from their true purpose.

Intrusion in the parish: priests' wives and concubines

One of the central issues of the reform movement of the eleventh century was the abolition of clerical marriage and the eradication of concubinage.[138] The campaign against clerical sexuality and marriage was based on doctrinal and practical considerations. The theological arguments against clerical marriage centred on the fact that sex was impure and sinful and would thus contaminate any liturgical action the priest performed.[139] The reformers also called for

133 Bonnin, pp. 8, 71 and *Register*, pp. 11, 80.
134 Bonnin, pp. 89–90 and *Register*, p. 102.
135 Appendix A, no. 41; Bonnin, pp. 69–70 and *Register*, p. 78.
136 Bonnin, p. 411 and *Register*, p. 468.
137 Bonnin, p. 361 and *Register*, p. 411.
138 I have discussed the problems of clerical celibacy previously in 'Exclusion as Exile', pp. 151–5.
139 Gerald of Wales, *The Jewel of the Church: a Translation of Gemma Ecclesiastica by Giraldus Cambrensis*, trans. J. F. Hagen, Davis Medieval Texts and Studies 2 (Brill, 1979), p. 132.

the liberation of clergy from their wives and concubines as a precondition for the liberation of church property from lay control as a whole: too much church property had disappeared into the hands of priests' offspring.[140] Peter Damian's disgust of marriage was rooted in his repugnance towards sexual relations, but was also formulated in arguments concerning the Church's property. He believed that the married clergy would be expensive to maintain as they had to provide for wives and children. This, he reasoned, was why priests alienated ecclesiastical property to their families.[141] The Church was determined to ensure the complete separation of priests from the laity. The priesthood had to be separate because of its divine function of the celebration of the Eucharist: as Christopher Brooke has described it 'helping in the creation of the body and blood of Christ on the altar'.[142] A series of synodal statutes cemented the Church's position. Prior to the First Lateran Council in 1123, the marriages of the clergy were recognised as illicit but valid. Canon twenty-one of this council changed the position and decreed that ordination to the three higher grades of holy orders created an impediment to marriage. All existing unions were stripped of legal status and the protection of the law.[143] Canons six and seven of Lateran II, 1139, went further and decreed that priests' marriages should be broken up, both parties were to do penance and those who resisted should be deprived of their benefices.[144] As clerical marriages were deemed invalid, any children of those marriages were stripped of their legitimacy. This continued to be the Church's policy for the remainder of the Middle Ages, though in practice, as we shall see, it was unworkable, as bishops often had no means to enforce the canon law in the localities.

So what of the women who, in the eyes of the Church, trespassed into this space devoted to male sacrality? In the early Middle Ages, women who entered into spiritual marriage, which did not involve sexual relations, with priests, had participated in sacral activity, for example, baking bread for the Eucharist, handling the altar vessels and lighting candles. Indeed, as McNamara has shown, clerical wives were set apart through special acts of consecration in Merovingian France.[145] Gradually attitudes towards clerical wives, regardless of their sexual status, hardened. In 1049, Pope Leo IX (1048–54) decreed that the concubines of Roman clerics should not only be separated from their lovers but also forced into servitude as chattels of the Lateran Palace.[146] Writing in the early thirteenth century, Thomas of Chobham (d.1233 x 36) observed

---

140 Brundage, *Law, Sex and Christian Society*, p. 214. See also P. Beaudette, '"In the World but not of it": Clerical Celibacy as a Symbol of the Medieval Church', *Medieval Purity and Piety: Essays on Medieval Clerical Celibacy and Religious Reform*, ed. M. Frassetto, Garland Medieval Casebooks 9 (New York and London), pp. 34–6.

141 Brundage, *Law, Sex and Christian Society*, p. 215. See also Gerald of Wales, *Jewel of the Church*, pp. 211–13.

142 C. Brooke 'Priest, Deacon and Layman from St Peter Damian to St Francis', in Brooke, *Churches and Churchmen*, pp. 234–5.

143 *Decrees*, p. 194.

144 *Decrees*, p. 198. This statute was repeated in canon eleven of Lateran III, pp. 217–18.

145 J. A. McNamara, 'An Unresolved Syllogism: the Search for a Christian Gender System', *Conflicted Identities and Multiple Masculinities*, ed. Murray, pp. 10–11.

146 Mansi, vol. 20, col. 724 and Brundage, *Law, Sex and Christian Society*, p. 218.

that the harsh penalties prescribed in the canons, notably enslavement, were no longer enforced. He argued that bishops should deal more firmly with the concubines: they should at least forbid these women to be given the kiss of peace during mass.[147] Some thirteenth-century English synods and decrees prescribed shaving the heads of concubines, denying them the sacraments, and ostracising them socially.[148] Brundage argues that this strategy marked a dramatic change from the Church first condoning then discouraging clerical concubinage and, finally, penalising the women who were its victims.[149] Certainly writers like Peter Damian spoke of priests' wives and concubines in the most vituperative language, calling them the 'Devil's choice tidbits' and 'wallowing pools of greasy hogs'.[150] Gerald of Wales stated 'that women who prevent our salvation and lead us to damnation should not be called our friends, but rather our dread enemies'.[151]

It was against this background of mistrust and fear of female sexuality and the threat it posed to the secular clergy not sheltered by the monastic cloister, that Archbishop Eudes sought to discipline the unchaste clergy in his province of Rouen. In this way he was following the lead of previous, but not always successful, prelates like Archbishop John of Rouen (1067–79) and Bishop Arnulf of Lisieux (1141–81).[152] Work on the gender implications of clerical celibacy in Normandy in particular and Europe in general has focussed on the priests, largely because the surviving evidence highlights lapses in ecclesiastical discipline.[153] The exception to this trend is Dyan Elliott's recent work on priests' wives that concentrates on the theological implications of their presence in the parish.[154] A consideration of the women and children involved here reveals some interesting points about the nature of the relationships between a supposedly celibate male clergy and their female parishioners, illustrating not only relationships that were marriages in all but name, but also the exploitative aspects involved.

What is immediately apparent from the surviving evidence is the large number of women who formed long-term relationships with clerics. These relationships involved women from across the social scale and members of the secular clergy from cathedral canons to parish priests. In forming such bonds, especially if they lived with priests, women put themselves outside the bounds of accepted ecclesiastical behaviour and space. As Elliott points out, at a time

---

147 Thomas of Chobham, *Summa confessorum*, pp. 385–7.
148 *Councils and Synods with Other Documents Relating to the English Church II 1205–1313*, ed. F. M. Powicke and C. R. Cheney, 2 vols (Oxford, 1964), vol. 1, pp. 62–3 for Salisbury, 1217x1219; pp. 154–5 for a decree for the province of Canterbury, 1225 and p. 180 for Worcester, 1229.
149 Brundage, *Law, Sex and Christian Society*, p. 405.
150 Peter Damian, *Contra intemperantes clericos*, PL 145, col. 410. See also Elliott, *Spiritual Marriage*, p. 103.
151 Gerald of Wales, *Jewel of the Church*, p. 133.
152 For Archbishop John and Bishop Arnulf see P. Bouet and M. Dosdat, 'Les évêques normands de 985 à 1150', *Les évêques normands du XIe siècle*, ed. P. Bouet and F. Neveux (Caen, 1995), pp. 20, 32.
153 For example, Swanson, 'Angels Incarnate', pp. 160–77.
154 Elliott, *Fallen Bodies*, especially pp. 81–106.

when the reformers were trying to institute a strict division between the clergy and the laity, priests' wives defied classification by being neither fully lay nor fully clerical. In addition, by virtue of their gender, they trespassed on to what was becoming an exclusively male space.[155] Archbishop John of Rouen was the first prelate in the province to try to impose celibacy on all the clergy above subdeacon. When, in 1072, he ordered those in major orders to abandon their concubines, he was stoned for his pains.[156] In a letter from Archbishop Lanfranc to John, dated to between April 1076 and July 1077, Lanfranc makes it clear that canons were prohibited from taking or keeping a wife unless they renounced their prebends.[157] Problems relating to clerical celibacy continued in the Rouen archdiocese during the first decades of the twelfth century. When Archbishop Geoffrey (1111–28) tried to enforce the canons of the council of Reims relating to clergy cohabiting with women, at a synod in 1119, he sparked a riot in Rouen cathedral.[158] The archbishop fled to his private apartments while his retainers physically attacked the protesting priests.[159] Opposition to clerical celibacy and a defence of the rights of priests' sons was articulated in a tract known as the 'Norman Anonymous'.[160] In c.1178–79, Bishop Arnulf of Lisieux encountered similar problems amongst the canons of his cathedral. In a letter to Pope Alexander III (1159–81) he wrote: 'I immediately from the beginning took steps to purge the wantonness customary to the church. To remove the old canons involved in concubinage required a hand of necessary severity. One day, for the assurance of their virtue, I caused eighteen concubines to be abjured publicly by the canons.'[161]Although 'the old canons' did not openly return to their concubines, their successors established new partners, and even children, in the cathedral neighbourhood:

> No evidence can easily be shown; I could not pass sentence from suspicion alone; and their very number defended them with a multitude of prevarications. Yet what had been committed by many could not be concealed. The labour pains of birth were making the new men stronger and the whole neighbourhood was celebrating the new cradles.[162]

The problem of clerical concubinage was not one that was going to be solved easily. If one looks at Archbishop Eudes's register, it is apparent that a great many women were involved in long-term relationships with the clergy at any one time. It is not always clear from the register what sort of relationships were involved. A number of entries, however, do refer to women who

---

155 Elliott, *Fallen Bodies*, pp. 83–4.
156 OV, vol. 2, p. 200.
157 *Letters of Lanfranc*, no. 41, p. 135.
158 For Archbishop Geoffrey, see Bouet and Dosdat, 'Les évêques normands de 985 à 1150', p. 21. This Rouen synod is known only from OV, vol. 6, p. 291 note 4.
159 OV, vol. 6, pp. 290–5.
160 The treatise, however, does not elaborate on the rights of concubines and wives so I do not discuss it here. For a discussion of the theology of the 'Norman Anonymous' see Barstow, *Married Priests*, pp. 157–73.
161 Barlow, no. 132, p. 198 and Schriber p. 256.
162 Barlow, no. 132, p. 199 and Schriber, pp. 256–7

were 'kept', or described as concubines, for a long time. These relationships seem to be marriages in all but name. For example, Richard, the priest at Rouxmesnil, had kept a woman for a long time and had a child by her.[163] The priest at Marcaise was said to have had a servant concubine, whereas Matthew, a canon of the chapter of St-Hildevert in Gournay, had kept a woman from Les Andelys for fourteen years and it was believed that she was still living in his house.[164]

Women established homes for these men much as they would for husbands who were laymen. One example from Eudes's register shows a glimpse of domestic life amongst women associated with the secular clergy. There were two women living in the house of the priest at Mesnil-David, though it is not known who they were. His concubine is recorded as living elsewhere, though his children were staying with him so perhaps the women involved were his daughters. Archbishop Eudes recorded them as they were causing a disturbance by fighting in the house, the reason being that 'one was fond of roses and the other had cut down the rose bushes'.[165] Women who had made homes for priests were most unwilling to have them broken up by the ecclesiastical authorities, as is brilliantly illustrated by one of Bishop Arnulf's letters to Pope Alexander III, dated 1178/9, about Hamon, one of his parish priests. The word 'concubine' does not do justice to the nature of this relationship. Hamon had apparently kept the anonymous woman 'in his house and table and bed' for more than thirty years and had fathered many children. The couple were quite open in their relations as Hamon did not keep his partner hidden by a veil and they had publicly celebrated the marriages of their daughters, clearly a sign that they considered their daughters to be legitimate.[166] Arnulf wanted Hamon to repudiate his partner and take up a life of celibacy. Not only was Hamon unwilling to do this, but his partner and their daughters actively sought to prevent the break-up of their family and home when they 'assaulted and atrociously laid impious hands on the two priests' Arnulf had sent to their house.[167] By taking such action, Hamon and his partner risked ostracising themselves and their family from the Church. In this case though, it would seem that the lay community accepted their relationship, judging from the fact that Hamon's daughters had found husbands and that it was only

---

163 Bonnin, p. 17 and *Register*, p. 20. Davis discusses the issue of concubinage, but only from the point of view of clerical discipline: *Holy Bureaucrat*, pp. 116–22.

164 Bonnin, pp. 26, 466 and *Register*, pp. 30, 531.

165 Bonnin, p. 20, and *Register*, p. 24.

166 Barlow, no. 115, pp. 177–8 and Schriber, p. 259. See also Kelleher, '"Like Man and Wife": Clerics' Concubines in the Diocese of Barcelona', p. 349 for a comparable case from 1314 in which 'witnesses asserted that [the priest] Gener shared both his table and his bed with Romia'.

167 Barlow, no. 115, pp. 177–8 and Schriber, p. 259. Outrage at members of the clergy blatantly flouting the rules on celibacy extended to England. John of Salisbury was furious that Walkelin, archdeacon of Suffolk, had called his son by a concubine Adrian, after the pope. Subsequently, Walkelin had gone on pilgrimage, leaving his partner, who was pregnant with another child, with instructions to name the child Benevento if a boy and if a girl, Adriana; *The Letters of John of Salisbury*, ed. and trans. E. Millor and C. Brooke, OMT, 2 vols (Oxford, 1979–86), vol. 1, no. 15, pp. 24–5.

the actions of a reforming bishop that sought to break up the family. Half a century earlier, in a letter dated c.1102 or 1103, from Anselm, archbishop of Canterbury, to Herbert Losinga, bishop of Norwich (1091–1119), Anselm states that the concubinary priests should be replaced with chaste priests. If the expelled priests then attacked their replacements, 'not only should they [the new priests] exclude them and their women from their community but also from the lands which they hold'.[168] To some priests then, the support and love offered by their relationships with women was worth risking something akin to exile, though the support of the lay community was clearly needed if the Church wished to ostracise them fully.

Not all relationships between women and the secular clergy followed the pattern set out above. There could be an exploitative side to the liaisons. Some of the clergy noted in Archbishop Eudes's register had abused their position, their access to certain places like churches and their freedom of movement, to engineer meetings with women. For example, a priest at Auberville caused 'a certain woman to marry one of his servants that he might have freer access to her'.[169] The priest at Biville 'followed a certain woman through the fields' so he could have intercourse with her.[170] The priest of St-Sulpice in the deanery of Envermeu held vigils in his church every Saturday night. Eudes instructed that the church was to be closed at night and no one was to keep vigil. Such practices were prohibited under canon fifteen of the Rouen council of 1231, which states that 'vigils are not to be held in churches except on the feast of the saint of the church'.[171] This legislation was designed in part to limit the opportunities for illicit activities after dark. Perhaps church vigils had become an excuse for raucous parties entailing not only an unacceptable use of sacred space and a perversion of the practices therein, but also an equally unaccept-able mingling of sections of society that should otherwise be kept separate, namely male clerics and laywomen.

In addition, there are a number of women recorded in Eudes's register who may have been considered particularly vulnerable to predatory priests. They include poor women, disabled women and widows. For instance, the priest at Auberville, in addition to carrying on an affair with his servant's wife, was rumoured to be involved with 'the daughter of a certain poor woman who lives near the cross'.[172] The priest at La-Rue-St-Pierre had kept 'a certain little old woman' for a long time, and the priest at Chars was illfamed of a certain widow.[173] Master John of St-Lô, a canon of the Rouen cathedral chapter, was 'defamed of incontinence with a certain woman who is almost blind'.[174] In response to these accusations, John maintained that he had had nothing to do with her since he had been ordained a priest. Eudes's instructions and

168 Schmitt, vol. 4, no. 254, pp. 165–6 and Fröhlich, vol. 2, no. 254, pp. 242–3. Prior to 1094, Herbert's see was located in Thetford.
169 Bonnin, p. 25 and *Register*, p. 29.
170 Bonnin, p. 28 and *Register*, p. 33.
171 Mansi, vol. 23, col. 216.
172 Bonnin, p. 25 and *Register*, p. 29.
173 Bonnin, pp. 32, 40 and *Register*, pp. 36, 43.
174 Bonnin, p. 122 and *Register*, p. 136.

John's response appear shocking to modern eyes in their treatment of this very vulnerable woman. Eudes stated that to avoid a scandal John should send this woman out of town, which he promised to do. Again, a relationship with a member of the secular clergy threatened expulsion from the community for the woman involved, in this case, possibly one who had no one else to support her. Yet ironically, the need for support, whether emotional or financial, may have been the very reason why these women formed relationships with priests in the first place. They were vulnerable and therefore easy targets for men officially debarred from an active sexual life.

Exploitation of a different kind occurred between members of the secular clergy and prostitutes.[175] Again, priests exploited access to their churches and the sacraments to engineer meetings in places that may have afforded some degree of privacy. For example, the dean of Eu churched two prostitutes 'as though they were virtuous women so that he might have to do with them'.[176] Walter, the priest of Bray-sous-Baudemont in the French Vexin, led the dancing at the celebrations for the marriage of a prostitute which he had performed. Later, in the evening, he and some of the neighbouring priests had sex with her. He had previously cohabited with another prostitute.[177] Robert, a member of the chapter of St-Mellon-de-Pontoise, also frequented prostitutes and openly walked 'before the door of a certain workroom' where they gathered.[178] As Karras points out, priests were often banned from brothels and this may have been the reason behind Robert's peculiar actions. These examples are a strong indication that not only the women but also the priests placed themselves on the margins of accepted behaviour when contracting sexual relations.[179] Where brothels were tolerated, priests, unlike other men, could not openly be seen to frequent them. Instead they were forced to lurk outside, which must have been a humiliating experience. The clergy did not always come out of meetings with prostitutes unscarred by their experiences. If caught, not only would they have to face the wrath of the archdeacon and bishop but the women also sometimes set them up for ridicule. Archbishop Eudes discovered that Denis, another member of the chapter of St-Mellon had had a 'certain loose woman' in his chamber who had 'seized his super-tunic and thrown it out of the window and into the street to another of her ribald friends'.[180] This was a very public shaming of an unchaste priest. Swanson

---

175 For a wider discussion of medieval prostitution see R. M. Karras, *Common Women: Prostitution and Sexuality in Medieval England*, Studies in the History of Sexuality (Oxford, 1996). Karras argues that some groups of prostitutes may have specialised in catering for priests or members of religious orders, especially in ecclesiastical cities such as York where the clergy made up a significant proportion of the potential client base: *Common Women*, p. 30.

176 Bonnin, pp. 25–6 and *Register*, p. 30. Eudes describes the women as 'mulieres meretrices' and so they are clearly prostitutes.

177 Bonnin, p. 379 and *Register*, p. 429.

178 'in quodam operatorio': Bonnin, p. 42 and *Register*, p. 47.

179 Karras, *Common Women*, p. 33.

180 Bonnin, p. 538 and *Register*, p. 611. An interesting later parallel to this case is discussed by Karras. Elizabeth Chekyn was convicted of prostitution in 1516 and was described as 'a common harlot, strumpet and also now lately strolling and walking by the streets

has argued that priests were caught in a contradiction between the Church's desire that the priests should be 'angels incarnate' and the priests' urges to assert their masculinity.[181] The prostitutes were mocking the priests' confusion and hypocrisy.

Not all sexual relationships between priests and women were based on mutual respect, affection or monetary exchange. Some priests who were unable to persuade women to agree to have a sexual relationship resorted to violent means, including rape and murder. Denis of St-Mellon, whom we have discussed above, was recorded as having beaten a girl called Alice of whom he was defamed and this may have been a case of rape.[182] Ralph Coypel, a canon in the cathedral chapter of Lisieux, was alleged to have 'offered violence to a certain woman' to force her into his house and rape her. The woman resisted but stood no chance as 'when she began to cry out, Ralph and his accomplices throttled her so hard' that she died shortly afterwards.[183] If a woman was raped or so threatened, then by law she had to cry out in order to bring people to her aid and to have her case accepted by the courts.[184] In this case it appears that the canon, who had not been alone but in the company of other men, panicked and, determined that the case should not come before the ecclesiastical authorities, he and his companions killed the woman. The fact that Archbishop Eudes recorded the crime shows that the murderer(s) did not escape justice. Not all women were as powerless as Ralph Coypel's victim. Simon, the chaplain of St-Hildevert in Gournay, was severely beaten by a woman called Haise because she was unwilling to turn her daughter over to him for sex. Unfortunately for mother and daughter, Haise's assertive action could not prevent the priest raping the girl.[185]

Not all women in priests' houses were necessarily their sexual partners: daughters or other female relatives acted as housekeepers. Female relatives were allowed to live with priests according to canon three of the first council of Nicaea in 325 which stated that bishops, priests and other clerics should not keep any women in their households 'save perhaps for a mother or a sister or aunt or such other person as may be immune from suspicion'.[186] This statute was reiterated by canon seven of the First Lateran Council in 1123.[187] Certainly up to the mid-twelfth century, the Church recognised the need for a woman to keep house for priests in lieu of the wives they were forbidden to take. However, by the thirteenth century, Archbishop Eudes found it necessary to act against the presence of female relatives in priests' houses. In Eudes's

---

of this city [London] in a priest's array and clothing, in rebuke and reproach of the order of the priesthood': *Common Women*, p. 78.
181 Swanson, 'Angels Incarnate', p. 161.
182 Bonnin, p. 535 and *Register*, p. 611.
183 Bonnin, p. 297 and *Register*, p. 336.
184 *Coutumiers de Normandie*, I, ed. Tardiff, pp. 40–2 and trans. *Women's Lives in Medieval Europe*, ed. E. Amt (London, 1993), p. 56.
185 Bonnin, p. 466 and *Register*, p. 531.
186 *Decrees*, p. 7 and Brundage, *Law, Sex and Christian Society*, p. 112.
187 *Decrees*, p. 191.

register, the majority of female relations in priests' houses were daughters.[188] The archbishop does not give us very much information regarding their activity though their presence was contrary to synodal legislation.[189] It is possible that some of these girls were very young and their fathers were bringing them up, either because their mothers were dead or had moved elsewhere. Instances of incest between priests and their female relatives were not unknown. Walter, the parish priest at Grandcourt, was illfamed of his own niece as was Ralph of St-Denis-des-Monts.[190] Dom Gilbert of the Rouen cathedral chapter even had children by his niece.[191] Closer blood ties were in evidence in the case of Richard, priest at Nesle, who was accused of incontinence with his own sister, Mary.[192] Clearly, according to contemporary opinion, female relatives posed just as much of a threat to a priest's fragile celibacy as any other woman.

For a number of women, a priest was a valid choice as a sexual partner and the Norman evidence has shown that they could enjoy long and happy relationships. For other women, especially those in vulnerable circumstances, the secular clergy were seen as preying on themselves or their daughters. These priests were willing to abuse their position in the Church to exploit their female parishioners. The most vulnerable group, amongst whom was the blind woman from Rouen, probably entered into relationships with priests in the expectation of finding support in a time of need. The Church, however, seemingly made no distinction between women who were happily married in all but name, women forced into sex and women in a vulnerable position. All women were held equally responsible for undermining the ideal of clerical celibacy and in complete contrast to modern scholarly opinion, the women were seen as predatory and the priests as victims. Moreover, some theologians perceived the women and the priests as committing a sexual as well as an ecclesiastical crime. Peter Damian believed that a priest had an intimate relationship with his church, of which he was the husband; consequently any relationship he had with one of his spiritual daughters, a female parishioner, was incestuous.[193] Although Peter Damian's views on the issue of clerical celibacy lay at the extremes of the Church's beliefs on the separation of the priesthood and the laity, it is true to say that, by being involved in a sexual relationship with a secular priest of whatever character, a woman was placing herself at the very limits of her spiritual community and indeed faith. Whereas some parishes might have accepted relationships, for example, that between

---

188 For example, Bonnin, pp. 29, 32, 329 and *Register*, pp. 33, 36, 377.
189 Mansi, vol. 22, col. 393. Sons as well as daughters were prohibited from living in priests' houses by the thirteenth-century council of Coutances, see Mansi, vol. 25, col. 33 and Taglia 'On Account of Scandal', p. 63.
190 Bonnin, pp. 21, 516 and *Register*, pp. 25, 589.
191 Bonnin, p. 561 and *Register*, p. 643.
192 Bonnin, p. 195 and *Register*, p. 210.
193 Brooke, 'Priest, Deacon and Layman', p. 235. See also Elliott, *Fallen Bodies*, p. 103, where she argues that by entering into a sexual relationship with a priest, a woman not only committed a sin against God but against the wider community as the sacramental benefits of the priest that rightly belonged to the community were being siphoned off by their wives, p. 106.

Hamon and his partner, if the ecclesiastical authorities decided to act, it was the women concerned who faced being turned out of their homes and expelled from their communities, not the priests. The Church had no place for them in contrast to the women who, like the widows of Bec or lay sisters, placed themselves under obedience to a male monastery.[194]

Conclusion

In this discussion of the notions of reception and intrusion into sacred space, it is apparent that religious communities and churches were involved in a careful balancing act. Intrusion was very much in the eye of the beholder and accommodations had to be reached. The Church as a whole needed lay support, especially in the case of monasteries that relied on the donations and benefactions of the laity in order to survive. At certain times, communities were more willing to accommodate large numbers of lay people than was strictly allowable by monastic statutes. For example, lay people were welcomed into cathedrals and monasteries at times of rebuilding in a reciprocal arrangement that allowed the community to acquire building materials and the pilgrims to pray and seek healing. Secular cathedrals welcomed pilgrims for the significant feasts of the church's dedication, in the case of Coutances, feasts associated with the Virgin Mary. In the example from St-Amand-de-Rouen, the fame of the saint for dealing with cases of mental illness provided the justification necessary to bring a laywoman into the nuns' community to such a great extent. Other forms of intrusion were questioned by the ecclesiastical authorities and by the time we reach the thirteenth century, they were less willing to accommodate what they saw as severe breaches of the monastic rule. Archbishop Eudes was concerned to ensure a separation between the professed religious in his care and the lay people, both men and women, who came to worship in monastic churches. In these cases, physical barriers were sometimes erected to underline the spatial separation between secular and religious.

Questions of gender are important in other forms of intrusion. Although it was impossible, and undesirable, to ensure that monastic communities were totally single-sex institutions, ecclesiastical visitors like Abbot Stephen and Archbishop Eudes aimed to limit the opportunities for men to enter communities of women and women to enter male houses. The visitors' concern is best reflected in the restrictions placed on hospitality and the regulations drawn up regarding the presence of servants. These questions go beyond a simple classification of visitors by biological sex. Old women were acceptable as maids in male monasteries as they were perceived as less of a sexual threat to the monks' chastity than young women. Eudes repeatedly made an exception in restrictions on hospitality for those 'whom it would be a scandal to keep out'. Presumably these people would be founders, benefactors and the higher nobility, who, by their status and association with the house, should have been

[194] See chapter four.

able to conduct themselves in a manner becoming to guests of a religious community. The presence of children presented a problem in nunneries because of the temptation for the nuns to identify with Mary's role as a mother, a very different gendered identity to her role as a spotless virgin.

The problem of celibacy and gender is central to the discussion of priests' wives and concubines. Here, the priests were not shielded from secular women by the walls of a religious community, but were living amongst their parishioners as celibate men. The attempts by the reform movement of the eleventh century to eradicate clerical concubinage were not successful, as is shown by the number of priests with partners in the pages of Archbishop Eudes's register. The women themselves were blamed for ensnaring the priests in the web of human relationships. The secular clergy, like their monastic brethren, were a separate order in medieval society: it was not the place of the laity to trespass into the spaces occupied by them.

3

Enclosure

The monastery should be so set up that everything necessary is carried on within the monastery, that is the water, the mill, the garden, and the various crafts so that there be no necessity for the monks to be wandering about outside: that is absolutely not good for their souls.[1]

The rule of St Benedict clearly shows that enclosure was the principal means by which religious communities sought to protect their vocation from any interference from the outside world: it was enforced by monastic rules and expressed in the monastery architecture. In the preceding chapter, we saw how the laity intruded on sacred space. Enclosure, and the rules and customs governing it, were not just designed to keep lay people out, but also to ensure professed religious remained within their monasteries as far as possible. In this chapter, we shall consider how enclosure worked in practice as against the statutes laid down by monastic rules and the expectation of ecclesiastical visitors like Abbot Stephen and Archbishop Eudes. Monks and nuns temporarily left their cloister for various reasons and some indeed turned apostate and left their monasteries for good. We will also look at the use of monastery buildings, which is necessary for a full understanding of the architectural practice of enclosure. Statutes relating to enclosure also ensured the separation of certain groups from the rest of society; in this context, the attitudes towards those with leprosy and the governance of hospitals have particular relevance. Enclosure did of course have its many problems and these are most readily identified in a discussion of male staff in houses of female religious. Nuns required male priests to perform the sacraments and the priests required somewhere to live. As the Church's attitude towards female religious hardened, men were also required to liaise with the secular world in the execution of the nuns' business. These factors set up significant tensions in the practice of monasticism and in the communities' relations with local lay society.

[1]   *Rule*, ch. 66, p. 303

The cloister: ideas and appearance

The language used in medieval sources relating to the cloister, as Christopher Brooke has highlighted, is confusing: St Benedict used the word *claustrum* for the enclosure as a whole, not just the claustral ranges, the more common meaning in historical and archaeological research.[2] Used in this second way, the cloister was at the heart of the monastic precinct. It took the form of a courtyard with an arcaded walk around the interior. It was here that all the buildings necessary for the spiritual and communal side of monastic life, church, chapter house, refectory and dormitory, were found. The kitchens, agricultural buildings and workshops for the exploitation of the houses' material resources were situated away from the cloister, either in the inner court in the case of domestic functions, or in the outer court of the precinct for those areas likely to cause more disturbance.[3] Both male and female houses in Normandy were generally orientated with the cloisters on the south side. There does not appear to have been use of the north cloister for female houses in Normandy except for functional reasons. This is in contrast to monastic sites in England where Gilchrist has identified such use as being of particular significance as she argues it harks back to Anglo-Saxon traditions of female spirituality and reflects customs that located women on the north side of the church.[4] The claustral orientation of enough Norman houses to make a comparison meaningful is unknown, but three houses, Montivilliers, St-Sauveur and La Trinité, possibly had cloisters to the north of their churches. Montivilliers' north cloister was replaced early in the abbey's history by the parish cemetery of St-Sauveur and the cloister was shifted to the south, presumably because the water supply, a branch of the river Lazarde, was situated there.[5] The growth of the local parish provided added impetus. The parish church was built into the north side of the nave of the nuns' church, and so a parish cemetery to the north was more appropriate than the nuns' cloister. The location of water was also the reason behind the positioning of the cloister at St-Sauveur in Évreux, if published plans are accurate.[6] The spatial distribution of the original site is unknown. The north cloister at La Trinité may have been so situated due

2   C. Brooke, 'Reflections on the Monastic Cloister', *Romanesque and Gothic: Essays for George Zarnecki*, ed. N. Stratford, 2 vols (Woodbridge, 1987), vol. 1, p. 19.

3   Gilchrist, *Norwich Cathedral Close*, p. 43. See F. Yvernault, 'Les bâtiments de l'abbaye de Montivilliers au moyen âge', *Montivilliers, hier, aujourd'hui, demain*, 9 (1997), p. 42, for a plan.

4   Gilchrist, *Gender and Material Culture*, pp. 128–48. The north side of the church was associated with iconography of the Blessed Virgin Mary and other female saints, making it a suitable location in the eyes of the Church for women during worship. For the separation of the sexes during worship see M. Aston, 'Segregation in Church', *Women in the Church*, ed. W. Sheils and D. Wood, Studies in Church History 27 (Oxford, 1990), p. 240.

5   G. Priem, *Abbaye royale de Montivilliers*, Abbayes et Prieurés de Normandie 14 (Rouen, 1979) p. 9.

6   Appendix B, no. 10. The monks' abbey of St-Taurin also had a cloister situated to the north: appendix A, no. 32.

to lack of space on the south side in which to build a commodious claustral range. Though as we saw in chapter one, La Trinité was a ducal foundation and the orientation of the cloister may be due to a desire on the part of Duke William and Duchess Matilda to construct a suitably impressive abbey in order to display their piety and power.[7]

In the standard south cloister plan the chapter house and dormitory were located in the east range. The refectory occupied the south range, opposite the church, which lay to the north of the cloister garth. The west range contained a variety of buildings, often dependent on the affiliation of a particular community. In Cistercian houses, the west range was generally taken up with the lay sisters' or brothers' quarters, namely their refectory and dormitory, so they could go about their manual work without disturbing the choir monks' and nuns' devotions: there are exceptions to this rule. In one such Cistercian house, Mortain, the lay sisters were housed in the north claustral range with their buildings extending westwards from the church.[8] In Benedictine houses, the use of the west range was more fluid; at Montivilliers the abbess had her apartments in the west range. Other houses might use the west range as guest accommodation. There seem to be no general rules concerning the location of the infirmary, but it was located outside the cloister: for example, to the east at Montivilliers and to the south at St-Etienne in Caen.[9]

Rules governing the status and use of the cloister may have differed from order to order, but broadly speaking male and female members of contemplative communities were required to stay within their chosen house. Nuns were more strictly enclosed, at least in theory, than monks. The cloister was at the heart of the monastery, but the definition of 'cloister' was not merely confined to the physical actuality of the inner court. As Jean Leclercq stated, 'it designates ... the material obstacle which marks the bounds of the property; the space reserved to those who enter or live there' and 'the body of ecclesiastical laws relative to this obstacle and this space'.[10] In other words, the cloister was a state of mind as much as a physical place, reflected in the rules regarding the appearance and behaviour of professed religious.[11]

In theory, the monastery was self-sufficient and so no monk or nun should have to leave its precincts, but in reality the practice of cloistering was different. There were times when it was absolutely necessary for a professed religious to journey beyond the gatehouse, while at other times, a more lax interpretation of the cloister rules allowed outings. It is clear though, that the practice of

---

[7]   See chapter one, section on topography.

[8]   Appendix B, no. 15.

[9]   Appendix B, no. 14; appendix A, no. 21; *Monasticon*, plate 104 dating to 1684.

[10] J. Leclercq, 'La clôiture points de repère historiques', *Collectanea Cisterciencia*, 43 (1981), p. 366 and J. T. Schulenburg, 'Strict Active Enclosure and its Effects on the Female Monastic Experience (ca. 500–1100)', *Medieval Religious Women vol. 1: Distant Echoes*, ed. J. A. Nichols and L. T. Shank, Cistercian Studies 71 (Kalamazoo, 1984), p. 51.

[11] This is a definition also followed by Megan Cassidy-Welch, 'the cloister was both material and metaphorical, physically located and mentally imagined': *Monastic Spaces and their Meanings*, p. 45.

claustration was interpreted differently for men and women.[12] Concern about the place of religious women in society and the Church was raised as early as the fourth century in the letters of St Jerome (c.350–c.420). The sixth-century rule for women written by Caesarius of Arles (469/70–542), however, was the first to impose a strict claustration based on the idea that nuns were to be kept apart: 'If anyone having left her parents, wishes to renounce the world and enter the holy fold, in order to evade, with God's help, the jaws of spiritual wolves, let her never leave the monastery until her death, not even into the church, where the door can be seen.'[13] Within our period, an active cloister was insisted upon in the charter for the first Cluniac monastery for women at Marcigny, founded in 1056, and was mandatory as a primary condition of acceptance into the Cistercian order for Coyroux (founded in 1142).[14] Attitudes towards a strict claustration for nuns culminated in the decretal *Periculoso* of 1298, promulgated by Pope Boniface VIII (1294–1303): 'We do firmly decree ... that nuns collectively and individually ... ought henceforth to remain perpetually cloistered in their monasteries, so that none of them, tacitly or expressly professed, shall or may for whatever reason or cause ... have permission hereafter to leave the same monasteries.'[15] The reasons for such stringent legislation lay partly in a fear of unregulated female spirituality and sexuality. The Church could theoretically keep an eye on nuns confined in monasteries as they were subject to male authority and regulated by one of the accepted monastic rules. Women who formed more informal groups, meeting in their own homes, placed themselves outside the structure of the Church and were considered a threat. This attitude is highlighted in conciliar legislation, particularly canon twenty-six of the Second Lateran Council, 1139:

> We decree that the pernicious and detestable custom of some women who though they live neither according to the Rule of the blessed Benedict nor according to the rules of Basil and Augustine, yet wish to be commonly regarded as nuns, be abolished ... These build their own retreats and private houses.[16]

---

12   These differences are usually articulated by historians in terms of a passive cloister for men, designed to prevent ingress by the laity and an active cloister for women that sought to prevent nuns from leaving except in times of necessity.

13   Caesarius of Arles, 'Règle des vierges (c.512–534)', *Oeuvres monastiques vol. 1: oeuvres pour les moniales*, ed. and trans. A. de Vogüé and J. Courreau, Sources Chrétiennes 345 (Paris, 1988), pp. 180–1 and translated into English in *Women's Lives in Medieval Europe*, ed. Amt, pp. 221–2. See also D. Hochstetler, 'The Meaning of the Cloister for Women According to Caesarius of Arles', *Religion, Culture and Society in the Early Middle Ages: Studies in Honor of Richard E. Sullivan*, ed. T. Noble and J. S. Cantreni (Kalamazoo, 1987), pp. 27–40.

14   E. Makowski, *Canon Law and Cloistered Women: 'Periculoso' and its Commentators 1298–1545*, Studies in Medieval and Early Modern Canon Law 5 (Washington DC, 1997), pp. 9–10 and Schulenburg, 'Strict Active Enclosure', p. 60; Barrière, 'Cistercian Convent of Coyroux', p. 76.

15   *Corpus iuris canonici*, ed. E. Friedberg, 2 vols (Leipzig, 1879–81; repr. Graz, 1959), vol. 2, cols 1053–4 and trans. Makowski, *Canon Law and Cloistered Women*, pp. 135–6.

16   *Decrees*, p. 203. We do not know who these women were, though they seem to prefigure the beguines in their lifestyle

An examination of ecclesiastical visitation records demonstrates that although nuns had their own place in a religious space given over to their needs, a nunnery, where they could be regulated and watched over by their ever wary male superiors, nuns, like monks, did venture out of their houses. Crucially, discussing the cloister with reference to the nuns' use of it in particular can reveal to a certain degree how religious men and women interpreted the strictures quoted above. What emerges is a picture of nuns especially attempting to adapt claustral spaces to suit their needs better, often in the face of concerted opposition from their male ecclesiastical superiors.[17]

Certain buildings and a degree of enclosure were also necessary prerequisites for the successful running of a leper house or hospital. All communities would have naturally required an infirmary for the sick; lodgings for the staff; in some cases, guest houses, and a chapel and farm buildings to ensure the agricultural exploitation of their demesne. The less structured nature of these communities and the lack of architectural survivals means that we know very little about the spatial layout of most of them in Normandy.[18] The statutes for most hospitals, which are so important for our knowledge, were based on the Augustinian rule and so the religious affiliation of these institutions was much looser than a congregation of Benedictine abbeys; consequently their ground plans were more varied. In Normandy, two broad types of ground plan can be discerned for leper houses: an ensemble of individual houses or simple wooden cabins, or a collection of communal lodgings.

Notre-Dame-de-Beaulieu in Caen belongs to the first category. A description of 1713 adjoining a coloured plan of 1667 gives a picture that is generally believed to represent approximately the establishment as it was in the Middle Ages.[19] The community comprised two enclosures: the first was entered by a gate with two houses for porters and was surrounded by fields cultivated by lepers and staff; the second enclosure contained the church, with the priest's house opposite and houses for the sick with gardens attached at the foot of the church. In addition, there were agricultural buildings such as stables and granges, and a well at the centre of the enclosure.[20] The earlier leper house of Nombril-Dieu was included in the grounds.[21] St-Nicolas-de-la-Chesnaie, near Bayeux, followed the second type of plan, namely communal lodgings. Again, it had two enclosures, that of the lepers and that of the immediate demesne of the community. In front of the chapel was the house of the monks who cared for the lepers with the lepers' house opposite it. The entrance was watched

17 See below.
18 Jeanne, 'Exclusion et charité', vol. 1, p. 64. Many hospital buildings were destroyed or suffered damage in the Hundred Years War.
19 Jeanne, 'Exclusion et charité', vol. 1, p. 89.
20 Jeanne, 'Exclusion et charité', vol. 1, p. 89. The site was also described by A. C. Ducarel during a tour of Normandy undertaken shortly before 1767. At the time of his visit, the site was being turned into a 'house of correction for the confinement of sturdy beggars and prostitutes', A. C. Ducarel, Anglo-Norman Antiquities Considered in a Tour Through Part of Normandy (London, 1767), p. 76.
21 Appendix C, no. 7.

over by a gatehouse. The surviving architecture within the present farm dates from the fourteenth century, after it was rebuilt following the English invasion, but it probably follows an earlier plan.[22] Hospitals and leper houses may not have adopted the standard monastic cloister, but it is clear that their architecture operated in a similar way to ensure the communities remained enclosed; and it is to the operation of the cloister that we shall now turn. In this instance, enclosure was necessary for the maintenance of self-sufficiency within the community to prevent mendicancy amongst the lepers.[23] The attitude of the Church towards the enclosure of lepers was similar to its approach to the cloistering of nuns: both were seen as groups in need of regulation, on the one hand through fear of a disease not properly understood and on the other through a fear of unregulated female sexuality.

Boundaries and thresholds

In the previous section, we established the layout of the monastic cloister and the ground plans of leper houses and hospitals, as well as the theory underpinning them. Here, we shall examine in more detail the idea that the cloister or enclosure was far from being an inviolable space, but actually involved a number of boundaries and thresholds throughout the precinct that regulated behaviour in a more nuanced fashion.

Access to the cloister, and thus to the monks and nuns within it, was supposed to be strictly controlled by a monastic official. According to the rule of St Benedict, written initially for men, this person was to be 'a wise old man' whose 'maturity will prevent his wandering about'.[24] This statute is echoed by Abbot Stephen of Lexington during his inspections of the nuns of the Savignac congregation, who stated the portress should be a 'mature' nun.[25] She should prevent any nun from talking alone to a lay person through the window and should either be present herself or assign another of 'praiseworthy reputation'.[26] During his visits to Norman houses, Archbishop Eudes expressed concern at the lack of security of the cloister in both houses of monks and nuns on a number of occasions. As far as the nuns at Bondeville were concerned, the doorkeeper was deemed to be indiscreet and so was to be replaced.[27] At Villarceaux the gate looking towards the fields was frequently

22 Jeanne, 'Exclusion et charité', vol. 1, pp. 93–6.
23 Saul Brody has observed that most of the land attached to the leper hospital at Reims was given over to farming: *The Disease of the Soul: Leprosy in Medieval Literature* (Ithaca and London, 1974), p. 74.
24 *Rule*, ch. 66, p. 303.
25 'Preficiatur custodie claustri aliqua monialis matura secundum statutum capituli generalis'; *Registrum epistolarum*, p. 239.
26 'nulla monialis loquatur ad fenestram sine socia matura moribus et laudabilis testimonii sibi assistente et audiente': *Registrum epistolarum*, p. 239, and Bonnin, pp. 43–5, 326 and *Register*, pp. 50, 373 for similar prescriptions for Villarceaux and St-Amand.
27 Bonnin, p. 112 and *Register*, p. 127.

open and so the archbishop ordered it to be closed off.[28] The gate was also
to be guarded more effectively at St-Amand.[29] In some male houses, such as
at Eu, and Aumale, the cloister was not well kept.[30] These regulations were
designed to keep undesirable persons from intruding upon professed monastics'
areas as much as keeping the monks and nuns themselves enclosed. If the
points at which access was controlled were not properly guarded, then the
spatial parameters of the enclosure became more permeable.[31] During several
visits, Eudes was anxious to ensure that monks' and nuns' access to the
outside world was strictly controlled. At St-Vigor-le-Grand, for example, the
monks were to 'go out by the front way' and at other houses, they were not
to wander beyond the gate, presumably any gate that led them out of the
cloister or precinct.[32] The purpose of his strictures was to ensure that points
of contact with the outside world were limited, ideally to the gateway or door,
allowing the comings and goings of the monks and nuns to be observed and
controlled.

Both monks and nuns were guilty of infringements regarding the rules
of claustration, but an analysis of the spatial areas that Eudes records is
illuminating as to the differences in their activities. It is clear that in terms
of minor infringements involving monastics heading to specified locations,
monks wandered further afield than nuns. Their destinations were quite
varied including towns, farms, granges and markets. Towns seem to have
been a particularly attractive location where the monks went to drink in
taverns, for example Brothers Lawrence and Geoffrey from Bacqueville, or to
trade at the local markets, as at Sausseuse.[33] More often Eudes criticises the
male religious in his care for unauthorised gallivanting in the local towns.[34]
Communities' farms and gardens are particularly interesting in determining
what consituted breaking the cloister. These were the areas that required
a degree of negotiation in their use: that is to say, areas where it might be
acceptable for an individual to be present depending on circumstances and
the permission of his or her superior. Monks and nuns were allowed access
to gardens within the precinct, as can be seen from Eudes's visit to Ouville
in 1254/5 where he noted that the canons left the cloister and the garden
without permission.[35] The archbishop was more concerned with monks' and
nuns' visits to agricultural areas outside the monastery precincts. At Valmont,
for example, the monks went out from the cloister to the farm without the

[28]   Bonnin, p. 281 and *Register*, p. 317.
[29]   Bonnin, p. 326 and *Register*, p. 373.
[30]   Appendix A, no. 4 for Aumale; Bonnin, pp. 48 and 608–9 and *Register*, pp. 54 and
        700.
[31]   See P. Johnson, 'The Cloistering of Medieval Nuns: Release or Repression, Reality
        or Fantasy', *Gendered Domains: Rethinking Public and Private in Women's History*, ed.
        D. O. Helly and S. M. Reverby (Ithaca, 1992), p. 39 where she also notes the perme-
        ability of the cloister.
[32]   Bonnin, p. 92 and *Register*, p. 107.
[33]   Appendix A, no. 6 for Bacqueville; Bonnin, pp. 10, 484 and *Register*, pp. 14, 552.
[34]   For example, at Ste-Gauberge and Alençon: Bonnin, pp. 233, 373 and *Register*, pp. 257,
        442.
[35]   Bonnin, p. 210 and *Register*, p. 230.

permission of their superior; at St-Fromond they went to the farm during the recreation hour; and at St-Georges-de-Boscherville the monks entered the orchards and farms without permission.[36] These three houses were located in rural areas, and so an excursion to town was out of the question for the monks, if we assume that their infringements of the cloister fell under the heading of minor misdemeanours rather than an indication of intended apostasy. The monastic farms thus provided an opportunity to slip away for an hour or two, with less chance of discovery. The fact remains, though, that as these farms were outside the cloister the monks needed their superiors' permission to visit them. Even if their intention was not to leave the community permanently, the cloister could not be so carelessly disregarded in the eyes of the Church.

We have noted that in Jean Leclercq's definition, the cloister was a mental as well as a physical space. This can be broadened out to include the cloister as custody of the body.[37] This was not only manifest in observance of the clothing regulations discussed below, but also through the observance of chastity. Although both monks and nuns were guilty of breaking their vow of chastity, such infringements had a more visible consequence for nuns in terms of a pregnancy.[38] Not only did such an infringement entail the breaking of a physical boundary and the transgression of mental barriers, the obvious physical fact of pregnancy also publicly highlighted the nuns' failure to keep custody of their bodies and remain faithful to their vows and status as brides of Christ. For monks, a failure in this respect would only become visible to the community if the mother of the child brought it the attention of the superior. Sexual relations led to further problems in maintaining the cloister as a sacred space. Not only might children be housed in a nunnery, but nuns also left their cloister to visit their sons and daughters, or, more gravely, to seek aid in ending an unwanted pregnancy. At St-Aubin, Eudes had removed the veils of Alice and Eustasia for repeatedly offending against their vows and he sent one Agnes of Pont to a leper house in Rouen because 'she had connived at Eustasia's fornication' and was rumoured to have aided the unfortunate woman in procuring an abortion.[39] At Villarceaux, nuns left their cloister for reasons connected to their children conceived during illicit liaisons, for example Joan of L'Aillerie, who at one time had left the cloister and cohabited with a man by whom she had a child.[40] It is unsurprising that some of the nuns' lovers were either the community's chaplain or a local parish priest, which caused problems in the maintenance of good monastic practice.[41] Nicola of Rouen, a

---

36   Appendix A, nos 100, 75, 77; Bonnin, pp. 135, 251, 191 and *Register*, pp. 152, 281, 205.
37   See particularly *Rule of Saint Augustine*, ed. van Bavel and trans. Canning, pp. 29–32, especially p. 31 'you are to consider yourselves responsible for one another's chastity'.
38   It is important to note that Penelope Johnson, who has analysed Archbishop Eudes's register quantitatively, found that the nuns were no more apt to break their vow of chastity than the monks: *Equal in Monastic Profession*, pp. 114–15.
39   Bonnin, p. 255 and *Register*, p. 285.
40   Bonnin, p. 43 and *Register*, p. 48.
41   See below for the discussion on male staff in houses of nuns.

nun of St-Saëns, formed an enduring bond with the father of her two children, Simon, the parson at St-Saëns.[42]

Despite the existence of regulations to ensure monks and nuns stayed put in their communities, there were times, however, when it was legitimate for professed religious to leave their cloister. Eudes took such circumstances into account in his statutes for Villarceaux when he forbade 'any sister to leave the cloister without permission and without respectable companionship, nor shall such permission be granted without patent and reasonable cause'.[43] First and foremost, professed religious, including nuns, ventured out of the cloister for the benefit of their community. Even Peter the Venerable had to accept that it might be necessary for the cellaress of Marcigny to leave the abbey on business. The Cistercian statutes stated that an abbess might go out on business with an escort of two nuns and for the cellaress one was sufficient.[44] A charter from the Benedictine abbey of St-Sauveur in Évreux, dated 1243, shows the abbess sending out the prioress and another nun to collect the tithes of their lands at Les Botteraux.[45] Nuns also left their cloisters in pursuit of less formal business arrangements. It is in this area that the contradictions between strict enclosure and monastic self-sufficiency are most apparent and where practice on the ground came into conflict with ecclesiastical expectations. Women were unable to support themselves in the same way as monks, through manual labour, and were thus dependent to a far greater degree on their benefactors for material support.[46] Some of the sisters from Bival sold their bread rations outside the abbey, while nuns from St-Aubin were missing at one of Archbishop Eudes's visits as they 'had gone to France in search of alms'.[47] Clearly, women in some of the Norman religious houses could not depend on their secular supporters and patrons to provide for all their needs, or through financial mismanagement had found themselves in straitened circumstances. Consequently, their poverty dictated that some community members would have to seek support from outside. The case of St-Aubin is particularly interesting as it implies a degree of mendicancy on the part of the

[42]   Bonnin, p. 338 and *Register*, p. 384.

[43]   Bonnin, p. 44 and *Register*, p. 50.

[44]   Johnson, 'Cloistering of Medieval Nuns', p. 29; Williams, *Cistercians in the Early Middle Ages*, p. 404 and *Statuta*, vol. 1, 1220, no. 4, p. 517.

[45]   This is the final charter in a pancarte, Évreux, AD H 1363 liasse for La Selle: 'Mittimus dilectam sanctimonialem nostram et priorissam Sancti Salvatoris Ebroicensis ad recipiendum possessionem nostram decimeram nostrarum de Boterell' de quibus agebatur inter nos coram officialem Ebroicensis'. I am grateful to John Walmsley for allowing me to use his transcription. For nuns' business activities see also Venarde, 'Praesidentes negotiis: Abbesses as Managers in Twelfth-Century France', pp. 189–205.

[46]   Heloise raises the problem of nuns engaging in manual work in a letter to Abelard; *Petrus Abelardus epistolae*, PL 178, col. 215 and *The Letters of Abelard and Heloise*, trans. B. Radice (Harmondsworth, 1974), pp. 161–2. For nuns' inability to be self-sufficient see Gilchrist, *Gender and Material Culture*, p. 90; J. A. McNamara, *Sisters in Arms: Catholic Nuns through Two Millenia* (Cambridge, MA and London, 1996), p. 260 and S. Thompson, *Women Religious: the Founding of English Nunneries after the Norman Conquest* (Oxford, 1991), pp. 12–13.

[47]   Bonnin, pp. 468, 471 and *Register*, pp. 532, 537. France in this case may mean the Île-De-France, or merely beyond the borders of Normandy.

nuns, deemed unacceptable by the Church. Indeed, the female branch of the Franciscan order, later known as the Poor Clares, was refused papal permission to adopt a rule adhering to the ideal of apostolic poverty as propounded by St Francis.[48]

It is noticeable that both the secular and ecclesiastical authorities made greater use of monks than nuns outside monasteries. The administrative and diplomatic abilities of some monks brought them to the attention of both their secular and spiritual superiors. Benedictine and Cistercian monks took vows of stability to a specific house at their profession and so their employment in the courts of kings and popes highlights the problems enclosure posed in the administration of the realm and papal curia. Highly educated monks, valued for their skills or wise counsel, were faced with having to leave their cloisters, perhaps unwillingly, and enter into the service of the pope their king. The two most notable figures in the Anglo-Norman world to have to deal with this dilemma encountered by monks who became bishops were Lanfranc, former prior of Bec and abbot of St-Etienne in Caen, and Anselm, abbot of Bec, who both became archbishops of Canterbury after the Norman Conquest. For both this meant leaving the quietude of their respective cloisters and entering the turbulent world of secular politics at a time when lay powers and Church were in often direct conflict. Lanfranc, whose administrative skills in building up the patrimony of Bec we have already noted, became one of the first counsellors to Duke William during the 1050s.[49] He had already had to leave his cloister to journey to Rome to plead William's case before Pope Nicholas II (1058–61) in relation to his possibly consanguineous marriage to Matilda of Flanders.[50] Anselm was also active in the duchy prior to his elevation to the see of Canterbury. In common with other abbots, he attended the ducal court to witness charters as well as synods. During his abbacy, Anselm had to defend Bec's privileges against Robert Curthose, by now duke, and Robert, count of Meulan, who was keen to exercise some degree of seigneurial control over the abbey.[51] Such activities could not be conducted wholly from within the cloister, and Lanfranc and Anselm both found that the positions of authority within a monastic community brought their talents to the attention of lay powers, drawing them out of the monastic world and into the world of politics.

Later dukes of Normandy and kings of England seem to have favoured the Cistericans as spiritual advisers and diplomats. When Henry II entered into negotiations to gain absolution for his perceived part in the murder of Thomas Becket, the by now Cistercian abbey of Savigny, home of his spiritual adviser Haimo, was chosen as the venue for discussion. Savigny was also an acceptable choice for the Cistercian party, as there was a strong pro-Becket faction

---

48   McNamara, *Sisters in Arms*, p. 311.
49   See chapter one.
50   Vaughn, *Abbey of Bec*, pp. 18–19
51   Vaughn, *Abbey of Bec*, p. 34 and S. N. Vaughn, *Anselm of Bec and Robert of Meulan: the Innocence of the Dove and the Wisdom of the Serpent* (Berkeley, 1987) for Anslem's relationship with Robert more generally.

within the order.[52] Although the Cistercians sought a greater withdrawal from the world, the able monks and abbots of the order found themselves called away from their cloister by popes who named them as members of commissions and required them to act in a judicial manner. Cisterican abbots headed preaching tours in the Langue d'oc as part of the campaign to extirpate heresy in the region.[53] These activites could prove burdensome to monastic communities. For example, Fountains in Yorkshire reported to Pope Lucius III (1181–85) that secular, or at least non-conventual, tasks burdened the monastery with expenses and earned it the emnity of powerful men.[54] For Norman Cistercians, service to lay rulers could lead to significant diplomatic problems and earn a community the emnity of not just the king of England, who, of course, was duke of Normandy until 1204, but also the king of France. The general chapter of 1197 had cause to censure two monks, Gilbert of Bonport and Robert of Perseigne, in the diocese of Mans, for becoming involved in the struggles between Philip Augustus and Richard I. It is not clear from the resulting statute what the monks had been doing, but it had clearly caused some kind of scandal since the punishment handed down by the chapter was severe. Both monks were expelled and instructed to stay clear of both kingdoms. In addition, they were to receive the discipline in chapter, incur the loss of their rank in the community, and were forbidden to celebrate mass. Their abbots were penanced by having to fast on bread and water for six days and through suspension of their abbatial functions for forty days. Should a similar flouting of the Cistercian customs occur again, the monks were to be expelled from the order.[55] Previously, the abbot of Mortemer, along with the abbot of Perseigne, had found himself in deep trouble at the general chapter of 1190 for attending King Richard I's coronation. It was only a plea by Richard himself that prevented the abbots from being punished.[56]

The involvement of a monk of Bonport in what were possibly negotiations on behalf of the English king is interesting in the light of the circumstances of the foundation of the abbey. At the time of its foundation by Richard in 1190, Bonport was the only abbey south of Rouen on the Seine, and as such Johnson has speculated that its location can be read as an initial attempt to fortify the region against Philip Augustus's efforts to reclaim Normandy.[57] Regardless of the affiliation of the house at the outset – there is speculation as to whether it was Benedictine or Cistercian – Johnson's suggestion that the abbey might serve as an intelligence post at a time when Richard did not have the resources to build a castle, as he later did at Château-Gaillard, seems

52   F.R. Swietek, 'King Henry II and Savigny', Cîteaux, 38 (1987), pp.14–15. In 1164 Becket had fled to Pontigny and had used Cistercian monks as messengers.
53   See B.M. Kienzle, Cistercians, Heresy and Crusade in Occitania, 1145–1229: Preaching in the Lord's Vineyard (Woodbridge, 2001).
54   Williams, Cistercians in the Early Middle Ages, p.73.
55   Twelfth-Century Statutes, 1197 no. 46, pp. 396–7.
56   Appendix A, no. 56; Twelfth-Century Statutes, 1190 no. 39, p. 205.
57   P. Johnson, 'Pious Legends and Historical Realities: the Foundations of La Trinité de Vendome, Bonport and Holyrood', Revue Bénédictine, 151 (1981), p.190.

plausible.[58] For monks of ability, regardless of their order, there was often a conflict between the needs of their vocation and spiritual life on the one hand and the demands of their king and pope on the other.

For the sick and religious who inhabited leper houses and hospitals, enclosure and the boundaries and thresholds it involved served a different purpose in some respects. These communities housed a wider variety of people, both lay and religious, than monasteries.[59] In some instances we know how these communities were structured. At Bolbec and Mont-aux-Malades (Rouen) the communities were split into four groups: priests, clerks and lay brothers, all of whom were presumably members of staff; male lepers; female lepers; and female staff consisting of healthy women and other servants.[60] It is possible that other mixed houses (such as Bellencombre, Gournay and Orbec) followed a similar structure.[61] At Salle-aux-Puelles, the house consisted of a variable number of leprous sisters under the authority of a prioress, and male staff under the authority of a prior to provide for their spiritual needs; it does not seem to have had a core of healthy sisters acting as cooks and nurses.[62] The structure at the hôtels-Dieu was similar, though only the staff took vows as the sick were not permanent members of the community. The hospital at Caen was staffed by five canons, three of whom maintained permanent residence with two looking after churches belonging to the hospital, and ten weak and aged sisters.[63] The hôtel-Dieu at Pontoise was staffed by a core of Augustinian sisters under a prioress and its liturgical needs were met by a prior and four brothers.[64] The community at Vernon was similarly structured and the hospitals at both Vernon and Pontoise had provisions for maidservants as necessary.[65] As we have noted, the Third Lateran Council in 1179 sought to place limits on the number of healthy staff. This was in part to limit contagion, but, more importantly, to reduce the opportunity of alms designated for the benefit of the sick poor being appropriated by the healthy. People who wished to be maintained at the expense of the hospital but without taking on religious obligations were to be excluded.[66]

Just as abbot and bishop visitors sought to limit the numbers of postulants seeking entry to monastic houses, there was no automatic guarantee of a place in a hospital or leper house for those in need. There are various reasons for this.[67] Social status determined access or exclusion, as is suggested by the statutes for Salle-aux-Puelles which reveal that the leftover food was to be

58   Johnson, 'Pious Legends', p. 191.
59   Touati, 'Les groupes de laics'.
60   Appendix C, no. 5 for Bolbec; Arnoux, p. 123 and Bonnin, pp. 203, 513 and *Register*, pp. 222, 585.
61   Appendix C, nos 3, 13, 19; Bonnin, pp. 230, 496, 499 and *Register*, pp. 253, 564, 569.
62   Bonnin, pp. 100–2 and *Register*, pp. 115–17.
63   Bonnin, p. 575 and *Register*, p. 662.
64   Appendix C, no. 21; Bonnin, p. 478 and *Register*, p. 545.
65   Appendix C, no. 28 for Vernon; *Statuts*, p. 162.
66   The council of Rouen (1214), Mansi, vol. 22, col. 913 and *Statuts*, pp. xii–xiii.
67   See also Rawcliffe, *Leprosy in Medieval England*, pp. 291–301 for the difficulties of finding a place in English leper houses.

carefully gathered up for the 'poor lepers outside'.[68] Salle-aux-Puelles had been founded for leprous noble women, consequently non-aristocratic women were unable to enter. The 'poor lepers outside' included non-noble women and men. It is interesting to note, however, that despite the presence of another house in Rouen, Mont-aux-Malades, that catered for lepers from the twenty-one parishes of Rouen, some lepers were still reduced to mendicancy. It appears that even in Normandy's capital there was insufficient provision for all those in need across the social spectrum. It is possible that leper houses demanded a fee for entry not unlike the dowries required for novice nuns and that the conciliar legislation concerning the acceptance of wealthy individuals at the expense of the sick was flouted. Attempts by a previous archbishop, Pierre de Collemezzo (1236–44), to reform Mont-aux-Malades, however, specifically forbade the canons to demand anything for the reception of lepers.[69] Alternatively, some establishments limited their intake to a specific catchment area, for example, the neighbouring parishes. This was certainly the case at St-Gilles-de-Pont-Audemer, which only accepted lepers from the parishes of St-Germain, St-Aignan, St-Ouen and Notre-Dame-du-Pré.[70] Beyond this we cannot say who was permitted entry and who was excluded, but it seems highly likely that it was easier for the well-off to gain access than for the poor. Charity towards lepers was not boundless. In addition to the segregation between men and women, healthy and sick, distinctions were also made between those lepers who had places within hospitals and those who were outside the reach of institutional charity. At Lisieux, lepers from outside the community were not allowed to come into the hospital to eat and drink and those inside were forbidden to receive hospitality from lepers outside a five-mile radius 'in quindena'.[71] The references to lepers outside the hospital of Lisieux again suggests that provision for leprous individuals was made strictly on a local basis, or it may be that some chose not to join communities and instead suffered a life of mendicancy. Mendicant lepers were, however, perceived as a great threat, as the Rouen and Coutances legislation makes plain. The attitude of these church councils contrasts with the compassion shown by some people, such as Gautier Maloiseau, who saw mendicant lepers as objects of pity rather than of fear. In 1188, Gautier brought the leper house at Bolbec, described as small and poor, under more formal regulation, as the lepers had been wandering from door to door in streets, squares and villages.

---

68   Bonnin, p. 101 and *Register*, pp. 115–17 and Bériac, *Histoire des lépreux au moyen âge*, pp. 257–8.

69   P. Langlois, *Histoire du prieuré du Mont-aux-Malades-lès-Rouen et correspondance du prieur de ce monastère avec saint Thomas de Cantorbéry 1120–1820* (Rouen, 1851), p. 330. For details on Archbishop Pierre see V. Tabbagh, *Diocèse de Rouen*, Fasti Ecclesiae Gallicanae 2 (Turnhout, 1998) pp. 84–5.

70   Appendix C, no. 20; Mesmin, 'The Leper House of Saint-Gilles de Pont-Audemer', vol. 1, p. 94.

71   *Status*, p. 205. The meaning of 'in quindena' is not clear. It could mean once every fifteen days (Lewis and Short, *A Latin Dictionary*, p. 1513) or a barrier or five mile radius (J.-F. Niemeyer, *Mediae latinitatis lexicon minus*, p. 880). I think the five-mile radius is the most likely definition, possibly referring to the catchment area of the leper house like that of St-Gilles-de-Pont-Audemer, above.

Gautier provided them with the necessities of life so they no longer had to beg.[72]

Hospitals admitted a wider variety of people, usually on a temporary basis: at Pontoise and Vernon the sick were allowed seven days' grace after recovery before they had to leave.[73] Both Vernon and Pontoise admitted pregnant women. Women in labour were allowed to come to the hospital for their confinement and could remain for up to three weeks after giving birth. After the infant had been baptised and the woman purified (that is to say churched), she was to leave the hospital.[74] Provision was made for the care of the child at the hospital in the absence of a father should its mother die in childbirth.[75] The women who sought aid in the hospitals were probably from a poor background or unmarried so could not count on any other support in their confinement either from their families or private physicians. These women are not censured in any way and the statutes do not moralise regarding their situation.[76] In addition to the sick, poor and pregnant women, the hôtel-Dieu at Vernon operated a guest house, presumably for travellers and pilgrims.[77] The hôtel-Dieu at Montivilliers also catered for a wide range of people including the poor, sick and travellers.[78]

With such a wide variety of people resident within their walls, the rules regarding the use of space within hospitals and leper houses not only regulated the relationship between the sick, religious and laity outside, but also created separate spheres of enclosures within the communities. Boundaries and thresholds were created to segregate men from women and, at the same time, the sick from the healthy. Mixed hospitals existed to a great extent in Normandy and where we know the make-up of a house it was invariably mixed, with only a few exceptions. Salle-aux-Puelles was a house devoted to the care of female lepers while the leprosaries of Évreux and Chaumont admitted men.[79] The lack of ground plans makes it difficult to establish the architectural separation of these groups. Written evidence and comparative archaeological material from England exists to illustrate how the manipulation of space operated to maintain segregation. Eadmer, St Anselm's biographer writing in the twelfth century, tells us that at the hospital of St John at Canterbury, Archbishop Lanfranc divided the building into two, 'putting men suffering from various

---

[72]   'Chronique de fondation de l'Île-Dieu', ed. M. Arnoux, Des clercs au service de la réforme, pp. 300–1.
[73]   Statuts, pp. 138, 161.
[74]   For the churching of women in the Middle Ages see, B. R. Lee, 'The Purification of Women after Childbirth: a Window into Medieval Perceptions of Women', Florilegium, 14 (1995–96), pp. 43–55. See also Touati, 'Les groupes de laïcs', p. 150.
[75]   This was also the case at St Bartholomew, Smithfield and St Mary, Bishopsgate, both in London: C. Rawcliffe, 'Women, Childbirth and Religion in Later Medieval England', Women and Religion in Medieval England, ed. D. Wood (Oxford, 2003), p. 96.
[76]   Statuts, pp. 139 and 162.
[77]   Statuts, p. 161.
[78]   Appendix C, no. 17; C. Duprey, J. Guez and L. Lefebvre, 'Histoire de l'hôpital de Montivilliers de la fondation de l'hôtel-Dieu (1241) au transfert de l'hospice (1924)', Montivilliers hier, aujourd'hui et demain, 4 (1991), p. 37.
[79]   Appendix C, nos 9, 10.

kinds of infirmity in one part and women who were ailing in the other'. He also provided clothing and food from his own funds and, more important, 'attendants and guardians to take particular care to see … that there should be no opportunity for the men to enter the women's quarters or the women the men's'.[80] At the hospital, there was also a chapel that men and women were able to enter from their separate quarters and maintain segregation in worship. Excavation of the hospital site has confirmed the divisions clearly described by Eadmer.[81] Similarly at Lanfranc's leper house, 'wooden houses' were assigned to the lepers and 'here as elsewhere the men were kept separate from the women'.[82] Lanfranc ideally wished for a strict gender division between sick men and women. It is possible that the 'attendants and guardians' were of the same sex as those they cared for, but evidence from other hospitals that we have looked at suggests that the majority of the nursing work was undertaken by women. The evidence from Canterbury shows the gender-based divisions in the hospital were reinforced by its architecture. Although these descriptions refer to buildings in England, prior to his elevation to the see of Canterbury, Lanfranc had been prior of Bec and abbot of St-Etienne, Caen where he may have founded the leper house of Nombril-Dieu.[83] It is, therefore, possible that he based the arrangements in Canterbury on those already existing in Normandy.

Like the leper house in Canterbury, the later foundation at Mont-aux-Malades began life as a collection of cabins forming a leper village.[84] It is possible that this settlement prompted the foundation of a more formal community, but the lepers maintained their isolated huts. A practical separation from the healthy staff was maintained, with access to the church provided by means of a covered gallery.[85] The community at Bellencombre in northern Normandy may also have had separate houses for the lepers, as Archbishop Eudes Rigaud had cause to mention that the buildings (domos) where the lepers lived were in a poor state of repair, despite a gift from King Louis IX of France for the upkeep of the architectural fabric.[86] Separation was also maintained in those houses that adopted a more communal architectural plan, with lepers confined to one floor of a building, as at Bois Halbout.[87] Here, the community lived together in the same building, with the staff inhabiting the ground floor of the living area and the lepers the first floor. The lodging was

---

[80]   Eadmeri historia novorum, pp. 15–16 and Bosanquet, Eadmer's History of Recent Events, p. 16.

[81]   Gilchrist, Contemplation and Action, p. 21.

[82]   Eadmeri historia novorum, p. 16 and Bosanquet, Eadmer's History of Recent Events, p. 16. Lanfranc originally intended the hospital to cater for thirty male lepers and thirty female lepers though this soon grew to over a hundred. See E. J. Kealey, Medieval Medicus: a Social History of Anglo-Norman Medicine, (Baltimore and London, 1981), p. 86.

[83]   See appendix C, no. 7.

[84]   Langlois, Histoire du prieuré du Mont-aux-Malades, p. 6.

[85]   Langlois, Histoire du prieuré du Mont-aux-Malades, p. 328.

[86]   Bonnin, p. 496 and Register, p. 564. See also appendix C, no. 3.

[87]   Appendix C, no. 4.

joined to the chapel. The refectory and kitchens were located opposite the chapel with a herb garden and granges behind them.[88]

Architectural segregation was reinforced by written statutes. Segregation of the sexes at the leper house in Lisieux was apparent in regulations designed to prevent accidental contact between men and women. Women were not allowed to spin in the porch nor under the vines or to dry linen clothes.[89] The porch and vineyard were open spaces where risk of contact was increased not only between the sexes but also between the leprous and non-leprous. If the laundry was dried flat, not only would it take up a great deal of space, but the women would have to move into an open space and occasion an unacceptable mingling of different groups of people. Hospitals and leper houses were also religious spaces and as such segregation had to be maintained between those inside the community and the laity, just like in monasteries. At Salle-aux-Puelles, a leper community run along monastic lines, Archbishop Eudes expressed concern that lay people entered the kitchens, cloister and workrooms, mingling freely with the sisters and talking without permission.[90] Not only did this mean that healthy interlopers were coming into contact with leprous sisters, but also that they disturbed the good running of the house and distracted the attention of the sisters away from monastic routine and thus the worship of God. In addition, the sisters were exhorted to keep the monastic silence in order to maintain the sacred nature of the space.[91] A later visit records that the sisters could not be compelled to rise for Matins and that they only attended this service when they wished.[92]

Spatial segregation was not uniform across leper houses and hospitals in Normandy. Despite the desire of various authorities to segregate according to gender and to maintain these institutions as quasi-monastic houses, provision was made in some institutions for marriage. Although there was a pronounced desire to segregate lepers on the grounds of sex, item six of the statutes for Lisieux decreed that lepers were not to marry healthy people but only other lepers.[93] The fact that one of the statutes specifically deals with the penalties for adultery suggests that marriage between lepers was common enough to warrant strictures against unlawful sexual relationships.[94] These statutes, in contrast to the experience of women at Salle-aux-Puelles who followed a monastic routine, show that not all lepers were held to a religious vocation. The sanctioning of marriage between lepers was a more pragmatic way of controlling their sexuality than enforced celibacy. We do not know whether the leprous spouses would have been allowed to cohabit, given the previous restrictions placed on the mixing of the sexes, but there was no bar in canon

---

88   Jeanne, 'Exclusion et charité', vol. 1, p. 96.
89   Statuts, p. 205.
90   Bonnin, p. 34 and Register, pp. 38–9.
91   Bonnin, p. 34 and Register, pp. 38–9.
92   Bonnin, p. 325 and Register, pp. 371–2.
93   Statuts, p. 204. The verb is contrahere. Brody, Disease of the Soul, p. 85, J. Imbert, Les hôpitaux en droit canonique, (Paris, 1947), p. 176 and Jeanne, 'Les lépreux et les léproseries', p. 44 all translate this as 'to marry'.
94   Statuts, p. 204.

law against lepers marrying. Letters from Pope Alexander III (1159–81) to the archbishop of Canterbury and the bishop of Bayeux state that lepers unwilling to live in continence could marry if they could find a willing partner. A leprous spouse could require a healthy partner to engage in sexual intercourse and, according to Alexander, leprosy was not a cause for the dissolution of marriage.[95] These provisions are interesting given the association between leprosy and sexual sin, which was one of the reasons why lepers were objects of revulsion, and the Church's desire generally to keep the healthy and leprous apart wherever possible. It suggests that the sanctity of the marriage vows over-rode any other legislation and underlines the importance of marital debt.[96] At least one pope, Urban III (1185–87), did rule, however, that the contraction of leprosy was grounds for a divorce.[97] There was, therefore, a contradiction between the Church's desire to segregate lepers and the need to maintain the sanctity of marriage. Provisions, like the statutes of Lisieux may also be a tacit recognition that not all those who were categorised as lepers felt the disease to be a vocation or wished to live in community.

Within less specialised establishments like the hôtels-Dieu, different groups of men and women were kept apart. In larger hospitals this included provision for pregnant women. The statutes for the hospital of St-Jacques at Lille in northern France show that expectant mothers had their own chamber.[98] It is likely that this was also the case at Vernon. Including the maternity ward in the main body of the infirmary hall, even if this was divided into men's and women's sections, would not have been sensible for a number of reasons. For women to give birth in the main hall, which often incorporated a chapel or altar where mass was celebrated, would have resulted in the pollution of a sacred space with the wages of sin; literally in the case of blood and metaphorically as the pain of childbirth was Eve's legacy from the Fall.[99] The disturbance caused by mothers in labour and babies crying would not have provided the restful environment needed by the rest of the sick. Indeed, it was for this reason that the hôtel-Dieu in Troyes would not receive pregnant

95   *Corpus iuris canonici*, ed. Friedberg, vol. 2, cols 690–1. Brody, *Disease of the Soul*, pp. 84–5 misquotes these sources as a canon of Lateran III and a letter from Pope Gregory IX to Alexander III, archbishop of Canterbury. For an example of a leprous marriage see the case of Marguerite of Flanders who married Raoul II of Vermandois who was a leper: L. Duval-Arnould 'Les dernières années de comte lépreux Raoul de Vermandois', *Bibliothèque de l'École des Chartes*, 142 (1984), pp. 81–2 and L. Napran, 'Marriage Contracts in Northern France and the Southern Low Countries in the Twelfth Century' (Ph.D. thesis, University of Cambridge, 2001), p. 90. Once married persons had consummated their union, Alexander was prepared to force them to continue sexual relations as long as either party desired them: Brundage, *Law, Sex and Christian Society*, p. 335.

96   The Church ruled that husband or wife had a duty to engage in sex if either partner demanded it. See C. N. L. Brooke, *The Medieval Idea of Marriage* (Oxford, 1989), pp. 132–4, 277–80 and Brundage, *Law, Sex and Christian Society*, pp. 241–2, 281–4, 358–60.

97   *Corpus iuris canonici*, ed. Friedberg, vol. 2, col. 691 and Brundage, *Law, Sex and Christian Society*, p. 269.

98   Imbert, *Les hôpitaux en droit canonique*, p. 125.

99   Rawcliffe, 'Women, Childbirth and Religion', p. 96.

women until they were assigned their own quarters.[100] We do not know how far medieval medical practice recognised the danger posed to newborn babies and their mothers from the spread of disease, but the risk of infection to them in a general infirmary would be another strong reason for separate provision. It therefore seems likely that separate labour wards in hospitals were the norm, if not on the scale of the lying-in room of the hôtel-Dieu in Paris, which could take twenty-four women.[101]

As well as spatial boundaries, limits were also placed on the types of work people within the hospital community did. Although it seems that the majority, if not all, of nursing care, including the care of men, was provided by sisters in religious vows, they were prevented from caring for different groups within hospitals, for example those seeking hospitality, like travellers and pilgrims. Contact between the sisters and male guests was prohibited at Vernon and Pontoise. Article twelve of the Vernon statutes states that the sisters of the house must not eat with or tend to male guests and that the male staff should likewise avoid the female staff.[102] Equally, women were not to minister to the needs of the male staff.[103] It is likely that the maidservants were deputed to care for those seeking hospitality and carry out household tasks such as the cooking and laundry for the male staff. The segregation of the sexes is much more explicit in the statutes for Pontoise. Unlike at Vernon where it seems that the refectory was used by all hospital staff, whether male or female, at Pontoise, the sisters had their own refectory, dormitory and infirmary and these areas were duplicated for the clerical and lay brothers.[104]

There was a profound need to separate the healthy and sick which was most marked in leper houses. Unlike hospitals where those who were fit enough could eat in the common refectory, lepers were prevented from having anything to do with food or goods that might come into contact with healthy members of staff or the population at large. A wall was to be constructed between the sick and the healthy at Grand-Beaulieu at Chartres, a leper house that provided the model for St-Gilles-de-Pont-Audemer in terms of its organisation. No leper was to live in the granges, in order to protect the health of the brothers and by extension the sisters who also lived there.[105] Contagion was further limited by prohibitions on washing the clothes of the sick with those of the healthy and on lepers preparing communal food.[106] The population at large was protected by statutes that prevented the free movement of lepers outside their houses. The leper house at Lisieux was situated in the parish of St-Désir, just outside the city walls near the river Touques. This river provided the first barrier beyond which lepers could not pass without the permission of

100   *Statuts*, p. 115 and Rawcliffe, 'Women, Childbirth and Religion' p. 113, note 30.
101   Rawcliffe, 'Women, Childbirth and Religion', p. 96.
102   *Statuts*, p. 161.
103   *Statuts*, p. 161.
104   *Statuts*, p. 136.
105   Cited in Avril, 'Le III concile de Latran et les lépreux', *Revue Mabillon*, 60 (1981), p. 50.
106   *Statuts*, p. 217 Avril, 'Le III concile de Latran et les lépreux', p. 51 and Bériac, *Histoire des lépreux au moyen âge*, p. 189.

their superior, according to the statutes dated 1256.[107] They were not to eat in the town nor drink in the taverns without the consent of the priest, nor go out after curfew unless absolutely necessary.[108] If they were granted permission to leave their house, they had to be properly attired in a closed cape or other reasonable clothes.[109] Regulations like this find echoes in conciliar legislation. Archbishop Maurice of Rouen (1231–35) in c.1231 forbade lepers to enter the city (castella).[110] If they contravened this decree and were molested then no pity was be taken on them.[111] The bishop of Coutances, in c.1300, likewise forbade lepers from entering populated places like markets, under pain of confiscation of their goods.[112] There were mitigating circumstances, however, in which lepers could gain leave of absence from their houses. One of the statutes for Lisieux reveals that lepers were able to spend the night at the houses of relatives who were dying.[113] This provision is indicative of an attitude of compassion towards those afflicted with leprosy and a recognition that separation did not necessarily entail a severence of all family ties. This compassion occasionally surfaces in the sources despite the emphasis in some material on segregation, as we saw above in the case of Gautier Maloiseau's reform of Bolbec. Interestingly, in all this evidence from Normandy for segregation between the lepers and non-lepers, no distinction is made on grounds of gender: the primary division is between the sick and the healthy.

Establishing a clear spatial domain regulated by written statutes and reinforced by architectural divisions was essential for the maintenance of the religious life. Striking similarities exist between professed religions and the men and women in hospitals and leper houses. Claustration was not uniform across all orders and houses, though some of those in vows, notably Augustinian canons who worked in parishes, and sisters who had a practical vocation caring for the sick, had a greater degree of movement. Contemplative nuns had less reason to travel outside their communities, at least in theory, than Benedictine monks who might travel outside their monastery due to the number of dependent priories under the care of the mother house. For the communities in hospitals and leper houses, the need to regulate contact between different groups of people within the houses defined the use of space. For monks, nuns, hospital staff and some lepers, pursuit of a vocation meant living in a religious community. Enclosure rules were therefore necessary to protect the sacred nature of the space and the lives of those within it.

---

[107] Statuts, p. 203.
[108] Statuts, pp. 204–5. See Rawcliffe, Leprosy in Medieval England, pp. 316–22.
[109] Statuts, p. 203. See also the diocesan statutes from Coutances c.1300: Mansi, vol. 25, col. 30.
[110] Tabbagh, Diocèse de Rouen, pp. 82–3.
[111] Mansi, vol. 23, col. 399 and Bériac, Histoire des lépreux au moyen âge, pp. 185–6.
[112] Mansi, vol. 25, col. 30 and Bériac, Histoire des lépreux au moyen âge, pp. 185–6.
[113] Statuts, p. 205. Presumably if one was dying the risk of catching leprosy from a diseased relative was irrelevant. See also Bériac, Histoire des lépreux au moyen âge, p. 185.

The use of community buildings

The correct use of space within the cloister was just as important as principles and rules relevant to the practice of enclosure and essential in maintaining a sacred space. Abbot Stephen of Lexington recognised the importance of spatial practice on his first visit to Mortain when he recorded that the nuns 'being of one mind under the inspiration of divine grace ... live in common according to the norms of the Cistercian order in all things, observing the exercises which are customary in the church, in the cloister, refectory, dormitory and in every other place'.[114] The monastic visitation records reveal that many houses in Normandy were in a state of disrepair. Archbishop Eudes recorded that the buildings at Bourg-Achard were badly roofed and uninhabitable in many places; the buildings of the Cluniac house of Mortemer-sur-Eaulne were 'somewhat decayed'; and all the buildings needed re-roofing at Ste-Gauberge and Tillières.[115] Eudes was not merely concerned with the ruinous fabric, but also the effect this would have on community life. Abbot Stephen also recognised the problem during a visit to Villers-Canivet in 1232, when he instructed that 'no building will be constructed inside or outside the nuns' cloister unless it is covered with a good roofing which prevents fire damage'.[116] Fire and other calamities could result in the dispersal of a community. No monks were at St-Hilare when Eudes visited in 1263 as the priory had been destroyed in a fire.[117] Stephen was anxious that this should not happen to any of the houses of female religious in his care and so he instructed that the community at Villers-Canivet should not be dissolved without his permission, even if the house had been destroyed.[118] At the other end of the scale, extravagance could cause equally severe problems. The number of monks at Envermeu had been reduced because their new prior had undertaken grandiose building projects that clearly reduced the income of the priory.[119]

The successful practice of the religious life depended on the ability to perform certain rituals in certain spaces. The nuns of Villers-Canivet petitioned Bishop Thomas de Fréauville (1232–38), asking that they be allowed to seek alms in his diocese for the rebuilding of their church. The previous edifice was dark and confined as well as threatening to collapse, presumably preventing them from observing the monastic offices fully.[120] The parishioners at Auffay, a priory dependent on St-Évroul, could not stand in the nave to hear services because the church was in such a bad state of repair

114 *Registrum epistolarum*, p. 234.
115 Appendix A, nos 18, 57, 76, 96; Bonnin, p. 514, 339, 307, 626 and *Register*, p. 581, 385, 345, 720.
116 *Registrum epistolarum*, p. 242.
117 Appendix A, no. 78; Bonnin, p. 459 and *Register*, p. 523. See also chapter four for the case of Almenèches.
118 *Registrum epistolarum*, p. 243.
119 Appendix A, no. 30; Bonnin, p. 543 and *Register*, p. 621.
120 *Registrum epistolarum*, p. 250.

it was exposed to the weather.[121] At St-Aubin the nuns' health had suffered because the buildings were so dilapidated: the 'houses badly needed repair, especially the roof of the main monastery where they could hardly stay when the weather was rainy'.[122] As a result the nuns 'did not chant their hours properly, especially Matins, because they had been ill for a long time', and the prioress was so ill, she was bedridden.[123] Other problems included doves flying through the chancel and choir during divine office at Bondeville and gusts of wind howling through the nave at Noyon-sur-Andelle; at both houses Eudes ordered the windows, which were clearly not glazed in anyway, to be blocked up.[124] Hospitals were also not immune from poorly maintained buildings: at Neufchâtel-en-Bray, the infirmary was on the verge of collapse.[125] These examples are at the extreme end of those problems relating to architectural fabric discovered by Eudes and Stephen, but they do reflect the importance of the integrity of the fabric of the monastery buildings to a successful and well-run community. The monastic life was a communal one and so it was absolutely vital that the community had adequate buildings in which to live and work.

The lack of necessary spaces led to the inappropriate use of other rooms within the monastery, further diminishing the quality of the monastic life. This leads us to a discussion of some of the main communal areas – the dormitory, infirmary and refectory – in which we will see that the incorrect use of space is often linked to a failure by the community to live in common.

The dormitory was often the largest conventual space in a monastic community, outranked in size only by the church.[126] It has also been the subject of differing interpretations. This space underlines the fact that a monastery was not just a place of prayer but also a home to the religious who made up the community. The dormitory was generally situated on the upper floor of the east range of the cloister. Gilchrist has argued from the late medieval English evidence that this location linked female monastic architecture with the practices of seigneurial architecture, in which living apartments were located on upper floors. The dormitory may also have offered a degree of protection in times of trouble.[127] She goes beyond this practical consideration by using techniques of spatial analysis which reveal the number of steps a person must take before reaching certain locations within a given complex of buildings, to show that nuns' dormitories were located in the deepest space of the monastery in contrast to male houses where the chapter house was

[121] Appendix A, no. 3; Bonnin, p. 508 and *Register*, p. 579.
[122] Bonnin, p. 500 and *Register*, p. 569.
[123] Bonnin, p. 500 and *Register*, p. 569.
[124] Bonnin, pp. 426, 512 and *Register*, pp. 486, 584.
[125] Appendix C, no. 18; Bonnin, p. 407 and *Register*, p. 462.
[126] V. Jansen, 'Architecture and Community in Medieval Monastic Dormitories', *Studies in Cistercian Art and Architecture vol. 5*, ed. M. P. Lillich, Cistercian Studies 167 (Kalamazoo, 1998), p. 59.
[127] Jansen, 'Architecture and Community', p. 64.

similarly situated.[128] She argues that the dormitories' position reinforced strict enclosure for women religious, but this does not account for the similarity in location for monks' sleeping quarters.[129]

The rule of St Benedict is clear that monks were to all sleep in one place if at all possible, but if the community was too large, in smaller groups of ten or twenty. To ensure good order, the senior monks were to be interspersed with the juniors. By sleeping in a communal dormitory, when the call to prayer came the brethren were in a position to encourage one another out of sleepiness, to ready themselves for duties in the church.[130] The dormitory was therefore a space in which accountability to the community was reinforced: by living publicly there was nowhere to hide. The same is true for dormitories in hospitals that followed versions of the Augustinian rule. At Vernon, the sisters were all to go to bed at the same hour in the dormitory, apart from the two sisters appointed to keep watch over the sick during the night and others who might be absent for reasons of necessity.[131] Although the rules explain the purpose of a communal dormitory, it does not explain its location. It is true that easier access to the church for the night offices was gained by locating sleeping quarters in the east range in proximity to the choir of the church. A consideration of evidence from letter collections suggests an additional reason. The nun had a special place within medieval religion as the bride of Christ. Bishop Arnulf of Lisieux in his letter dated to circa 1150, to the nun G., following the death of her fiancé, makes this plain: 'therefore the betrothal was not stolen from you but altered. Now you are joined with a bond not to a man but to a holy God, whose desirable embrace warms you and draws you closer, so that "His left hand may rest on your head and His right hand may embrace you"'.[132] Other letter writers made the connection between nun and bride of Christ more explicit. Anselm, in one of his letters to Gunhilda, exhorts her to return to the monastic life and Christ her 'spouse, who promises the kingdom of heaven as dowry' so that 'even though he [Christ] has been spurned by you, recalls you who spurn him in order to lead you to his royal bedchamber'.[133] Chastity was of course equally important for monks, and so it is possible to speculate that the dormitory was thus situated in one of the most secluded places to emphasise a monk or nun's relationship with God. For women, this was articulated in terms of marriage; for men it symbolised their renunciation of secular ideas of masculine behaviour like the creations of wealth and a family.

---

[128] Gilchrist, *Gender and Material Culture*, p. 166. This technique of access analysis was formulated by B. Hillier and J. Hanson, in *The Social Logic of Space* (Cambridge, 1984). See also J. Grenville, *Medieval Housing*, The Archaeology of Medieval Britain (London, 1997), pp. 17–20 for a critique of the method.

[129] Gilchrist, *Gender and Material Culture*, p. 166.

[130] *Rule*, ch. 22, p. 154.

[131] *Statuts*, pp. 162–4.

[132] Barlow, no. 5, p. 8 and Schriber, pp. 28–9. Biblical quotation, Song of Songs 2:6. See also Bos, 'Gender and Religious Guidance', pp. 59, 147–8.

[133] Schmitt, vol. 4, no. 168 p. 44, 46 and Fröhlich, vol. 2, no. 168, pp. 67, 69.

As ever, practice on the ground conflicted with the ideals upheld by rules and visitors. Both Archbishop Eudes and Abbot Stephen discovered irregular practices relating to the dormitory. The nuns at Villarceaux and Almenèches had their own rooms, in the latter case with locks; the Augustinian canons at St-Lô in Rouen also had private rooms.[134] The dormitory at Briouze was too small for the community, but there seems to have been no such excuse at St-Martin-d'Es, where Eudes instructed the monks to sleep in the same room 'as becoming and properly as they should'.[135] The importance of communality was underlined by the archbishop's visit to St-Pierre-des-Préaux, where he discovered a monk sleeping alone in the cellar. There was obviously a good reason for this behaviour as Eudes instructed the abbot either to send him a companion or recall him to the dormitory as it was 'unbecoming for a monk to sleep alone'.[136] These examples raise interesting questions as to the modification of space by communities. We do not know the exact layout of the private rooms discovered by Eudes; it is possible they were located in a purpose-built area but it seems more likely that the religious divided up the common dormitory into a series of separate cubicles. This was clearly the arrangement forbidden by Stephen at Villers-Canivet where he ordered the nuns 'under pain of grave fault of disobedience' not to divide their dormitory up by means of hangings round the bed.[137] Separate cubicles may also have existed at Fontaine-Guérard as indicated by a series of changes in tile pattern on the floor. The dormitory was divided by a central aisle. Down either side, cells were situated as signified by a change from square tiles laid straight, to a diamond pattern. These examples are indicative of two things: a desire for a degree of privacy amongst the religious and the tensions inherent in communal living. Contemplative communities were made up of a group of people who desired to live apart from the world and devote themselves to God, yet they were constantly in the company of others. The division of communal dormitories into cells suggests a need for a private place of prayer and devotion.[138] David Bell has argued that technological advances such as chimneys and fireplaces set into the wall, which allowed smaller rooms to be heated, aided the development of a concept of privacy.[139] The evidence also shows that the ecclesiastical visitors were determined to maintain the common dormitory and with it the openness and accountability that was essential to

---

[134] Appendix A, no. 69 for St-Lô in Rouen; Bonnin, pp. 44, 235, 374, 280 and *Register*, pp. 49, 260, 424, 314.

[135] Appendix A, nos 19, 82; Bonnin, pp. 374, 489 and *Register*, pp. 424, 557.

[136] Bonnin, p. 198 and *Register*, p. 231.

[137] *Registrum epistolarum*, p. 243.

[138] It is possible that this links in with developments in castle architecture in which the separation of the hall and chamber, was also occasioned by the need for more privacy. See L. Hicks, 'Women and the Use of Space in Normandy, c.1050–1300' (Ph.D. thesis, University of Cambridge, 2003), pp. 56–61.

[139] Around the time of the foundation of the Carthusian order at the turn of the eleventh and twelfth centuries, we begin to see an increase in the numbers of anchorites and recluses along with the provision of private rooms in monasteries: D. N. Bell, 'Chambers, Cells and Cubicles: the Cistercian General Chapter and the Development of the Private Room', *Perspectives for an Architecture of Solitude*, ed. Kinder, pp. 188.

monasticism. Archbishop Eudes and Abbot Stephen may have feared that the division of dormitories into individual cells might encourage laziness, illicit sexual relations putting monks and nuns' chastity at risk, and other such unmonastic behaviour.

The rule of St Benedict states that 'a separate cell shall be set aside for ... sick brethren and an infirmarian who is God-fearing, diligent and assiduous'.[140] Lanfranc of Canterbury in his eleventh-century constitutions also instructed that the infirmarian was to have his own cook and a separate kitchen if the plan of the buildings and resources allowed. Brethren were only to go to the infirmary if they were too ill to remain with the community.[141] According to the rule, the infirmary was therefore a place apart and this is reflected in its location. For example, Cistercian infirmaries in England and Wales were not only placed to the east of the cloister but towards the south; therefore they were usually situated near the monastery's water supply.[142] From what we know of the location of infirmaries at Montivilliers and Fontaine-Guérard, the same is true for Normandy. Water was essential in an infirmary for flushing latrines, cleaning and bathing. In addition, locating the infirmary at some distance from the main body of the community was a practical move to separate the sick and the healthy, which, as we have seen, was of paramount importance in the regulation of hospitals and leper houses.[143] In Cistercian houses there might be two or more infirmaries catering for monks, *conversi*, and sometimes a third for the sick poor.[144] Rules governed the correct use of infirmary space as much as any other location within the monastery and the ecclesiastical visitors were anxious to apply them.

The faults found in the use of the infirmary differed in respect not just to communities of monks and communities of nuns, but also between the Benedictine and Cistercian orders. In the houses of Benedictine monks that Eudes Rigaud visited, it seems that irregular practices in the infirmary were largely connected with a failure to provide sufficient care for the sick monks. Eudes noted that at St-Lô the sick were not well cared for and he ordered the removal of the current building, described as 'shabby'.[145] The situation was equally desperate at St-Wandrille as the archbishop recorded that the sick were not properly cared for and that a new building should be constructed as the current one was in 'a wretched state'.[146] Other grumbles included superiors neglecting their duty to visit the sick as at Mont-Deux-Amants, and lack of

140 *Rule*, p. 193. I discussed the use of the infirmary in the context of exile in 'Exclusion as Exile', pp. 155–8.
141 *Monastic Constitutions*, pp. 132–3, 176–7.
142 D. N. Bell. 'The Siting and Size of Cistercian Infirmaries in England and Wales', *Studies in Cistercian Art and Architecture* vol. 5, ed. Lillich, pp. 211–12.
143 Bell, 'Siting and Size of Cistercian Infirmaries', p. 219.
144 Cassidy-Welch, *Monastic Spaces and their Meanings*, p. 137. See also chapter two for the discussion of alms giving and charity.
145 Bonnin, pp. 86–7 and *Register*, p. 99.
146 Bonnin, p. 293 and *Register*, p. 331.

proper food for convalescents at Mont-Ste-Catherine.[147] In contrast to the concern expressed by Eudes regarding monks who neglected the sick, Abbot Stephen's visits to houses of the Savignac congregation and Archbishop Eudes's visits to nunneries reveal very different interpretations of what constituted the proper use of the infirmary by the monks and nuns staying in it.

The main reason for monks or nuns spending time in the infirmary, according to both the Benedictine rule and the Cistercian statutes, was if they were unable to fulfil their roles within the community, whether through illness, during recovery after blood letting, or through old age. There was therefore an emphasis on separation both in terms of the location of the infirmary and the practices conducted within it.[148] Normal regulations, like those regarding diet, did not apply here. It was this fact that led to many of the problems in observance within Norman female houses and Cistercian monasteries. Abbot Stephen was very concerned that removal from the community due to illness should not turn into an excuse to move into a private room. He found it necessary to state that 'no nun was to be assigned a small chamber' at Mortain 'but she should lodge honestly in the infirmary or infirmary chamber when illness requires or manifest weakness will have demanded'.[149] This injunction is echoed in his command at one of the male monasteries in his care that sought to prevent the building of separate cells.[150] In addition to lodging communally, Stephen also emphasised the necessity of taking meals in the proper manner. The nuns at Mortain were not to eat together but singly and next to their own beds, but the prioress could have four companions at her table and the subprioress two.[151] Stephen clearly thought it was impossible to live a full communal life in the infirmary; monks and nuns were there precisely because illness or old age meant that they were prevented from living the full monastic life. Some allowances had to be made therefore, through the mitigation of the full rigour of the monastic rule.

The practices followed in the houses visited by Eudes were slightly different. Here the main problem was the use of the infirmary as a soft option: healthy nuns went to the infirmary for meals as this was the only place in the monastery where meat was served, hence the provision for a separate kitchen in Lanfranc's Constitutions. For example, Eudes recorded that the nuns ate meat freely in the infirmary at St-Amand and that the healthy sometimes ate with the sick, 'two or three with one sick sister'.[152] The sick and those who waited on them ate in scattered groups at Montivilliers rather than the healthy together in one group and the sick in another.[153] Eudes ordered that the nuns who were not confined to bed should all eat at one table at St-Sauveur, whilst

[147] Appendix A, no. 53 for Mont-Deux-Amants; Bonnin, pp. 264, 195 and *Register*, pp. 295, 210.
[148] Cassidy-Welch, *Monastic Spaces and their Meanings*, pp. 134 and 141.
[149] *Registrum epistolarum*, p. 235.
[150] The monastery of Chalocé in the diocese of Anjou: *Registrum epistolarum*, p. 217. See also Williams, *Cistercians in the Early Middle Ages*, p. 250.
[151] *Registrum epistolarum*, p. 239.
[152] Bonnin, pp. 15–16 and *Register*, p. 19.
[153] Bonnin, pp. 518, 564 and *Register*, pp. 591, 647.

at St-Amand he complained that no one read the divine office to the infirmary occupants.[154] For Eudes, illness did not prevent the monastics in his care living as much of a common life as they could manage. Whereas for Stephen the infirmary was a cross between a hospital and an old people's home, presumably visited by the chaplain who would say mass and hear confession, Eudes regarded it as a community in miniature where the rigours of the rule were mitigated but the principle of the common life remained.[155]

The use of the infirmary in this way resulted in neglect of the common table in the refectory. Only at St-Saëns, where there was no refectory, did Eudes tolerate this behaviour.[156] At St-Amand nuns would gather to eat in small groups around each patient in the infirmary, possibly in a show of spiritual support for their sick sister.[157] At Almenèches, Bival, Montivilliers and St-Léger the nuns had their own food and ate in 'friendly groups', whilst at Villarceaux and Montivilliers they ate apart in chambers.[158] The women were able to do this as in some communities, for example, Almenèches, they held private property, including casseroles and copper kettles, and money was allotted to each individual to provide herself with cooked food and victuals. Although monks also neglected the common table, they did so in a different way from nuns. Whereas nuns used their infirmary as an alternative to the refectory in which to eat meat or gather in smaller more sociable groups, monks used different spaces. The monks ate in the prior's chamber at St-Fromond, and at St-Martin-de-Pontoise they even created their own bar in 'Bernard's Room'.[159] In large abbeys, monks used their outside priories as places of refreshment: men resident in the dependent priories of St-Etienne in Caen, St-Pierre-des-Préaux and St-Ouen in Rouen did not fast and regularly ate meat.[160] It seems then, that the priories fulfilled a similar role in male houses to the infirmary in female communities. Both places provided loopholes in the rules as they were areas that could be used as recreational spaces where religious could be sent for refreshment. The idea that priories could act as rest houses for the monks is supported by the presence of hunting dogs at houses dependent on St-Etienne in contravention of Eudes Rigaud's instructions.[161] The nunneries had fewer outside houses and, perhaps with the restrictions on leaving the cloister, it would have been impractical for the nuns to be sent out to them. As a result, they adapted internal spaces within their abbeys for refreshment. The importance of the sharing of a communal meal to religious life is underlined by the provision of refectories in the statutes for hospitals.

---

154 Bonnin, pp. 220, 285 and *Register*, pp. 241, 322.
155 I note here that Adam Davis takes a slightly different line, focusing on the association between sin and disease expressed in canon 22 of Lateran IV: Davis, *Holy Bureaucrat*, pp. 80–1 and *Decrees*, pp. 245–6.
156 Bonnin, p. 170 and *Register*, p. 188.
157 Bonnin, p. 16 and *Register*, p. 19.
158 Bonnin, pp. 235–6, 374, 146, 472, 197, 572 and *Register*, pp. 260, 424, 165, 538, 212, 658.
159 Bonnin, pp. 557, 275 and *Register*, pp. 638, 309.
160 Bonnin, pp. 94, 198 57 and *Register*, pp. 109, 212, 63.
161 Bonnin, p. 262 and *Register*, p. 293.

At Vernon, the refectory was a shared space where not only did the sisters and male clerics eat, but also the sick who were well enough to leave their beds. Aside from the bedridden, sisters and clerics were to eat only in the refectory and not in the hall, cellar, chamber or any other place within the hospital.[162] Hospitals were religious places and so similar standards to those applied to contemplative monastics were to be upheld.

In our discussion of practices relating to the dormitory, infirmary and refectory, we can see clearly that the monks and nuns of many of the monastic communities in Normandy neglected a central tenet of the monastic life: they were not living in common. At times, communal living degenerated to the extent that some groups were almost living in separate households, as at Almenèches.[163] The pursuit of the common life was not aided by a number of superiors who refused to or could not live in common alongside their flocks. At times it was absolutely essential that heads of communities should have their own room. The multiple roles of the superior dictated separate lodgings: superiors were the spiritual leaders, business managers and administrators of their houses, not to mention their duty as host to visiting dignitaries.[164] Although a superior might have a separate room in which to conduct business, he or she was still supposed to sleep in the common dormitory. Several heads of house possessed their own lodgings in Normandy and there is much variation in the location of these rooms. The abbess of the Benedictine community at Montivilliers had her own apartments and chapel in the west range of the cloister.[165] At Cistercian Fontaine-Guérard, the abbess had a separate room situated above the eastern portion of the chapter house and separated from the main dormitory by a low, wide arch.[166] In contrast, the abbot's lodging at Cerisy was the upper floor of the gatehouse.[167] Abbot's lodgings are also known at Foucarmont and Cherbourg.[168]

The physical separation of the superior from the community could have a detrimental affect on the leadership of the monastery and consequently for the rest of the monks or nuns: as the Augustinian rule states, the superior

---

162   *Statuts*, p. 159, 169. See also Pontoise, p. 136.
163   This is a development that has also been observed in both male and female communities in England in the later Middle Ages at, for instance, Godstow and Ramsey. See also Gilchrist, *Gender and Material Culture*, pp. 122- 3 and N. Bradley Warren, *Spiritual Economies: Female Monasticism in Later Medieval England*, The Middle Ages (Philadelphia, 2001), p. 19.
164   Kinder, *Cistercian Europe*, p. 359 and S. Bonde and C. Maines, 'A Room of One's Own: Elite Spaces in Monasteries of the Reform Movement and an Abbot's Parlour at Augustinian St-Jean-des-Vignes, Soissons (France)', *Religion and Belief in Medieval Europe*, ed. G. de Boe and D. Verhaeghe, Papers of the Medieval Europe Brugge 1997 Conference 4 (Zellik, 1997), p. 43.
165   Bonnin, p. 517 and *Register*, p. 591.
166   J. Fournée, 'Deux abbayes cisterciennes de la région de l'Andelle', *Annuaire des Cinq Départments de Normandie*, (1986), p. 88.
167   Bonde and Maines, 'A Room of One's Own', p. 45.
168   *Registrum epistolarum*, p. 214; Bonnin, pp. 89–90 and *Register*, pp. 102–3. The prior of Ste-Barbe-en-Auge (appendix A, no. 73) may also have had his own room: Bonnin, p. 303 and *Register*, p. 344.

was to set an example.[169] The prior of Ouville was described as a drunkard who sometimes 'lies out in the fields' and at Cherbourg, the abbot, also a drunkard, did not ensure that the rule was observed, sleep in the dormitory, rise for Matins, or eat in the refectory, although he was 'physically able to do all these things'.[170] The abbot of St-Ouen was criticised for negligence in attending chapter and rising for Matins.[171] The provision of separate apartments for the abbess of Montivilliers ensured that she rarely mixed with the community or attended crucial communal activities like chapter.[172] The abbess of St-Amand stood accused of eating with her favourites instead of in the refectory with the rest of the community, and the abbess of St-Léger only ate in the refectory at the great feasts of the Church, presumably because the nuns ate different or better food in celebration of the feast.[173] Whatever the reasons for the separation of the superior from the rest of the community, the result was a decline in the standard of monastic practice at some houses.

The superiors of troublesome houses may have felt the need to get away from their communities from time to time; after all, monasteries were made up of human beings and their associated failings, and at times living in such proximity to quarrelsome people could prove too much. Comtesse, the prioress at Bondeville who was largely responsible for turning the community around and raising the level of observance, was criticised by Eudes for standing in the courtyard out of doors after Compline.[174] It seems likely that she wanted, or needed, time to herself. At Mont-Deux-Amants, the prior was accused of leaving the house more often than was necessary, while his counterpart at Le Tréport rode abroad 'altogether too much and with the baldest of excuses'.[175] As at least some of the heads of Norman houses were drawn from the nobility, it may be that their desire for separation was rooted in their previous secular status. In the early history of the ducal foundations, heads of house were even members of the ruling family. Cecilia, daughter of William the Conqueror and Matilda, became abbess of Caen, and Duke Robert the Magnificent's aunt, Beatrice, was the first head of the refounded community at Montivilliers, with a half-sister of Empress Matilda, also called Matilda, becoming abbess there in the twelfth century. In contrast, a superior who was too severe could have been responsible for strife within the community and affect its willingness to live in common. The abbot of Mont-Ste-Catherine was a 'wrathful and bitter man', who caused problems in chapter as the monks were too frightened to accuse one another of faults; and at Mont-St-Michel the superior was ordered to be more considerate of the sick and weak.[176] Constance, a nun of Montivilliers, was removed from her abbey after complaining to Archbishop

169 *Rule of Saint Augustine*, ed. van Bavel and trans. Canning, pp. 37–8.
170 Bonnin, pp. 9, 89–90 and *Register*, pp. 13, 102–3.
171 Bonnin, p. 202 and *Register*, p. 220.
172 Bonnin, p. 517 and *Register*, p. 591. See also appendix B no. 14.
173 Bonnin, pp. 285, 197 and *Register*, pp. 322, 212.
174 Bonnin, p. 410 and *Register*, p. 468.
175 Appendix A, no. 98 for Le Tréport; Bonnin, pp. 444, 229 and *Register*, pp. 506, 251.
176 Appendix A, no. 55 for Mont-St-Michel; Bonnin, pp. 195, 246 and *Register*, pp. 210, 274. See also Burton, *Yorkshire Nunneries*, p. 30 for a comparative example from Swine

Robert Poulain (1208–21) of the punishment inflicted upon her by the abbess. She was placed in a different community.[177]

The formation of small groups and the activities outlined above in all areas of the monastery inevitably led to tensions within the community. After all, the antithesis of small friendly groups was nuns or monks at loggerheads with each other. Groups of nuns were in dispute at Almenèches, Bival, St-Aubin and Villarceaux, where Joan of Hauteville and Ermengarde of Gisors actually came to blows.[178] Brother John Chicaut of St-Sulpice and John of Baudre and Thomas of Ostrehan at St-Etienne in Caen were all 'sowers of discord'.[179] Two monks at the Cluniac priory of Mortemer-sur-Eaulne were dwelling in rancour, not charity, to the extent where Brother Eudes of Mortemer 'was not eating with Brother William the Englishman, nor was he singing his day or night hours with him'; perhaps it is not hard to guess why these two men, one French and one English, had fallen out.[180] Such behaviour, contrary as it was to monastic ideals, resulted in the troublemakers placing themselves outside the community through their actions, both spiritually and physically.[181] In extreme circumstances perpetrators were liable to be imprisoned, as we have discussed above. Although neither Eudes nor Stephen record the incarceration of any nuns, communities did make the necessary provisions, as can be seen at Montivilliers.[182] In contrast, Brother William of Modec, a monk at St-Wandrille, was ordered to remain alone in a 'certain room, entirely shut off … from all association with the community and the monks for that he had inadvisedly and evilly spoken words in open chapter which had scandalised and disturbed the community'.[183] Only after they had made restitution would rebellious religious be able to take up their former places. It is possible that the tensions identifiable within the community

where the prioress was criticised in the mid-thirteenth century for unjust and inconsistent punishments.

[177] Johnson, *Equal in Monastic Profession*, p. 75, citing P. Le Cacheux, *L'exemption de Montivilliers* (Caen, 1929), pp. 8–9. For Robert, see Tabbagh, *Diocèse de Rouen*, pp. 79–80.

[178] Bonnin, pp. 82, 229, 207, 43 and *Register*, pp. 93, 252, 226, 49. A similar case occurred at Swine: J. Burton, *The Yorkshire Nunneries in the Twelfth and Thirteenth Centuries*, Borthwick Papers 56 (York, 1979), p. 30.

[179] Appendix A, no. 88 for St-Sulpice; Bonnin, pp. 70–1, 94 and *Register*, pp. 79, 109.

[180] Bonnin, p. 339 and *Register*, p. 385.

[181] See *Rule of Saint Augustine*, ed. van Bavel and trans. Canning, pp. 25, 35–7 for the importance of maintaining harmony in the monastic community. The question of sin and penance is discussed more fully in chapter one.

[182] Appendix B, no. 14. Monastic imprisonment is further discussed by J. Dunbabin, *Captivity and Imprisonment in Medieval Europe, 1000–1300*, Medieval Culture and Society (Basingstoke, 2002), pp. 145–6; Cassidy-Welch, *Monastic Spaces and their Meanings*, pp. 122–3 and 'Incarceration and Liberation: Prisons in the Cistercian Monastery', *Viator*, 32 (2001), pp. 23–42.

[183] Bonnin, p. 516 and *Register*, p. 589. Illness could also result in incarceration as was possibly the case at Notre-Dame-du-Val, a canon described as a 'simpleton' and given to 'vociferation and unbridled vituperation' was kept in a prison which Archbishop Eudes instructed should be constructed further away from the main community: Bonnin, p. 578 and *Register*, pp. 665–6.

were reinforced by secular ties outside the community. We know from other evidence that family groups were located within these houses. For example, two abbesses of Almenèches, Emma and Matilda, were aunt and niece. At St-Amand three of the abbesses in the thirteenth century came from the same family.[184] The eleventh-century pancarte of St-Léger records five nuns with possible links to the founding family of Humphrey of Vieilles, whilst two daughters of Richer II, the founder of Chaise-Dieu-Du-Theil, were prioresses at the house.[185] I speculate that some of the groupings we have encountered may reflect such family or seigneurial ties.[186]

In this section, we have seen how closely related the quality and provision of spaces with a defined purpose was to the practices performed within them. Dilapidated buildings had a negative effect on the health of the community, rendering members unable to complete the services properly, as well as possibly placing certain areas out of use. The lack of specific areas, for example a refectory or dormitory, meant that monks and nuns were unable to live in common, a fact exacerbated by the devolution of the community into separate households. Professed religious, nuns especially, often had a different conception of the correct use of monastic space from that of their ecclesiastical superiors. They were active in reorganising areas like the infirmary or dormitory to suit their needs better; however, monasticism as understood by men like Abbot Stephen and Archbishop Eudes depended on the repetition of certain actions in certain spaces. Without a rule, which recognised the need for private space within a cloistered community, a community that did not follow these practices could not be regarded as properly monastic at all.

The use of liturgical space

Archbishop Eudes especially was keen to ensure that the liturgy was performed correctly in the monasteries in his care. We have already discussed some of the practices he condemned but other things attracted his attention, ranging from everyday faults like the incorrect recitation of offices to the inappropriate celebration of feast days, such as Holy Innocents (28 December) and Mary Magdalene (22 July). Again there are similarities between monks and nuns,

---

184 L.-R. Delsalle, 'Un monument oublié: l'abbaye de Saint-Amand', *Bulletin de la Société des Amis des Monuments Rouennais* (1979–80), p. 56.
185 *Regesta regum*, no. 217 and Martin, 'Un couvent des femmes, le prieuré de la Chaise-Dieu', p. 290. Comparative material exists from the Yorkshire nunneries where Maud, daughter of the founders of Nun Monkton – William and Juetta de Arches – became prioress, and at Marrick where the daughter of the founder, Roger de Aske, entered the priory: Burton, *Yorkshire Nunneries*, pp. 19–20.
186 Mary Laven has noted that the prelates who visited renaissance Venetian nuns 'found them asserting their individual and familial interests and fashioning their identities in wilful opposition to the common life': *Virgins of Venice: Enclosed Lives and Broken Vows in the Venetian Convent* (London, 2002), p. 2.

but also important differences that stem from the increase in the numbers of monks who became priests during the Middle Ages.

In order to perform liturgical practices correctly, monastery churches had to be furnished properly with vestments and vessels. The church also had to be kept in good order. While this may be self-evident, Archbishop Eudes found it necessary on occasion to remind the religious he visited to maintain the church in a state befitting the most sacred place in the community and centre of the monastic life. We can imagine the consternation with which Eudes greeted the beams and boxes in the church at La Lande-Patry, not to mention the three casks of wine discovered at Heudreville.[187] As well as failing to keep the church clean and uncluttered, he criticised many male monastic communities for failing to keep the vessels and vestments to a sufficient standard. The problems encountered in having to make spatial provision for multiple masses are discussed below, but in terms of vessels, this meant that each community had to own multiple chalices and patens in order for the priests to be able to say mass. The communities at Ivry and Hambye had insufficient chalices and the priory of Tournai-sur-Dives was without vestments, chalices and books.[188] Some communities, like Ticheville, tried to get round the problem by using the parish vessels, which was of course unacceptable, as mass could not be said at the same time.[189] Providing multiple sets of vessels and vestments was expensive, and for communities like Muzy, which had pawned its copes in order to have bells made, impractical.[190]

In Cistercian communities, concerns regarding the correct apparatus for and performance of the liturgy centred on simplicity. Part of the rationale behind the foundation of the order was to return to the original sentiment of the rule of St Benedict, in reaction to the elaborate liturgy and practices perceived to be worldly as at, for example, Cluny. Chapter twenty-five of the *Exordium Cistercii* lays down what sort of vessels and vestments were suitable. Pure gold vessels were prohibited, as were those ornamented with silver or precious stones except the chalice and *fistula*, which could be of silver or gold plate.[191] Vestments and altar cloths should be made of linen or wool and not contain silk, except the stole and maniple; copes were to be of one colour.[192] In addition, a statute of the general chapter in 1180 banned the use of copes in the interests of simplicity, though an exception was made for use during an abbatial blessing.[193] Simplicity extended to other aspects of the church and

---

[187] Appendix A, no. 43 for La Lande-Patry; Bonnin, pp. 577, 625 and *Register*, pp. 665, 720.

[188] Appendix A, no. 97 for Tournai; Bonnin, pp. 69–70, 86, 232 and *Register*, pp. 77, 98 and 256.

[189] Appendix A, no. 95; Bonnin, p. 200 and *Register*, p. 216.

[190] Copes were ecclesiastical vestments worn in procession. Bonnin, p. 70 and *Register*, p. 78.

[191] *Narrative and Legislative Texts*, p. 413. The *fistula* is a tube through which the Cistercians took wine from the chalice.

[192] *Narrative and Legislative Texts*, p. 413. See also Williams, *Cistercians in the Early Middle Ages*, p. 229.

[193] *Twelfth-Century Statutes*, 1180, no. 3, p. 87.

monastery as well. Floor tiles had to be plain and not patterned in any way. A statute of 1210 described a pavement made by a monk of Beaubec (though not actually at that abbey) as 'lacking in gravity and out of the ordinary', while the tiles at Bonport exhibited a fleur-de-lys pattern.[194] Stephen found cause to admonish the monks in his care to observe Cistercian simplicity in their liturgical celebrations. He stated that the altar cloths at Beaubec had to be white, and coloured altar cloths were to be removed at Aunay.[195] In addition, the coloured glass and pavement used in the infirmary at Aunay were to be removed by the feast of St Denis.[196] For Stephen, in common with the principles of his Cistercian order, the use of colour, excessive ornamentation and precious stones was most definitely a profanation of a sacred space that distracted monks from their proper worship.

Both houses of monks and nuns in Eudes's care experienced problems performing the daily offices in the correct manner. We have already noted that the poor state of buildings at St-Aubin meant that the nuns could not rise in the middle of the night for Matins.[197] This office proved to be problematic for male houses as well. Matins was said without modulation at Ticheville, presumably because it would take less time and the monks could get back to bed quicker, and, at St-Martin-d'Es, the monks did not chant it because of thieves.[198] This reference is ambiguous: perhaps the monks thought that activity in the middle of the night would attract the attention of undesirable characters abroad in the small hours. Although it is perhaps understandable that religious wanted to hurry through the night office, it did mean that they were not giving the prayers, and by extension God, their full attention. Other offices were rushed, due to pressures of work or infirmity, at several houses, including the male Benedictine houses of St-Saëns, Planches, Gasny and Beaussault.[199] The main fault encountered by Eudes was in the failure of priests to say masses. Each priest was supposed to perform the mass each day and this led to problems as the number of monks who were also priests increased: monastic churches simply did not contain enough altars. The importance of having sufficient altars predated Eudes's episcopate. In 1099, the church of St-Évroul was dedicated under Abbot Roger and its seven altars consecrated by Bishops Gilbert of Lisieux (1077–1101), Gilbert of Évreux (1071–1112) and Serlo of Sées (1091–1123) in the presence of the abbot of Bec and many lords.[200] An additional altar was consecrated to

194 Williams, *Cistercians in the Early Middle Ages*, p. 220 and *Statuta*, vol. 1, 1210, no. 34, p. 375.
195 Appendix A, no. 5; *Registrum epistolarum*, pp. 206 and 210.
196 *Registrum epistolarum*, p. 211.
197 See the section on the use of buildings above.
198 Appendix A, no. 82; Bonnin, pp. 63, 489 and *Register*, pp. 72, 557.
199 Appendix A, nos 86, 64, 35, 11; Bonnin, pp. 58, 78, 166 and *Register*, pp. 65, 88, 181. The monks at St-Sever were also censured for rushing the office and omitting their morning mass entirely: Bonnin, p. 248 and *Register*, p. 276. See Appendix A, no. 87 for St-Sever.
200 OV, vol. 5, pp. 264–7. The high altar was dedicated to the Blessed Virgin Mary, St Peter and St Évroul. Other altars were dedicated to the apostles, all martyrs, St Giles, all saints, all confessors and all virgins. For details about the bishops see Bouet and Dosdat, 'Les évêques normands de 985 à 1150', pp. 29, 31–2, 34–5.

Mary Magdalene in 1124.[201] Although St-Évroul was well supplied with altars in the twelfth century, during a visit to St-Wandrille in 1249 Eudes recorded that there were only three altars in the church, which were insufficient for the brothers to celebrate mass. Some monks at Beaumont-en-Auge did not even celebrate once a fortnight and at Cormeilles the brothers rarely sang private masses, a fault that was to be corrected.[202] The necessity for multiple masses entailed a reorganisation of the timetable and monastic space to accommodate all the priests. As women were barred from ordination, there was not the same need for more than one or two altars if the church was shared by a parish; multiple masses in nunneries entailed financial expense though, as is discussed below.

Liturgical practice extended to the correct placing of monks or nuns in the choir to ensure an appropriate recitation of the offices. The choir arrangements at La Trinité and St-Amand caused problems during the divine office. At St-Amand the choir was deemed to be unbalanced as there were, according to Eudes, too many juniors on one side.[203] Parts of the office would be said or sung alternately by the two sides of the choir, with the result that a large number of inexperienced nuns on one side might lead to mistakes or delays. At La Trinité, one group of nuns was located outside the choir and one inside, as opposed to two rows opposite each other.[204] Again the unorthodox placing of nuns in this part of the church led to problems in Eudes's eyes with their main task, the continual round of prayer in the offices. Whereas the archbishop did not criticise any male communities for unbalanced choirs, he did castigate cathedral chapters for not remaining in the choir during services. Secular clerics in cathedral chapters were not subject to the monastic rule, but had their own statutes and were expected to uphold certain standards of behaviour. The clerks-choral and canons of Lisieux clearly failed to do this when they left their choir and 'wandered gossiping through the church' during services, and similar problems were experienced at Coutances where, in addition to leaving their stalls, the canons talked loudly enough to be heard on the other side of the choir.[205]

The celebration of the feasts of Holy Innocents and Mary Magdalene caused more obvious problems. The nuns celebrated these feast days at Villarceaux with 'farcical improvisations'; they dressed up in secular clothes and danced and sang with each other and with lay folk.[206] The festivities caused an unacceptable mixing of lay and religious as well as the nuns shedding the outward sign of their profession, the habit. The nuns were in breach of many of the things that Eudes saw as essential in the practice of monasticism, like maintenance of the cloister, custody of the body and the proper performance of monastic offices. In addition, this was a feast of misrule when the junior

---

[201]   J. Thiron, 'L'abbaye de St-Évroul', *Congrès archéologique de France*, 157 (1954), p. 359
[202]   Appendix A, no. 26 for Cormeilles; Bonnin, pp. 55, 198 and *Register*, pp. 60, 213.
[203]   Bonnin, p. 486 and *Register*, p. 555.
[204]   Bonnin, p. 575 and *Register*, p. 662. We do not know why the nuns chose this arrangement. Perhaps the choir was in disrepair or the nuns felt the acoustics were better.
[205]   Bonnin, pp. 61, 87 and *Register*, pp. 69, 100.
[206]   Bonnin, p. 45 and *Register*, p. 50.

nuns assumed control of the abbey for the day, as for example, at St-Amand where the juniors remained in the choir, chanting the offices after the seniors had retired.[207] It seems that the nuns were following the tradition of the 'boy bishop' feasts observed in cathedrals on the feast of Holy Innocents. As Susan Boynton observes, the feast demonstrated an opposition between the daily liturgical structure and release from routine.[208] This involved a chorister being elected as bishop for the duration of the festival and making laws for the day to be obeyed by the whole cathedral chapter. As a thirteenth-century ordinal from Bayeux shows, in addition the boys sang the appropriate liturgy from the high stalls normally reserved for the cathedral canons and the canons themselves took the place of the boys.[209] At first this was welcomed by the Church as it was seen to encourage Christian behaviour and humility. However, throughout the thirteenth century, efforts were made to control what were seen as excesses and it gradually faded out, for example the Bayeux ordinal insisted that the cathedral clergy and boys should celebrate their feasts 'as solemnly as they can'.[210] Observance of the feast of Holy Innocents in this manner had meant that the normal order of the house was subverted and was thus contrary to the rule.[211]

It is interesting to note here that Archbishop Eudes did not criticise any male houses for observing feast days with a celebration of misrule. It is possible that Holy Innocents in particular was regarded as a feast best commemorated by boys: the twelfth-century liturgist John Beleth stated that the boys performed the office on the feast day because the Innocents, traditionally regarded as male, had been killed for Christ.[212] Significantly, in the thirteenth century, Archbishop John Pecham of Canterbury (1279–94) issued a mandate forbidding the celebration of Holy Innocents by children in nunneries.[213] Shulamith Shahar has speculated that the reason for this prohibition and criticism of the practice in nunneries lay in the fact that the feast was one of an inversion of hierarchy. Medieval society was aware of varying status and roles, but these were largely defined in relation to men, and thus women were excluded; therefore, a reversal of female roles as articulated through nuns' cele-

---

[207] Bonnin, p. 486 and *Register*, p. 534. The abbeys of St-Léger and La Trinité celebrated these feasts. The nuns of Montivilliers in addition celebrated the feasts of St John and St Stephen in a similar manner: Bonnin, pp. 197, 261, 384 and *Register*, pp. 212, 293. 436.

[208] S. Boynton, 'Work and Play in Sacred Music and its Social Context, c.1050–1250', *The Use and Abuse of Time in Christian History*, ed. R. N. Swanson, Studies in Church History 37 (Woodbridge, 2002), p. 57.

[209] *Ordinaire et coutumier de l'église de Bayeux*, ed. U. Chevalier (Paris, 1902), p. 67 and Boynton, 'Work and Play in Sacred Music', p. 72.

[210] *Ordinaire et coutumier de l'église de Bayeux*, p. 64 and Boynton, 'Work and Play in Sacred Music', p. 72. The boy bishop's feast was also celebrated in English cathedrals, notably Salisbury where the practice has been resurrected in recent years.

[211] K. MacKenzie, 'Boy into Bishop', *History Today*, 37 (December, 1987), pp. 10–11.

[212] S. Shahar, 'The Boy Bishop's Feast: a Case-study in Church Attitudes towards Children in the High and Late Middle Ages' *The Church and Childhood*, ed. D. Wood, Studies in Church History 31 (Woodbridge, 1994), p. 244.

[213] Shahar, 'Boy Bishop's Feast', p. 247.

bration of the feast of Innocents had no meaning.[214] In other words, whereas it was acceptable for male roles to be reversed in the context of a cathedral chapter, as all women regardless of age were regarded as inferior to all men in general, then nothing was to be gained by a similar reversal in a community of nuns. In this respect, Eudes's condemnations are as much to do with what was considered acceptable in relation to gender roles as it was to do with 'farcical improvisations'. Eudes's emphasis on feasts of misrule in nunneries contrasts with his concern that monks who were priests had the opportunity to celebrate mass correctly and on a regular basis.[215] I speculate here that the practice of feasts of misrule at certain times in the Church's year was a conscious attempt by the nuns to forge their own liturgical traditions outside the mainstream celebration of the mass in which they could only participate in a very limited and passive way as recipients of the host.[216]

Problems of enclosure: male staff in houses of nuns

The Church's attempts to enforce strict enclosure on houses of nuns brought a very real problem to houses of female religious in the number of male staff they had to employ. We have already seen that male communities did employ women, but their number was small, their role limited to various housekeeping tasks and the ecclesiastical visitors tried to remove them wherever possible. Both nunneries and monasteries had to employ secular administrators to help in the running of their estates, but nuns found it necessary to employ men for a variety of tasks, both temporal and spiritual.[217] Unlike houses of male religious, which could provide their own priests to minister to their sacramental needs, nunneries had to employ men for the purposes of saying the mass and hearing confession. The sacramental needs of the nuns at La Trinité, for example, were taken care of by four canons.[218] Lay brothers or seculars were necessary for heavy manual labour and other duties. Abbot Stephen of Lexington included a special section on the duties of the male religious in the nunneries in his care. It is apparent that the nuns were provided with a

---

[214] Shahar, 'Boy Bishop's Feast', p. 247.

[215] As for example at St-Etienne and St-Ouen, Bonnin, pp. 262, 57 and *Register*, pp. 293 and 63.

[216] I note here Caroline Walker Bynum's argument regarding some holy women who engaged in extreme fasting in the later Middle Ages to wield power over the priests who gave them communion by vomiting or otherwise rejecting the host which was taken as a sign of the priest's impurity; *Holy Food and Holy Fast*, p. 228. Ascetic food practices were not a primary concern of Norman nuns, as can be seen from the previous discussion of the refectory.

[217] For a consideration of the relations between nuns and men, see P. S. Gold, 'The Charters of Le Ronceray d'Angers: Male/Female Interaction in Monastic Business', *Medieval Women and the Sources of Medieval History*, ed. J. T. Rosenthal (Athens, GA, 1990), pp. 122–32. For seculars in the employ of monasteries more generally see Berkhofer, *Day of Reckoning*, pp. 130–43.

[218] *Regesta regum*, no. 62.

male community in miniature, made up of professed monks from the same order numbering around three. This group was headed by a prior who acted as a procurator and liaised with the secular world and thus negated the need for the nuns to leave their cloister.[219] For example, he was to provide a 'faithful and mature burgher or other man' who could go to market under the supervision of the prioress who presumably furnished him with a list of the community's requirements.[220] Other monks were in charge of the grain and its transportation between the grange and the mill.[221] Lay brothers were present in some of the houses Eudes visited. At St-Amand we know that a lay brother was in charge of the bakery and another, by the name of Eudes, was a cook.[222] Richard of Pontoise converted from Judaism and became a *conversus* at St-Amand on condition that the community would support his wife, Oda, and daughter, Joanna, whom he would be leaving without any income.[223] At Bondeville, Robert, the donor who made provision for his Genevieve to retire to the priory, became a monk there in 1290.[224] St-Saëns also had lay brothers but Eudes does not often say much about them other than recording their presence.[225]

Sometimes it is impossible to determine the exact status of a member of the monastic household: for example, whether they were a lay brother, someone living in retirement or a paid servant, as was the case with Guillaume de St-Amand and his son, Geoffrey, who were admitted to the house of St-Amand in Rouen in June 1295 by Abbess Beatrice d'Eu II. The charter that records their entrance does set out the work they were to do for the benefit of the community. In return for living in the enclosure, that is to say the monastic precinct, receiving the same food as the nuns as well as suitable clothes and shoes, they were to guard the gate of the abbey and give to it forty livres tournois, possessions in land and revenue at Fresne-le-Plan.[226] It is not known if these two men took any kind of formal vows, but it is clear that they felt some affinity with the nuns and provided a useful service for them. Such staff, including bailiffs and priests, also acted as witnesses to the nuns' charters at St-Amand and elsewhere, for example St-Saëns and Fontaine-Guérard.[227]

219 *Registrum epistolarum*, p. 235, and p. 242. He was responsible for bread, drink, butter, food portions and clothing.
220 *Registrum epistolarum*, p. 236.
221 *Registrum epistolarum*, p. 243.
222 Bonnin, p. 586 and *Register*, p. 678 and Le Cacheux, 'Histoire de l'abbaye de Saint-Amand de Rouen', p. 126. He appears in a charter of William of Varenne.
223 Johnson, *Equal in Monastic Profession*, p. 179 and Le Cacheux, 'Histoire de l'abbaye de Saint-Amand de Rouen', pp. 259–61. The charter is dated 1249. The nuns, however, reneged on the agreement. Richard went to court and won the case, forcing the abbey to pay him reparation of £5 and to support his wife and daughter with a payment of £2 a year.
224 Johnson, *Equal in Monastic Profession*, p. 180 and note 43, citing an unpublished charter. See chapter two.
225 For example Bonnin, p. 273 and *Register*, p. 306.
226 Le Cacheux, 'Histoire de l'abbaye de Saint-Amand de Rouen', pp. 135–6.
227 Eudes, the cook, appears in a charter of William of Varenne for St-Amand, whilst Tostain, a priest, and his brother, William, a monastery servant, appear in a charter

It is clear from Abbot Stephen's statutes that the monks charged with the nuns' spiritual care had their own areas, along with the lay brothers, within the precinct in order to prevent undue contact with the women. The monks had their own living area and no nun was to enter it or its surroundings.[228] Male staff also seem to have had their own areas in some of the communities that Eudes visited: at St-Aubin the nuns are recorded as eating in the priest's house.[229] Eudes forbade this in future and both he and Stephen regarded the priest's house as separate and distinct from the cloister and thus out of bounds to the nuns. The monks, too, were to observe the monastic offices, but in their own oratory. The sole exception was the mass which they celebrated for the nuns in the monastic church, though they were allowed in the church for private prayer when it was not in use by the nuns.[230] The monks also had their own refectory. Rules governing this were similar to those observed by the nuns. No seculars were to be admitted to the table; instead they were to eat in the guest house. Visiting abbots might dine with the monks but other religious were to take their food in the guest house.[231] Further restrictions were placed on the monks' movement within the female houses of the order. They were not to go into the nuns' outer court nor speak to the nuns without permission. The prior was to give permission only after ascertaining the name of the nun with whom the monk wished to speak. He was then to join them in case the monk took the opportunity to speak with other women. In addition, no monk was to speak with any of the nuns in the absence of the prioress, subprioress or other senior nun. The reason for this concern for Stephen lay in the fact that 'malevolent men invent fraudulent occasions in the custom of sly little foxes so they can cloak undertaken malice'.[232] He was concerned that prompting by less than holy desires might lead those in his charge into sin if too much contact was allowed between monastics of the opposite sex.

Archbishop Eudes records some of the practical problems associated with the male staff in a house of women religious. Far from being supportive of their vocations, male priests could in fact have a detrimental impact on the nuns' monastic experience: for example, Brother Roger, a lay brother at Bondeville, was rebellious and caused problems for the prioress.[233] Much, of

of Girard de Mauquenchy for the same house: Le Cacheux, 'Histoire de l'abbaye de Saint-Amand de Rouen', p. 126. The names of four monks who acted for St-Saëns are known: Robert de Montivilliers in the 1220s; Roger in the 1230s, Herbert of Rouen in the 1240s and Simon in the 1280s; Rouen, AD 56 HP 1 and 56 HP 5. Hugh, prior of Fontaine-Guérard, is recorded in a charter dated 1221, preserved in a later copy, Rouen, AD 80 HP 5. I am grateful to John Walmsley for these references.

228   *Registrum epistolarum*, p. 256.

229   Bonnin, p. 412 and *Register*, p. 471. This could be a case of the nuns sharing their chaplain with the local parish. In which case, the house could be located within the nunnery precincts or the parish.

230   *Registrum epistolarum*, p. 253. This measure observes the prohibition laid down in canon twenty-seven of the Second Lateran Council of 1139 that nuns should not sing the divine office in the same choir as monks or canons: *Decrees*, p. 203.

231   *Registrum epistolarum*, p. 253.

232   *Registrum epistolarum*, p. 254.

233   Bonnin, p. 348 and *Register*, p. 396.

course, depended on the characters of the individuals concerned, but it seems that for those men with unscrupulous desires, the opportunities to create havoc were legion. A number of nuns were cited for being 'illfamed' of their chaplains, that is to say there was a degree of suspicion surrounding their relationship. A woman by the name of Jacqueleine had to leave the priory of Villarceaux after she became pregnant by the chaplain who was then expelled.[234] The priest at St-Saëns was also removed due to rumours about his chastity.[235] In this climate, visits that might otherwise be perfectly innocent came under suspicion. The abbot of Jumièges was warned not to visit the nuns of Villarceaux casually as he was causing scandal by his familiarity.[236] Those charged with the spiritual care of the nuns seem to have been instrumental in reducing the sacred nature of the community by possibly abusing their position of trust.[237] Other problems involved the lack of a sufficient number of male clerics to ensure the nuns could hear mass and go to confession. In 1254, Eudes recorded that a nun at St-Saëns assisted the priest at mass and that this was to be prevented in future.[238] Not only were women barred from ordination, they could not act as servers during services. For a woman to assist a priest she would have to enter that place in the church reserved for male clerics, the sanctuary, thus placing herself outside her proper place in the ecclesiastical hierarchy.

It is possible that male ecclesiastics were unwilling to minister to the needs of the nuns, perceiving them to be a potential threat to their own vocations. The problems experienced by Cistercian and Premonstratensian sisters in being accepted by their male brethren have been well documented.[239] In Normandy, Bival, which had been founded as a daughter house of the male Cistercian abbey of Beaubec, had a troubled early history. In the late twelfth century, the monks abused their position and appropriated most of the nunnery's goods to their own use.[240] The tensions this caused prompted some women to leave the abbey to found communities at Bondeville and St-Saëns, despite Hugh of Gournay, one of their secular supporters, issuing a charter

234 Bonnin, p. 43 and *Register*, p. 49.
235 Bonnin, p. 142 and *Register*, p. 158. The priest at St-Saëns continued to be a problem at many of Eudes's further visits.
236 Bonnin, p. 585 and *Register* p. 674.
237 An extreme example, dating from 1279, of male clerics' abuse of their position in a house of female religious involves the Dominican convent of Zamora in Spain. The Dominican friars charged with the nuns' spiritual care were so persistent in their sexual advances that some of the nuns hid in the oven to escape the men: P. Linehan, *The Ladies of Zamora* (Manchester, 1997), pp. 1, 48–58.
238 Bonnin, p. 187 and *Register*, p. 199.
239 For example, B. Bolton, 'Mulieres Sanctae', *Sanctity and Secularity: the Church and the World*, ed. D. Baker, Studies in Church History 10 (Oxford, 1973), pp. 77–95; C. H. Lawrence, *Medieval Monasticism: Forms of Religious Life in Western Europe in the Middle Ages* 3rd edn (Harlow, 2001) *passim* and Thompson, 'Problem of Cistercian Nuns'.
240 J. R. Strayer, 'A Forged Charter of Henry II for Bival', *Speculum*, 34 (1959), p. 232.

warning off the abbot.[241] In such circumstances, the necessity of having male staff was as burdensome to the nuns as it was to some male religious.

Conclusion

Enclosure was central to the practice of monasticism: it served as a barrier which protected professed religious' vocations and marked out an area as devoted to God. Enclosure was about control, both in terms of the outside world's access to monastic and other religious precincts, and monks, nuns and lepers' ability to move into the secular world. The practice of claustration was not limited to the physical actuality of the inner court but encompassed dress, the monks' and nuns' mental observance of the cloister and, in some circumstances, the laity's respect for it. Enclosure did, however, bring some very real problems to religious communities. The tension between maintaining the cloister but also a profile visible enough to ensure sufficient donations in order that the house should survive, seems to have been particularly acute for some of the later and smaller foundations. This had a more severe effect on nuns due to the Church's stricter interpretation of the rules regarding enclosure for women. Gendered differences are also apparent in the need for male priests in female houses, leading to further tensions and expense. The communities which inhabited leper houses and hospitals faced different problems relating to the lack of charitable provision, that meant that control of lepers in particular was only confined to those within a community. Equally, regulations regarding which lepers could be accepted prevented those who needed the support of a community from obtaining it, Although there were distinctions between lay brothers and sisters and choir monks and nuns, total enclosure was not possible for the latter or even desirable. The status and power of heads of house ensured that a significant proportion of their time would be spent away from spiritual duties and often this was linked to their family networks.

[241] Johnson, *Equal in Monastic Profession*, p. 45. Comparable evidence exists from the nunnery of Swine in Yorkshire where the misuse of funds by the canons and *conversi* charged with looking after the nuns' finances, plunged the nunnery into debt and deprived the nuns of food: Burton, *Yorkshire Nunneries*, p. 31.

4

Family

The family is central to our understanding of the interaction between the laity and religious.[1] Monks, nuns and priests all had blood relations as well as their new religious family within the cloisters and churches of Normandy. Families were also the first point of contact between the religious and secular spheres and were thus both of benefit and disadvantage to the religious life. Relatives – parents, siblings and children – founded monastic institutions, contributed to their endowment and provided their professed members.[2] But the family could also be a burden on already stretched financial resources and make demands on the monks' and nuns' time.

In Normandy, the families of monks and nuns blurred spatial boundaries in a number of ways, both in terms of the physical barriers of the monastic precincts and the abstract barriers induced by enclosure.[3] Kinfolk were found in the cloister making demands on hospitality. They caused professed religious to leave the cloister for a variety of reasons. Some families developed a network of vocations within specific houses, establishing a religious branch of the family interest dedicated to the maintenance of its spiritual well-being. Other families used their monastic foundations as private mausolea, displaying their wealth and patronage through tombs in churches, cloisters and chapter houses. Gender is crucial in this discussion. Although an individual's biological sex remained the same after taking vows, their gendered identity changed. This is particularly true of those individuals who were married prior to committing themselves to a life of celibacy. By considering the family and use of space through the interaction between the Norman laity and religious, this book's other themes of display, reception and intrusion, and enclosure, come together.

---

1   For recent work on the family in the Middle Ages see R. Fossier, 'The Feudal Era (Eleventh – Thirteenth Century), A History of the Family Vol. 1: Distant Worlds, Ancient Worlds, ed. A. Burguière et al. (Cambridge, 1996), pp. 407–29 and T. K. Harevan, 'The History of the Family and the Complexity of Social Change', American Historical Review, 96 (1991), pp. 95–124.

2   See the activities of the Giroie and Grandmesnil families later in this chapter and J. C. Ward, 'Fashions in Monastic Endowment: the Foundations of the Clare Family 1066–1314', Journal of Ecclesiastical History, 32 (1981), pp. 427–51.

3   See chapter three.

Family interests and monastic needs

By entering a religious house, be it a monastery or a hospital, a man or woman was suppressing his or her will to that of a corporate body of like-minded people connected by their desire to fulfil a vocation dedicated to the service of God. Vocations also entailed a certain degree of renunciation of secular family ties outside the monastic community. An entire renunciation of these ties was impossible given the symbiotic relationship between monasticism and its benefactors, but writers of monastic rules, as well as bishops and abbots in their visitation records, were firm: in their opinion the religious family came first. As we have seen, within Norman monasticism as elsewhere, accommodation of, and conflict between, different interest groups was apparent.[4] The material evidence for family involvement in monasticism is unfortunately scanty and so of necessity we are reliant to a greater degree on documentary sources. Evidence for the accommodation of conflicting needs comes from a variety of sources including Orderic Vitalis's *Ecclesiastical History*, episcopal letters and visitation records.

The necessity to accommodate the needs of both professed religious and lay people within monastic precincts arose because lay support was vital to the maintenance of the religious life. Monks and nuns played their part in society by praying for others and quiet contemplation, but to do so they needed endowments sufficient for their material needs. As Emma Cownie has indicated, concern for the salvation of one's soul and the souls of ancestors was crucially important to all men and women, and this motivated them to endow monasteries for the benefit of themselves and their families. Other benefits could be accrued through religious patronage, namely fraternity, burial or reception of the habit for a donor or a donor's kinsman or woman.[5] Patronage of a particular house was closely linked with family strategies. Of course, to engage in contemplation and prayer, male and female monastics needed to maintain the quietude of the cloister. Contact could not be severed completely as this would risk losing donations, impoverishing the monastery and making the monastery less attractive to potential recruits. After all, donors did not just endow religious houses for spiritual benefit; the secular prestige of a particular family was also enhanced. Family support, whether it be through the oblation of kin or material donations, was vital.

Relatives affected the use of space in monasteries in two ways: first, their physical presence within the monastery, for example when seeking hospitality or visiting, made demands on the financial resources of the institution; second, through interference in the vocations of monks and nuns by recalling them from the cloister. Gender is important here, both in the conception of what it meant to be a monk or nun, but also in how family members were received.

---

[4]   See chapter two.
[5]   E. Cownie, *Religious Patronage in Anglo-Norman England 1066–1135*, Studies in History, new series (Woodbridge, 1998), pp. 151–2.

The families of professed religious caused most upheaval when their actions resulted in the dispersal of a community through brutal incursions, something to which nuns were particularly vulnerable. Orderic Vitalis records that the abbey of Almenèches suffered in this way in 1100, in the disorder following the return of Duke Robert Curthose (1087–1106) from the Holy Land. The nunnery's troubles stemmed from the fact that Abbess Emma (d.1113) was the daughter of Roger of Montgomery (d.1094) who founded the monastery, and the sister of Robert of Bellême with whom the duke was in dispute. Clearly she was a woman with important family and political connections and this jeopardised the safety of her community. Orderic records that Duke Robert and his men had gathered in the nunnery and 'turned the consecrated buildings into stables for their horses'. Robert of Bellême 'rushed to the spot and, setting fire to the buildings burned the nunnery to the ground'. As a consequence, the nuns were dispersed and 'each one retired to the home of kinsfolk or friends' with Abbess Emma and three of her nuns seeking shelter at Orderic's monastery of St-Évroul, another religious house with which her family had connections: her father had supported the monks.[6] Given the political situation and the enmity that existed between the duke and Robert of Bellême, it would not have been in the interests of the community for Emma to return to her family as did some of the other nuns. The abbey of St-Évroul thus provided a safe retreat.

In these exceptional circumstances, the sanctity of an individual's vocation was of secondary importance to their family's connections and its political network. Almenèches continued to endure many vicissitudes after the departure of the warring lords. Although Emma regrouped her community in the following year and rebuilt the abbey, its buildings were destroyed by another fire under her successor and relative Matilda (1113–after 1157).[7] Despite the destruction occasioned by the nunnery's close association with the Montgomery-Bellême family, it continued to choose family members to lead it. Almenèches was not the only abbey to have been burned down, but the net

---

6   OV, vol. 6, pp. 34–7. Though as we have already noted in chapter two, Emma's mother, Mabel, was less than charitable towards the monastery of St-Évroul. For the family of Bellême more generally see K.Thompson, 'Family and Lordship to the South of Normandy in the Eleventh Century: the Lordship of Bellême', JMH, 11 (1985), pp. 215–26. Isolation also caused similar upheavals for religious communities. During the Hundred Years War, the nuns at Moutons were forced to move from the forest of Lande Pourrie to Avranches, as the isolated site proved too dangerous. See appendix B, no. 16.

7   OV, vol. 6, pp. 36–7 and note 3. Matilda was Emma's niece, and daughter of Philip 'the Grammarian', described by Marjorie Chibnall as the most obscure of Roger of Montgomery's sons. This fire occurred during the struggles between the count of Anjou and Robert of Bellême. The community suffered another fire in 1308, G.-M. Oury, Abbaye Notre-Dame d'Almenèches-Argentan, Abbayes et Prieuriés de Normandie 8 (Rouen, 1979) pp. 3, 9–12. Damage like this was not limited to houses of female religious in Normandy. The nunnery at Laon was burned during civil upheavals and the abbess of a local house was killed by one of her serfs: A Monk's Confession: the Memoirs of Guibert of Nogent, ed. and trans. J. Archambault (Philadelphia, 1996), pp. 190–1 and Johnson, Equal in Monastic Profession, p. 58.

result was the same.[8] Actions which resulted from the activities of lay kin like Robert of Bellême, resulted in both a profanation of the sacred space of the monastery and the disruption of the daily round of offices. Since monasteries were not only deemed to be sacred because of acts of consecration, but also because of the activities of prayer and contemplation that were undertaken within them, the sacred space and the religious practices that give that space meaning are inextricably linked: damage to one, in the case of Almenèches the physical buildings, caused damage to the other, the nuns.[9] A monastic community cannot exist without its buildings or its members.

On a more individual level, relatives interfered in the pursuit of vocations through either recalling relatives from the cloister or putting obstacles in their way to making their profession. Archbishop Anselm of Canterbury wrote about two cases where the desire on the part of a husband or wife to become a monk or nun led to problems for their spouse. In his letter to a lady named Ermengard, dated c.1079/92, Anselm entreats her to allow her husband to become a monk. Her permission was necessary if her husband was to renounce marriage for the cloister, but Ermengard's reasons for refusing it are not made explicit. Anselm hints that her refusal was due to 'the glory and temporal privileges' which she loved and hoped to keep through her husband.[10] Archbishop Anselm believed that only monks had a realistic chance of salvation, and, from his perspective, Ermengard's failure to grant permission could only lie in a love of worldly things.[11] Ermengard, however, may have simply loved her husband or was fearful of the consequences of being left alone and unprovided for once he had entered the cloister. Ermengard would not have been able to remarry once her husband had entered the monastery of his choice by virtue of the fact that he was still alive.[12]

In a letter dated 1103 to Eustace, father of Gosfrid, one of the monks of Bec, Anselm illustrates the problems that could arise when one spouse entered the cloister whilst the other remained in the world. Eustace had apparently given his wife permission to become a nun and had himself made a vow of

---

[8]   See chapter three.

[9]   Michel de Certeau considers that places are only made meaningful and transformed into spaces by the people who live in them and move through them: de Certeau, *Practice of Everyday Life*, pp. 97–8, 105 and Lefebvre, *Production of Space*, p. 217.

[10]   Schmitt, vol. 1, no. 134, pp. 276–8 and Fröhlich, vol. 1, no. 134, pp. 310–12. Ermengarde and her husband are not identified. This case is discussed by Sally Vaughn in *St Anselm and the Handmaidens of God*, pp. 105–11. From three possible Ermengardes, Vaughn identifies Anselm's correspondent as Ermengarde of Bourbon, the third wife of Count Fulk le Rechin of Anjou who was estranged from her husband by c.1089. I am not convinced that such a positive identification is possible, given that Fulk did not seem to be interested in entering a monastery, but was more intent on marrying Bertrade de Montfort. See OV, vol. 4, pp. 260–3 for Orderic's account of Fulk's relationship with Bertrade and her later abduction by Philip I (1060–1108) of France.

[11]   R. W. Southern, *St Anselm and his Biographer: a Study of Monastic Life and Thought 1059–c.1130* (Cambridge, 1963), p. 101.

[12]   Brundage, *Law, Sex and Christian Society*, p. 202. See also OV, vol. 2, pp. 290–1 for a similar proscription in which a man whose wife has taken the veil is not to remarry as long as she is alive, from the Council of Rouen 1072. Orderic's record of this council is the only one that survives.

chastity, but he married again and indeed had a son by his new wife. Anselm points out that even if Eustace had not made this vow, he was still at fault, because while his first wife was still alive, he could not marry someone else.[13] The desire on the part of one half of a married couple to enter the religious life placed considerable burdens on the other half. If they refused the request, they laid themselves open to charges of loving worldly things above God. If they granted their permission, then they were expected to observe the same state of chastity as their spouse but without the support of a monastic community and its practices. In this context, monastic space extended well outside the monastery walls into the world. It also cut across considerations of gender as men and women exchanged their position as a married and sexually active couple for a new gendered identity as a celibate monk or nun, an identity also imposed on their lay spouse. Lay kin were brought into the sphere of monastic influence whether they liked it or not. We have already noted the confusion priests may have experienced regarding conceptions of their masculinity.[14] Men whose wives took the veil may well have experienced a similar psychological crisis, but without the benefit of a priestly vocation to support their newly celibate status. For women in a similar position, they effectively had to live out their lives in what amounted to a chaste widowhood.

Many monks and nuns continued to enjoy a close relationship with their natal families even after profession. Their immediate family seem to have had no hesitation in recalling them from the cloister as needed. Significantly, nuns were more susceptible to such family requests than monks: I have not found any comparable examples of monks being called away to serve their families in similar capacities. Archbishop Eudes's register contains a number of cases of nuns returning home for a variety of reasons. One woman from the priory of Villarceaux left to be married.[15] Eudes does not explain why. There are two likely reasons: first, she had been sent to the priory as a child oblate and once she reached the age of majority she decided to exercise her right not to take vows; second, her parents decided that it was now more advantageous to them for her to be married off rather than remain in the nunnery. An example from outside, though not unconnected with, Normandy supports this conjecture. Marie of Boulogne, the daughter and heiress of King Stephen (1135–54) and Queen Matilda III (d.1152), was forced to leave her place as the abbess of Romsey Abbey in Hampshire to marry Matthew of Flanders in 1160 in order to rescue the Boulogne lineage. After giving birth to two daughters, she eventually returned to the religious life at Ste-Autreberte in Montreuil.[16] At one of Eudes's visits to Lisieux, a nun was away nursing a sick relative, whilst

---

13   Schmitt, vol. 4 no. 297, pp. 217–18 and Fröhlich, vol. 2 no. 297, pp. 314–15. Eustace and his wife are not identified.

14   See chapter one, section on clothing, and chapter two on priests and their wives and concubines.

15   Bonnin, p. 117 and *Register*, p. 132.

16   *La chronique de Gislebert of Mons*, ed. L. Vanderkindere (Brussels, 1904), p. 90 and trans. L. Napran, *Chronicle of Hainaut* (Woodbridge, 2005), pp. 52–3 and Robert of Torigni, *Chronicon*, p. 207. See also L. Napran, 'Marriage and Excommunication: the Comital House of Flanders', *Exile in the Middle Ages*, ed. Napran and van Houts, pp. 74–8

a nun from St-Léger-des-Préaux was staying with her mother at Argoulles.[17] Eudes does not specify whether the nun and her mother were at the family home, but this seems likely.

Nuns continued to be useful to their natal families even after profession. It was not just their spiritual support that was valued but also their practical skills, like nursing, which they had no doubt picked up in their communities. Their abilities as nurses and biological potential for motherhood sometimes meant that nuns had to leave their cloisters either permanently or temporarily. Leaving the cloister led to a reaffirmation of secular ties with their lay kin and again, in some cases a change of gendered identity. In the case outlined above, a previously celibate, and presumably virginal woman, gave up her place in the cloister in order to fulfil an alternative role as a wife and mother. Whether departure from the community was permanent or temporary, the nuns' male ecclesiastical superiors disapproved. In a letter to a nun named Mabilia, dated c.1106–07, Archbishop Anselm of Canterbury admonished her to remain in her community and not to visit her family for:

> What need is there for you to visit any of your relatives since they do not need your advice or help in any way, nor can you receive any advice or help from them regarding your intention and profession which you could not find in your cloister ... Do not go to them because you are not allowed to leave the monastery except for a necessity which God may make known.[18]

Intriguingly, he does not elaborate on what such a necessity might be, either for women or for men. Anselm expresses similar sentiments in his letter, written before 1074, to Henry, a monk at Christ Church Canterbury, who wanted to travel to Italy to help his sister as 'some rich man has deceitfully subjected her to undeserved servitude'. Anselm admonishes Henry that:

> Even if it is good to want to free a person bound to difficult circumstances, yet what you intend is not good enough to be worth looking back after having held on to Christ's plough for so long; worth having a monk break his vow by such an interruption.[19]

It is not known how the nuns and monks felt about such visits. Some may have welcomed the chance to leave their communities for a while and see old familiar faces; certainly the cases discussed above suggest that monks and nuns had very strong links with their parents and siblings. Others may have found their removal from the daily round of prayer an unsettling and disorienting experience and experienced great distress at being reunited with their immediate family, especially if their vocation had been a bone of contention at the time of their entrance into a monastic community. Once again, this

---

and E. van Houts, *Memory and Gender in Medieval Europe 900–1200*, Explorations in Medieval Culture and Society (Basingstoke, 1999), p. 75.

17   Bonnin, pp. 296, 591 and *Register*, pp. 335, 680.

18   Schmitt, vol. 4, no. 405, p. 350 and Fröhlich, vol. 3, no. 405, p. 171. Mabilia and her community are not identified

19   Schmitt, vol. 3, no. 17, pp. 122–4 and Fröhlich, vol. 1, no. 17, pp. 105–7

intrusion by families caused a blurring of spatial boundaries between the lay and monastic worlds and shows the conflict that existed between the desire of the professed religious to pursue their vocation and the ties they still felt to their families.

Despite the provisions within monastic rules to limit contact between professed religious and their lay kin, family members found their way into the cloister, causing disruption and resulting in a diminution of the sacral nature of monastic space. The importance of the relationship between professed religious and their relatives, as well as the specific problems posed by the presence of lay kin in the cloister, was recognised by the ecclesiastical visitors who treated relatives as a category separate from guests as a whole. Abbot Stephen of Lexington stated that the nuns' relatives (*parentes*) were to be kept at an unspecified 'proper distance' from the abbey of Mortain and its granges.[20] At Aunay-sur-Odon, he ordered that the monks were to speak with their relatives only rarely.[21] Stephen's statutes were specifically designed to prevent unnecessary contact between monks or nuns and their relatives by establishing a physical buffer zone between the religious houses and the secular spaces of the lay world, which would ensure that contact between lay and religious was limited to occasions of absolute necessity. Unfortunately, like Archbishop Anselm in the example cited above, Stephen does not elucidate what these circumstances might be. The need to limit contact is explained further by some of the entries in Archbishop Eudes's register. Relatives disturbed the daily religious routine in some nunneries by eating, drinking and sleeping within the precincts.[22] In addition, the recitation of the daily offices suffered from the necessity to attend to the needs of the nuns' relatives. At Bival, kin were so disruptive that the nuns missed Compline.[23] Under the precepts of the monastic rule, the nuns had to ensure that their guests were received in a fitting manner, but it was unacceptable to the ecclesiastical superiors for the nuns to miss part of the monastic office in order to meet the demands of their families.[24]

Cases from the visitation records indicate that the visitors were more concerned about how nuns were interacting with lay kin within the monastic precincts than monks, reflecting the stricter enclosure female religious experienced.[25] In houses of monks there is a shift of emphasis to the use of the communities' financial resources and property by relatives. In many of the cases recorded by Archbishop Eudes, these activities resulted in serious financial abuses of the communities' resources and, in some instances, brought superiors into direct conflict with their brethren. In 1264, the archbishop recorded that the financial state of St-Ouen in Rouen was not good because Abbot Nichol de Beauvais's sister and her husband, Master William, had

---

20   *Registrum epistolarum*, p. 239.
21   *Registrum epistolarum*, p. 212.
22   For example, at Bival, St-Aubin, St-Sauveur, St-Saëns and Bondeville. See Bonnin, pp. 146, 207, 220, 338, 348 and *Register*, pp. 165, 226, 241–2, 384, 395.
23   Bonnin, p. 146 and *Register*, p. 165.
24   See chapter two for hospitality.
25   See chapter three for a more detailed discussion of this aspect of monastic life.

made demands on the abbey's supplies of 'wine, wheat, food, oats and other things'.[26] At a subsequent visitation in 1266, Eudes stated that 'against the wishes of the community, many things had been given to the abbot's sister by the administrators in order to gain the good will of the abbot'. The community also believed that the abbot had some nephews who 'were living at the expense of the monastery', though Eudes is not specific as to whether they were merely living on the income of the house or within the precincts.[27] Clearly, bad leadership on the part of the abbot had led to a situation whereby members of his immediate and extended family profited from his access to the income of St-Ouen to the detriment of the community. Similar problems were discovered at Mont-St-Michel in 1256 where complaints were made to Eudes in chapter that Abbot Richard III's actions were diminishing the financial resources of the monastery. He had gone so far as to provide dowries for several of his nieces and had maintained one of his nephews at great expense in the secular schools and had also bought him an expensive book, the entire Corpus legum.[28] Alienation of monastery property was completely forbidden by monastic statutes. The statutes of Pope Gregory IX (1227–41) specifically forbade abbots to transfer immovable property belonging to their monasteries to relatives in need. Movable property could only be bestowed in small amounts as alms.[29] In the case of the abbot of Mont-St-Michel, Archbishop Eudes and the community had good reason for serious complaint. Not only were the abbot's relatives profiting at the expense of the monks' material needs, but the diversion of revenue meant that there would be less money to spend on enhancing the spiritual side of monastic life, the giving of alms and the maintenance of buildings.[30] Certainly, providing dowries for nieces was not an acceptable use of funds in a community made up of celibate men devoted to the worship of God.

Family members could also be found in monastic houses as servants. In these cases it was their physical presence and actions within the monastic precincts that caused conflict. In many cases, servants were relatives of the superior of the house which added another dimension to the problem. At Beaulieu in 1253, the prior had two nephews who performed their duties in a much more rebellious way than did the other servants. One of the nephews, by the name of Thomas, was illfamed of incontinence and dined on sumptuous

26 Bonnin, p. 495 and Register, p. 563. See also P. E. Pobst, 'Visitation of Religious and Clergy by Archbishop Eudes Rigaud of Rouen', Religion, Text and Society in Medieval Spain and Northern Europe: Essays in Honour of J. N. Hillgarth, ed. T. E. Burman, M. D. Meyerson and L. Shopkow, Papers in Medieval Studies 16 (Toronto, 2002), p. 233.
27 Bonnin, p. 551 and Register, p. 631.
28 Bonnin, p. 246 and Register, p. 274. For Abbot Richard see Gallia Christiana, vol. 11, cols 522–3. See also Johnson, Equal in Monastic Profession, p. 27. In contrast, the prior of St-Hymer-en-Auge (appendix A, no. 79) apparently had permission from his abbot (of Bec) to support a nephew in Paris from the community's resources: Bonnin, p. 296 and Register, p. 355.
29 Bonnin, p. 646 and Register, p. 742.
30 We have already seen how poorly maintained buildings caused a reduction in the quality of sacred space in chapter three.

food in his own room. According to Archbishop Eudes, Thomas's association with Beaulieu damaged the reputation of the community.[31] At Lierru, Eudes ordered the prior to send his brother away, a man who was both dishonest and of bad reputation.[32] More serious abuses were perpetrated by Thomas, a relative of the prior of Liancourt. Not only did he bestow the goods of the priory on his concubines in the village, he also brought one woman into the dormitory and had sex with her in front of a novice.[33] Community reputations, like personal reputations, were fragile and, furthermore, were vital in attracting additional material support from potential donors. Again the symbiotic relationship between physical space and the practices performed in it are underlined: inappropriate behaviour by either professed monks and nuns or lay persons meant that the sacred space was profaned.

Close relatives were welcomed into the monastic community under certain circumstances and provided they behaved in an appropriate manner. At the Augustinian house at St-Lô, Archbishop Eudes chided the abbot for being too severe towards the canons' families when they came to visit.[34] At Aumale, a Benedictine house, the mothers of the novices were allowed to dine at the house occasionally, but only in the 'great common hall', presumably the hall in the abbey's guest house. Their presence in any other rooms was specifically forbidden.[35] Some of the novices were quite possibly still young boys. Allowing their mothers to visit was a kindness to both the boys and women concerned and these visits may have fallen into the category of necessity that Archbishop Anselm did not define in his letter to Mabilia, discussed above. Clearly the archbishop recognised the need for some contact between professed religious and their closest relatives, mothers in particular. To maintain endowments and benefactions the potential donors had to be allowed some access to religious communities otherwise it might be all too easy to forget about those monks and nuns shut away in their cloisters and allowed only limited contact with the outside world. It was a fine line that professed religious had to tread between maintenance of a sacred space within the world and the need to attract the financial support for that maintenance.

Family vocations

The most acceptable form of contact between religious houses and their lay supporters was of course through the giving up of a family member to the service of God. At the most obvious level, families were a source of potential recruits for new foundations. Patronage of religious houses and the reasons behind it have been discussed in detail by scholars elsewhere, so I shall only

---

31   Bonnin, p. 169 and *Register*, p. 186.
32   Appendix A, no. 46; Bonnin, p. 306 and *Register*, p. 348.
33   Bonnin, p. 192 and *Register*, p. 207.
34   Bonnin, p. 87 and *Register*, p. 99.
35   Bonnin, p. 497 and *Register*, p. 566.

consider a few examples here.[36] Concentration of members of the same family can be found in the early histories of some of the Norman nunneries. Two abbesses of Almenèches, Emma and Matilda, were aunt and niece. The eleventh-century pancarte of St-Léger records two nuns from the founding family of Humphrey of Vieilles, and three nuns from the family of one of Humphrey's vassals, whilst two daughters of Richer II, the founder of Chaise-Dieu-du-Theil, were prioresses there: Julienne in the mid-twelfth century and Félicie in the early thirteenth.[37] I have speculated that some of the groupings we have encountered in chapter three may reflect similar family ties. The importance of ensuring a relative was located in the cloister is reflected in the record of a quitclaim of Robert of Tosny to the abbey of Marmoutier, near Tours. The document is a record of Robert's renunciation of some land of which he had previously challenged the monks' possession. In return, the abbey granted that either Robert or his brother, Berengar, could become a monk. If both chose not to enter the cloister, Robert's son could enter in their place.[38] Emily Tabuteau argues that this agreement was intended to ensure that at least one member of the family benefited from the grant through reservation of a place in the community.[39] By allowing the option of one of three different men becoming a monk, Robert hoped that should he or his brother not be so inclined, then his son would, thus ensuring the presence of a relative within the cloister and the provision of the wider spiritual benefits this would entail for the rest of the family.

The most remarkable and interesting way in which families were received into monastic space is illustrated by the widows who entered male monasteries.[40] These women had been wives and mothers before deciding to pursue a religious vocation. Their gendered identity as mothers proved important in their choice of vocation.[41] Among the most prominent of these widows were Heloise, mother of Herluin (d.1070), founder and first abbot of Bec; Eve, wife of William Crispin and mother of Gilbert Crispin (d.1117/18) another monk of Bec and later abbot of Westminster; Basilia of Gournay and her niece

[36]   See, for example, Cownie, *Religious Patronage*; Johnson, *Equal in Monastic Profession*; Potts, *Monastic Revival* and S. Thompson, *Women Religious*. For more localised studies of individual families and houses see, D. Bates and V. Gazeau, 'L'abbaye de Grestain et la famille d'Herluin de Conteville', AN, 40 (1990), pp. 5–30; S. F. Hockey, 'William fitz Osbern and the Endowment of his Abbey of Lyre', ANS, 3 (1980), pp. 95–105; J. Potter, 'The Benefactors of Bec and the Politics of Priories', ANS, 21 (1998, 1999), pp. 175–92 and Ward, 'Fashions in Monastic Endowment'. For Lyre, see Appendix A, no. 50. For comparative material from England, see Pestell, *Landscapes of Monastic Foundation*, pp. 175–82 and J. Burton, *The Monastic Order in Yorkshire 1069–1215*, Cambridge Studies in Medieval Life and Thought, 4th series 40 (Cambridge, 1999), pp. 182–215.
[37]   For St-Léger see *Regesta regum*, no. 217 and for Chaise-Dieu see Martin, 'Un couvent des femmes', p. 290.
[38]   Fauroux, no. 157, pp. 342–3.
[39]   E. Z. Tabuteau, *Transfers of Property in Eleventh-Century Norman Law* (Chapel Hill and London, 1988), p. 17.
[40]   Michel Parisse's study of widowhood focuses on women who retired to nunneries, M. Parisse, 'Des veuves au monastère', *Veuves et veuvage dans le haut moyen âge*, ed. M. Parisse (Paris, 1993), pp. 255–74.
[41]   See below.

Ansfrida who likewise retired to Bec;[42] Eulalia, *sanctimonialis* of St-Wandrille, and her daughter;[43] and Emma, wife of Arnold of Echauffour, who took the veil at Lessay.[44] However, instances of women entering houses of men were not limited to the early part of our period nor just to noble women. From the thirteenth century, Archbishop Eudes records another cluster of women who entered houses of Augustinian canons at Corneville, Beaulieu, Sausseuse, St-Laurent-en-Lyons, and Mont-Deux-Amants, and one Benedictine house, St-Martin-de-Pontoise, as lay sisters.[45] Informal groups of women located at male monasteries were not a phenomenon confined to Normandy. In the second half of the eleventh century, Hersend gave the abbey of St-Jean-d'Angely a substantial allod with the provision that she would later become a nun and stay in Vayres with her son who was a monk there; and Ludolf, a monk of St-Laurent in the province of Reims, took his sister with him to live in the abbey where she took the veil.[46] In eleventh-century England, several male houses had communities of women attached to them.[47]

Information regarding which spaces within the monastic precincts these women occupied is scarce, though some details survive as to where they might have lived or worked. The presence of Herluin's mother, Heloise, at Bec's original site of Bonneville is recorded in Gilbert Crispin's *Life* of Herluin where he notes that she performed 'the duty of a handmaid, washing the garments of God's servants and doing most scrupulously all the extremely hard work imposed on her'.[48] On one occasion, she was the subject of divine intervention when the building in which she was baking bread caught fire. Despite Herluin initially giving thanks to God that his mother's life had been taken whilst engaged in sacred work within the monastery, Heloise survived the blaze.[49] The information regarding Eulalia comes from St Vulfran's miracle collection, written at St-Wandrille. One of the monks had given Eulalia's daughter a picture of Christ which she had entrusted to her mother for safekeeping. Eulalia hid the picture under the mattress where it was discovered and then removed by their pet fox. Miraculously the picture was recovered

---

42 See A. Porée, *Histoire de l'abbaye du Bec*, 2 vols (Évreux, 1901), vol. 1, pp. 182–4; K. Quirk, 'Experiences of Motherhood in Normandy, 1050–1150' (Ph.D. thesis, University of Cambridge, 1997), p. 144; van Houts, *Memory and Gender*, p. 55 and Vaughn, *St Anselm and the Handmaidens of God*, pp. 70–5, 91–8. Basilia, Ansfrida and Eve are recorded in *Chronicon Beccensis*, PL, vol. 150, col. 648.

43 *Miracula sancti Vulfranni*, p. 158.

44 Appendix A, no. 44 for Lessay; OV, vol. 2, pp. 124–7.

45 For example, Bonnin, pp. 8, 130, 190, 318, 513, 475 and *Register*, pp. 119, 202, 10, 363, 586, 542. St-Martin-de-Pontoise was not in Normandy but did fall within the archdiocese of Rouen and so probably had strong links with religious communities within our sphere of study.

46 Johnson, *Equal in Monastic Profession*, p. 29.

47 S. Foot, *Veiled Women*, Studies in Early Medieval Britain 2 vols (Aldershot, 2000), vol. 1, pp. 172–9 and vol. 2, pp. 49–52, 79–81 and 157–8. As with Normandy, the evidence for religious women in male communities is often fragmentary and some only survives in very late sources, for example the presence of women at St Albans is reported by the thirteenth-century chronicler Matthew Paris.

48 Gilbert Crispin, *Vita Herluini*, p. 193 and trans. *Normans in Europe*, p. 73.

49 Gilbert Crispin, *Vita Herluini*, p. 193 and trans. *Normans in Europe*, pp. 73–4.

three days later outside the house.[50] It would appear from these two texts that the widows living under obedience to a male monastery inhabited small houses somewhere in the monastic precinct. The evidence for Heloise is more ambiguous, as she probably baked the bread in the monastery's kitchen and not in her own little house. Kitchens, as Gilbert's story reminds us, were prone to catch fire and thus would have been situated away from the main cloister.

The laity were prohibited from entering the cloister, with more specific injunctions against women in houses of monks and men in houses of nuns.[51] These general prohibitions make the presence of these women in some of the most important abbeys of the time even more intriguing. Provision must have been made for these women to participate in the spiritual life of their chosen monastery to some extent. It is probable that Heloise, Eulalia and other widows had access to the monks' church where they would have sat in the nave during the daily office as it was the most accessible part of the church and did not entail entrance through the cloister. Although these women may not have had access to the monks' areas within the church and cloister, enough contact existed between them for one of the monks of St-Wandrille to give Eulalia's daughter the picture mentioned above, presumably a rejected piece of parchment from the monastery's scriptorium. Lay sisters in other monasteries probably had similar arrangements. Alternatively, such women might have inhabited a mini cloister or small chapel somewhere in the monastic precincts in which they could recite the offices. Orderic Vitalis records that on at least two occasions a small chapel attached to his monastery of St-Évroul 'where the blessed father Évroul had devoted himself in solitude to heavenly meditation' provided temporary shelter for nuns.[52] It seems that these women lived at the site in a chapel near the source of the river Ouche, so we can speculate that the building took the form of a small oratory with living accommodation attached.

Why women like Heloise, Eve, Basilia, Eulalia and her daughter retired to male monasteries in their widowhood remains a matter of speculation and cannot be attributed to a single reason. The most likely motive was an economic one. By making a donation of land, goods or services in return for living space and maintenance, the women made safe provision for their retirement.[53] Following the death of their husbands, their sons and daughters-in-law might have considered their presence in the marital home superfluous.

---

[50]   *Miracula sancti Vulfranni*, p. 158.

[51]   See chapter two.

[52]   OV, vol. 2, pp. 102–3 and vol. 6, pp. 36–7. Judith and Emma, sisters of Abbot Robert of Grandmesnil sheltered there following their brother's exile in c.1061, though they later renounced the veil and joined him in Italy. Later, Abbess Emma and three nuns came to St-Évroul following the destruction of their abbey of Almenèches by fire in 1103. See also OV, vol. 2, p. 76 and note 7 above.

[53]   See also Foot, *Veiled Women*, vol. 1, p. 172. In this way, they would be similar to people known as corrodians later in the Middle Ages (discussed in chapter two), but their commitment to the spiritual side of their life at Bec and St-Wandrille seems to have been greater than that of corrodians more generally.

By making donations to a religious house, not only could they provide for their old age, but also follow a religious path that might have been denied them earlier in their lives in favour of marriage. Widowhood freed these women from the biological constraints imposed by marriage and motherhood enabling them to pursue a life of chastity and religious service. Both Heloise and Eve Crispin handed over goods to the abbey where they were to spend the rest of their lives; Bec was in fact founded on Heloise's dower lands.[54] As late as the thirteenth century other women made similar arrangements. In a contract with the canons of Cherbourg, dated 1284, Jean le Goupil and his wife, Églatine, of the nearby parish of Octeville, made a donation to the canons. Jean and Églatine were to provide services in return for three white loaves, a pitcher of beer and a portion from the abbey's kitchens per day. Jean was to serve as the abbey's porter, provost and baker whilst Églatine was to cultivate and spin linen and hemp as well as feeding the animals.[55] Rihaut, the widow of Sanson Le Palefoi gave the canons of Cherbourg all her goods and inheritance at Gouberville when she entered as a lay sister in 1255.[56]

In considering why these widows chose to retire to male houses, one must also consider why they did not choose to become nuns in a house of women religious. There is a crucial difference between living as a semi-religious in a fairly independent manner, as did the widows discussed above, and becoming a fully professed nun and playing a full part in the life of the community by taking one's place in the choir and chapter. Examples do exist from the early part of our period indicating that women did retire to nunneries as widows and after they had been active in the world. The names of several women described as wives or mothers are recorded in the charters for the abbey of La Trinité in Caen and are listed by Lucien Musset.[57] The husbands of at least two of these women, Havise, wife of Fulk of Aunou, and Avicia, wife of Robert son of Ansfrey, were still alive when their wives entered the abbey.[58] The other women mentioned are possibly widows. The mother of the monk Gundulf also settled to the religious life in the abbey of La Trinité.[59] At Montivilliers, three possible widows, Wimer, wife of Ansfrey the seneschal, Hadvise, and Benselina, wife of Ralph Giffard, entered the community along

---

54 For Heloise, Abulafia and Evans, 'Introduction', *Works of Gilbert Crispin*, p. xxii; Gilbert Crispin *Vita Herluini*, p. 185, note 2; Fauroux, no. 98, p. 251. For Eve, Milo Crispin, *Miraculum quo b. Mariae subvenit Guillelmo Crispino Seniori: ubi de nobili Crispinorum genere agitur*, PL 150, cols 741–2 and trans. *Normans in Europe*, p. 88.

55 Arnoux, p. 162, citing an original charter.

56 Arnoux, p. 162, citing an original charter.

57 *Les actes de Guillaume le Conquérant et de la reine Mathilda pour les abbayes caennaises*, ed. L. Musset, MSAN 37 (1967), p. 48 and nos 8 (1082) and 27 (1109–13). The 1082 charter is also published in *Regesta regum*, no. 59, pp. 271–86. See also J. Walmsley, 'The Early Abbesses, Nuns and Female Tenants of the Abbey of Holy Trinity, Caen', *Journal of Ecclesiastical History*, 48 (1997), pp. 425–44.

58 *Les actes … pour les abbayes caennaises*, no. 8 and *Regesta regum*, no. 59.

59 *The Life of Gundulf Bishop of Rochester*, ed. R. Thomson, Toronto Medieval Latin Texts (Toronto, 1997), p. 31 and translated as *The Life of the Venerable Man, Gundulf, Bishop of Rochester*, by the nuns of Malling Abbey (Malling Abbey, 1968), p. 10.

with Adela, whose husband, Gerald Boctoy, was still alive.[60] It is possible that in the late eleventh century not enough places were available for those women who wished to pursue the religious life and so some noble women chose to retire to male houses. By the thirteenth century, however, there was greater provision for women who wished to become nuns in Normandy so why did women enter houses of Augustinian canons? In the case of Églatine and Rihaut, family considerations may have been mixed in with the fact that no houses of female religious existed in the Cherbourg area at this time.[61] As regards the women in Eudes's register mentioned as having retired to houses of Augustinian canons, both Corneville and Mont-Deux-Amants were situated near the female communities of St-Léger-des-Préaux and Fontaine-Guérard. If there were no obvious family connections, why did these women choose to go to a male house? The answer lies in a combination of economic circumstances and the character of the religious life as a lay sister or choir nun. The relatively unregulated and more independent life of a lay sister was probably more attractive to women used to being in charge of their own households as it did not involve the same degree of enclosure or regulation.[62] For those women who came from backgrounds lower down the social scale to the predominantly noble choir nuns, entrance to a community as a lay sister was a much cheaper option as the dowry required for a choir nun was substantial.

Family ties rooted in the ownership of land combined with the presence of a male relative, particularly a son, were the primary motives for women to attach themselves to a male monastery.[63] The identity of these widows as mothers continued to be important after their acceptance of the semi-religious life. It is possible that they felt a stronger attachment to a male house with which their families had long-standing relations as benefactors than they did to any of the female abbeys to which their families had no connection. After marriage, women, as mothers of the succeeding generation of sons, identified strongly with the ethos of their husbands' families. This allegiance extended beyond political and military ambitions to include religious aspirations too. Eve Crispin's conversion to some form of religious life at Bec was the final expression of her long devotion to the monastery with which her husband's family was so closely connected, and indeed of her adoption of her husband's customs.[64] Basilia's husband, Hugh of Gournay, was also a monk at Bec and their son Gerard later joined the abbey.[65] Moreover, the reputation of monks like Lanfranc and Anselm may well have been a contributing factor to Eve

---

[60]   *Regesta regum*, no. 212, pp. 654–63, dated 1068 x 1076.

[61]   The nearest female community was St-Michel-de Bosc.

[62]   This argument has also been put forward by Patricia Halpin for later Anglo-Saxon England in P. Halpin, 'Women Religious in Late Anglo-Saxon England', *Haskins Society Journal*, 6 (1994), p. 104. See also Foot, *Veiled Women*, vol. 1 p. 173 who argues that the case remains unproven.

[63]   Quirk, 'Experiences of Motherhood', p. 143.

[64]   Milo Crispin, *Miraculum quo b. Mariae subvenit Guillelmo Crispino Seniori*, cols 741–2 and trans. *Normans in Europe*, p. 88.

[65]   GND, vol. 2, pp. 214–15 and notes.

and Basilia's decision to retire to Bec and other women may have felt the same. Kathleen Quirk has suggested that Anselm's interest in the imagery of spiritual motherhood may have played a role in this development.[66] The widows who took up the religious life in male monasteries were not only biological mothers to their own sons, but became spiritual mothers to every monk in the community. Like Lanfranc, his predecessor as archbishop of Canterbury, Anselm had also been a monk of Bec and both men wrote with great warmth about the Bec widows. Lanfranc, in a letter to Gilbert Crispin, written in about the winter of 1073, speaks of Eve's care for his nephew who was a monk at Bec, in calling him her son.[67] Anselm likewise refers to the affection that existed between Eve and the monks of Bec.[68]

This idea of spiritual motherhood is also present in Anselm's letters concerning Basilia of Gournay whom he describes explicitly a number of times as 'mother'.[69] Other Bec monks also took up the theme: Milo Crispin wrote, in c.1140, that even before her conversion to the monastic life, Eve had 'embraced the abbot and the monks, admiring them with deep devotion, as if they were her own children. Clothes, and all that she possessed in precious ornaments she handed over for the use of the church and the brethren'.[70] Stephen of Rouen (c.1169) records that the Empress Matilda too became known as 'the mother of the monks' following her long association with the abbey of Bec and its priory of Notre-Dame-du-Pré. She was buried at Bec after her death.[71] Anselm's theology of spiritual motherhood in conjunction with the family connections may well have fostered a particular sense of vocation for the widows at Bec. This vocation may well have been perceived as a more attractive option on the part of women who had been mothers and active in the world, than the more strictly cloistered life of a choir nun. Churchmen may also have seen spiritual motherhood as more acceptable than mixing virgins and widows in the same community. The fact that some houses notably Marcigny, a Cluniac nunnery, were founded with the specific aim of giving older aristocratic women, including widows and married women who had agreed with their husbands to enter religious houses, an opportunity to pursue a vocation lends strength to this very likely

---

66 Quirk, 'Experiences of Motherhood', p. 34.
67 *Letters of Lanfranc*, no. 20, p. 101.
68 Schmitt, vol. 3, no. 22, p. 129 and no. 98, pp. 228–9 and Fröhlich, vol. 1, no. 22, pp. 113–14 and no. 98, p. 247.
69 Schmitt, vol. 3, e.g. no. 118, p. 256 and no. 147, p. 294 and Fröhlich, vol. 1, no. 118, pp. 282–4 and no. 147, pp. 233–4. See also S. N. Vaughn, 'St Anselm and Women', *Haskins Society Journal*, 2 (1990), pp. 88–91.
70 Milo Crispin, *Miraculum quo b. Mariae subvenit Guillelmo Crispino Seniori*, cols 741–2 and trans. *Normans in Europe*, p. 88.
71 Stephen of Rouen, *Draco Normannicus* in *Chronicles*, ed. Howlett, vol. 2, pp. 711–14. For Matilda's relations with Bec see M. Chibnall, 'The Empress Matilda and Bec-Hellouin', *ANS*, 10 (1987), pp. 35–48 and *The Empress Matilda: Queen Consort, Queen Mother and Lady of the English* (Oxford, 1991), pp. 15, 61, 136, 177, 189–90. Matilda gave jewels and relics to the abbey.

explanation that a mother's emotional ties continued throughout her life and crossed spatial and gendered divisions.[72]

Women were not the only family members who took monastic vows, either in full or in part, at monastic houses that had strong links with their family, though it appears that only they took vows or affiliated themselves to a house inhabited by the opposite sex. Orderic Vitalis records a number of boys and men who became monks in houses with family connections at his own monastery of St-Évroul. Reginald, the youngest son of Arnold of Echauffour and thus the grandson of William Giroie, the founder, was given to St-Évroul as an oblate, aged five; another descendant of the Giroie family, William, called Gregory, was given as an oblate, aged nine.[73] Men who had followed a military career came to the cloister late in life, just as did women who had been wives and mothers. In c.1050, Robert of Grandmesnil, son of Robert of Grandmesnil and Hawise, daughter of Giroie, became a monk of St-Évroul under Abbot Thierry: Robert had previously been a knight.[74] Ralph, the son of Giroie and known as the 'Ill-tonsured', became a monk of Marmoutier near Tours late in life. After his final vows he received permission to transfer to St-Évroul where his nephew, Robert of Grandmesnil, was then abbot. Ralph asked God to afflict him with leprosy and having contracted the disease, he lived in a chapel for a long time with a monk named Goscelin and gave counsel to many people.[75] Family ties were obviously important to Ralph rather than an attachment to a particular place, as after Robert of Grandmesnil was expelled and sent into exile in Italy, Ralph returned to his original house of Marmoutier.[76]

Family vocations and ties were not just confined to houses of contemplative monks and nuns. From the twelfth century onwards, there exist examples of family members entering the service of hospitals and leper houses. For example, Ralph, son of Guido, not only made provision for the upkeep of his leprous daughter upon her entry to the hospital of St-Gilles in Pont-Audemer, but also made arrangements for his own entry into the brotherhood at St-Gilles.[77] Ralph's actions suggest a desire on the part of the family to have a share in the care of its afflicted relative and shows that the ties between a father and his daughter were just as strong as those between mother and child. Despite the practice of separation, familial ties did not end with the diagnosis of leprosy.[78] Just as we have seen in the case of the Augustinian houses, pursuing a vocation within a leper house or hospital could provide a

---

[72]   N. Hunt, *Cluny under Saint Hugh, 1049–1109* (London, 1967), pp. 186–191 and Thompson, *Women Religious*, pp. 84–7. Marcigny was founded in 1056 by Geoffrey, the lord of Semur and his brother Hugh, later abbot of Cluny.

[73]   OV, vol. 2, pp. 126–7 and pp. 84–5.

[74]   OV, vol. 2, pp. 40–1.

[75]   OV, vol. 2, pp. 28–9 and 76–7.

[76]   This is possibly because it was too dangerous to stay in Normandy. See E. Johnson, 'The Process of Norman Exile into Southern Italy', *Exile in the Middle Ages*, ed. Napran and van Houts pp. 31–2 and OV, vol. 2, pp. 104–5.

[77]   Mesmin, 'The Leper House of St-Gilles de Pont-Audemer', vol. 1, p. 106 and vol. 2, no. 34.

[78]   For the practice of separation see chapter 2.

means by which a couple could remain together whilst serving God. Engeran and his wife who entered the service of the leper house of St-Gilles together were just such a couple.[79]

The presence of married couples within religious communities caused particular tensions and could lead to conflict, just as nepotism on the part of a superior could. In the case of the widows of Bec, the ties between mother, husband and son, were seen as a positive force as they provided the impetus for a woman to take up a semi-religious life and become a mother not only to her own son, but to the entire community. In the case of married couples in hospitals and leper houses, the exclusive nature of the relationship between husband and wife caused a reduction in the common life of the community. The staff at the mixed hospital in Gournay neglected their spiritual well-being to the extent of not observing any rule at Eudes's visit in 1257. Although the men and women ate together, they clearly did not sleep communally 'in one and the same place', as some of the brothers slept with their wives whenever they pleased.[80] In other words, instead of having separate dormitories allocated to the male and female staff, rooms seem to have been allocated according to marital status. We have already seen in the case of St-Gilles that husbands and wives entered the hospital fraternity together. The married couples at Gournay may be another manifestation of married people taking simple vows, including chastity and obedience, rather than making a profession entailing a lifetime commitment. If this were the case, then they did not uphold the rule on sexual abstinence, one of the vows they were supposed to have taken on entry into the hospital. Despite attempts to regulate the mingling of the sexes, in practice cohabitation presented a real danger to the maintenance of the hospital as a sacred space. Just as not all contact with unprofessed relatives was considered altogether bad, then not all family connections amongst the professed were considered to be good. All contact was subject to the strictures of the various rules laid out for the governance of religious institutions.

I have shown to some extent the variety available to the men and women who wished to pursue the religious life and have also raised questions as to the role of gender and the motivation behind vocations. The evidence challenges some of our preconceived notions of which individuals could enter which houses. At first glance, the presence of noble widows in male communities is indicative of a lack of provision for the number of women wishing to take up the religious life in Normandy. When considered alongside a theology of spiritual motherhood, the presence of Heloise, Eve, Basilia and their contemporaries in monasteries like Bec reveals the existence of an alternative form of vocation in which they could draw on their experiences as wives and mothers to counsel the monks, including their sons and husbands. The presence of such close relatives had the added advantage of providing some form of comfort in their old age. For non-noble women and women who did not wish to pursue the heavily cloistered life of a choir nun, the vocation of a lay sister

79   Mesmin, 'The Leper House of St-Gilles de Pont-Audemer', vol. 1, pp. 107–8 and vol. 2, nos 4, 28, 40 and 102.
80   Bonnin, p. 283 and *Register*, p. 319.

was available. These women, however, would not have had as much freedom as their sisters in nunneries to have a say in the running of the community. Their presence in male communities was tolerated, valued and possibly even encouraged, but they were still on the margins of those communities. The spaces they inhabited were not at the heart of the cloister but elsewhere in the precincts and marginal to the central liturgical areas of the church and chapter house. Like the female followers of Christ, they were liminal and on the margins of accepted religious practice.

For men, however, even those that had been active as soldiers in the secular world before turning to the cloister, the type of religious life practiced by the widows of Bec was not available. Whereas women could use the emotional bonds with their children to pursue a vocation of spiritual motherhood, rooted in their own identity as biological mothers, men were not in the same respect able to be spiritual fathers. Ralph the 'Ill-tonsured', as we have seen, could choose a semi-reclusive life at St-Évroul, but was still very much part of his former monastic community, as is shown by his eventual return to Marmoutier after his nephew and abbot of St-Évroul, Robert of Grandmesnil was exiled. Of course, other religious vocations were open to men. By the end of the eleventh century, soldiers were able to literally take up arms for Christ in order to go on crusade to the Holy Land. Despite the involvement of women in the crusades, notably as the administrators of family estates, in encouraging the men folk and occasionally as fighters, this was not an option that was generally available to them.[81] Both women and men could, however, enter leper houses and hospitals on a more or less equal footing and this seems to have been an attractive option for those couples who, perhaps after having raised a family of their own, wished both to remain together and serve God for the remainder of their days. The examples I have discussed all reveal that for some individuals, close emotional bonds to the nuclear family and monastic vocations were not mutually exclusive: indeed, they were positively beneficial. At Bec especially, the widows' relationship with their husbands and sons in the cloister allowed the sacred space of that monastery to expand and bring more souls within its sphere of influence.

Burial

The families of monks and nuns influenced the architecture and internal arrangement of both the church and claustral areas of the monastic houses in which their relatives were pursuing vocations in one very important respect, burial. Much work has been done on monastic burial, but little from an explicitly gendered or spatial perspective. Some scholars like Philippe Ariès

[81] For a discussion of women in the crusades see M. Bennet, 'Virile Latins, Effeminate Greeks and Strong Women: Gender Definitions on Crusade?' and K. Caspri-Reisfeld, 'Women Warriors during the Crusades, 1095–1254' both in Gendering the Crusades, ed. S. B. Edgington and S. Lambert (Cardiff, 2001), pp. 16–30 and 94–107.

and Paul Binski have argued that the burial of the dead within churches and monasteries was a cause of conflict between the competing needs of the groups that used the church, for example a religious community on the one hand and the laity on the other, and that the Church periodically tried to resist claims by the laity to be buried in such areas.[82] Various Cistercian abbots across Europe were punished by the general chapter of the order for burying lay persons within the claustral areas of their abbeys, before it ruled that the laity could be received for burial within Cistercian monasteries. The abbot of Vallis Sanctae Mariae in the diocese of Paris was punished in 1205 for burying a noble man in his church and the abbot of Vieuville for burying a woman in 1201.[83] Brian Golding in contrast emphasises the benefits of burial to both parties, in terms of prestige and endowments.[84]

The cases I have identified in Normandy – all from the eleventh and twelfth centuries – show that burial within monasteries was considered as being inextricably linked with the prerogative acquired by a donor or founder after a large benefaction. In this way the living and the dead were brought into closer fellowship and the ties between sacred and secular, heavenly and earthly space were strengthened.[85] Monastic foundations welcomed the chance to bury a great patron or founder, no doubt because of the prestige this would bring to the house. For example, Juhel de Mayenne and most of his family had agreed to be buried at the abbey of Savigny. When Juhel later founded Fontaine-Daniel in c.1200 and wished to be buried there, Savigny tried in vain to insist that his earlier promise be respected after his death in April 1220.[86] For some monastic houses, a founder or benefactor's choice to be buried elsewhere was seen as disloyal.[87] Family allegiance functioned the other way around too. In the twelfth century, Empress Matilda wished to be buried at the abbey of Bec, a foundation with which she had enjoyed a long association, contrary to the expectations of her father Henry I, who regarded Rouen cathedral, where previous members of the ducal house were buried, as

82   P. Ariès, *The Hour of our Death* (Harmondsworth, 1981), pp. 45–51 and P. Binski, *Medieval Death: Ritual and Representation* (London, 1996), pp. 57–8 and 74–7. For a survey of English evidence, particularly archaeological material, see R. Gilchrist and B. Sloane, *Requiem: the Medieval Monastic Cemetery in Britain* (London, 2005), especially pp. 56–70.

83   Cassidy-Welch, *Monastic Spaces and their Meanings*, p. 232 and *Statuta*, vol. 1, 1205, no. 15, p. 465; 1201, no. 15, p. 266 and 1217, no. 3, p. 310.

84   Brian Golding has written extensively on Norman and Anglo-Norman burial amongst the higher ranks of society. See, for example, B. Golding 'Burials and Benefactions: an Aspect of Monastic Patronage in Thirteenth-Century England', *England in the Thirteenth Century: Proceedings of the 1984 Harlaxton Symposium*, ed. W. M. Ormrod (Woodbridge, 1985), pp. 64–75 and 'Anglo-Norman Knightly Burials', *The Ideals and Practice of Medieval Knighthood*, ed. C. Harper-Bill and R. Harvey (Woodbridge, 1986), pp. 35–48.

85   See also P. Geary, *Living with the Dead in the Middle Ages* (Ithaca and London, 1994).

86   G. Day, 'Juhel III of Mayenne and Savigny', *Analecta Cisterciensia*, 34 (1980), pp. 103–28.

87   Golding, 'Burials and Benefactions' p. 64.

more suitable, even though no dukes had been buried there since William Longsword.[88]

If a founder or patron was wealthy enough, then construction of an abbatial church might be designed so as to incorporate a grand tomb at the heart of the liturgical space of the monastery.[89] Bishop Hugh of Lisieux died in 1077 and was buried in the nuns' choir of the abbey of St-Désir in Lisieux, which he had founded with his mother, Lesline, countess of Eu. We have already noted that provision for Hugh's eventual burial may have been made right from the start of the building's construction in the shape of an ornamental Romanesque pavement at St-Désir which possibly formed a symbolic access towards Hugh's tomb and the altar beyond. Given the conflict between the nuns and the cathedral canons who both claimed Hugh's body for burial, the pavement was perhaps designed so that the nuns could express due reverence to their founder in a suitably impressive liturgical manner. Thanks to William the Conqueror's adjudication in their favour, the community was able to do so.[90] The destruction of this church in the mid-twelfth century by Angevin soldiers means that we do not know whether other burials had taken place within it and whether the nuns would have continued to use the pavement in a similar way on later occasions.[91]

Monastic churches did not have to be designed in a particular manner for founding families and other important benefactors to use them as a burial place. Indeed, graves were not confined to the church, but can be found in the cloister and chapter house. We know of several families in Normandy who favoured particular religious houses as burial places, but I wish to focus on the burials in two houses in particular: St-Évroul and St-Pierre-des-Préaux.[92]

The monastery of St-Évroul was closely connected with the Giroie family.[93] Although a Merovingian community had existed in the forest of Ouche for over two centuries, the civil wars of the tenth century had caused the commu-

---

[88] GND, vol. 2, pp. 246–7 and Chibnall, Empress Matilda, p. 61.

[89] Gilchrist and Sloane also argue that burial intentions could directly affect church design, citing the Augustinian priory of Kirkham as an example. The lords of Helmsley, the de Roos family, funded the rebuilding of the east end and at least four generations of the family were buried there: Gilchrist and Sloane, Requiem, p. 57.

[90] OV, vol. 3, pp. 16–17.

[91] Deshayes, 'Le pavement roman', p. 471. I think it is possible that the original structure was designed to be incorporated into a larger cruciform building. G. Simon argued that it was this later structure that was the first church and was replaced in the mid-sixteenth century when the bell tower collapsed; G. Simon, 'L'abbaye de St-Désir de Lisieux et ses églises successives', Annuaire des Cinq Départements de la Normandie (1927), p. 32.

[92] For monastic burial in Normandy more generally see Cownie, Religious Patronage, p. 214 in which she includes a list of known burials in the region, and Golding, 'Anglo-Norman Knightly Burials'.

[93] For the Giroie family see P. Baudin, 'Une famille chatelaine sur les confines normanno-manceaux: les Géré (Xe–XIIIe siècles), Archéologie médiévale, 22 (1992), pp. 309–56 and J.-M. Maillefer, 'Une famille aristocratique aux confins de la Normandie les Géré au XIe siècle', Autour du pouvoir ducal Normand Xe–XIIe siècles, ed. L. Musset, J.-M. Bouvris and J.-M. Maillefer, Cahiers des Annales de Normandie 17 (Caen, 1985), pp. 175–206. For Hugh of Grandmesnil see, M. Hagger, 'Kinship and Identity in

nity to scatter. William Giroie and the Grandmesnil brothers later established a new community in the mid-eleventh century and Duke William formally approved the foundation and granted the first privileges sometime in 1050.[94] St-Évroul was the home of Orderic Vitalis whose history records in great detail the persons buried and the locations of their tombs within the precincts of the monastery. The community, by allowing burial in the cloister and the chapter house, honoured members of the Giroie family. Robert Giroie, Arnold of Echauffour, Ralph of Montpinçon, and Robert of Rhuddlan were all buried in the cloister, in the case of Robert of Rhuddlan, on the south side of the church, that is to say the north cloister walk.[95] Hugh of Grandmesnil, who was received into the fraternity of the monks, and his closest family including his wife, sons and daughters-in-law, were all buried in the chapter house.[96] According to Orderic, Hugh's wife, Adeliza of Beaumont, was buried on the right hand side of Abbot Mainer.[97] It is interesting to note that either the monks' desire to honour their founders or the power of the founding family was so great as to allow the burial of women, albeit carefully selected women, in such an honoured position within the monastery. The chapter house in a male community was an area that women would rarely, if ever, be allowed to enter. Close members of the founder's family, regardless of their biological sex, were welcomed into the fellowship of the monks at their death. The family members of Giroie and Grandmesnil were buried in a location that was denied to the vast majority of monks who would have been interred within the cemetery, usually located to the north of the abbey church which was a burial place open to all members of the community in keeping with their common life. The chapter house was where the daily business of the monastery was conducted, where the monks gathered to hear chapters of the rule read and where they received visiting dignitaries: it was at the very heart of monastery life. An indication of the importance of this space and the honoured place it held in the life of the community is illustrated by the fact that the only monks that Orderic records has having been granted burial in this area were figures greatly honoured within the community: Abbot Mainer, Abbot Osbern and Guitmund, Osbern's companion. Osbern was originally buried in the cloister before his body was translated to the chapter house by Abbot Mainer.[98]

Eleventh-Century Normandy: the Case of Hugh de Grandmesnil, c.1040–1098', JMH, 32 (2006), pp. 212–30.

[94] For more information regarding the early years of St-Évroul see OV, vol. 1, pp. 11–14 and M. Chibnall, 'Ecclesiastical Patronage and the Growth of Feudal Estates at the Time of the Norman Conquest', AN, 4 (1958), pp. 105–8. Golding also discusses the association between the families and the monastery in 'Anglo-Norman Knightly Burials'.

[95] OV, vol. 2, pp. 80–1, 124–5; vol. 3, pp. 164–5, and vol. 4, pp. 142–3. Three generations of the Montpinçon family were associated with St-Évroul. See M. Chibnall, 'Liens de fraternitas entre l'abbaye de St-Évroult et les laics (XIe–XIIe siècles)', Les mouvances laïques des orders religieux, p. 238.

[96] OV, vol. 4, pp. 338–9. For the fraternity of St-Évroul, see Chibnall, 'Liens de fraternitas entre l'abbaye de St-Évroult et les laics', p. 237.

[97] OV, vol. 4, pp. 338–9.

[98] OV, vol. 4, pp. 338–9, vol. 2, pp. 134–5.

The tradition of family burial at St-Évroul was replicated in some of its daughter houses: Gilbert of Auffay and members of his family were buried at Notre-Dame in Auffay in the Pays de Caux, a priory of monks dependent on St-Évroul. Gilbert and his wife Beatrice were buried in the church.[99] Their son, Walter and his wife Avice were buried in the cloister by the door of the church, presumably the door in the south wall through which the monks would enter.[100] Touchingly, Orderic records that Walter was buried at his wife's feet.[101] Again, we see how lay people were received into the monks' areas in their choice of burial location. In the case of Walter and Avice, their tombs were located in a part of the monastery that the monks would constantly be passing through on their way in and out of the church. Their tomb acted as a reminder to the monks to pray for the souls of their benefactors. In addition, Richard, the son of Walter and Avice, was also buried at the priory, though Orderic does not record the location of this particular tomb.[102] In this last case, the relationship between the dead person and the original founder, although close enough to be honoured by the monks was also distant enough not to merit burial in one of the more significant areas of the priory like the chapter house, cloister or church.

The tombs created for the burial of the founder and close members of his or her family, for example sons, daughters and spouses, as well as other important benefactors, not only acted as a final resting place for their earthly remains, but also as important reminders of their secular power. Although the tombs themselves have long gone, a woodcut survives of five such monuments in the Benedictine abbey of St-Pierre-des-Préaux, a house of monks founded in 1035 by Humphrey of Vieilles of the Beaumont family.[103] Humphrey's sons, Roger Beaumont (d. c.1093) and Robert fitz Humphrey (d. after 1054),[104] were buried in the chapter house of the abbey where they were later joined by Roger's sons, Count Robert I of Meulan who had died 5 June 1118 in England, and Henry Beaumont (d.1119). Waleran II of Meulan, son of Robert (d.1118?) became a monk of St-Pierre before he died in April 1166 and was also interred in the chapter house. The tombs were later capped with carved slabs, dating from the twelfth century, decorated with effigies in relief. David Crouch has suggested that these tombs were commissioned either by Waleran in his own lifetime or by his son after his death.[105] The tombs provided a focus for the remembrance of the founder and his descendants as well as visual representations of the power of the Beaumonts and the protection they offered to the monastery.

99   OV, vol. 4, pp. 112–13.
100 OV, vol. 3, pp. 256–9.
101 OV, vol. 3, pp. 256–7.
102 OV, vol. 3, pp. 258–9.
103 J. Mabillon, *Annales Ordinis S. Benedicti occidentalium monachorum patriarchae*, 6 vols (Paris, 1703–39), vol. 5, pp. 328–9.
104 For the date of Robert's death see D. Bates, 'The Conqueror's Adolescence', ANS, 25 (2003), pp. 1–18.
105 D. Crouch, *The Beaumont Twins: the Roots and Branches of Power in the Twelfth Century*. Cambridge Studies in Medieval Life and Thought, 4th series 1 (Cambridge, 1986), pp. 3, 78.

The liturgical function of the chapter house has already been discussed, but it was also the prime location where a large part of the monastery's secular business was conducted and where benefactors might be received.[106] For visiting dignitaries to St-Pierre-des-Préaux or St-Évroul, the presence of tombs as visible reminders of the monasteries' patrons would serve to instil awe and demonstrate that the monastery had some very powerful protectors. As Brian Golding has argued, the body of a great magnate was a potent symbol and was regarded as 'almost a secular relic'.[107]

The examples I have discussed above date from the eleventh and early twelfth centuries. It is not the purpose of this work to discuss in detail the changing patterns of patronage in the Norman and Anglo-Norman world, as this has been considered extensively elsewhere.[108] It is clear, however, that patronage did change as time moved on from the initial foundation of a religious house. Many of the Norman nobles also held land in England after 1066 and for some families, like the Clares, their English lands became the basis of their patrimony. Although grants might still be made to Norman houses, newer English foundations received their patrons' bodies for burial. The creation of new religious orders also affected the choice of burial place, as landholders might choose to endow a new house rather than an existing Benedictine one. The final factor which could influence burial practice was a change in dynasty, as in the case of a female heir marrying. We have already seen how Eve Crispin adopted her husband's customs after her marriage; other women did the same, favouring their marital families' religious houses over those of their natal family.

Whereas important supporters and vassals of the dukes of Normandy established their own mausolea in monasteries with which they had strong connections as we have seen at St-Évroul, Auffay and St-Pierre-Des-Préaux, the ducal house itself never really established a specific burial place for its family members.[109] The first two Norman dukes, Rollo (d. 931) and William Longsword, were buried in the cathedral church at Rouen. Richard I (d.996) and Richard II (d.1027) were both buried in Richard I's foundation at Fécamp: the same site held a ducal palace. Richard III (d.1027) was buried at St-Ouen in Rouen where his son, Nicholas, later became abbot.[110] The death of Robert

106 See chapter three.
107 Golding, 'Burials and Benefactions', p. 74. See also A. Martindale, 'Patrons and Minders: The Intrusion of the Secular into Sacred Spaces in the Late Middle Ages', The Church and the Arts, ed. D. Wood, Studies in Church History 28 (Oxford, 1992), pp. 143–78.
108 See for example, Chibnall, 'Ecclesiastical Patronage and the Growth of Feudal Estates'; Cownie, Religious Patronage and Golding, 'Burial and Benefactions'.
109 For the burial places of the Norman dukes see 'The Brevis relatio de Guillelmo nobilissimo comite Normannorum written by a Monk of Battle Abbey', ed. and trans. E. van Houts, History and Family Traditions in England and the Continent 1000–1200, Variorum Collected Studies (Aldershot, 1999) VII, pp. 40a–40 and L. Musset, 'Les sépultures des souverains normands: un aspect de l'idéologie du pouvoir', Autour du pouvoir ducal normand Xe–XIIe siècles, ed. Musset, Bouvris and Maillefer, pp. 19–44.
110 GND, vol. 2, pp. 46–7 and note 1. Nicholas was an illegitimate son of Duke Richard III. He was originally an oblate of Fécamp before enjoying a long abbacy at St-Ouen

the Magnificent (d.1035) whilst on pilgrimage to the Holy Land, meant that his body was buried overseas in Nicaea. After Robert's death, the dukes tended to be buried in the churches of their own foundations or at abbeys they particularly favoured; however, William of Malmesbury records how William the Conqueror made an attempt through a special envoy to bring back the body of his father, presumably so that he could be reinterred at Fécamp. The envoy, hearing of William's death on the way home, settled in Apulia and buried Robert there.[111]

As far as Duke William the Conqueror, and his wife, Matilda, are concerned, Orderic Vitalis provides us with some information regarding their burial. Instead of electing to be buried either in Rouen, the capital of the duchy, or at Fécamp, founded by his ancestors, William chose to be buried in his own foundation of St-Etienne in Caen when he died in 1087. Orderic's *Ecclesiastical History* and Wace's *Roman de Rou* which was based on Orderic's account, record the funeral in detail, because great drama surrounded William's burial.[112] The funeral took place amid a fire and a claim to the land on which the abbey had been built. The solemnities descended into farce when it became apparent that the grave prepared for William was too small. When the monks used force to squeeze the Conqueror's body into the hole, the swollen corpse exploded. Eventually, William's mortal remains were interred in the sanctuary between the choir and the altar. More importantly Orderic and Wace record that the funeral was the occasion for a grand procession. Less information survives regarding the burial of Matilda, who died on 1 November 1083. She was buried between the choir and the altar of the nuns' church at the abbey of La Trinité which she had founded, a similar location to her husband's tomb in St-Etienne. This space was outside the main body of the church to which the laity would have had access, namely the nave, and was in fact located in the most sacred place in the church. William and Matilda were thus buried at opposite sides of the town, underlining the power and patronage of the ducal house. It is possible that similar practices to those suggested for Bishop Hugh at St-Désir were followed at La Trinité. No doubt Matilda's funeral would have been an occasion for a grand procession of nuns including one of her daughters, Cecilia, a nun since 1075 who later became abbess of La Trinité. The burials of William and Matilda show that at the highest social level, burial was very much a matter of personal choice, especially when the men and women concerned were founders of new religious houses.

Burial within monastic precincts was an important benefit accorded to the founding family following the initial outlay and sometimes continuing expense endowing a religious foundation occasioned because they were brought into fellowship with the monks and nuns who continued to pray for them after

---

from 1034–92.

[111] William of Malmesbury, *Gesta regum Anglorum*, ed. and trans. Mynors, Thomson and Winterbottom, vol. 1, pp. 504–5.

[112] OV, vol. 4, pp. 104–9 and Wace, *Roman de Rou*, trans. G. Burgess, pp. 294–7, lines 9257–82.

their death. Splendid tombs in impressive abbey churches and buildings were seen as suitable resting places for people of the highest social status, regardless of gender. However, in the examples considered above, women tended to be buried in religious foundations connected with their husband's family. The Empress Matilda is an obvious exception, though her position and ability to exercise her own choice were strengthened in that her father and son were kings. Even so, Matilda still had to argue her case with Henry I before she gained his blessing for her chosen burial site of Bec.

The religious community concerned in turn benefited from this mark of favour by having visible signs, in the form of elaborate tombs, of the power that their protectors could command. For the individual monks or nuns concerned, such burials would have proved disruptive, though at the same time a welcome diversion, to the daily monastic routine. As we have seen, the continued involvement of the family in the life of a foundation placed heavy financial burdens and constraints on time on the houses concerned. By allowing the founders' family to use the precincts as a mausoleum, the potential for more intrusion to visit graves was exacerbated and so gratitude to the founders came at a price. For both the monastic community and the lay benefactors, lay burial equated to a strengthening of ties: boundaries between categories of lay and religious were blurred whilst the living and the dead were brought into closer fellowship within a sacred space on earth.

Conclusion

It is clear that contact between lay kin and religious did not end either abruptly or irrevocably just because a relative had taken vows for the whole period under inspection. Monasteries, hospitals and leper houses were religious places where it was simply impossible and in many ways undesirable to obtain a complete separation from the world. While the institutions were spaces set apart specifically for the worship of God, worldly concerns inevitably intruded on a day-to-day level. Usually these concerns consisted of small annoyances, like relatives visiting on journeys, but, at their most extreme, the affairs of the lay kin seriously disrupted the smooth running of the daily round of monastic offices.

Both lay men and women could be an intrusive presence in religious space, but intrusion did not necessarily involve a lay person entering the precincts of a monastic house. Gendered differences are apparent in this interaction. Nuns could be called away from their cloister to attend to domestic family needs, no doubt because the skills, like nursing, that they learned in their communities were highly valued by the lay world. Monks were less likely to be called away by their families, but men who had entered the cloister found the secular authorities disrupting their monastic vocation in other ways. Robert of Grandmesnil was exiled from Normandy and Lanfranc and Anselm both became archbishop of Canterbury, which entailed them having to leave their cloister.

Close relatives of monks and nuns, for example parents and siblings, were received into the cloister in a variety of ways, notably claiming hospitality or seeking advancement through misappropriation of the communities' revenues. The differences in provision for men and women wishing to take up the religious life also led to the reception of close family members into the cloister, most notably in the cases of widows who entered male communities. These women established informal groupings at male monasteries which housed their husbands and sons. By pursuing a semi-religious life in these surroundings, women like Eve Crispin and Basilia of Gournay exchanged their roles as biological mothers to their sons for one as spiritual mothers to entire communities of monks, with archbishops – Lanfranc and Anselm – in the fraternity of those communities. At one level, this vocation still involved the intrusion of women into a community of celibate men, but the Norman Church welcomed it, presumably because the women brought very real benefits to the monastery in terms of counsel and their skills previously employed in running a household.

In the case of the burial of the founder of their community and the founder's spouse and children, monks and nuns experienced an overlapping of religious and lay space, and it is in this respect that the accommodation between the needs of families and the communities they founded is most apparent. The desire to have close links with professed religious extended beyond the initial foundation of the community to fellowship with it in death, although this desire is not so well documented for the later period. The reasons may lie in the fact that other interests or new orders like the Franciscans and Dominicans attracted the patronage of later members of the founding families of the earlier Norman religious houses. Burials within the monastic precincts entailed the reception of groups of lay people, for example at the funeral of William the Conqueror, into the community. Religious communities and churches were places where boundaries met and were transgressed. The families' involvement with religious houses did not end with a bequest or with the profession of a single member; for those who either could not or wished not to take vows, some share in the spiritual benefits of the sacred space of the cloister was desirable. Links with monasteries, both through the vocations of living relatives and the burial of the dead, provided a link between the earthly world and the spiritual world beyond.

Conclusion

The duchy of Normandy experienced great variety in the forms of the religious life. Although our story begins with the re-establishment of Benedictine monasticism in the tenth and eleventh centuries, this renewal of spiritual life gave the impetus for further developments and the foundation of new orders. By the mid-twelfth century several Savignac and Cistercian houses were in existence, founded in response to the more ascetic ideals of figures like Robert of Molesme, founder of the Cistercian order, and Vitalis of Savigny. As the century progressed, the number of hospitals and leper houses increased, founded in a spirit of charity and, perhaps, as an alternative outlet for those people for whom a contemplative vocation was not attractive. For the laity, whose main point of contact with organised religion in many respects was their parish priest, there were also several ways of expressing religious devotion, most notably through pilgrimage to shrines housed in monasteries, parish churches and cathedrals.[1] However, all forms of religious life and devotion depended on the active cooperation between the clergy, professed religious and the laity. The relationship was one of mutual support. Clergy, monks and nuns provided services and prayers; the laity provided material support through the foundation and ongoing benefaction of religious houses and the payment of tithes.

In this book, we are concerned with how this relationship was made manifest through the use of space. Our discussion has involved the reading of familiar sources like the *miracula*, chronicles and Eudes Rigaud's register in new ways to try and get beyond an institutional history of the Church in Normandy to how Christian religion functioned on a daily basis. By necessity, some aspects of the religious life, most notably the economic, have not been discussed fully here as other scholars have dealt with them in detail.[2] The questions I have addressed concern how people lived; how men and women built the houses in which they or their relatives spent their lives; how they organised those buildings in order to serve God. How far men and women, both lay and religious, were able to do this depended on local circumstances, especially the political situation; their relationships with ecclesiastical superiors, like Archbishop Eudes Rigaud or Abbot Stephen of Lexington; whether

---

1   See the discussion of pilgrimage in chapter two.
2   See, for example, the work of Marjorie Chibnall, Cassandra Potts and John Walmsley.

there was a war going on and whether, in time of peace, the money and other resources were available to realise their plans. The period considered here also raises questions about how the use of space might change over time; how much freedom people had to create and adapt sacred spaces in medieval Normandy and how different groups of people came into conflict over the use of space. The creation and maintenance of sacred space in Normandy was therefore an ongoing process, in which the active cooperation of both laity and religious was paramount.

We noted in the introduction that the use of sacred space in Normandy is best discussed through the four areas of spatial practice, accommodation and conflict, namely display, reception and intrusion, enclosure and the family. Through our examination of these different areas it is possible to reach some conclusions regarding how professed religious, clergy and the laity met and interacted and how this interaction was influenced by conceptions of gender. It is also clear from our discussion, that problems relating to control of space, particularly which groups had access to different parts of churches or monasteries, and the differences in ideas of how space should be used between professed religious and their superiors are also tremendously important. Control does not just relate to buildings and other spaces, but also to people and their behaviour. Equally pertinent to our discussion is how much freedom professed religious, the clergy and the laity had in the ways they organised and used sacred spaces and how this usage may have changed over time.

It may seem strange to speak in terms of conflict in the use of sacred space and different ideas about it, but the fact that different groups of people with differing needs had to share and cooperate in the use, for example, of monastic churches as parish churches meant the potential for conflict was there. At an institutional level, conflict was apparent on a national and international scale through the political implications of church reform, particularly attempts by the reform papacy to free the Church from lay control and maintain a clear distinction between religious and laity. In our sources, we see conflict at the level of individual communities, particularly in the pages of Archbishop Eudes Rigaud's register and of Abbot Stephen's visitations. Eudes recorded instances of monastic communities and parishes striving to reach a suitable accommodation between their often conflicting needs. In our discussion of intrusion, we saw how the bishop sought to maintain the separation of professed religious and laity in his injunction that the canons of Corneville should create a partition in the bell tower so that both the community and parish could ring their bells and avoid undue contact.[3] Sometimes these spatial conflicts could have a profoundly negative effect on one of the parties as shown by Eudes's instruction to the nuns of Montivilliers to sing their prayers and antiphons in the choir, rather than moving through the church where they would come into contract with the laity in the parish section.[4] A proper configuration of space, maintaining a degree of separation, was necessary in order that the community could function and that the laity would not be excluded from the sacraments,

---

3   Bonnin, p. 280 and *Register*, p. 315.
4   Bonnin, p. 472 and *Register*, pp. 538–9.

in particular the celebration of the mass. These compromises involved the use of space on many levels and demonstrate temporal differences. Not only did a parish require access to the church for services, but also access to physical space and time in which to sound the parish bells or attend mass, reinforcing the local parish identity.

The existence of conflict in the use of space raises in turn questions about how the various different groups of people within the Norman Church sought to control space, both in terms of people's access to it and use of it, and indeed the local environment in which they lived. We began our discussion of display by looking at the topographical locations and external architecture of some religious communities. Some communities sought isolated or liminal places for reasons of asceticism, but too much harsh living was detrimental to the pursuit of a vocation as the tribulations of Herluin's nascent community of Bec make clear.[5] Choice of site was also a means of declaring intent. In the case of the Benedictine abbey of Jumièges, the monks' desire to resettle their previous site maintained a link with the past.[6] For the nuns of Fontaine-Guérard, their choice of a secluded location in the Andelle valley made a case for their affiliation with a specific order, in this case of the Cistercians.[7] On the other hand, geographic isolation was sometimes spurned. Duke William and Duchess Matilda's foundation of the abbeys of La Trinité and St-Etienne in Caen reflects the preference of the secular founders for a suburban location and therefore to give impetus to a new economic centre. These foundations also demonstrate their personal piety and the importance of the Church in wider Norman society.[8] The physical appearance of monastic houses articulated through their architectural design was another means of controlling space. Architecture was the most visible and probably easily understood means of conveying messages to a wider population at a basic level. For example, a church was recognisably a church and the bigger and more splendid it was proved a good indication of its wealth and perhaps importance. How far the subtleties of features like the west end of the church at Jumièges, with its Carolingian echoes, were understood by all is a matter of debate. The fact that communities sought to display aspects of their history, patronage or affiliation, suggests someone may have been on hand to explain to those who wished it. Lanfranc made provision in his *Monastic Constitutions* for lay visitors to undertake guided tours, demonstrating how communities made attempts to protect their image and exert a measure of control on wider perceptions of their purpose and position in society.[9] A monastic public relations exercise in this vein could convey a particular message and thus attract support in a very immediate way.

The Christian life, whether lived by pious lay people or through a monastic or priestly vocation, entailed self-control and discipline in varying degrees. As

---

5 Gilbert Crispin, *Vita Herluini*, p. 192 and trans. Vaughn, 'Life of Herluin', p. 73.
6 Appendix A, no. 42.
7 Appendix B, no. 11.
8 Appendix A, no. 21 and appendix B, no. 5.
9 *Monastic Constitutions*, pp. 130–3.

such, control meant the Church exercising influence over men and women, not only through the practice of penance as we saw in our discussion of display, but also in a gendered way. This was arguably greater for monastics and greater still for parish priests. Men who became priests responsible for the care of souls in a parish were required to live up to a very different ideal of behaviour from that expected of other men. In secular society, masculine behaviour, expectations of what a man in a particular position or social rank should or should not do, was dictated by conceptions of honour, military activity, the creation of wealth and the fathering of children. Priests, who were confronted with these concepts on a daily basis, were gendered differently and their manliness was evident through their control and sublimination of worldly appetites. Similar control was needed by monks and nuns, whose nature as enclosed professed religious may have protected them to a small degree from the realities of secular gendered expectations on a daily basis. The Church, however, headed by a male pope and staffed by celibate men, feared female sexuality both in terms of its effect on clergy and also on nuns. Laywomen therefore presented a threat to both groups. To monks, laywomen, and in the eyes of some theologians, even nuns, presented the ultimate temptation of potential sexual attraction, reminding them of what they had promised to renounce in taking a vow of chastity. For nuns too, lay women were a reminder of all they had renounced in the pursuit of their vocation: marriage and having children. As a consequence, we see prohibitions against women not only spending the night in houses of monks, but also in nunneries.[10] Control also had an additional negative side. Some men and women undoubtedly entered the religious life through a very clear sense of vocation: equally others had no choice at all. For those men and women who found pursuit of a vocation too difficult, or indeed had no vocation, personal control and the control exercised by the community would have been stifling, leading in the most extreme cases to apostasy.

In terms of the written monastic rules, how the use of space is controlled is made obvious both on a large and small scale. Monks and nuns in cloistered communities needed to maintain control of the boundaries and thresholds within which they operated. Of particular importance was the need to restrict access to the cloister, something that the ecclesiastical visitors like Archbishop Eudes Rigaud and Abbot Stephen of Lexington looked into on a regular basis. These visitors not only ensured that the physical cloister itself was closed off, but also that a fit and suitable person was in charge as porter or portress.[11] The cloister of course did not just refer to a physical actuality, but also the mental state of the monks and nuns, both individually and as a collective. Professed religious were to maintain the cloister in terms of custody of their own bodies through proper behaviour, dress and observance of the rule. For example, our discussion of incorrect monastic dress in the context of display revealed how the monks' and nuns' adoption of elaborate clothing and secular

---

[10]   *Registrum epistolarum*, p. 242; e.g. Bonnin, pp. 208, 209 and *Register*, pp. 228, 230. See the discussion on hospitality in chapter two.

[11]   *Rule*, ch. 66, p. 303; *Registrum epistolarum*, p. 239; Bonnin, p. 281 and *Register*, p. 317.

hairstyles was an unwelcome reminder of previous secular status and a indicator of potential apostasy. Joan Martel riding out to see her relatives in her 'sleeved gown', flaunted her disregard of the monastic vocation in a wholly unacceptable way.[12] Boundaries and thresholds were also vitally important in leper houses and hospitals on several levels.

Like monks and nuns, people in religious vows who worked with the sick poor and lepers had a duty of maintaining these institutions as sacred places. Similar restrictions on the entry of lay people had to be in place to protect not only the vocation of brothers and sisters within hospitals, but also to ensure that the financial resources of the house were directed towards their proper purpose, the maintenance of the sick.[13] In addition, the nature of hospitals and leper houses with different communities and groups of people living on the same site meant that it was necessary to ensure a separation of sick and healthy and lay and religious. This separation was not only maintained in the written rules governing which spaces may or may not be used at different times and by different groups of people, for example, the ban on women drying laundry at Lisieux, but also architecturally as the different groups inhabited either different sections of a building or separate edifices.[14] Control of people and space within leper houses especially was closely bound up with the Church's attitude to people afflicted with the disease. As we have noted, the Church did have, at least in the twelfth century, a degree of compassion in its attitude towards those afflicted with leprosy: they were seen as being in need of protection and the illness as almost being a vocation in itself. There was still a need, however, to ensure control over a group that caused anxiety in society for various reasons. Lepers not only aroused fear through the nature of their disease, which was not fully understood either in terms of how it was spread or its symptoms, but also in terms of their tendency to wander from place to place, either due to insufficient provision for them in institutions – particularly poor lepers who did not have the necessary material wealth to enter some houses – or an unwillingness on the part of some lepers to be confined in one place.

Although historians have tended to emphasise the coercive elements of enclosure, especially in regard to women religious, rules that control the movement of men and women, especially in the monastic context, and the use of space were as much about the freedom of men and women to pursue their vocation without undue interference from the secular world. Again, medieval ideas about gender, particularly women's sexuality, link very closely with spatial practice here. Theologians and churchmen emphasised that when a man or woman took religious vows, the main consequence was the surrendering of individual freedom. The renunciation of personal liberty had a beneficial effect: for the professed religious themselves this meant, at least in theory,

12   Bonnin, p. 338 and Bonnin, p. 383.
13   Mansi, vol. 22, cols 835–6, 913.
14   See the discussion in chapter three. The lepers at Mont-aux-Malades in Rouen inhabited their own houses, whereas at St-Nicholas-de-la-Chesnaie near Bayeux, they had communal lodgings.

some degree of protection from undue secular demands, though as we have seen this was not always the case. Lanfranc and Anselm had profound anxieties about leaving their cloisters to become, as archbishops of Canterbury, head of the English Church.[15] The Cistercian order enacted harsh penalties on monks it perceived to be too caught up in secular affairs.[16] Nuns found themselves subject to family demands even after they had taken vows, whether to return to the family home to nurse sick relatives, as in the case of a nun from St-Léger-des-Préaux, or to leave their community permanently to marry, as did a nun of Villarceaux.[17] Equally though, women may have found freedom within a vocation from the biological demands of marriage and motherhood. We have noted that a number of women retired to both male and female houses in their widowhood, particularly to the monastery of Bec, and these actions may perhaps be indicative of vocations felt earlier in life, but put on one side, due to family needs and political strategies.[18] For lepers, the controls in place within hospitals and leper houses meant freedom from possible molestation, something which became increasingly important as the Church and society's attitude to the disease hardened. We have seen how some statutes, for example those promulgated for Rouen, specifically included a clause stating that lepers who contravened them laid themselves open to public abuse.[19] In terms of hospitals, the more active vocation and greater interaction between different groups of people meant greater freedom of choice for people who may have not considered themselves suitable for a contemplative vocation: it seems as if some brothers and sisters could take simple vows, that is to say not be professed to a particular house for life. Married couples might enter for a short while, taking temporary vows, but had the option to leave and return to secular life as may have been the case at the hospital in Gournay.[20]

By exploring the use of sacred space we have established that the laity experienced ownership of monasteries, nunneries and parish churches. Archbishop Eudes Rigaud's injunctions ensuring the proper repair and organisation of such spaces reflect this. That there was a need for such statutes demonstrates the practical ambiguity in the status of churches, cloisters and other monastic buildings through the laity laying claim to sacred spaces at times of pilgrimage. Laymen and laywomen regarded sacred spaces as belonging to the local secular community, as shown in the provisions that only lepers from a certain parish or groups of parish might enter a particular leper house.[21] Religious communities were also regarded as particular to persons or places. We began this book with the funeral of William the Conqueror and his burial in the choir

---

[15]   See the discussion on the cloister in chapter three.
[16]   For example, Gilbert of Bonport and Robert of Perseigne who lost their rank and the privilege of celebrating mass in their communities among other punishments: *Twelfth-century Statutes*, 1197, no. 46, pp. 396–7.
[17]   Bonnin, pp. 296, 117 and *Register*, pp. 335, 132.
[18]   See the discussion of the widows of Bec in chapter four.
[19]   Mansi, vol. 23, col. 399.
[20]   Bonnin, p. 283 and *Register*, p. 319.
[21]   For example St-Gilles in Pont-Audemer.

of St-Etienne.[22] Powerful patrons seemed to regard their institutions with a proprietorial air. The power of the ducal house was ably demonstrated through the construction of La Trinité and St-Etienne in Caen, though these buildings worked on many levels, also illustrating the place of Benedictine monasticism within Normandy and the growth of the town. Non-ducal monasteries, for example Orderic's house at St-Évroul, reflect the close relationship between community and founding aristocratic family. Pride in the monastery worked both ways and was reciprocal. Not only was the local noble family proud of its monastery, but also the monastic community itself was equally proud of its powerful secular patrons and protectors. Both groups were dependent on each other and were interlinked, valuing their relationship that illustrated the essential nature of the interaction between religious and laity. Families were anxious to ensure the monks' or nuns' prayers and join the confraternity, and monasteries were keen to safeguard what they saw as certain privileges in terms of burial of significant benefactors and the income these entailed. At a less exalted level, lay people, coming into monasteries at festival times, for example at Ivry, or to hear anniversary masses for their dead friends at Notre-Dame-du-Pré, reflect this sense of, if not technical ownership of space, then at least the laity's feeling that they had a real stake in it.[23] Services provided by various monastic houses and other communities may well have contributed to the laity's sense of co-ownership of sacred space. For example, we noted in our discussion of reception and intrusion that monasteries were a favoured place for laymen and laywomen to seek hospitality or alternatively as a school for the education of their children. Older laymen and laywomen also made provision for their retirement in monastic houses. Again such arrangements were clearly reciprocal: lodging and food was provided for the old people in return for an income or substantial endowment given to the monastic community, as was the case with Genevieve, whose husband made provision for her at St-Amand in Rouen.[24]

It is crucial to realise that questions regarding the ownership of sacred space could easily lead to exploitation on the part of both the laity and religious. Hospitality, though a requirement of the Benedictine and other rules, was extremely burdensome on communities if lay patrons and visitors took undue advantage, for example Mabel of Bellême and her large retinue of knights descending on St-Évroul.[25] Whereas the provision for taking in guests had its spiritual precedent in the Gospels, too many guests staying for too long could reduce the sacred nature of monastic space for both religious and laity in two ways. On a practical level, food, and other resources, such as fodder and bedding for horses, could run out; while at the same time, tending to the guests would disturb the peace of the cloister and distract monks and nuns from contemplation and prayer. Exploitation was not confined to

---

[22] OV, vol. 4, pp. 104–9.
[23] Bonnin, pp. 69–70, 411 and *Register*, pp. 78, 468.
[24] See the discussion on hospitality in chapter two and Johnson, *Equal in Monastic Profession*, pp. 179–80.
[25] OV, vol. 2, pp. 54–5.

contemplative communities but also to leper houses and hospitals. Conciliar legislation continuously developed to ensure that all the healthy members of communities would take some form of vows so they would not divert monies designated for the care of the sick towards comfortable living for themselves. For parish priests, potential exploitation worked the other way round. Some men used their ecclesiastical position within the parish to exploit freer access to vulnerable women, with whom they could have casual sex or some kind of relationship, for a variety of relationships that easily extended beyond the officially sanctioned role of pastoral care. Sometimes these relationships were long-term and marriage in all but name, others were more casual. It is no surprise that many of the women in such situations were poor or vulnerable in other ways, for example through physical disability, as their partners were men officially debarred from an active sexual life.[26]

In our discussion of the construction and use of sacred spaces by both laity and religious, we have seen how space as a concept was not static, but was socially constructed and historically specific. Despite the gaps in the evidence, we can see that the ideas about space changed over time and its use and construction was fluid. We need only consider the example of the Fécamp ordinal to support this conjecture. The Fécamp ordinal – a document recording the liturgical practices followed in the abbey at different points in the Church's year – includes in its manuscript pages a wide margin to facilitate annotations on the use of liturgical space in the church, cloisters and precincts of the abbey of Fécamp, demonstrating how liturgical practice changed over time.[27] Although the core of what it meant to be a monk or a nun (leading a life of contemplation vowed to poverty, chastity and obedience) did not change and was articulated clearly in the monastic rule, external circumstances in the sense of politics, social norms and economic developments did change. We only have to look at the development of architecture, whether Romanesque or Gothic, to realise that on a very basic level things changed. Churches built in 1050 did not look the same as churches built in 1300: building techniques allowed for a greater flamboyance in architecture, for example, much larger windows or thinner walls by the end of our period. As more monks became priests, developments over time in the liturgy and in doctrine resulted in the multiplication of side chapels; there was a need to ensure the laity had access to relics; and an increase in the number of masses that were said for the dead. The greater separation of clergy from laity following on from the reform movement also ensured practical and physical changes in church architecture, such as the erection of screens between the laity in the nave and priests or communities in the choir.

The period c.1050–1300 saw a reduction in communal living, despite its importance in a monastic context, revealing changes in the configuration of space through how communities used monastic buildings. This was generally regarded with a negative attitude by the Church. In some circumstances, for example in the use of the infirmary as a place of refreshment where monks or

---

[26] See the discussion on clerical celibacy in chapter two.
[27] *The Ordinal of the Abbey of the Holy Trinity Fécamp*, vol. 1, pp. 2–4 and plate X.

nuns might indulge in food otherwise forbidden by the rule, it is possible that these developments did reflect a perceived decline in standards.[28] In the case of the division of the communal dormitory, as at Villers-Canivet for example, something else might be apparent.[29] For both monks and nuns, their chaste status and position, especially for nuns, as a spouse of Christ, may have led individuals to a realisation of the need for a more private space within the monastery for private devotion and contemplation. Equally, the human reason of needing a place of one's own to escape to if life got too difficult explains these developments: the practices and ideals described in the monastic rules put an impossible burden on many individuals. Certainly superiors of monastic communities developed their own lodgings in order to accommodate both their spiritual role as head of the community and more secular role as administrator, negotiator and business man or woman. Certainly for the latter roles, they would need at the very least an office in order not to distract the rest of the community.[30]

Movement through space also changed and this is most obviously revealed in a close examination of the experience of nuns in the central medieval period. The sources we have examined from St-Amand especially reveal the changing nature of the Church's view of the nuns as opposed to the nuns' views of what they could and could not do. In the eleventh and early twelfth centuries, the community at St-Amand was a visible one as shown through its connections with the archbishops of Rouen and activities in caring for the depressed woman from Lisieux. By the thirteenth century, the Church authorities were trying to limit that visibility through prohibitions on processions, silencing of bells and limiting the ways in which the nuns could chant the office.[31] Other houses too suffered from similar strictures, notably Montivilliers, prevented from processing in the church due to the presence of the parish in the northern aisle of the nave. How far these rules were followed we will never know, but in these cases at least, coercion overrode communities' liberties in the need to control sacred space.

Over the course of this book we have considered various aspects of spatial practice – the use and construction of space in relation to the religious life and parish churches – in order to show that it was fluid and allowed for an interaction of different groups in society generally considered to be very separate entities. All too often debates surrounding the use of space seem rather sterile, centred on institutions or conducted in highly abstract terms and becoming depopulated. I have tried to show how the use of space in theory and practice was instrumental in determining relations between people. Space may have been demarcated as sacred to God, but it was lived space – lived, worked and worshipped in by men and women, lay and religious.

28   For example, at St-Amand in Rouen, Bonnin, p. 16 and *Register*, p. 19.
29   *Registrum epistolarum*, p. 243.
30   As we have seen, superiors had separate lodgings at Fontaine-Guérard, Montivilliers, Foucarmont and Cherbourg among others.
31   See the discussion of the bull of Innocent IV in chapter one and Johnson, *Equal in Monastic Profession*, p. 141.

Appendix A: Male religious houses[1]

1. Alençon, St-Leonard (St-Giles)[2]
dép.: Orne, chef-lieu
Benedictine priory, Sées diocese
Founded between 1020 and 1025 by William Talvas and dependent on Lonlay.[3]

Sources:
Bonnin, pp. 80, 234–5, 373; *Register*, pp. 90–1, 259, 422

References:
Cottineau, vol. 1, col. 53

2. Ardenne, Notre-Dame
dép.: Calvados, arr. and cant.: Caen, comm.: St-Germain-la-Blanche-Herbe
Premonstratensian abbey, Bayeux diocese
Initially given to a certain Gilbert in 1138 by Aiulphe du Four and his wife Asceline. In 1144 Philippe de Harcourt brought the community under the Premonstratensian rule and it became an abbey in 1150, affiliated to La Lucerne.

Sources:
'Chronique de foundation de Notre-Dame d'Ardenne', ed. Arnoux[4]

References:
Ardura, *Abbayes*, pp. 74–8
Beck, 'Recherches sur les salles capitulaires', p. 346
Cottineau, vol. 1, cols 137–8
GC, vol. 11, cols 459–62

Plates and photographs:
Courtauld Institute of Art, Conway Collection, R31/31(18a) showing bomb damage to the site[5]

---

[1] These appendices are not exhaustive lists of religious houses in Normandy, nor do they list all sources and secondary works relating to them.
[2] Cottineau, vol. 1, col. 53 also lists a priory with similar foundation details, but dedicated to Notre-Dame. In the English edition of Eudes's register the priory is identified as St-Leonard's: *Register*, p. 258.
[3] See no. 48.
[4] Shortened references are given in the appendices; for full references see the bibliography.
[5] The Courtauld Institute of Art has made many of its images available on a web-based data base at <http://www.artandarchitecture.org.uk> date accessed 28 November 2006. All subsequent references to the Courtauld Institute are taken from this website.

3. Auffay, Notre-Dame

dép.: Seine-Maritime, arr.: Dieppe, cant.: Totes
Canons regular, then Benedictine priory, Rouen diocese
Originally a house of canons regular in the eleventh century. In 1067, it was refounded as a Benedictine priory of St-Évroul by Gilbert of Auffay.

Sources:
Bonnin, pp. 47, 145, 223, 508; *Register*, pp. 53, 164, 246, 579
OV, vol. 2, pp. 134–5, vol. 3, pp. 256–9, vol. 4, pp. 338–9

References:
Cottineau, vol. 1, col. 195

4. Aumale, St Martin

dép. : Seine-Maritime, arr.: Neufchâtel-en-Bray, cant.: chef-lieu
Collegiate then Benedictine abbey, Rouen diocese
Originally a collegiate foundation dedicated to St Martin in the eleventh century by Guérinfroid. The canons were replaced with Benedictines from St-Lucien-de-Beauvais by Stephen, count of Aumale, and in 1120, the foundation became an abbey. Situated on the Bresle.

Sources:
Bonnin, pp. 76, 118–19, 229, 268, 300, 359, 542, 497 608–9; *Register*, pp. 85–6, 133–4, 252, 300, 340, 386, 515, 566, 700

References:
Cottineau, vol. 1, cols 204–5
GC, vol. 11, cols 274–78

5. Aunay-sur-Odon

dép. : Calvados, arr. and cant.: Vire
Savignac/Cistercian abbey, Bayeux diocese
Founded in 1131 by Jouradan de Say and his wife Lucie and affiliated to Clairvaux in 1157. The church was consecrated on 29 April 1190.

Sources:
Registrum epistolarum, pp. 197, 210–12, 214, 219–21

References:
Beck, 'Recherches sur les salles capitulaires', pp. 24–7
Cottineau, vol. 1, cols 201–2
GC, vol. 11, cols 443–5

6. Bacqueville-en-Caux, Notre-Dame

dép. : Seine-Maritime, arr.: Dieppe, cant.: chef-lieu
Benedictine priory, Rouen diocese
Founded in 1131 by William Martel, it became a priory of Tiron in 1133.

Sources:
Bonnin, pp. 10, 54, 110, 145, 171, 301, 542; *Register*, pp. 14, 59, 125, 163, 188, 340, 619

References:
Cottineau, vol. 1, col. 238.

7. Barbery:

dép. : Calvados, arr.: Falaise, cant.: Bretteville-sur-Laize
Savigniac/Cistercian, priory then abbey, Bayeux diocese

Founded in 1140 by Robert Marmion as a grange of Savigny, then affiliated to Clairvaux. It became an abbey between 1176 and 1181 when his son, also called Robert Marmion, increased the endowment.

Sources:
Registrum epistolarum, pp. 197, 210, 213, 221
Twelfth-Century Statutes, 1200, no. 52

References:
Beck, 'Recherches sur les salles capitulaires', pp. 33–4
Cottineau, vol. 1, col. 261
GC, vol. 11, cols 452–6
Twelfth-Century Statutes, p. 766

8. Beaubec, St-Laurent

dép. : Seine-Maritime, arr.: Neufchâtel-en-Bray, cant.: Forges-les-Eaux
Savigniac/Cisterican abbey, Rouen diocese
Founded 1118 x 1127 by Hugh II of Gournay then affiliated to Clairvaux. It was located near the source of the Epte.

Sources:
Registrum epistolarum, pp. 195–6, 200, 206–7, 221–2
Twelfth-Century Statutes, 1194, no. 23 and 1199, no. 55

References:
Deck, 'Le temporal de l'abbaye cistercienne de Beaubec I'
Cottineau, vol. 1, cols 289–90
GC, vol. 11, cols 301–4
Twelfth-Century Statutes, p. 766

9. Beaulieu, Notre-Dame

dép. : Seine-Maritime, arr. Rouen, cant.: Darnetal, comm.: Préaux
Augustinian priory, Rouen diocese
Founded in 1189 by Jean de Préaux.[6]

Sources:
Bonnin, pp. 49, 127, 169, 363, 597; *Register*, pp. 55, 141, 186, 414, 686

References:
Arnoux, p. 22
Cottineau, vol. 1, col. 300

10. Beaumont-en-Auge, Notre-Dame

dép. : Calvados, arr. and cant.: Pont-l'Evêque
Benedictine priory, Rouen diocese
Founded in 1060 by Robert Betrand 'Le Tors' and his wife Suzanne; dependent on St-Ouen.

Sources:
Bonnin, pp. 60, 198, 296, 593; *Register*, pp. 67–8, 213, 335, 683

References:
Cottineau, vol. 1, col. 305

Plates and photographs:
Monasticon, plate 113

6   Cottineau has a foundation date of 1200.

11. Beaussault: St-Maur

dép. : Seine-Maritime, arr.: Neufchâtel, cant.: Forges-les-Eaux
Benedictine priory, Rouen diocese
Founded before 1141 and dependent on Bec.

Sources:
Bonnin, pp. 146, 207, 268; *Register*, pp. 165, 227, 299–300

References:
Cottineau, vol. 1, col. 312.

12. Bec-Hellouin, Le, Notre-Dame

dép. : Eure, arr.: Bernay, cant.: Brionne
Benedictine abbey, Rouen diocese
Founded by Herluin c.1030 after a career as a soldier in the service of Count Gilbert of
Brionne. After relocating twice, shortly after foundation, the community eventually settled
at Bec. Nothing of the medieval fabric survives from this house apart from a fifteenth-
century tower. The abbey is once again home to a community of Benedictine monks.

Sources:
Bonnin, pp. 104, 197, 280, 623; *Register*, pp. 120, 212, 314, 717
Chronicon Beccensis
Fauroux, nos 98, 178–81, 189
Gilbert Crispin, *Vita Herluini*
Regesta regum, nos 166–8

References:
Beck, 'Recherches sur les salles capitulaires', pp. 68–9
Cottineau, vol. 1, cols 316–9
GC, vol. 11, cols 216–39
Normans in Europe, p. 69
Porée, *Histoire de l'abbaye du Bec*

Plates and photographs:
Monasticon, plate 114

13. Belle-Étoile (Cerisy-Belle-Étoile), Notre-Dame

dép. : Orne, arr.: Argentan, cant.: Flers
Premonstratensian abbey, diocese of Bayeux
Founded in c.1190 by Henri de Beaufou and affiliated to La Lucerne. The community
originally comprised a group of hermits. The church and claustral buildings date from the
thirteenth century.

References:
Ardura, *Abbayes*, pp. 108–13
Beck, 'Recherches sur les salles capitulaires', pp. 41–2
Cottineau, vol. 1, col. 329
GC, vol. 11, cols 462–5

14. Bernay: Notre-Dame

dép. : Eure, arr.: chef-lieu
Benedictine abbey, Lisieux diocese
Founded initially in 1008 by Judith of Brittany, wife of Richard II, duke of Normandy,
on her dower lands.[7] Work on the monastery's construction was delayed until after her

---

[7]   Beck gives the date of foundation as c.1015.

death in 1017. The conventual buildings to the south of the church were rebuilt in the sixteenth and seventeenth centuries and the church was reworked between the fifteenth and seventeenth centuries, though part of the nave, south transept and choir survives from the eleventh century. In 1249, fire severely damaged the community, resulting in a decrease in the number of monks from thirty-five to fifteen.

Sources:
Bonnin, pp. 64, 200, 297; *Register*, pp. 72, 217, 337
Fauroux, no. 35
Regesta regum, no. 30

References:
Bayle, 'Bernay, abbatiale Notre-Dame'
Beck, 'Recherches sur les salles capitulaires', pp. 67–8
Cottineau, vol. 1, cols 356–7
Musset, *Normandie romane*, vol. 2, pp. 45–57

Plates and photographs:
Courtauld Institute of Art, Conway Collection, B78/3625 and B78/3624, abbey church
Monasticon, plate 109
Musset, *Normandie romane*, vol. 2, plates 1–23

15. Beuvron: St-James

dép. : Manche, arr.: Avranches, cant.: chef-lieu
Benedictine priory, Avranches diocese
Founded by Robert, count of Avranches, in 1105 and dependent on St-Benoît-sur-Loire.

Sources:
Bonnin, pp. 246, 459; *Register*, pp. 273, 523–4

References:
Cottineau, vol. 1, col. 372

16. Blancheland (Neufmesnil), Notre-Dame and St-Nicolas

dép. : Manche, arr.: Coutances, cant.: La Haye-du-Puits
Premonstratensian abbey, Coutances diocese
Originally a group of hermits living at St-Jacques-de-Brocqueboeuf on land given by Guillaume d'Orval in 1154–55. In August 1155, the community was transferred to Blancheland and the Premonstratensian order by Richard de la Haye-du-Puits and his wife Matilda of Vernon.

References:
Ardura, *Abbayes*, pp. 131–7
Beck, 'Recherches sur les salles capitulaires', p. 53
Cottineau, vol. 1, col. 388
GC, vol. 11, cols 944–9

17. Bonport (Pont-de-l'Arche), Notre-Dame

dép. : Eure, arr.: Louviers, cant.: chef-lieu
Cistercian abbey, Évreux diocese
Founded 1190/91 by Richard I from Le Val. Parts of the cloister, including the kitchen and refectory survive.

Sources:
Twelfth-Century Statutes, 1190, no. 7; 1194, no. 50; 1195, no. 56; 1197, no. 46; 1198, no. 23

References:
Beck, 'Recherches sur les salles capitulaires', p. 87
Cottineau, vol. 1, cols 432–3
GC, vol. 11, cols 667–71
Johnson, 'Pious Legends and Historical Realities', pp. 189–92
Twelfth-Century Statutes, p. 770

Plates and photographs:
Courtauld Institute of Art, Conway Collection, L181/19(58) for the kitchen and 997/15/19
and L18/19(50) for the refectory

18. Bourg-Achard, St-Lô

dép. : Eure, arr.: Pont-Audemer, cant.: Routout
Augustinian priory, Rouen diocese
Nivelon du Bosc established four prebends for secular canons in the parish church of St-Lô
in 1136 and the community was brought under the Augustinian rule. In 1142, Archbishop
Hugh of Rouen confirmed the foundation.[8]

Sources:
Bonnin, pp. 8, 58, 104, 172, 281, 514, 585, 622; *Register*, pp. 11, 65, 119, 190, 316, 587, 674,
716

References:
Arnoux, p. 21
Cottineau, vol. 1, col. 459
Gazeau, 'Les chanoines réguliers de Corneville et de Bourg-Achard au XIIe siècle',
pp. 198–206

19. Briouze, St-Gervais

dép. : Orne, arr.: Argentan, cant.: chef-lieu
Benedictine priory, Sées diocese
Founded in 1080 by William, the local seigneur, and dependent on St-Florent-de-Saumur.

Sources:
Bonnin, pp. 236, 374; *Register*, pp. 261, 424

References:
Cottineau, vol. 1, col. 507

20. Bures-en-Bray (Londinières), St-Etienne

dép. : Seine-Maritime, arr.: Neufchâtel-en-Bray, cant.: Londinières
Benedictine priory, Rouen diocese
Dependent on Notre-Dame-du-Pré

Sources:
Bonnin, pp. 48, 100, 170, 208, 338, 541–2; *Register*, pp. 54, 114, 188, 228, 384, 514

References:
Cottineau, vol. 1, col. 531

21. Caen, St.-Etienne

dép. : Calvados, chef-lieu
Benedictine abbey, Bayeux diocese

---

[8]   Cottineau gives a foundation date of 1143.

Founded 1063 by William the Conqueror.[9] The abbey church was originally built in c.1060. The façade and towers of the church date from the eleventh century and parts of the nave are also Romanesque. A Gothic choir replaced the original structure in the thirteenth century. The monastery buildings were pillaged by the Huguenots in the sixteenth century and in the eighteenth century the abbey was rebuilt to a design of Guillaume de la Tremblaye. As a consequence, very little architecture other than the church exists from the Middle Ages.

Sources:
Les actes ... pour les abbayes caennais, nos 1, 3–7, 10, 13–14, 18–20, 23–4, 26, 28, 30
Bonnin, pp. 94, 262, 575; Register, pp. 109, 293, 661
Fauroux, no. 223
Regesta regum, nos 45–57

References:
Baylé, 'Caen: abbatiale Saint-Étienne (Abbaye-aux-Hommes)'
Beck, 'Recherches sur les salles capitulaires', pp. 13–17
Cottineau, vol. 1, cols 1550–3
GC, vol. 11, cols 420–9
Grant, 'Caen: abbatiale Saint-Étienne'
Jean-Marie, Caen aux XIe et XIIe siècles, pp. 34–6
Musset, Normandie romane, vol. 1, pp. 54–61

Plates and photographs:
Courtauld Institute of Art, Conway Collection, B77/5166 for the church; B36/4654 for the west front
Monasticon, plate 104
Musset, Normandie romane, vol. 1, plates 1–21

22. Cerisy-la-Fôret, St-Vigor

dép. : Manche, arr.: St-Lô, cant.: St-Clair
Benedictine abbey, Bayeux diocese
Originally founded in the sixth century by St Vigor, bishop of Bayeux, it was restored between 1030 and 1032 by Duke Robert the Magnificent. A former monk of St-Ouen in Rouen was the first abbot. Most of the surviving structure of the church is Romanesque with a thirteenth-century façade. The conventual buildings were rebuilt in the eighteenth century after the community was reformed by the Maurists.

Sources:
Bonnin, pp. 91, 260–1; Register, pp. 106, 291
Fauroux nos 64, 99, 167–70, 195–6
Regesta regum, nos 89–97

References:
Baylé, 'Cerisy-la-Forêt: abbatiale Saint-Vigor
Beck, 'Recherches sur les salles capitulaires', pp. 48–9
Cottineau, vol. 1, col. 656
GC, vol. 11, cols 408–13
Potts, Monastic Revival, pp. 31–2

Plates and photographs:
Courtauld Institute of Art, Conway Collection, negative no. 2583 for the abbey church, 2585 for the choir and 2587 for the nave

---

9   This is the date given by Jean-Marie.

23. Chaumont-en-Vexin, Notre-Dame-l'Aillerie

dép. : Oise, arr.: Beauvais, cant.: chef-lieu
Benedictine priory, Rouen diocese
Dependent on St-Germer-de-Flay.

Sources:
Bonnin, pp. 41, 167, 193, 241, 529, 567; *Register*, pp. 45, 182, 207, 268, 604, 651

References:
Cottineau, vol. 1, col. 36

24. Cherbourg, Notre-Dame-du-Voeu

dép. : Manche, arr.: chef-lieu
Augustinian abbey,[10] Coutances diocese
Founded after 1145. The Empress Matilda was a benefactor.

Sources:
Bonnin, pp. 89–90, 250; *Register*, pp. 102, 279–80

References:
Arnoux, p. 21
Beck, 'Recherches sur les salles capitulaires', pp. 37–8
Cottineau, vol. 1, cols 759–60
GC, vol. 11, cols 940–44

25. Conches-en-Ouche, St-Pierre

dép. : Eure, arr.: Évreux, cant.: chef-lieu
Benedictine abbey, Évreux diocese
Founded in 1035 by Roger of Tosny. The first monks, including the first two abbots, were
from Fécamp. The cloister was situated to the north of the church.

Sources:
Bonnin, pp. 71, 219, 306, 626; *Register*, pp. 80, 241, 347, 721

References:
Beck, 'Recherches sur les salles capitulaires', pp. 86–7
Cottineau, vol. 1, cols 852–3
GC, vol. 11, cols 637–44
Potts, *Monastic Revival*, p. 117

Plates and photographs:
Monasticon, plate 105

26. Cormeilles, Notre-Dame and St-Pierre

dép. : Eure, arr.: Pont-Audemer, cant.: chef-lieu
Benedictine abbey, Évreux diocese
Founded around 1055 x 1060 by William of Breteuil (d.1072) who was buried there.
Situated on the Calonne.

Sources:
Bonnin, pp. 8, 60, 198, 296; *Register*, pp. 11, 67, 213, 335

References:
Cottineau, vol. 1, col. 875
GC, vol. 11, cols 846–50
Henry, 'L'abbaye de Notre-Dame de Cormeilles'

---

[10]   Of the congregation of St-Victor in Paris.

27. Corneville-sur-Risle

dép: Eure, arr. and cant.: Pont-Audemer
Augustinian priory then abbey, diocese Rouen
Founded in 1143 in the Risle valley by Gilbert, nephew of Waleran of Pont-Audemer, his wife Matilda and their daughters Crispine, wife of Nicolas de Tanay, and Eustachie, wife of Richard de la Mare. The community was raised to abbatial status between 1147 and 1155.

Sources:
Bonnin, pp. 59, 201, 280, 515, 548; *Register*, pp. 65, 217, 315, 588, 626

References:
Arnoux, p. 21
Cottineau, vol. 1, col. 879
Gazeau, 'Les chanoines réguliers de Corneville et de Bourg-Achard', pp. 191–7
GC, vol. 11, cols 298–301

28. Croix-St-Leufroy, La

dép. : Eure, arr.: Louviers, cant.: Gaillon
Benedictine abbey, Évreux diocese
Originally founded in 692 by St Leufroy and restored before 1035. Ralph of Tosny was a benefactor. Situated on the Eure.

Sources:
Bonnin, pp. 73, 221, 304; *Register*, pp. 82, 243, 345
Regesta regum, no. 165

References
Cottineau, vol. 1, col. 922
GC, vol. 11, cols 632–7

29. Désert, Le

dép. : Calvados, arr.: Vire, cant.: Vassy
Benedictine priory, Bayeux diocese
Situated on a tributary of the Vire.

Sources:
Bonnin, pp. 92, 260; *Register*, pp. 107, 291

References:
Cottineau, vol. 1, col. 959
Power, *The Norman Frontier*, pp. 30–7

30. Envermeu, St-Laurent

dép. : Seine-Maritime, arr.: Dieppe, cant.: chef-lieu
Benedictine priory, Rouen diocese
Dependent on Bec and founded in 1052 by Turold, bishop of Bayeux, and his brother Hugh of Envermeu.

Sources:
Bonnin, pp. 5, 139, 228, 543; *Register*, pp. 5, 157, 250, 621

References:
Cottineau, vol. 1, col. 1054

31. Eu, Notre-Dame

dép. : Seine-Maritime, arr.: Dieppe, cant.: chef-lieu
Augustinian abbey,[11] Rouen diocese
Founded in 1119 by Henry, count of Eu and Archbishop Geoffroy. Situated on the Bresle.

Sources:
Bonnin, pp. 48, 99, 139, 300, 361, 408, 453; *Register*, pp. 54, 113, 158, 340, 411, 463, 516

References:
Arnoux, p. 20
Cottineau, vol. 1, cols 1084–5
GC, vol. 11, cols 293–8

32. Évreux: St-Taurin

dép. : Eure, chef-lieu
Benedictine abbey, Évreux diocese
Restored by Richard I, duke of Normandy, possibly following the treaty of Gisors in 965, to house the relics of St-Taurin, a fourth-century bishop of Évreux. Most of the Romanesque abbey was destroyed by fire in 1195 when Philip Augustus took the town. The cloister, which was on the north side of the church, was destroyed in 1825.

Sources:
Bonnin, pp. 73, 220, 305, 624; *Register*, pp. 82, 241, 347, 718
Fauroux, no. 5

References:
Cottineau, vol. 1, cols 1088–9
GC, vol. 11, cols 624–32
Musset, *Normandie romane*, vol. 2, p. 26

Plates and photographs:
Monasticon, plate 106

33. Fécamp, Ste-Trinité

dép. : Seine-Maritime, arr.: Le Havre, cant.: chef-lieu
Benedictine abbey, Rouen diocese
This community was originally a community of nuns in the late ninth century. Refounded as a male community, and the church was consecrated in 990. In 1001, Richard II brought William of Volpiano to the duchy to reform Fécamp and subsequently other houses. The abbey itself was situated within the grounds of the ducal palace and was exempt from episcopal visitation.[12] It has been fully excavated by Annie Renoux.

Sources:
Fauroux, nos 4, 9, 25, 31, 34, 38, 54, 70–2, 85, 87, 93–4, 139, 145, 218
The Ordinal of the Abbey of the Holy Trinity Fécamp
Regesta regum, nos 139–48
Sauvage, 'Des miracles advenus en l'église de Fécamp'

References:
L'abbaye bénédictine de Fécamp: ouvrage scientifique du XIIIe centenaire
Beck, 'Recherches sur les salles capitulaires', pp. 84–5
Cottineau, vol. 1, cols 1116–20
GC, vol. 11, cols 201–15

---

[11]   Of the congregation of St-Victor in Paris.
[12]   This is why it does not figure in Archbishop Eudes Rigaud's register of visitations.

Potts, *Monastic Revival*, pp. 26–9
Renoux, *Fécamp: du palais ducal au palais de Dieu*

Plates and photographs:
Courtauld Institute of Art, Conway Collection, B78/3445 for the choir and A78/1514
A78/1511 and L12/14(3A) for the sarcophagus
Monasticon, plates 115–16

34. Foucarmont

dép. : Seine-Maritime, arr.: Neufchâtel-en-Bray, cant: Blagny
Savigniac/Cistercian abbey, Rouen diocese
Founded in 1130 by Henry, count of Eu, who became a monk and died in 1139. Later affili-
ated to Clairvaux. The church was rebuilt in 1201.

Sources:
Registrum epistolarum, pp. 196, 214–15
Twelfth-Century Statutes, 1194, no. 23, 1198, no. 27

References:
Cottineau, vol. 1, cols 1202–3
Twelfth-Century Statutes, p. 783

35. Gasny, St-Nicaise

dép. : Eure, arr.: Les Andelys, cant.: Écos
Benedictine priory, Rouen diocese
Dependent on St-Ouen.

Sources:
Bonnin, pp. 45, 98, 131, 166, 188, 227, 264, 345, 390, 567; *Register*, pp. 51, 112, 148, 181, 201,
249, 295, 393, 444, 650

References:
Cottineau, vol. 1, col. 1258

36. Graville: Ste-Honorine

dép. : Seine-Maritime, arr. and cant.: Le Havre
Augustinian priory, Rouen diocese
Founded from Ste-Barbe-en-Auge; founded before 1200 by William Malet.[13] The monastic
buildings date from the thirteenth and eighteenth centuries, though parts of the church
date from the eleventh. Situated on a cliff on the northern side of the Seine estuary, the
priory suffered damage in during the wars of religion and in 1944.

Sources:
'Chartes et documents relatifs aux activités pastorales des chanoines regulier', ed. Arnoux,
pp. 333–5
Bonnin, pp. 110, 137, 225, 266, 293, 353, 472, 517; *Register*, pp. 126, 155, 247, 298, 331, 401,
538, 591

References:
Arnoux, p. 22
Baylé, 'Graville-Saint-Honorine: église Sainte-Honorine'
Cottineau, vol. 1, cols 1337–8.
Musset, *Normandie romane*, vol. 2, pp. 195–201
Priem, 'L'église Ste-Honorine de Graville au Havre'

---

[13] Cottineau gives a date of 1203.

Plates and photographs:
Musset, *Normandie romane*, vol. 2, plates 92–6

37. Grestain, Notre-Dame

dép. : Eure, arr.: Pont-Audemer, cant.: Beuzeville, comm.: Fatouville-Grestain
Benedictine abbey, Rouen diocese
Founded by Herluin of Conteville, husband of William the Conqueror's mother, Herleva, in 1050 and with the consent of Duke William, for the souls of his family. Both Herluin and Herleva were buried there. Robert of Mortain was a major benefactor and both he and his first wife, Matilda, were also buried at the abbey.

Sources:
Barlow, no. 47 and Schriber, p. 108
Bonnin, pp. 60, 197, 295; *Register*, pp. 67, 212, 333
Regesta regum, no. 158

References:
Cottineau, vol. 1, cols 1342–3
Bates and Gazeau, 'L'abbaye de Grestain et la famille d'Herluin de Conteville'
GC, vol. 11, cols 842–6
Golding, 'Robert of Mortain'

38. Hambye, Notre-Dame

dép. : Manche, arr.: Coutances, cant.: Gavray
Benedictine abbey, Coutances diocese
Founded in 1145 by William Paisnel and Bishop Algare of Coutances. The chapter house and abbey church are the main architectural survivals.

Sources:
Bonnin, pp. 86, 248; *Register*, pp. 98, 276

References:
Beck, 'Hambye: abbaye Notre-Dame'
Beck, 'Recherches sur les salles capitulaires', pp. 36–7
Cottineau, vol. 1, cols 1374–5

39. Heudreville-sur-Avre (now Mesnil-sur-l'Estrée), St-Martin

dép. : Eure, arr.: Évreux, cant.: Nonancourt
Benedictine priory, Évreux diocese
Dependent on Tiron.
Bonnin, pp. 70, 221, 307, 625; *Register*, pp. 79, 243, 349, 720

References:
Cottineau, vol. 1, col. 1413

40. Île-Dieu, L' (Perruel), Notre-Dame

dép. : Eure, arr.: Les Andelys, cant.: Fleury-sur-Andelle
Premonstratensian abbey, Rouen diocese
Originally a group of hermits who were brought into one community by Gilbert de Vascoeuil and Réginald de Pavilly in 1187.

Sources:
'Chronique de fondation de l'Île-Dieu', ed. Arnoux, pp. 297–306

References:
Ardura, *Abbayes*, pp. 297–300
Cottineau, vol. 1, cols 1447–8

GC, vol. 11, cols 340–3

41. Ivry, Notre-Dame

dép. : Eure, arr.: Évreux, cant.: St-André
Benedictine abbey, Évreux diocese
Founded in 1076 by Roger, lord of Ivry. All that remains of the abbey is a carved doorway
dating from the third quarter of the twelfth century.

Sources:
Bonnin, pp. 69–70, 221, 307–8; *Register*, pp. 77–8, 244, 351

References:
Cottineau, vol. 1, cols 852–3
Musset, *Normandie romane*, vol. 2, p. 291

Plates and photographs:
Courtauld Institute of Art, Conway Collection, B56/1147 for the carved doorway
Monasticon, plate 107

42. Jumièges, St-Pierre

dép. : Seine-Maritime, arr.: Rouen, cant.: Duclair
Benedictine abbey, Rouen diocese
Originally founded in the seventh century by St Philibert, the community was restored
in 941 by William Longsword and the church was consecrated in 1067 by Archbishop
Maurillius. Parts of the church of St-Pierre may date from as early as the ninth century.
The church of Notre-Dame dates from the eleventh century, though the choir is Gothic.
The cloister was reconstructed in the 1530s, though the remains of the chapter house date
as far back as the late eleventh or early twelfth centuries as well as a twelfth-century guest
house in the west range.

Sources:
Bonnin, pp. 4, 56, 102, 231, 265–6, 324, 584–5, 606–7; *Register*, pp. 3, 61, 117, 253, 297, 370,
674, 698
Fauroux, nos 14, 26, 36, 51, 59, 63, 74–5, 92, 100, 113, 188, 213, 220
GND, vol. 1, pp. 18–19, 84–7, 108–11, vol. 2, pp. 172–3
Regesta regum, nos 159–64

References:
Baylé, 'Jumièges: église Saint-Pierre'
Baylé, 'Jumièges: abbatiale Notre-Dame
Beck, 'Recherches sur les salles capitulaires', p. 67
Cottineau, vol. 1, cols 1496–9
GC, vol. 11, cols 185–210 and 949–81
Jumièges: congrès scientifique du XIIIe centenaire
Le Maho, *Jumièges Abbey*
Musset, *Normandie romane*, vol. 2, pp. 61–3, 107–22

Plates and photographs:
Courtauld Institute of Art, Conway Collection, negative no. 1109 by James Austin, of the
west front
Monasticon, plate 118
Musset, *Normandie romane*, vol. 2, plates 24–43

43. Lande-Patry, La, St-Vincent

dép. : Orne, arr.: Domfront, cant.: Flers
Benedictine priory, Bayeux diocese
Dependent on St-Vincent-du-Mans.

Sources:
Bonnin, pp. 260, 577; *Register*, pp. 290, 665

References:
Cottineau, vol. 1, cols 1548–9

44. Lessay, Ste-Trinité and Notre-Dame

dép. : Manche, arr.: Coutances, cant.: chef-lieu
Benedictine abbey, Coutances diocese
Founded in 1056 with monks from Bec by Richard, known as Thurstan Haldup, vicomte of the Cotentin, his wife Anna and their son Eudo. Eudo's sister, Emma, wife of Ernaud Giroie d'Echauffour took the veil there. Eudo himself was buried in the middle of the choir. The church was badly damaged in 1944 and has since been restored. The conventual buildings, which were built to the north of the church, were remodelled in the eighteenth century.

Sources:
Bonnin, pp. 88, 249; *Register*, pp. 100, 278
OV, vol. 2, pp. 124–5
Regesta regum, no. 175

References:
Baylé, 'Lessay: abbatiale de La Trinité'
Beck, 'Recherches sur les salles capitulaires', pp. 18–19
Cottineau, vol. 1, col. 1592
GC, vol. 11, cols 916–22
Herval, 'L'abbaye de Lessay'
Musset, *Normandie romane*, vol. 1, pp. 169–71

Plates and photographs:
Courtauld Institute of Art, Conway Collection, negative no. 1125 by James Austin, abbey church and negative no. 1147 by James Austine, choir
Musset, *Normandie romane*, vol. 1, plates 76–87

45. Liancourt, St-Pierre

dép. : Oise, arr.: Beauvais, cant.: Chaumont-en-Vexin
Benedictine priory, Rouen diocese
Founded in 1065 by Gautier, count of Meulan. Dependent on St-Père-de-Chartres.

Sources:
Bonnin, pp. 41, 105, 133, 254, 529; *Register*, pp. 45, 120, 150, 284, 604

References:
Cottineau, vol. 1, cols 1600–1

46. Lierru (Ste-Marguerite-de-l'Autel)

dép. : Eure, arr.: Éverux, cant.: Breteuil
Augustinian priory, Évreux diocese
This community had its origins in a group of hermits located in the forest of Conches from c.1150 and was founded as an Augustinian priory between 1170 and 1180. Roget of Tosny was a protector of the hermits.

Sources:
Bonnin, p. 306 and *Register*, p. 348
'Chartes concernent la prieuré de Ste-Barbe-en-Auge', ed. Arnoux, pp. 295–6

References:
Arnoux, pp. 13, 21

47. Longueil: St-Pierre

dép. : Seine-Maritime, arr.: Dieppe, cant.: Offranville
Benedictine priory, Rouen diocese
Dependent on Bec and according to Cottineau founded before 833.

Sources: Bonnin, p. 209; *Register*, pp. 229–30

References:
Cottineau, vol. 1, col. 1648.

48. Lonlay

dép. : Orne, arr. and cant.: Domfront
Benedictine abbey, Mans diocese
Founded in c.1020 by William Talvas of Bellême. The remains of the Romanesque transept
and Gothic choir were adapted to parish use.

References:
Baylé, 'Lonlay-l'Abbaye: abbatiale Notre-Dame'
Beck, 'Recherches sur les salles capitulaires', p. 86
Cottineau, vol. 1, col. 1651
Musset, *Normandie romane*, vol. 1, p. 34
Thibout, 'L'abbaye de Lonlay'

49. Lucerne, La (La Lucerne-d'Outremer)

dép. : Manche, arr.: Avranches, cant.: La Haye-Pesnel
Premonstratensian abbey, Avranches diocese
Founded in 1146 by Hasculphe de Subligny and his brother, Bishop Richard of Avranches.
The community moved site twice before settling at La Lucerne. The church was destroyed
at the beginning of the Hundred Years War and rebuilt by Abbot Jean du Rocher
(1396–1407).

References:
Ardura, *Abbayes*, pp. 360–4
Baylé, 'La Lucerne: abbatiale de La Trinité'
Beck, 'Recherches sur les salles capitulaires', pp. 29–30
Cottineau, vol. 1, cols 1686–7 as La Luzene
GC, vol. 11, cols 556–63

50. Lyre (La Vieille-Lyre), Notre-Dame

dép. : Eure, arr.: Évreux, cant.: Rugles
Benedictine abbey, Évreux diocese
Founded by William of Breteuil and Adeline, his wife. The church and conventual build-
ings were constructed in the second half of the twelfth century. Situated on the Risle.

Sources:
Bonnin, pp. 218, 306, 626; *Register*, pp. 239–40, 348, 721
Fauroux, no. 120
Regesta regum, no. 192

References:
Beck, 'Recherches sur les salles capitulaires', pp. 72–3
Cottineau, vol. 1, col. 1694
GC, vol. 11, cols 644–52

Plates and photographs:
Monasticon, plate 108

51. Mondaye (Juaye-Mondaye), St-Martin

dép. : Calvados, arr.: Bayeux, cant.: Balleroy
Premonstratensian abbey, Lisieux diocese
Founded in 1202 by the Percy family. It was originally a community of hermits, but Premonstratensian by 1216. The monastery was rebuilt in the eighteenth century.

References:
Ardura, *Abbayes*, pp. 380–7
Arnoux, p. 21
Beck, 'Recherches sur les salles capitulaires', p. 54
Cottineau, vol. 2, col. 1882
GC, vol. 11, cols 860–2

52. Montaure: Notre-Dame

dép. : Eure, arr.: Louviers, cant.: Pont-l'Arche
Benedictine priory, Évreux diocese
Dependent on St-Ouen and founded in 1063 by Eudes Stigand.

Sources:
Bonnin, pp. 74, 218, 304, 627; *Register*, pp. 84, 238, 345, 722
Fauroux, no. 57

References:
Baylé 'Montaure: église Notre-Dame'
Cottineau, vol. 2, col. 1933

53. Mont-Deux-Amants (Amfreville-sous-les-Monts)

dép. : Eure, arr.: Les Andelys, cant.: Fleury-sur-Andelle
Augustinian priory, Rouen diocese
Founded before 1150. Situated at the confluence of the Seine and the Andelle.

Sources:
Bonnin, pp. 47, 197, 264, 340, 378, 444, 513; *Register*, pp. 53, 212, 295, 387, 428, 505, 586

References:
Arnoux, p. 21
Cottineau, vol. 1, cols 960–1

54. Montmorel (Poiley), Notre-Dame

dép. : Manche, arr.: Avranches, cant.: Ducey
Augustinian abbey, Coutances diocese
Founded 1162 x 1171 by Raoul, canon of St-Victor, Paris. Jean de Subligny, son of Hasculphe founder of La Lucerne, and Rualen du Homme were two of the earliest patrons. Situated on the Sélune.

Sources:
Bonnin, pp. 83–4; *Register*, p. 95

References:
Arnoux, p. 151
Beck, 'Recherches sur les salles capitulaires', pp. 42–3
Cottineau, vol. 2, col. 1927

55. Mont-St-Michel

dép. : Manche, arr.: Avranches, cant.: Pontorson
Benedictine abbey, Avranches diocese

Refounded 966 by Richard I, duke of Normandy and confirmed by King Lothar. The church was originally built in the eleventh century and then rebuilt in the fifteenth after the choir collapsed. Due to its location, the abbey was not built around a cloister, but on three levels below the abbey church.

Sources:
Baylé, 'Mont-Saint-Michel: église Notre-Dame-sous-Terre'
Baylé 'Mont-Saint-Michel: abbatiale romane'
Bonnin, pp. 246–7; *Register*, p. 274
Fauroux, nos 12, 16–17, 47, 49, 65, 73, 76–7, 110–11, 132–3, 148, 232
Regesta regum, nos 213–14

References:
Beck, 'Recherches sur les salles capitulaires', p. 56
Cottineau, vol. 2, cols 1897–1908
GC, vol. 11, cols 510–33
Millénaire monastique du Mont-St-Michel
Potts, *Monastic Revival*, pp. 81–2

Plates and photographs:
Courtauld Institute of Art, Conway Collection, B36/4878, by F.R.P. Sumner, thirteenth-century cloister arcade; B78/3644, nave and B78/3664, thirteenth-century refectory

56. Mortemer-en-Lyon (Lisors)

dép. : Eure, arr.: Les Andelys, cant.: Lyons-la-Fôret
Cistercian abbey, Rouen diocese
Founded before 1130 and definitely Cistercian by 1137. Construction began under Abbot Adam (1138–54) with the lay brothers' range.

Sources:
Twelfth-Century Statutes, 1190, no. 7, 1193, no. 57

References
Arnoux and Maneuvrier, *Deux abbayes*
Beck, 'Recherches sur les salles capitulaires', pp. 70–1
Cottineau, vol. 2, cols 1990–1
GC, vol. 11, cols 307–13
Gosse-Kishinewski, 'Lisors: Abbaye Notre-Dame de Mortemer'
Twelfth-Century Statutes, p. 793

57. Mortemer-sur-Eaulne, Notre-Dame

dép. : Seine-Maritime arr. and cant.: Neufchâtel-en-Bray
Benedictine (Cluniac) priory, Rouen diocese
Founded in the eleventh century. Situated on the Eaulne near its source.

Sources:
Bonnin, p. 339; *Register*, p. 385

References:
Cottineau, vol. 2, col. 1991

58. Muzy

dép. : Eure, arr.: Évreux, cant.: Nonancourt
Benedictine priory, Évreux diocese
Dependent on Coulombs and founded c.1128 by Rahier de Muzy. Situated on the Avre.

Sources:
Bonnin, pp. 70, 221, 307; *Register*, pp. 78, 243, 350

References:
Cottineau, vol. 2, col. 2024

59. Neufmarché-en-Lyons, St-Pierre

dép. : Seine-Maritime, arr.: Neufchâtel-en-Bray, cant.: Gournay
Benedictine priory, Rouen diocese
In c.1070–80, Hugh of Grandmesnil expelled the canons and replaced them with monks
from St-Évroul. In c.1128, William Roumare increased the size of the community and
according to Orderic Vitalis this occasioned the building of a new choir.

Sources:
Bonnin, pp. 13, 67, 114, 146, 254, 282, 413, 544, 620; *Register*, pp. 16, 76, 129, 166, 284, 318,
471, 622, 713

References:
Cottineau, vol. 2, col. 2057
Musset, *Normandie romane*, vol. 2, p. 30

60. Notre-Dame-du-Val (St-Omer)

dép. : Calvados, arr.: Falaise, cant.: Thury-Harcourt
Augustinian abbey, Bayeux diocese
Founded by Goscelin de la Pommeraye in 1125.

Sources:
'Documents relatifs à l'abbaye Notre-Dame du Val', ed. Arnoux, pp. 347–62
Bonnin, p. 578; *Register*, pp. 665–6

References:
Arnoux, pp. 21, 214
Beck, 'Recherches sur les salles capitulaires', p. 52
Cottineau, vol. 2, col. 3254
GC, vol. 11, cols 440–1

61. Noyon-sur-Andelle/Nogion (Charleval), Notre-Dame

dép. : Eure, arr.: Les Andelys, cant.: Fleury-sur-Andelle
Benedictine priory, Rouen diocese
Dependent on St-Évroul. Founded in 1108 by William, count of Évreux, at the instigation
of his wife Helvise, daughter of William, count of Nevers, and under Abbot Roger.

Sources:
Bonnin, pp. 49, 168, 192, 426, 465; *Register*, pp. 55, 184, 206, 486, 530

References:
Cottineau, vol. 2, col. 2085

62. Ouville (Ouville l'Abbaye), Notre-Dame

dép. : Seine-Maritime, arr.: Yvetot, cant.: Yerville
Augustinian abbey, Rouen diocese
Charters show that this community was in existence before the end of the twelfth
century.[14] Founded by William of Ouville.

Sources:
Bonnin, pp. 9, 53–4, 119, 171, 210, 385, 432, 519, 600; *Register*, pp. 13, 59, 134, 188–9, 230,
438, 492–3, 593, 691

[14] Cottineau gives a thirteenth-century date.

References:
Arnoux, pp. 22, 156
Cottineau, vol. 2, col. 2161

63. Pavilly

dép. : Seine-Maritime, arr.: Rouen, cant.: chef-lieu
Benedictine, priory, Rouen diocese
Dependent on Montreuil-sur-Mer from 1037.

References:
Cottineau, vol. 2, cols 2238–9

64. Planches, Notre-Dame

dép. : Orne, arr.: Argentan, cant.: Le Merlerault
Benedictine priory, Lisieux diocese
Dependent on St-Père-de-Chartres and founded before 1065.

Sources:
Bonnin, pp. 78, 233; *Register*, pp. 88, 256

References:
Cottineau, vol. 2, col. 2295

65. Pontoise, St-Martin[15]

dép. : Seine-et-Oise, arr.: chef-lieu
Benedictine abbey, Rouen diocese
Founded around 1050 by Amaury and received a confirmation from Philip I of France in 1090.

Sources:
Bonnin, pp. 41, 105, 132, 165, 193, 241, 275, 312, 447, 536; *Register*, pp. 46, 120, 149, 180, 207–8, 267, 309, 355, 508, 611–12

References:
Cottineau, vol. 2, cols 2334–5

66. Pré: Notre-Dame

dép. : Seine-Maritime, arr.: Rouen, faubourg St-Sever
Benedictine, priory, Rouen diocese
Founded in c.1063 by Duke William and Duchess Matilda. It was given to Bec in 1093.

Sources:
Bonnin, pp. 34–5, 271, 411; *Register*, pp. 39, 303, 468

References:
Cottineau, vol. 2, col. 2546
GC, vol. 11, cols 239–44

67. Préaux: St-Pierre

dép. : Eure, arr. and cant.: Pont-Audemer
Benedictine abbey, Lisieux diocese
Originally founded in the eighth century and restored in 1034 by Humphrey de Vieilles. This community has left no archaeological trace.

---

[15] Although not in Normandy, this house was in the Rouen archdiocese during the Middle Ages.

Sources:
Bonnin, pp. 60, 198, 295, 591; *Register*, pp. 66, 212–13, 334, 680
Fauroux, nos 88–9, 87, 121, 174–5
Regesta regum, nos 218–19
Rouet, 'Le patrimoine anglais et l'Angleterre vus à travers les actes du cartulaire de St-Pierre de Préaux', pièces justicatives, pp. 113–15

References:
Cottineau, vol. 2, cols 2356–7
GC, vol. 11, cols 834–42
Gazeau, 'Le temporal de l'abbaye de St-Pierre de Préaux au XIe siècle'
Henry, 'Les abbayes de Préaux', pp. 191–216

Plates and photographs:
Monasticon, plate 112

68. Rouen, La Trinité-du-Mont and later Mont-Ste-Catherine

dép. : Seine-Maritime, chef-lieu
Benedictine, abbey, Rouen diocese
Founded before 1030 by Goscelin of Arques. The church was consecrated in 1030 by Archbishop Robert.

Sources:
Bonnin, pp. 7, 103, 133, 168, 195, 302, 346, 382; *Register*, pp. 9, 118–19, 150, 184–5, 210–11, 342; 394, 433
Fauroux, nos 60–1, 81–4, 96, 101, 104, 118–19, 123, 130, 135, 138, 143, 200–2, 206, 221, 233
Regesta regum, nos 231–6

References:
Cottineau, vol. 2, cols 2544–5

69. Rouen, St-Lô

dép. : Seine-Maritime, chef-lieu
Augustinian priory, Rouen diocese
Reformed in 1132 by Bishop Algare of Coutances. Most of the church was destroyed in 1944.

Sources:
Bonnin, pp. 48, 133–4, 169, 204, 280, 524; *Register*, pp. 54, 151, 185, 222–3, 314, 598

References:
Arnoux, p. 21
Cottineau, vol. 2, col. 2545

70. Rouen, St-Ouen

dép. : Seine-Maritime, chef-lieu
Benedictine abbey, Rouen diocese
Originally founded in the middle of the sixth century and dedicated to St Peter. Restored in the eleventh century after destruction by the Normans in 841. The community was damaged by fires in 1156, 1201 and 1248; most of the existing architecture dates from the fourteenth century onwards. The cloister appears to have been located on the northern side of the church and most of the medieval buildings were destroyed during rebuilding in the eighteenth century.

Sources:
Bonnin, pp. 56–8, 121, 202–3, 265, 326–7, 401, 456, 495, 551–2, 585; *Register*, pp. 62–4, 136, 219–21, 296–7, 373–4, 415–16, 457, 519, 563, 630–1, 675

Fauroux, nos 13, 19, 21, 24, 37, 39, 40–5, 53, 57, 78–9, 103, 105, 107, 112, 158, 191, 193, 204–5, 210–12
Regesta regum, nos 243–8

References:
Baylé, 'Rouen: abbatiale Saint-Ouen'
Beck, 'Recherches sur les salles capitulaires', pp. 69–70
Cottineau, vol. 2, cols 2547–50
Fouré, 'Rouen, abbatiale St-Ouen'
GC, vol. 11, cols 135–55
Le Maho, 'Recherches sur les origines des quelques églises de Rouen', pp. 178–9
Musset, *Normandie romane*, vol. 2, p. 31
Musset, 'Ce qu'enseigne l'histoire d'un patrimoine monastique: St-Ouen de Rouen du IXe au XIe siècle'

Plates and photographs:
Monasticon, plate 121

71. Sacey: St-Martin

dép. : Manche, arr.: Avranches, cant.: Pontorson
Benedictine priory, Avranches diocese
Dependent on Marmoutier and founded by Count Robert de Bodiac. Situated on the Guerge.

Sources:
Bonnin, pp. 84, 246; *Register*, pp. 96–7, 273–4

References:
Cottineau, vol. 2, col. 2572

72. St-André-de-Gouffern (La Hoguette)

dép. : Calvados, arr. and cant.: Falaise
Savigniac/Cistercian abbey, Bayeux diocese
Founded in 1131 then affiliated to Clairvaux.

Sources:
Registrum epistolarum, pp. 196–7, 207–8, 213, 221
Twelfth-Century Statutes, 1191, no. 30, 1193, no. 57

References:
Beck, 'Recherches sur les salles capitulaires', pp. 85–6
Cottineau, vol. 2, col. 2588
GC, vol. 11, cols 743–7
Twelfth-Century Statutes, p. 800

73. St-Barbe-en-Auge (Écajeul)

dép. : Calvados, arr.: Lisieux, cant.: Mézidon
Augustinian priory, Lisieux diocese
Originally founded as St-Martin-d'Écajeul by Stigand Mézidon in 1055. William, a former canon of Rouen cathedral and a hermit in the forest of Breteuil imposed the Augustinian rule and reformed the community. Situated on the Dives.

Sources:
Bonnin, pp. 63, 199, 303; *Register*, pp. 71, 215, 344
'Chartes concernant le prieuré de Saint-Barbe-en-Auge', ed. Arnoux, pp. 295–7
'Chronique de Sainte-Barbe-en-Auge', ed. Arnoux, pp. 275–93
'Deux lettres de Geoffrey de Breteuil, sous-prieur', ed. Arnoux, pp. 293–5
Fauroux, no. 22 (Écajeul)

References:
Arnoux, p. 11
Beck, 'Recherches sur les salles capitulaires', p. 87
Cottineau, vol. 2, col. 2604

74. St-Évroul

dép. : Orne, arr.: Argentan, cant.: La Ferté-Fresnel
Benedictine priory, Lisieux diocese
Originally founded in the sixth century and restored by Abbot Thierry in 1058. Situated on the river Charentonne in the forest of Ouche. The church was originally built in the late eleventh century and rebuilt in the thirteenth following the earlier plan: it is known only from drawings.

Sources:
Bonnin, pp. 63, 200, 303; *Register*, pp. 72, 216, 345
Fauroux, nos 122, 155
OV, passim
Regesta regum, no. 255

References:
Beck, 'Recherches sur les salles capitulaires', pp. 73–4
Cottineau, vol. 2, cols 2669–71
GC, vol. 11, cols 813–30
Le Maho, 'Autour de la foundation de l'abbaye de Boscherville, p. 138
Monasticon, plate 111
Thiron, 'L'abbaye de St-Évroul'

75. St-Fromond

dép. : Manche, arr.: St-Lô, cant.: St-Jean-de-Daye
Benedictine priory, Coutances diocese
Dependent on Cérisy and founded in the eleventh century.[16]

Sources:
Bonnin, pp. 91, 251, 557; *Register*, pp. 104, 281, 638

References:
Cottineau, vol. 2, col. 2682
Musset, 'Les origines du prieuré de St-Fromond: un acte negligée de Richard II'

76. Ste-Gauberge (St-Cyr-la-Rosière)

dép. : Orne, arr.: Montagne, cant.: Nocé
Benedictine priory, Sées diocese
Founded before 1024 as dependent on St-Florentin de Bonneval. Bishop Yves de Bellême (1034–70) gave it to St-Père de Chartres.

Sources:
Bonnin, pp. 233–4; *Register*, pp. 257

References:
Cottineau, vol. 2, col. 2961

77. St-Georges-de-Boscherville (St-Martin-de-Boscherville)

dép. : Seine-Maritime, arr.: Rouen, cant.: Duclair
Secular canons/Benedictine abbey, Rouen diocese

---

[16]   Cottineau gives a date of 1179.

Originally a college of canons founded in 1050 by Raoul of Tancarville. The Benedictine abbey was founded in 1113 by William of Tancarville with monks from St-Évroul. The vestiges of the college church and small cloister were discovered during excavations. The later Benedictine church was possibly inspired by St-Évroul. The chapter house was constructed at the end of the twelfth century by Abbot Victor (1157–1211) who was buried there.

Sources:
Bonnin, pp. 56, 103, 134, 191, 266, 501; *Register*, pp. 61–2, 118, 151, 205, 297, 571
Fauroux, no. 197 for the college of canons

References:
Baylé, 'Saint-Martin-de-Boscherville: abbatiale Saint-Georges'
Beck, 'Recherches sur les salles capitulaires', pp. 71–2
Cottineau, vol. 2, cols 2701–2
GC, vol. 11, cols 267–73
Le Maho, 'Autour de la foundation de l'abbaye de Boscherville', pp. 192–42
Le Maho, 'Une collégiate normande au temps de Guillaume le Conquérnat: St-Georges-de-Boscherville, d'après les fouilles de 1981'
Le Maho, 'Saint-Martin-de-Boscherville: collégiale Saint-Georges'
Morrison, 'The Figural Capitals of the Chapterhouse of Saint-Georges-de-Boscherville'
Musset, *Normandie romane*, vol. 2, pp. 143–56

Plates and photographs:
Courtauld Institute of Art, Conway Collection, B36/5382, church; 18L/19(19a), chapter house and A771/1418, chapter house doorway
Monasticon, plate 117
Musset, *Normandie romane*, vol. 2, plates 64–91

78. St-Hilaire-du-Harcourt

dép. : Manche, arr.: Mortain, cant.: chef-lieu
Benedictine priory, Avranches diocese
Founded in c.1083 and dependent on St-Benoit-sur-Loire.

Sources:
Bonnin, pp. 245, 459; *Register*, pp. 273, 523

References:
Cottineau, vol. 2, col. 2728

79. St-Hymer-en-Auge:

dép. : Calvados, arr. and cant.: Pont-l'Évêque
Canons/Benedictine priory, Lisieux diocese
Originally founded in 1066 as a college of canons. In 1147 it became a priory of Bec by Hugh IV of Montfort.

Sources:
Bonnin, pp. 61, 198, 296; *Register*, pp. 68, 214, 335
Regesta regum, no. 258

References:
Cottineau, vol. 2, col. 2733

80. St-Laurent-en-Lyons (Fleury-la-Fôret)

dép. : Eure, arr.: Les Andelys, cant.: Lyons-la-Fôret
Augustinian priory, Rouen diocese
Founded before 1151 by Enguerrand le Portier. It had been a college of canons from c.1015.

Sources:
Bonnin, pp. 66, 115, 206, 363–4, 412, 582; *Register*, pp. 75, 129, 224, 415, 470, 671
'Confirmation des biens de Saint-Laurent-en-Lyons', ed. Arnoux, pp. 345–6

References:
Arnoux, p. 21
Cottineau, vol. 2, col. 2760

81. St-Lô: Ste-Croix

dép. : Manche, chef-lieu
Augustinian abbey, Coutances diocese
Reformed in 1132 or 1139 by Bishop Algare.

Sources:
Bonnin, pp. 86–7, 557; *Register*, pp. 99, 638

References:
Arnoux, p. 21
Beck, 'Recherches sur les salles capitulaires', pp. 28–9
Cottineau, vol. 2, cols 2768–9
GC, vol. 11, cols 935–40

82. St-Martin-d'Es [17]

dép. : Oise, arr.: Beauvaise, cant.: chef-lieu
Benedictine priory, Rouen diocese
Dependent on St-Magloire in Paris.

Sources:
Bonnin, pp. 282, 319, 489; *Register*, pp. 318, 365, 557

83. St-Martin-la-Garenne [18]

dép. : Seine-et-Oise, arr.: Mantes, cant.: Limay
Benedictine priory, Rouen diocese
Founded in 1141 by Archbishop Hugh of Amiens and dependent on Bec.

Sources:
Bonnin, pp. 45, 132, 166, 189, 302; *Register*, pp. 51, 148, 181, 202, 343

References:
Cottineau, vol. 2, col. 2832

84. St-Pierre-sur-Dives

dép. : Calvados, arr.: Lisieux, cant.: chef-lieu
Benedictine abbey, Sées diocese
Founded in 1046 by Lesceline, the sister-in-law of Duke Richard II.

Sources:
Bonnin, pp. 59, 77, 232, 371; *Register*, pp. 66, 87, 255, 419
Haimon

References:
Cottineau, vol. 2, cols 2851–3
GC, vol. 11, cols 728–35

---

[17]   Although not in Normandy, this community was part of the Rouen archdiocese.
[18]   Although not in Normandy, this community was part of the Rouen archdiocese.

Plates and photographs:
Monasticon, plate 131

85. Ste-Radegonde, Neufchâtel-en-Bray

dép. : Seine-Maritime arr.: Neufchâtel-en-Bray, chef-lieu
Benedictine priory, Rouen diocese
Dependent on St-Pierre-des-Préaux.

Sources:
Bonnin, p. 208; *Register*, p. 227

References:
Beck, 'Recherches sur les salles capitulaires', p. 72
Rouet, 'Une dépendance de l'abbaye St-Pierre de Préaux: le prieuré Ste-Radegonde'

86. St-Saëns

dép. : Seine-Maritime, arr.: Neufchâtel, cant.: chef-lieu
Benedictine priory, Rouen diocese
Dependent on St-Wandrille by 1150.

Sources:
Bonnin, pp. 7, 58, 325, 516, 599, 637; *Register*, pp. 8, 64–5, 371, 589, 689, 733

References:
Cottineau, vol. 2, cols 2873–4

87. St-Sever

dép. : Calvados, arr.: Vire, cant.: chef-lieu
Benedictine abbey, Coutances diocese
Originally founded in 523 and refounded in the eleventh century.[19] The first abbot was
Ascelin.

Sources:
Bonnin, pp. 85, 248; *Register*, pp. 97, 276

References:
Beck, 'Recherches sur les salles capitulaires', pp. 43–4
Cottineau, vol. 2, cols 2887–8
GC, vol. 11, cols 913–16
Musset, 'Les origines et le patrimoine de l'abbaye de St-Sever'

88. St-Sulpice-sur-Risle (L'aigle)

dép. : Orne, arr.: Mortagne, cant.: chef-lieu
Benedictine priory, Évreux diocese
Dependent on St-Laumer-de-Blois.

Sources:
Bonnin, pp. 70–1, 219, 306, 626; *Register*, pp. 79, 240, 348, 720

References:
Cottineau, vol. 2, cols 2897–8

89. St-Vigor-le-Grand

dép. : Calvados, arr. and cant.: Bayeux
Benedictine abbey, Bayeux diocese

---

[19]   Musset suggests a date of between 1066 and 1070.

Originally founded in the sixth century by St Vigor, the community was restored after destruction during the Viking incursions by Bishop Odo (1050–97). The claustral ranges were to the north of the church.

Sources:
Bonnin, pp. 92, 261; *Register*, pp. 106–7, 292

References:
Beck, 'Recherches sur les salles capitulaires', pp. 22–4
Cottineau, vol. 2, cols 2916–17

Plates and photographs:
Monasticon, plate 103

90. St-Wandrille, SS Pierre and Paul

dép.: Seine-Maritime, arr.: Yvetot, cant.: Caudebec-en-Caux
Benedictine abbey, Rouen diocese
Originally founded in 648 and restored in 1033. The refectory dates from the second half of the twelfth century.

Sources:
Bonnin, pp. 55, 111, 134, 171, 224, 266, 293, 325, 352; *Register*, pp. 60, 126–7, 152, 189–90, 247, 297–8, 331, 371, 400
Fauroux, nos 7, 30, 46, 52, 55, 69, 80, 95, 102, 106, 108–9, 124–6, 128–9, 134, 152–4, 177, 190, 207, 234
Regesta regum, nos 261–4

References:
Cottineau, vol. 2, cols 2921–4
GC, vol. 11, cols 155–85
Musset, *Normandie romane*, vol. 2, pp. 259–61

Plates and photographs:
Courtauld Institute of Art, Conway Collection, B89/1145, church and a clipping of the twelfth-century refectory
Monasticon, plate 130
Musset, *Normandie romane*, vol. 2, plates 130–8

91. Sausseuse (Tilly)

dép.: Eure, arr.: Les Andelys, cant.: Écos
Augustinian priory, Rouen diocese
Founded in 1118 or 1119.

Sources:
Bonnin, pp. 45, 104, 131, 190, 271, 484; *Register*, pp. 51, 120, 148, 202–3, 304, 552

References:
Arnoux, p. 20
Cottineau, vol. 2, cols 1960–1

92. Savigny

dép.: Manche, arr.: Mortain, cant.: Le Teilleul
Savigniac/Cistercian abbey, Coutances diocese
Founded in 1112 by Raoul de Fougères and his wife Amicia for Vital of Mortain and then affiliated to Clairvaux. A new church was begun in 1173 and consecrated in 1220 to house the relics of its saints. The surviving refectory door is Romanesque.

Sources:
Registrum epistolarum, pp. 224–32

Twelfth-Century Statutes 1189, no. 4, 1190, no. 53, 1191, nos 1, 16; 1192, nos 18, 30; 1193, nos 22, 55; 1194, nos 23, 40, 51, 54; 1195, nos 59, 66, 76; 1198, nos 27, 40; 1199, nos 17, 19, 54; 1200, nos 54, 1201, nos 25, 26, 49

References:
Beck, 'Recherches sur les salles capitulaires', pp. 31–3
Cottineau, vol. 2, col. 2966
Grant, 'Savigny and its Saints'
Musset, *Normandie romane*, vol. 1, p. 42
Suydam, 'Origins of the Savignac Order'
Swietek, 'King Henry II and Savigny'
Twelfth-Century Statutes, p. 803.

93. Sées, St-Martin

dép. : Orne, arr.: Alençon, cant.: chef-lieu
Benedictine abbey, Sées diocese
Restored in 1060 by Roger of Montgomery and his wife Mabel.

Sources:
Bonnin, pp. 80, 235; *Register*, pp. 91, 260
Regesta regum, no. 271

References:
Cottineau, vol. 2, cols 2992–3
GC, vol. 11, cols 712–28

94. Sigy, St-Martin and St-Wulgan

dép. : Seine-Maritime, arr.: Neufchâtel-en-Bray, cant.: Argueil
Benedictine abbey, Rouen diocese
Founded in c.1052 by a certain Hugh I. Given as a priory of St-Ouen in Rouen in the twelfth century by Hugh II. Situated on the Andelle.

Sources:
Bonnin, pp. 541, 480, 551; *Register*, pp. 512, 547, 630

References:
Cottineau, vol. 2, col. 3034

95. Ticheville: Notre-Dame

dép. : Orne, arr.: Argentan, cant.: Vimoutiers
Benedictine priory, Lisieux diocese
Dependent on St-Wandrille.

Sources:
Bonnin, pp. 63, 303; *Register*, pp. 72, 344

References:
Cottineau, vol. 2, cols 3157–8

96. Tillières-sur-Avre, St-Hilarie

dép. : Eure, arr.: Évreux, cant.: Verbeuil-sur-Avre
Benedictine priory, Évreux diocese
Dependent on Bec, founded in 1077 by Gilbert Crispin.

Sources:
Bonnin, p. 626; *Register*, p. 720

References:
Cottineau, vol. 2, col. 3160

97. Tournai-sur-Dives

dép. : Orne, arr.: Argentan, cant.: Trun
Benedictine priory, Sées diocese
Dependent on La Croix-Ste-Leufroy.[20]

Sources:
Bonnin, pp. 78, 232, 371–2; *Register*, pp. 88, 255–6, 420–1

References:
Cottineau, vol. 2, col. 3188

98. Le Tréport, St-Michel

dép. : Seine-Maritime, arr.: Dieppe, cant.: Eu
Benedictine abbey, Rouen diocese
Founded in 1053 by Robert I, count of Eu. Situated on the Channel at the mouth of the Bresle.

Sources:
Bonnin, pp. 48, 99–100, 139, 228–9, 269, 496, 609; *Register*, pp. 54, 113–14, 157, 251, 302, 565, 701
Fauroux, nos 215–17

References:
Cottineau, vol. 2, col. 3209
GC, vol. 11, cols 244–53

99. Valasse, le (Gruchet-le-Valasse), Notre-Dame de Voeu

dép. : Seine-Maritime, arr.: Le Havre, cant.: Bolbec
Cistercian Rouen diocese
Founded 1157 by Mortemer-en-Lyon. Remains of the chapter house are in existence.

Sources:
Twelfth-Century Statutes, 1190, no. 54; 1194, no. 44; 1199, no.17

References:
Cottineau, vol. 2, cols 3268–9
GC, vol. 11, cols 313–16
Twelfth-Century Statutes, p. 808

Plates and photographs:
Courtauld Institute of Art, Conway Collection, L75/3/24, twelfth-century chapter house

100. Valmont, Notre-Dame

dép. : Seine-Maritime, arr.: Yvetot, cant.: chef-lieu
Benedictine abbey, Rouen diocese
Founded in 1169 by Nicolas d'Estouteville. Parts of the twelfth-century church survive.

Sources:
Bonnin, pp. 31, 110, 135, 225, 266, 293, 353, 600, 630; *Register*, pp. 35, 125, 152, 248, 298, 332, 401–2, 690–1, 725

References:
Cottineau, vol. 2, col. 3289

[20] See no. 28.

GC, vol. 11, cols 278–81

Plates and photographs:
Courtauld Institute of Art, Conway Collection, B65/819, church

101. Val-Richer (St-Ouen-le-Pin)

dép. : Calvados, arr.: Pont-l'Évêque, cant.: Cambremer
Cistercian abbey, Bayeux diocese
Founded 1147 by Robert Tesson and affiliated to Clairvaux. It was the only Cistercian community founded in Normandy before the incorporation within the order of the Savignac congregation. The community moved from its original site at Soulevre to Val-Richer before 1150.

Sources:
Arnoux and Maneuvrier, *Deux abbayes*
Twelfth-Century Statutes, 1197, no. 47; 1198, no. 35; 1199, no. 19

References:
Beck, 'Recherches sur les salles capitulaires', pp. 40–1
Cottineau, vol. 2, col. 3264
Twelfth-Century Statutes, p. 809

102. Vernonnet, St-Michel

dép. : Eure, arr.: Évreux, cant.: chef-lieu
Benedictine priory, Rouen diocese
Dependent on Montebourg.

Sources:
Bonnin, pp. 109, 214; *Register*, pp. 124–5, 235–6

References:
Cottineau, vol. 2, cols 3340–1

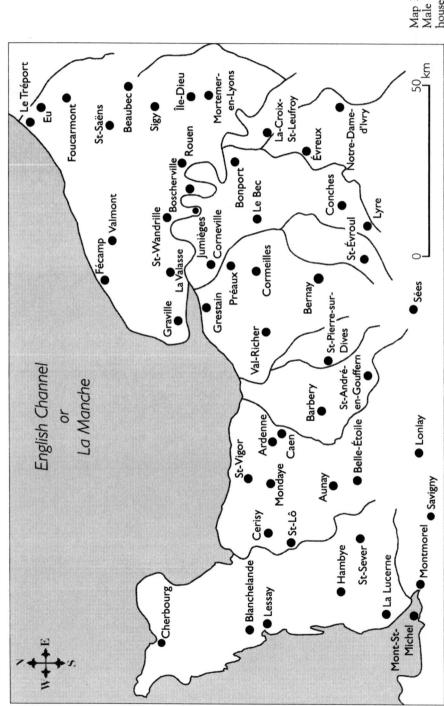

Map 1
Male religious
houses.

Appendix B: Nunneries[1]

1. Acquigny

dép. : Eure, arr. and cant.: Louviers
Fontevraud priory, Lisieux diocese
Founded in the mid-1120s by the Conches-Tosny family, but defunct by 1136. This was the first priory of Fontevraud in Normandy and has generally been ignored by historians. The community was probably dispersed after a fire, started by Waleran of Meulan, destroyed the castle and village in May 1136.

References:
Bienvenu, 'L'ordre de Fontevraud et la Normandie au XII siècle'

2. Almenèches

dép. : Orne, arr.: Argentan, cant.: Mortée
Benedictine abbey, Sées diocese
Originally founded in the sixth century but ceased to exist by the tenth. Refounded by 1063–66 by Roger of Montgomery.[2] After its refoundation, the house suffered three fires, the last shortly after Easter in 1308. As a consequence, little of a documentary or material nature survives for its early years. In the sixteenth century the community was attached to Fontevraud and founded priories at Argentan (1623) and Exmes (1630). In 1736 the abbey moved to Argentan.

Sources:
Bonnin, pp. 82, 235–6, 374; *Register*, pp. 93, 260, 424
GND, vol. 2, pp. 132–3
Haskins, *Norman Institutions*, p. 328
OV, vol. 4, pp. 32–7
Regesta, ed. Cronne and Davis, vol. 3, nos 17–18

References:
L'abbaye d'Almenèches-Argentan et Sainte-Opportune: sa vie et son culte, ed. Chaussy
Bouvris, 'En marge de l'année des abbayes normandes: la date de la restauration de l'abbaye d'Almenèches'
Cottineau, vol. 1, cols 62–3
GC, vol. 11, cols 735–40
Musset, 'Les premiers temps de l'abbaye d'Almenèches des origines aux XIIe siècle'
Oury, *Abbaye Notre-Dame d'Almenèches-Argentan*

---

[1] Dates of foundation follow John Walmsley's unpublished list of Norman nunneries unless otherwise noted. I am very grateful to Dr Walmsley for allowing me to use this material.
[2] Around 1060 according to Robert of Torigny.

3. Bival

dép. : Seine-Maritime, arr. and cant.: Neufchâtel
Savignac/Cistercian abbey, Rouen diocese
Founded by William and Robert of Bival in 1128, originally as a daughter house of Beaubec
but tensions quickly surfaced between the nuns and the abbots of Beaubec and Savigny.
This dissent resulted in some of the women leaving to help form new houses at Bondeville
and St-Saëns. In 1175, the abbey submitted to the authority of the ordinary, the archbishop
of Rouen.

Sources:
Bonnin, pp. 6, 9, 27, 117, 146, 226–7, 229, 268, 299, 339, 407, 468, 523, 550–1, 610, 635;
Register, pp. 6–7, 12, 23, 131, 165, 207, 252, 300, 339, 386, 462, 532, 596–7, 629–30, 702,
732

References:
Cottineau, vol. 1, col. 385
GC, vol. 11, cols 316–19
Strayer, 'A Forged Charter of Henry II for Bival'

4. Bondeville

dép. : Seine-Maritime, arr.: Rouen, cant.: Maromme
Savignac/Cistercian priory, Rouen diocese
Founded from Bival by Richard de Rouvres, his wife Matilda and their children 1128 x
1148. A drawing of this house survives in the seventeenth-century Gaignières collection. It
shows the church of St-Denis in the foreground, which appears to date from the thirteenth
and fourteenth centuries. It was still standing in 1844 but was then destroyed.

Sources:
Bonnin, pp. 15, 111–12, 217, 298–9, 348, 410, 455, 487, 512, 571, 615; *Register*, pp. 18, 127,
237, 337–8, 395–6, 467–8, 518–9, 556, 656, 584, 707–8
Walmsley, 'Two Lost Charters for the Nunneries of Villers-Canivet and Bondeville'

References:
Cottineau, vol. 1, col. 419
GC, vol. 11, cols 319–22

Plates and photographs:
Desmarchelier, 'L'architecture des églises de moniales cisterciennes', p. 106 for the drawing
in the Gaignières collection.

5. Caen, La Trinité

dép. : Calvados, chef-lieu
Benedictine abbey, Bayeux diocese
Founded in c.1059 by William, duke of Normandy and Duchess Matilda. La Trinité was
the parallel foundation to St-Étienne. The church was dedicated in June 1066, the date
of which coincided with a meeting of barons to prepare for the expedition to England.
Situated at the summit of a hill over the confluence of the Orne and the Odon, the only
survival from the medieval period is the abbey church which underwent three major
building campaigns, the last in 1130. Much of the fabric was restored in the nineteenth
century by Ruprich-Robert. Also in the nineteenth century, the remains of a Romanesque
porter's lodge and a building, termed Queen Matilda's palace, were demolished. The latter
was probably a guest house or some form of lodging. The location of the cloister is debateable but was probably situated on the north, due to a lack of space on the south side of
the church. Baylé argues that a plan of Caen by Bignon, dated 1672, shows square-shaped
buildings to the north of the church which were possibly indicative of a cloister.

Sources:
Les actes … pour les abbayes caennais, nos 2, 8–9, 11–12, 15–17, 21–2, 25, 27, 29
Bonnin, pp. 94, 261, 575; Register, pp. 110, 293, 662
Charters and Custumals of the Abbey of Holy Trinity Caen: the English Estates
Charters and Custumals of the Abbey of Holy Trinity Caen: the French Estates
Fauroux, no. 231
GC, vol. 11, Instrumenta, cols 59–61, 68–72, 75–6
GND, vol. 2, pp. 132–3
OV, vol. 2, pp. 10–11; vol. 3, pp. 8–11; vol. 4, pp. 44–7
Regesta Regum, nos 58–65

References:
Baylé, 'La Trinité de Caen'
Baylé, La Trinité de Caen, sa place dans l'histoire de l'architecture et du décor Romans
Baylé, Abbaye aux Dames La Trinité de Caen
Cottineau, vol. 1, cols 553–4
GC, vol. 11, cols 431–40
Walmsley, 'The Early Abbesses, Nuns and Female Tenants of the Abbey of Holy Trinity, Caen'

Plates and photographs:
Baylé, 'Caen: abbatiale de la Trinité (Abbaye-aux-Dames)'
Courtauld Institute of Art, Conway Collections, B36/4670, A77/1252, B36/4528 views of the church

6. La Caine, Notre Dame

dép. : Calvados, arr.: Caen, cant.: Evrecy
Benedictine priory, Bayeux diocese
Probably founded in 1066 by Roger Malfillâtre and dependent on the abbey of Beaumont-les-Tours. The elevation from priory to abbey was anticipated by a provision that the abbess should be nominated by the abbess of Beaumont but this was never realised.

Sources:
Fauroux, no. 227

References:
Bouvris, 'En marge de l'année des abbayes normandes: la date de la restauration de l'abbaye d'Almenèches', p. 116, note 9
Cottineau, vol. 1, col. 558

7. Chaise-Dieu-du-Theil, Notre-Dame

dép. : Eure, arr.: Évreux, cant.: Rugles
Fontevraud priory, Évreux diocese
Founded between 1128 and 1132 by Richer II of L'Aigle. The priory of Chaise-Dieu-du-Theil became closely associated with the male community of Le Désert and received endowments from a wide area of south Normandy and England.[3] Bienvenu treats the two houses as the same foundation. Surviving architecture includes part of the south wall of the church, the sanctuary of St-Jean which was possibly the brothers' chapel and part of the west range of the cloister.

References:
Bienvenu, 'L'ordre de Fontevraud et la Normandie au XII siècle'
Cottineau, vol. 1, col. 669
Martin, 'Un couvent des femmes'
Power, The Norman Frontier, pp. 306–7

[3]   See appendix A, no. 29.

8. Clairruissel (Gaillefontaine)

dép. : Seine-Maritime, arr.: Neufchâtel, cant.: Forges-les-Eaux
Fontevraud priory, Rouen diocese
Possibly founded in 1140 by Hugh IV of Gournay and Melisande.

References:
Bienvenu, 'L'ordre de Fontevraud et la Normandie au XII siècle'
Cottineau, vol. 1, cols 798–9

9. Cordillon (Lingèvres), St-Laurent

dép. : Calvados, arr.: Bayeux, cant.: Balleroy
Benedictine abbey, Bayeux diocese
Founded in 1190 by William de Soliers, knight.[4]

Sources:
GC, vol. 11, *Instrumenta*, cols 93–4 and 100

References:
Beck, 'Recherches sur les salles capitulaires', pp. 51–2
Cottineau, vol. 1, col. 872
GC, vol. 11, cols 438–40

10. Évreux, St-Sauveur

dép. : Eure, chef-lieu
Benedictine abbey, Évreux diocese
Founded in c.1060 by Richard, count of Évreux. Originally this abbey was situated inside the town in the *rue St-Nicolas* about twenty metres from the junction with the *rue de la Petite-Citeé*. It was destroyed by the fire of 1194 when King Philip Augustus captured the town. As a result, the nunnery was refounded outside the walls on land given by the cathedral near a branch of the river Iton. Little of the architecture now remains, most of it having been destroyed by a conversion following the Revolution. However, plans survive from the nineteenth century as well as a drawing from the seventeenth-century Gaignières collection. The cloister was situated on the north though it was extensively rebuilt in the sixteenth century.

Sources:
Bonnin, pp. 73, 220, 305, 624; *Register*, pp. 82–3, 241–2, 347, 718–19
Fauroux, no. 208
GC, vol. 11, *Instrumenta*, cols 125–7, 134–6, 141–2
GND, vol. 2, pp. 132–3
OV, vol. 6, pp. 228–9, 368–9

References:
Anchel, 'Quelques notes sur l'abbaye de Saint-Sauveur, d'Évreux à propos de la demolition du Quartier Tilly' with plans
'Chronique de fouilles médiévales', *Archéologie médiévale*, 1992, p. 447
'Chronique de fouilles médiévales', *Archéologie médiévale*, 1994, pp. 431–2
Cottineau, vol. 1, cols 1088–9
GC, vol. 11, cols 655–9

11. Fontaine-Guérard (Radepont)

dép. : Eure, arr.: Les Andelys, cant.: Fleury-sur-Andelle
Cistercian priory then abbey, Rouen diocese

---

4   According to Beck before 1198.

Founded between 1184 and 1190 by Robert, earl of Leicester, and Petronilla of Grandmesnil. Originally a priory, it was raised to abbatial status in 1253 and Ida was blessed as the first abbess on 20 June by Eudes Rigaud, archbishop of Rouen. Both King John of England and Louis IX of France were great benefactors. Fontaine-Guérard has some of the best surviving monastic architecture in Normandy. There are substantial remains of the abbey church and the east range of the cloister, including the sacristy, chapter house, dormitory, parlour and work room. In addition, a document entitled *État de situation de la maison de Fontaine-Guérard*, which dates from the time of the Revolution, gives a report of the buildings as they existed in 1792. The west range of the cloister housed a building used as a cellar and a kitchen with granaries above it. A warming room, refectory and a dormitory above were located in the south range. The infirmary was situated to the east of the cloister and the precinct contained granaries, stables and houses along with meadows, gardens and orchards. We do not know however, whether the arrangements detailed in this document date from the medieval period or later.

Sources:
GC, vol. 11, *Instrumenta*, cols 29–30

References:
Aubert, *L'architecture cistercienne en France*, vol. 2, pp. 177, 197–200
Cottineau, vol. 1, col. 1173
Fournée, *Abbaye de Fontaine-Guérard*
GC, vol. 11, cols 320–2

Plates and photographs:
Grant, *Architecture and Society*, pp. 113–14

12. Fumechon

dép. : Eure, arr.: Les Andelys, cant.: Fleury-sur-Andelle
Fontevraud priory, Rouen diocese
Founded from Clairruissel in c.1190.

References:
Bienvenu, 'L'ordre de Fontevraud et la Normandie au XII siècle'

13. Lisieux, St-Désir and Notre-Dame-du-Pré

dép. : Calvados, arr.: chef-lieu
Benedictine abbey, Lisieux diocese
Founded in c.1050 by Hugh, bishop of Lisieux, and his mother, Lesline, countess of Eu, who entered the house according to Potts. Originally founded at St-Pierre-Sur-Dives, at some stage in the first half of the eleventh century the nuns were transferred to Lisieux and replaced at St-Pierre by monks. The house was destroyed by bombing in 1944, but refounded after the war. Very little of the architecture has survived. The church was rebuilt in the sixteenth century following the collapse of the bell tower. It is possible that the medieval church comprised two phases. The first building, which contained a decorated Romanesque pavement, was partially destroyed by Angevin soldiers in the mid-twelfth century. It was rebuilt and a charter of Henry II purports to record the dedication.

Sources:
Bonnin, pp. 62, 199, 296, 592; *Register*, pp. 71, 214, 335–6, 682
Fauroux, no 140
GC, vol. 11, *Instrumenta*, cols 203–4
GND, vol. 2, pp. 132–3
OV, vol. 3, pp. 16–19
Regesta regum, no. 179

References:
Cottineau, vol. 1, cols 1626–7

Deshayes, 'Le pavement roman'
GC, vol. 11, cols 855–7
Potts, *Monastic Revival*, p. 112
Simon, *L'abbaye de Saint-Désir de Lisieux et ses fondateurs avec la liste des abbesses*
Simon, 'L'abbaye de Saint-Désir de Lisieux et ses églises successives'

14. Montivilliers, Notre-Dame

dép. : Seine-Maritime, arr.: Le Havre, cant.: chef-lieu
Benedictine abbey, Rouen diocese
Originally founded at Fécamp in 682 where the community was destroyed by Viking incursions, the community was refounded in 1035 by Robert, duke of Normandy. The claustral buildings have been restored recently, though the cloister arcade itself is a hypothetical reconstruction. Survivals from the Middle Ages include the dormitory dating from the turn of the twelfth and thirteenth centuries, the eleventh-century chapter house and thirteenth-century refectory in the east range and cellars and the continuation of the dormitory in the south. The abbess's apartments were located in the west range but nothing survives from the medieval period. The outer court of the monastery contained service buildings. In addition, the abbey church survives. It was originally built in the Romanesque style but has been much altered since the eleventh century. The parish church of St-Sauveur was later inserted into the north side of the nave. One of the most significant aspects of this building is the sculpted arch in the south transept. Various interpretations exist as to the meaning of the carvings such as scenes from the life of David or the entrance to a chapel dedicated to St Nicaise, one of the earliest bishops of Rouen.

Sources:
Bonnin, pp. 4, 66, 110, 137, 225, 266, 293, 353, 383–4, 431, 472, 517–18, 564, 600, 630;
Register, pp. 2, 60, 126, 155, 247, 298, 331, 401, 434–6, 490–1, 538–9, 590–1, 647, 690, 725
Fauroux, nos 164, 166, 171–3, 198, 203, 226
GND, vol. 2, pp. 136–7
Hall and Sweeney, 'An Unpublished Privilege of Innocent III in Favour of Montivilliers'
Le Cacheux, *L'exemption de Montivilliers*
Regesta regum, nos 210–11

References:
Cottineau, vol. 2, cols 1958–60
GC, vol. 11, cols 281–6
Hall and Sweeney, 'The Licentia de Nam of the Abbesses of Montivilliers'
Musset, 'Un document americain sur l'abbaye de Montivilliers'
Priem, *Abbaye royale de Montivilliers*
Yvernault, 'Les bâtiments de l'abbaye de Montivilliers au moyen âge' and plan, p. 42

Plates and photographs:
Baylé, 'Montivilliers: abbatiale Notre-Dame'
Franklin, 'The Romanesque Sculpted Arch at Montivilliers'

15. Mortain (Les Blanches), La Trinité

dép. : Calvados, arr.: chef-lieu
Savignac/Cistercian, abbey, Avranches diocese
Probably founded in 1105 by William, count of Mortain. The origins of this community lie in the foundation of a parallel female house to Savigny for Adeline, sister of Vitalis of Savigny (d.1122). When Savigny became a daughter house of Clairvaux and thus Cistercian, the nuns left their original site at Neufbourg and came to Mortain. Architectural survivals from the Middle Ages include the church, some of the claustral buildings such as the sacristy, chapter house, lay sisters' quarters and Romanesque cloister arcade. In an unusual arrangement these are housed in the north arm of the cloister. The church dates from the last quarter of the twelfth century and is cruciform in plan.

Sources:
GC, vol. 11, *Instrumenta*, cols 108–10
Registrum epistolarum, pp. 234–7, 239–40, 241–2, 245–7, 250

References:
Aubert, *L'architecture cistercienne*, vol. 2, pp. 174–5, 196 and 202–4
Beck, 'Recherches sur les salles capitulaires', pp. 30–1
Cottineau, vol. 1, cols 388–9
GC, vol. 11, cols 554–6
Le Cacheux, 'La date de la fondation de l'Abbaye Blanche de Mortain'
Poulle, 'Les archives et la dédicace de l'abbatiale de l'Abbaye Blanche'

16. Moutons (Aries), St-Clement

dép. : Manche, arr. and cant.: Mortain
Benedictine priory, Avranches diocese
Founded between 1100 and 1135 by Henry I. The house was originally situated in the forest of Lande Pourrie but this isolation proved dangerous during the Hundred Years War and so the community moved to Avranches. All that remains of this house is a small section of the dormitory, part of the cloister and a grange.

Sources:
Bonnin, pp. 244–5; *Register*, p. 272

References:
Beck, 'Recherches sur les salles capitulaires en Normandie', p. 54
Cottineau, vol. 2, col. 2006
GC, vol. 11, cols 533–5
de Prat, 'Le prieuré royal des bénédictines de Moutons à Saint-Clément'

17. Préaux, St-Léger and Notre-Dame

dép. : Eure, arr.: Évreux, cant.: Pont-Audemer
Benedictine abbey, Lisieux diocese
Founded in c.1040 by Humphrey of Vieilles and Albreda. As Gazeau noted, this abbey has received scant attention from historians. She argues that the reasons for this are threefold. Firstly, it was a female house, secondly, it was eclipsed by its male counterpart, St-Pierre, and thirdly, the sources are scarce.

Sources:
Bonnin, pp. 60, 197, 295–6, 591; *Register*, pp. 66, 212, 334, 680–1
Fauroux, no. 149
GND, vol. 2, pp. 132–3
OV, vol. 2, pp. 12–13
Regesta regum, no. 217

References:
Cottineau, vol. 2, col. 2357
GC, vol. 11, cols 853–5
Gazeau, 'Le domaine continental de l'abbaye de Notre-Dame et Saint-Léger des Préaux au XI siècle'
Henry, 'Les abbayes de Préaux', pp. 216–27

18. Rouen, St-Amand

dép. : Seine-Maritime, chef-lieu
Benedictine abbey, Rouen diocese
Founded in c.1030 by Goscelin, viscount of Arques, and Emmelina. The community was located in the north-east angle of the Gallo-Roman city enclosure, placing it near the centre of medieval Rouen. The first church was consecrated by John of Avranches, arch-

bishop of Rouen, in 1068. It was destroyed by a fire in September 1136 which ravaged the north-east quarter of the town. The abbey again suffered fire damage in 1248. Only part of the cloister wall and occasional vestiges of the buildings survive. From published plans it can be determined that the cloister was on the south of a cruciform church. In addition, the crosiers of four abbesses have been recovered. These date from the end of the eleventh to the late thirteenth centuries and have been tentatively associated with Abbesses Marsilia, Agnes, Beatrice of Eu and Emmeline of Eu.

Sources:
Bonnin, pp. 15–16, 121, 202, 285, 326, 396, 456, 486, 512, 589, 638; *Register*, pp. 18–19, 135, 218–19, 321–2, 372, 457, 579, 554, 583–4, 677–8, 734
Fauroux, nos 116, 182–7, 192
GND, vol. 2, pp. 134–5
Haskins, *Norman Institutions*, p. 295
Historia mulieris suspensae. Printed in Platelle and trans. in *Normans in Europe* pp. 80–4
Le Cacheux, 'Histoire de l'abbaye de Saint-Amand de Rouen', pièces justicatives
OV, vol. 6, pp. 466–7
Regesta, ed. Cronne and Davis, vol. 2, nos 829, 1221 and 1962 and vol. 3, no. 732.
Regesta regum, nos 237–42
Walmsley, 'Les revenus de l'abbaye de Saint-Amand de Rouen'

References:
Chirol, 'Crosses de deux abbesses de Saint-Amand'
Cottineau, vol. 2, cols 2543–5
Delabarre, 'L'abbaye de Saint-Amand'
Delsalle, 'Un monument oublié; l'abbaye de Saint-Amand'
GC, vol. 11, cols 286–90
Le Cacheux, 'Histoire de l'abbaye de Saint-Amand'
Le Maho, 'Recherches sur les origines de quelques églises de Rouen (VI–IX siècles)', pp. 163–72

19. St-Aubin (Gournay-en-Bray)

dép. : Seine-Maritime, arr.: Neufchâtel, cant.: chef-lieu
Cistercian priory, Rouen diocese
Founded in 1200 by Hugh de Gournay.

Sources:
Bonnin, pp. 114–15, 146, 207, 255, 283, 319, 361, 412, 466, 471, 500, 550, 585, 619; *Register*, pp. 129, 165, 225–6, 285, 319, 364, 411, 470–1, 531, 537, 569, 628–9, 676–7, 712

References:
Cottineau, vol. 2, col. 2599

20. Ste-Marguerite-en-Gouffern [5]

dép. : Calvados, arr.: Falise, cant.: Norteaux-Couliboeuf, comm.: Vignats
Benedictine priory, Sées diocese

Sources:
Bonnin, p. 83; *Register*, p. 94

References:
Cottineau, vol. 2, col. 2782

[5]   This is possibly the same house as Vignats, taking into consideration dedication and geographical location.

21. St-Michel-du-Bosc (Lithaire)

dép. : Manche, arr.: Avranches, cant.: La Haye-du-Puits
Benedictine priory, Coutances diocese
Founded between 1151 and 1183 by Raoul, abbot of Lessay and Richard de la Haye

References:
Cottineau, vol. 2, col. 2815

22. St-Saëns, Ste-Madeleine

dép. : Seine-Maritime, arr.: Neufchâtel, cant.: chef-lieu
Cistercian priory,[6] Rouen diocese
Founded in c.1167 from Bival.

Sources:
Bonnin, pp. 100, 142, 170, 187, 273, 310, 338, 380, 419, 451, 490, 522, 566, 598, 634; *Register*,
pp. 115, 158, 187–8, 199, 306, 353, 383–4, 430–1, 477–8, 513, 559, 595–6, 649–50, 687, 729

References:
Cottineau, vol. 2, col. 2874
GC, vol. 11, cols 324–5

23. Le Trésor (Bus-St-Remy)

dép. : Eure, arr.: Les Andelys, cant.: Ecos
Cistercian abbey, Rouen diocese
Founded in c.1227 by Raoul de Bus, knight. The foundation was confirmed by Louis IX
of France and both he and his mother, Blanche of Castille, were generous patrons. The
first nuns of the new foundation came from the house of Hispania in the diocese of
Amiens. The church was consecrated in 1234 by Archbishop Maurice of Rouen (1231–35).
Architectural remains included the south transept of the church up to the level of the
vaults and the entire east range of the cloister. The east wing seems to have conformed to
the standard Cistercian plan. The church is flanked by a small room which is probably the
sacristy. Adjoining this is the chapter house. Further chambers extend beyond this. The
dormitory was located on the first floor.

References:
Cottineau, vol. 2, cols 3209
Fournée, 'L'abbaye du Trésor'
GC, vol. 11, cols 325–7

Plates and photographs:
Grant, *Architecture and Society*, pp. 143–4

24. Vignats, Ste-Marguerite [7]

dép. : Calvados, arr.: Falaise, cant.: Morteaux-Coulibeouf
Benedictine priory, Sées diocese
Founded in 1130 by Robert of Bellême.

References:
Cottineau, vol. 2, col. 3375
GC, vol. 11, cols 740–2

---

6   This priory is incorrectly listed as Benedictine in Johnson, *Equal in monastic profession*,
    p. 269.
7   Possibly the same as Ste-Marguerite-de-Gouffern.

25. Villarceaux[8]

dép. : Seine-et-Oise, arr.: Mantes, cant.: Magny-en-Vexin
Benedictine priory, Rouen diocese
Founded in 1164 or earlier by Louis VII (1137–80).[9]

Sources:
Bonnin, pp. 43–5, 117, 167, 194, 281, 323, 402, 490, 534, 572, 602; *Register*, pp. 48–50, 132, 182, 209, 317, 368–9, 458, 558–9, 608–9, 658, 692–3

References:
Cottineau, vol. 2, col. 3381

26. Villers-Canivet

dép. : Calvados, arr. and cant.: Falaise
Savigniac/Cistercian priory, Sées diocese
Founded by 1133–35 by Roger of Mowbray. Nothing pre-dating the fourteenth century survives at this house. An eighteenth-century drawing shows that the church was cruciform. The rest of the plan shows the reconstructed abbey after the medieval buildings had fallen into ruin. It is believed that the cloister shown on the plan was in a different place to the medieval structure.

Sources:
Haskins, *Norman Institutions*, p. 308
Registrum epistolarum, pp. 242–3, 250–1, 296–8
Walmsley, 'Two lost charters for the nunneries of Villers-Canivet and Bondeville'

References:
Cottineau, vol. 2, col. 3398
GC, vol. 11, cols 752–4
'Procès-verbaux des séances du 5 mai 1939'
Rocher, *Abbaye de Villers-Canivet: sauvons les dernières pierres!*

---

8   This priory was not in medieval Normandy. It was dependent on the abbey of St-Cyr.
9   Venarde, *Women's Monasticism and Medieval society*, p. 204

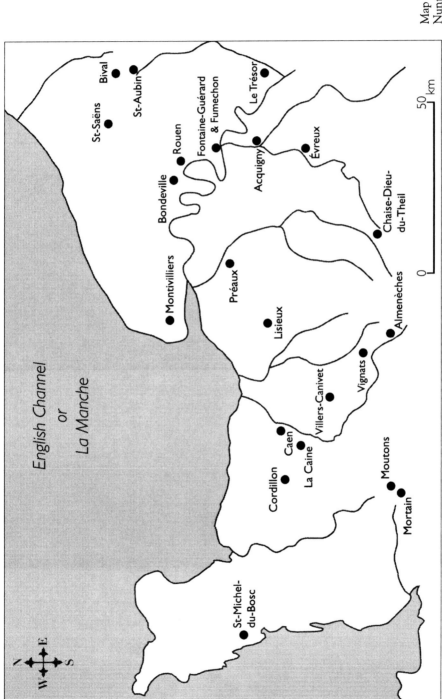

English Channel
or
La Manche

Bival
St-Saëns
St-Aubin
Fontaine-Guérard & Fumechon
Le Trésor
Rouen
Bondeville
Acquigny
Évreux
Montivilliers
Chaise-Dieu-du-Theil
Préaux
Lisieux
Almenèches
Villers-Canivet
Vignats
Caen
Cordillon
La Caine
Moutons
Mortain
St-Michel-du-Bosc

N
E
S
W

0   50 km

Map 2
Nunneries.

Appendix C: Hospitals and leper houses

1. Avranches, St-Nicholas

dép.: Manche, arr.: chef-lieu
Leper house, Avranches diocese
In existence by the end of the twelfth century. The community was situated only 625 metres from the town ramparts.

References:
Jeanne, 'Les lépreux et le léproseries en Normandie', p. 32
Fauchon, 'Les maladreries ou léproseries dans l'Avranchin et le Mortainais'

2. Bayeux (St-Vigor-le-Grand), St-Nicolas-de-la-Chesnaie

dép.: Calvados, arr.: chef-lieu
Augustinian leper house, Bayeux diocese
The exact date of foundation is unknown. The first mention of this community occurs in a confirmation by Henry II in 1173 of William the Conqueror's gifts to the house. The lepers were in the care of a prior and four monks. The house comprised two enclosures, that of the lepers and that of the immediate environment of the community. The surviving architecture within modern farm buildings probably dates from the fourteenth century, after it was rebuilt following the English invasion. The leper house was located 1.5 kilometres outside the ramparts of Bayeux, a position it shared with the abbey of St-Vigor-le-Grand.

Sources:
Letters and Charters of Henry II, no. 153[1]

References:
Jeanne, 'Exclusion and charité', vol. 1, pp. 42–3, 93–6
Jeanne, 'Quelques problématiques pour la mort du lépreux?'

3. Bellencombre, Tous-les-Saints

dép.: Seine-Maritime, arr.: Dieppe, cant.: chef-lieu
Augustinian leper house, Rouen diocese
Founded in 1130 by the châtelaines of Heuze. The church was consecrated in 1135 by Hugh of Amiens, archbishop of Rouen (1129–64). By 1177, the community had become a leper house and may have been founded as such originally. At some time before 1248 it became affiliated to the Augustinian order. The choir of the church survives and possibly dates from the first half of the thirteenth century. In addition, a large building aligned north–south exists on the north side of the enclosure. It was probably a living space for

---

[1] Currently in preparation. I am grateful to Judith Everard for providing me with copies of the relevant charters. Not all charters have yet been numbered so some entries in this appendix just list the *Letters*.

either the lepers or the staff. The building may have been communal, though evidence from Eudes's register suggests the lepers had separate houses.

Sources:
Letters and Charters of Henry II, no. 187
Bonnin, pp. 230, 496 and *Register*, pp. 253, 564

References:
Arnoux, p. 22.
Coutan, 'Description archéologique du prieuré de Tous-les-Saints près de Bellencombre'

4. Bois-Halbout (Cesny), St-Jacques

dép.: Calvados, arr.: Falaise, cant.: Thury-Harcourt
Augustinian leper house, Bayeux diocese
Founded 1165 x 1171 by Robert Taisson. This house was given to the canons of Notre-Dame-du-Val after its foundation.[2] Remains of the chapel survive. The staff and lepers lived communally on separate floors of the same building. The hospital was also provided with a herb garden and granges.

Sources:
Arnoux and Maneuvrier, *Deux abbayes*, pp. 47–53.

References:
Arnoux and Maneuvrier, *Deux abbayes*
Jeanne, 'Exclusion et charité', vol. 1, p. 96.

5. Bolbec, (Val-au-Gris)

dép.: Seine-Maritime, arr.: Le Havre, cant.: chef-lieu
Augustinian leper house, Rouen diocese
Founded in 1188 and reformed by Gauthier Maloiseau. Gauthier regrouped the mendicant lepers and provided them with the necessities of life to prevent them wandering. The community was of four orders: 1) priests, clerks and lay brothers, 2) lepers, 3) sick women and 4) healthy women and other servants.

References:
Arnoux, pp. 22, 123

6. Caen, hôtel-Dieu:

dép.: Calvados, chef-lieu
Augustinian hospital, Bayeux diocese
Possibly founded by Henry II, this community was first mentioned in around 1184, though may date from the mid-twelfth century. The hospital was located on a branch of the river Orne close to the porte Milet in the St-Jean quarter of Caen.

Sources:
Bonnin, p. 575; *Register*, p. 662

References:
Arnoux, p. 22
Jean-Marie, *Caen aux XIe et XIIe siècles*, pp. 87–8

7. Caen, Notre-Dame-de-Beaulieu and Nombril-Dieu

dép.: Calvados, chef-lieu
Leper house, Bayeux diocese

---

[2]   See appendix A, no. 60.

There is some doubt as to whether the hospital was founded by Henry II (1154–89) or pre-dates his reign. The house was under the direction of a prior. The institution also included within its grounds the leper house of Nombril-Dieu possibly founded by Lanfranc in c.1079. These leper houses in Caen were situated in the hamlet of Venoix, only 500 metres from the parish church. The complex comprised two enclosures. The first contained fields, Nombril-Dieu and houses for the porters. The second enclosure housed the community of Notre-Dame.

Sources:
Robert of Torigni, *Chronicon*, p. 209

References:
Jean-Marie, *Caen aux XIe et XIIe siècles*, pp. 88–91 and plan, p. 90
Jeanne, 'Exclusion et charité', vol. 1, p. 64
Jeanne, 'Les lépreux et les léproseries en Normandie', p. 32

8. Caen, St-Thomas

dép. : Calvados, chef-lieu
Augustinian hospital, Bayeux diocese
Founded after 1170. Located in the village of Calix in the *bourg l'abbesse*, approximately 1250 metres from La Trinité.

References:
Jean-Marie, *Caen aux XIe et XIIe siècles*, pp. 91–2
Jeanne, 'Les lépreux et les léproseries en Normandie', p. 28

9. Chaumont-en-Vexin

dép. : Oise, arr.: Beauvais, cant.: chef-lieu
Hospital, Rouen diocese

Sources:
Bonnin, p. 168 and *Register*, pp. 183–4

10. Évreux, St-Nicholas

dép. : Eure, chef-lieu
Leper house, Évreux diocese
The community appears in the records in c.1137 when a certain Richard gave land to the lepers of Évreux and it gradually came under more formal control. It was situated in the parish of Gravigny and appears to have been a community of men.

Sources:
Tabuteau, B., 'Une léproserie normande au Moyen Âge. Le prieuré de Saint-Nicolas d'Évreux du XII–XVI siècles. Histoire et corpus des sources'

References:
Tabuteau, 'De l'expérience érémitique à la normalisation monastique'

11. Falaise, St-Jean Baptiste

dép. : Calvados, arr.: Caen, cant.: chef-lieu
Augustinian/Premonstratensian hospital, Sées diocese
In 1127, Roger of Falaise built a hospital at the gates of the town with the consent of Henry I. In c.1133, the community adopted the Augustinian rule and then in 1159 that of the Premonstratensians.

Sources:
'Notice de fondation de St-Jean de Falaise', ed. Arnoux, pp. 310–11

References:
Ardura, *Abbayes*, pp. 248–51
Cottineau, vol. 1, col. 1102
GC, vol. 11, cols 754–8

12. Gournay, hôtel-Dieu

dép. : Seine-Maritime, arr.: Neufchâtel, cant.: chef-lieu
Hospital, Rouen diocese
Founded by 1256.

Sources:
Bonnin, pp. 255, 283, 319, 361, 413, 499, 587, 619; *Register*, pp. 285, 319, 364, 410, 471, 569, 676, 712

13. Gournay-en-Bray, St-Ladre

dép. : Seine-Maritime, arr.: Neufchâtel, cant.: chef-lieu
Leper house, Rouen diocese
Founded by 1128. Although the leper house as a whole was dedicated to St Ladre, its chapel was under the patronage of Ste Madeleine.

Sources:
Bonnin, pp. 283, 361, 413, 499, 620; *Register*, pp. 319, 410, 472, 469, 712–13

References:
Fournée, 'Contribution à l'histoire de la lèpre en Normandie: les maladreries et les vocables de leurs chapelles', p. 94

14. Isigny-sur-Mer

dép. : Calvados, arr.: Bayeux, cant.: chef-lieu
Leper house, Bayeux diocese
First mentioned in 1210.

References:
Jeanne, 'Les lépreux et léproseries en Normandie', p. 33

15. Lisieux, St-Blaise and St-Clair

dép. : Calvados, arr.: chef-lieu
Leper house, Lisieux diocese
Founded in c.1150, The leper house at Lisieux was in the same parish as the nunnery, St-Désir, 1.5 kilometres from the walls.

Sources:
Statuts, pp. 203–5

References:
Jeanne, 'Les lépreux et les léproseries en Normandie', pp. 32, 44

16. Mandeveille-en-Bessin

dép. : Calvados, arr.: Bayeux, cant.: Trévières
Leper house, diocese of Bayeux

References:
Jeanne, 'Les lépreux et léproseries en Normandie', p. 33

17. Montivilliers

dép. : Seine-Maritime, arr. and cant.: Le Havre
Hospital, Rouen diocese
Founded in 1241 by Abbess Marguerite de Sargines of Montivilliers.

References:
Duprey, Guez and Lefebvre, 'Histoire de l'hôpital de Montivilliers'

18. Neufchâtel-en-Bray, St-Thomas Becket

dép. : Seine-Maritime, arr.: chef-lieu
Augustinian hospital, Rouen diocese
Founded 1200–10.

Sources:
Bonnin, pp. 170, 362, 407, 452, 582–3; Register, pp. 188, 412, 462, 514, 671

References:
Arnoux, p. 22
GC, vol. 11, col. 293

19. Orbec, Ste-Madeleine

dép. : Calvados, arr. and cant.: Lisieux
Leper house, Lisieux diocese
Possibly founded in 1107 with the help of Henry I. References in the pancarte (1107–35)
to leprous women suggest that this was a mixed community. The principal benefactor was
Roger de Bienfaite, grandson of Gilbert of Brionne.

Sources and references:
Arnoux, 'Aux origines d'une léproserie la pancarte de la Madeleine d'Orbec', pp. 209–20

20. Pont-Audemer, St-Gilles

dép. : Eure, arr.: chef-lieu
Leper house, Augustinian in the fourteenth century, Lisieux diocese
Founded in c.1135 by Waleran, count of Meulan. The organisation of this house was based
on the leper house at Grand-Beaulieu, Chartres. Despite its foundation by Waleran, the
local count, the community had strong links with the town. However, if the townsfolk did
not keep up their alms donations they lost the right to nominate people to the house. It
was a mixed house as is shown by the donations on behalf of a number of female lepers.

Sources:
Mesmin, 'The Leper House of St Gilles de Pont-Audemer', cartulary

References:
Arnoux, p. 22
Mesmin, 'The Leper House of St Gilles de Pont-Audemer'

21. Pontoise

dép. : Seine-et-Oise, arr.: chef-lieu
Augustinian hospital, Rouen diocese
Founded by 1256 by Louis IX of France.

Sources:
Bonnin, pp. 478, 510, 536–7, 569–70, 603, 253–4; Register, pp. 545, 580–1, 612, 654, 694,
283
Statuts, pp. 128–50
William de Saint-Pathus, Vie de St Louis, p. 88

References:
Hallam and Everard, *Capetian France*, pp. 301–2

22. Putot-en-Bessin

dép. : Calvados, arr.: Caen, cant.: Tilly
Leper house, Bayeux diocese

References:
Jeanne, 'Les lépreux et léproseries en Normandie', p. 33

23. Rouen, La Madeleine

dép. : Seine-Maritime, chef-lieu
Augustinian hospital, Rouen diocese
Founded in 1154.

Sources:
Letters and Charters of Henry II
Bonnin, pp. 500, 563; *Register*, pp. 570, 645

References:
Arnoux, p. 22
Cottineau, vol. 2, col. 2545

24. Rouen, Mont-aux-Malades

dép. : Seine-Maritime, arr.: Rouen, cant.: Maromme
Augustinian leper house, Rouen diocese
Founded before 1135. The community certainly existed before the end of the reign of
Henry I as he issued a charter in its favour. After the death of Thomas Becket, Henry
II built a new church at the priory, dedicated in 1174. This house does not seem to have
observed a claustral plan. It began life as a collection of cabins forming a small village. It
is probable that this arrangement persisted throughout the Middle Ages.

Sources:
Letters and Charters of Henry II
Bonnin, pp. 203, 325, 513; *Register*, pp. 222, 371, 585
Langlois, *Histoire du prieuré du Mont-aux-Malades-lès-Rouen*, pièces justicatives
Regesta, ed. Cronne and Davis, vol. 3, no. 730

References:
Langlois, *Histoire du prieuré du Mont-aux-Malades-lès-Rouen*

25. Rouen, Salle-aux-Puelles

dép. : Seine-Maritime, arr.: Rouen, cant.: Le Grand-Couronne
Augustinian leper house, Rouen diocese
Founded by Henry II 1185 x 1188 for leprous noble women on the site of his manor on
the outskirts of Rouen. The chapel of St Julien survives and dates from c.1160. A remarkable series of wall paintings survive in the interior depicting scenes from the infancy of
Christ in a series of ten medallions. Evidence from Eudes's register suggests that this house
adopted a claustral plan.

Sources:
Letters and Charters of Henry II
Bonnin, pp. 34, 100–2, 325, 538; *Register*, pp. 38–9, 115–17, 371–2, 614–15

References:
Stratford, 'The Wall Paintings of the Petit-Quevilly'

26. St-Lô, Ste-Madeleine

dép. : Manches (chef-lieu)
Leper house, Avranches diocese
Founded at the beginning of the thirteenth century by Hugh de Morville, bishop of Coutances (1208–38).

References:
Jeanne, 'Les lépreux et léproseries en Normandie', p. 33

27. Tour-en-Bessin

dép. : Calvados, arr.: Bayeux, cant.: Trévières
Leper house, Bayeux diocese
First mentioned in 1263.

References:
Jeanne, 'Exclusion et charité', vol. 2, no. 66
Jeanne, 'Les lépreux et léproseries en Normandie', p. 33

28. Vernon, hôtel-Dieu

dép. : Eure, arr.: Évreux, cant.: chef-lieu
Augustinian hospital
Founded by 1260. Like Pontoise, King Louis IX refounded this hospital. According to William of Saint-Pathus, the cost was more than £30,000 because it was rebuilt in the best part of town and the king provided the sisters with all their needs.

Sources:
Statuts, pp. 151–79
William of Saint-Pathus, *Vie de Saint Louis*, p. 87

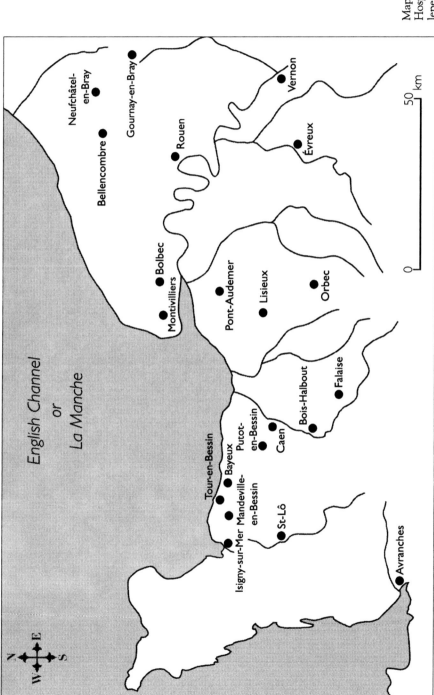

Map 3
Hospitals and
leper houses.

English Channel
or
La Manche

Neufchâtel-
en-Bray

Bellencombre

Gournay-en-Bray

Rouen

Vernon

Évreux

Bolbec

Montivilliers

Pont-Audemer

Lisieux

Orbec

Bois-Halbout

Falaise

Tour-en-Bessin

Bayeux

Putot-
en-Bessin

Caen

Isigny-sur-Mer Mandeville-
en-Bessin

St-Lô

Avranches

0   50 km

Bibliography

Unpublished primary sources
Évreux, AD H 1363
Rouen, AD 56 HP 1 and 56 HP 5
Rouen, AD 80 HP 5

Primary sources printed
Les actes de Guillaume le Conquérant et de la reine Mathilda pour les abbayes caennaises, ed. L. Musset, MSAN 37 (1967)
'The *Brevis relatio de Guillemo nobillismo comite Normannorum* written by a Monk of Battle Abbey', ed. and trans. E. van Houts, *History and Family Traditions in England and the Continent 1000–1200*, Variorum Collected Studies (Aldershot, 1999), VII
Caesarius of Arles, *Règle des vierges* (c.512–534) in *Oeuvres monastiques vol. 1: oeuvres pour les moniales*, ed. and trans. A. de Vogüé and J. Courreau, Sources Chrétiennes 345 (Paris, 1988), 35–273
Charters and Custumals of the Abbey of Holy Trinity Caen: the English Estates, ed. M. Chibnall, Records of Social and Economic History, new series 5 (Oxford, 1982)
Charters and Custumals of the Abbey of Holy Trinity Caen: the French Estates, ed. J. Walmsley, Records of Social and Economic History, new series 22 (Oxford, 1994)
'Chartes concernant le prieuré de Saint-Barbe-en-Auge', ed. Arnoux, *Des clercs au service de la réforme*, 295–7
'Chartes et documents relatifs aux activités pastorales des chanoines regulier', ed. M. Arnoux, *Des clercs au service de la réforme*, 333–5
Chrétien de Troyes, *Arthurian Romances*, trans. W. Kibler (Harmondsworth, 1991)
Chronicles of the Reigns of Stephen, Henry II and Richard I, ed. R. Howlett, RS 82, 4 vols (London, 1885)
Chronicon Beccensis, PL 150, 639–96
'Chronique de fondation de l'Île-Dieu', ed. M. Arnoux, *Des clercs au service de la réforme*, 297–306
'Chronique de fondation de Notre-Dame d'Ardenne', ed. M. Arnoux, *Des clercs au service de la réforme*, 306–10
La chronique de Gislebert of Mons, ed. L. Vanderkindere (Brussels, 1904) and *The Chronicle of Hainaut*, trans. L. Napran (Woodbridge, 2005)
'Chronique de Sainte-Barbe-en-Auge', ed. M. Arnoux, *Des clercs au service de la réforme*, 275–93
Cistercian Lay Brothers' Twelfth-Century Usages with Related Texts, ed. C. Waddell, Studia et documenta 10 (Brecht, 2000)
'Confirmation des biens de Saint-Laurent-en-Lyons', ed. M. Arnoux, *Des clercs au service de la réforme*, 345–6
Corpus iuris canonici, ed. E. Friedberg, 2 vols (Leipzig, 1879–81; repr. Graz, 1959)
Councils and Synods with Other Documents Relating to the English Church II 1205–1313, ed. F. M. Powicke and C. R. Cheney, 2 vols (Oxford, 1964)

Coutumiers de Normandie, I: Le très ancien coutumier de Normandie, ed. E.-J. Tardif, Société de l'Histoire de Normandie (Rouen, 1881)

Decrees of the Ecumenical Councils vol. 1: Nicaea I to Lateran V, ed. and trans. N. P. Tanner (London, 1990)

Delisle, L., 'Lettre de l'abbé Haimon sur la construction de l'église de Saint-Pierre-sur-Dives en 1145', Bibliothèque de l'École des Chartes, 5e série 1 (1860), 113–39

'Deux lettres de Geoffrey de Breteuil, sous-prieur', ed. M. Arnoux, Des clercs au service de la réforme, 293–5

'Documents relatifs à l'abbaye Notre-Dame du Val', ed. M. Arnoux, Des clercs au service de la réforme, 347–62

Eadmeri historia novorum in Anglia et opuscula duo de vita sancti Anselmi et quibusdam miraculis ejus, ed. M. Rule, RS 81 (London, 1884) and trans. G. Bosanquet, Eadmer's History of Recent Events in England (London, 1964)

Les ecclesiastica officia Cisterciens du XIIe siècle, ed. D. Choisselet and P. Vernet, La documentation cistercienne 22 (Reiningue, 1989)

The gesta Normannorum ducum of William of Jumièges, Orderic Vitalis and Robert of Torigni, ed. and trans. E. van Houts, OMT, 2 vols (Oxford, 1992–5)

Gerald of Wales, The Jewel of the Church: a Translation of Gemma Ecclesiastica by Giraldus Cambrensis, trans. J. F. Hagen, Davis Medieval Texts and Studies 2 (Brill, 1979)

Gilbert Crispin, Vita Herluini in The Works of Gilbert Crispin, Abbot of Westminster, ed. A. Sapir Abulafia and G. R. Evans, Auctores Britannici Medii Aevi 8 (London, 1986), 183–212 and trans. S. N. Vaughn, 'The Life of Lord Herluin, Abbot of Bec by Gilbert Crispin', Vaughn, The Abbey of Bec and the Anglo-Norman State, 67–86

Historia mulieris suspensae ad vitam revocatae descripta a Marsilia abbatissa Rotomagensi ..., AA SS, Febr., I, 902–3

Introductio monachorum et miracula insigniora per Beatum Michaelem archangelum patrata in ecclesia quae dicitur Tumba in periculo maris situ, nomine ipsius Archangeli fabricata, ed. E. de Robillard de Beaurepaire MSAN 2 (1877), 864–92

Inventio et miracula sancti Vulfranni, ed. Dom. J. Laporte, Mélanges publiés par la Société de l'Histoire de Normandie 14 (Rouen, 1938), 9–87

Le Marchant, Jean, Les miracles de Notre-Dame de Chartres, ed. P. Kuntsmann, Publications Médiévales de l'Univerisité d'Ottawa 1: Société Archéologique d'Eure-et-Loire 26 (1973)

The Letters and Charters of Henry II, ed. J. Holt and N. Vincent, British Academy-AHRC Acta of the Plantagenets' Project (Oxford University Press, forthcoming)

The Letters of Arnulf of Lisieux, ed. F. Barlow, Camden third series 61 (London, 1939), and The Letter Collections of Arnulf of Lisieux, trans. C. P. Schriber, Texts and Studies in Religion 72 (Lampeter, 1997)

The Letters of John of Salisbury, ed. and trans. E. Millor and C. Brooke, OMT, 2 vols (Oxford, 1979–86)

The Letters of Lanfranc Archbishop of Canterbury, ed. and trans. H. Clover and M. Gibson, OMT (Oxford, 1979)

The Life of Gundulf Bishop of Rochester, ed. R. Thomson, Toronto Medieval Latin Texts (Toronto, 1997) and The Life of the Venerable Man, Gundulf, Bishop of Rochester, trans. by the nuns of Malling Abbey (Malling Abbey, 1968)

Marie de France, Lais, ed. A. Ewert, with an introduction and bibliography by G. S. Burgess, French Texts (London, 1995) and The Lais of Marie de France, trans. R. Hanning and J. Ferrante (Durham, NC, 1978)

Milo Crispin, Miraculum quo b. Mariae subvenit Guillelmo Crispino Seniori: ubi de nobili Crispinorum genere agitur, PL 150, 735–44

Milo Crispin, Vita beati Lanfranci, PL 150, 19–58 and trans. Vaughn, 'The Life of Lanfranc', Vaughn, The Abbey of Bec and the Anglo-Norman State, 67–86

Miracula sancti Vulfranni episcopi, AA SS, Martii, III, 150–61

The Monastic Constitutions of Lanfranc, ed. and trans. D. Knowles and C. N. L. Brooke, OMT (Oxford, 2002)

A Monk's Confession: the Memoirs of Guibert of Nogent, ed. and trans. J. Archambault (Philadelphia, 1996)

Narrative and Legislative Texts from Early Cîteaux, ed. and trans. C. Waddell, Studia et Documenta 9 (Cîteaux, 1999)

The Normans in Europe, ed. E. van Houts, Manchester Medieval Sources (Manchester, 2000)

'Notice de fondation de St-Jean de Falaise', ed. M. Arnoux, *Des clercs au service de la réforme*, 310–11

Orderic Vitalis, *The Ecclesiastical History*, ed. and trans. M. Chibnall, OMT, 6 vols (Oxford, 1969–80)

Ordinaire et coutumier de l'église de Bayeux, ed. U. Chevalier (Paris, 1902)

The Ordinal of the Abbey of the Holy Trinity Fécamp, ed. D. Chadd, Henry Bradshaw Society 3, 2 vols (Woodbridge, 1999)

Pastors and the Care of Souls in Medieval England, ed. J. Shinners and W. J. Dohar, Notre Dame Texts in Medieval Culture 4 (Notre Dame, IN, 1998)

Patrologia latina, ed. J.-P. Migne, 221 vols (Paris, 1844–64)

Peter Damian, *Contra intemperantes clericos*, PL 145, 387–424

Petrus Abelardus Epistolae, PL 178, 113–379 and *The Letters of Abelard and Heloise*, trans. B. Radice (Harmondsworth, 1974)

Pigeon, E. A., 'Miracula ecclesiae Constantiensis', *Histoire de la cathédrale de Coutances* (Coutances, 1876), 367–83

Recueil des actes des ducs de Normandie, 911–1066, ed. M. Fauroux, MSAN 36 (Caen, 1961)

Regesta ponitificum Romanorum 1198–1304, ed. A. Potthast, 2 vols (Berlin, 1875)

Regesta regum Anglo-Normannorum, ed. H. A. Cronne and R. H. L. Davis, 4 vols (Oxford, 1968)

Regesta regum Anglo-Normannorum: the Acta of William I 1066–87, ed. D. Bates (Oxford, 1998)

Regestrum visitationum archiepiscopi Rothomagensis: journal des visites pastorals d'Eude Rigaud, archevêque de Rouen (1248–69), ed. T. Bonnin (Rouen, 1852) and *The Register of Eudes of Rouen*, ed. J. F. O'Sullivan and trans. S. M. Brown, Records of Civilisation Sources and Studies 72 (New York, 1964)

Registrum epistolarum Stephani de Lexinton Pars II. Epistolae et tempus regiminis in Savigniaco pertinentes (1230–1239), ed. P. Bruno Greisser, Analecta Sacri Ordinis Cisterciensis, 8 (1952), 181–378

Robert of Torigny, *Chronicon*, Chronicles, ed. Howlett, vol. 4

Rodulfus Glaber, *Vita domni Willelmi abbatis* in *Historiarum Libri quinque et Vita domni Willelmi abbatis*, ed. N. Bulst and trans. J. France and P. Reynolds, OMT (Oxford, 1989), 254–99

The Rule of St Augustine, trans. T. J. van Bavel and R. Canning, Cistercian Studies 138 (Kalamazoo, 1996)

The Rule of St Benedict: a Guide to Christian Living, ed. G. Holzherr and trans. the monks of Glenstal Abbey (Dublin, 1994)

S. Anselmi Cantuariensis archiepiscopi opera omnia, ed. F. S. Schmitt, 6 vols (Edinburgh, 1946–61) and *The Letters of Anselm of Canterbury*, trans. W. Fröhlich, Cistercian Studies 96–7 and 142 (Kalamazoo, 1990–95)

Sacrorum conciliorum nova et amplissima collectio, ed. J. D. Mansi, 31 vols (Venice, 1759–98)

Sauvage, A., 'Des miracles advenus en l'église de Fécamp', *Mélanges de la Société de l'histoire de Normandie*, 2e série 2 (Rouen, 1893)

Statuta capitulorum generalium ordinis Cisterciencis 1116–1786, ed. J.-M. Canivez, 8 vols (Louvain, 1933–41)

Statuts d'hôtels-Dieu et de léproseries, ed. L.-F. Le Grand (Vernon, 1901)

Stephen of Rouen, *Draco Normannicus*, Chronicles, ed. Howlett, vol. 2, 581–781

Thomas of Chobham, *Summa confessorum*, ed. F. Broomfield, Analecta Mediaevalia Namurcensia 25 (Louvain and Paris, 1968)

Twelfth-Century Statutes from the Cistercian General Chapter, ed. C. Waddell, Studia et documenta 12 (Brecht, 2002)

Vita Amandi, AA SS. Febr. I, 815–89

Wace, *Roman de Rou*, trans. G. Burgess with the text of A. J. Holden and notes by G. Burgess and E. van Houts (St Helier, Jersey, 2002)

Walmsley, J., 'Les revenus de l'abbaye de Saint-Amand de Rouen un rouleau de "rentes" des années 1220–1240', *Histoire et sociétés rurales*, 13 (2000), 143–74

Walmsley, J., 'Two Lost Charters for the Nunneries of Villers-Canivet and Bondeville in Normandy', *Archives*, 23 (1998), 168–71

William of Malmesbury, *Gesta regum Anglorum*, ed. and trans. R. A. B. Mynors, R. M. Thomson and M. Winterbottom, OMT, 2 vols (Oxford, 1998)

William of Poitiers, *Gesta Guillelmi*, ed. and trans. R. C. H. Davis and M. Chibnall, OMT (Oxford, 1988)

William of Saint-Pathus, *Vie de Saint-Louis*, ed. H. F. Delaborde (Paris, 1899)

Women's Lives in Medieval Europe: a Sourcebook, ed. E. Amt (London, 1993)

Secondary literature, unpublished

Bos, E., 'Gender and Religious Guidance in the Twelfth Century' (Ph.D. thesis, University of Cambridge, 1999)

Hicks, L., 'Women and the Use of Space in Normandy, c.1050–1300' (Ph.D. thesis, University of Cambridge, 2003)

Jeanne, D., 'Exclusion et charité: lépreux et léproseries dans le diocèse de Bayeux aux XII–XV siècles', 3 vols (mémoire de maîtrisse, Université de Caen, 1990–92)

Kerr, J., 'Monastic Hospitality: the Benedictines in England c.1070–1245' (Ph.D. thesis, University of St Andrews, 2000)

Mesmin, S. C., 'The Leper House of Saint-Gilles de Pont-Audemer: an Edition of its Cartulary and an Examination of the Problem of Leprosy in the Twelfth and early Thirteenth Centuries', 2 vols (Ph.D. thesis, University of Reading, 1978)

Napran, L., 'Marriage Contracts in Northern France and the Southern Low Countries in the Twelfth Century' (Ph.D. thesis, University of Cambridge, 2001)

Quirk, K., 'Experiences of Motherhood in Normandy, 1050–1150' (Ph.D. thesis, University of Cambridge, 1997)

Satchell, M., 'The Emergence of Leper Houses in Medieval England, 1100–1250' (D.Phil. thesis, University of Oxford, 1998)

Tabuteau, B., 'Une léproserie normande au Moyen Âge. Le prieuré de Saint-Nicolas d'Évreux du XII–XVI siècles. Histoire et corpus des sources' (Ph.D. thesis, Université de Rouen, 1996)

Secondary literature, published

L'abbaye bénédictine de Fécamp: ouvrage scientifique du XIIIᵉ centenaire, 3 vols (Fécamp, 1959–61)

L'abbaye d'Almenêches-Argentan et Sainte-Opportune: sa vie et son culte, ed. Y. Chaussy (Paris, 1970)

Adhémar, J., 'Les tombeaux de la collection Gaignières', *Gazette des Beaux-Arts*, 84 (1974), 5–192

Anchel, D., 'Quelques notes sur l'abbaye de St-Sauveur d'Évreux à propos de la demolition du Quartier Tilly', *Bulletin des amis des arts d'Eure*, 25 (1909), 26–47

L'architecture normande au moyen age: actes du colloque de Cerisy-la-Salle, ed. Maylis Baylé, 2 vols, 2nd edn (Caen, 2001)

Ardura, B., *Abbayes, prieurés et monastères de l'ordre de Prémontre en France des origines à nos jours. Dictionnaire historique et bibliographique*, Collection Religions (Nancy, 1993)

Ariès, P., *The Hour of our Death* (Harmondsworth, 1981)

Arnold, J. H., *Belief and Unbelief in Medieval Europe* (London, 2005)

Arnoux, M., 'Aux origines d'une léproserie la pancarte de la Madeleine d'Orbec (1107–1135)', *Recueil d'études offert en hommage à Michel Nortier, Cahiers Léopold Delisle*, 44 (1995), 209–20

Arnoux, M., 'Les origines et le développement du mouvement canonial en Normandie', ed. Arnoux, *Des clercs au service de la réforme*, 11–172

Arnoux, M., and C. Maneuvrier, *Deux abbayes de Basse-Normandie: Notre-Dame du Val et le Val Richer (XII–XIII siècles)*, Le Pays Bas-Normand, 93 (2000)

Asad, T., 'On Ritual and Discipline in Medieval Christian Monasticism', *Economy and Society*, 16 (1987), 159–203

Aston, M., 'Segregation in Church', *Women in the Church*, ed. W. Sheils and D. Wood, Studies in Church History 27 (Oxford, 1990), 237–94

Aubert, M., *L'architecture cistercienne en France*, 2 vols, 2nd edn (Paris, 1947)

Autour du pouvoir ducal Normand Xe–XIIe siècles, ed. L. Musset, J.-M. Bouvris and J.-M. Maillefer, Cahiers des Annales de Normandie 17 (Caen, 1985)

Auvry, C., *Histoire de la congregation de Savigny*, Société de l'histoire de Normandie, 3 vols (Rouen 1896–98)

Avril, J., 'Le III concile de Latran et les communautés des lépreux', *Revue Mabillon*, 60 (1981), 21–76

Bader, W., 'Eine Art Einleitung zur Geschichte des Essener Kanonissenstiftes', *Bonner Jahrbücher*, 167 (1967), 300–22

Barrière, B., 'The Cistercian Convent of Coyroux in the Twelfth and Thirteenth Centuries', *Gesta*, 31 (1992), 76–82

Barstow, A. L., *Married Priests and the Reforming Papacy: the Eleventh-Century Debates*, Texts and Studies in Religion 12 (New York and Toronto, 1982)

Bartlett, R., 'Symbolic Meanings of Hair in the Middle Ages', *Transactions of the Royal Historical Society*, 6th series 4 (1994), 43–60

Bates, D., 'The Conqueror's Adolescence', *ANS*, 25 (2003), 1–18

Bates, D., *Normandy Before 1066* (London, 1982)

Bates, D., and V. Gazeau, 'L'abbaye de Grestain et la famille d'Herluin de Conteville', *AN*, 40 (1990), 5–30

Baudin, P., 'Une famille châtelaine sur les confines normanno-manceaux: les Géré (Xe–XIIIe siècles), *Archéologie médiévale*, 22 (1992), 309–56

Baylé, M., *Abbaye aux Dames La Trinité de Caen*, Abbayes et Prieurés de Normandie 6 (Rouen, 1979)

Baylé, M., 'L'architecture romane en Normandie', *L'architecture normande*, vol. 1, 13–35

Baylé, M., 'Bernay, abbatiale Notre-Dame', *L'architecture normande*, vol. 2, 27–31

Baylé, M., 'Caen: abbatiale de la Trinité (Abbaye-aux-Dames)', *L'architecture normande*, vol. 2, 50–5

Baylé, M., 'Caen: abbatiale Saint-Étienne (Abbaye-aux-Hommes)', *L'architecture normande*, vol. 2, 56–61

Baylé, M., 'Cerisy-la-Forêt: abbatiale Saint-Vigor' *L'architecture normande*, vol. 2, 65–8

Baylé, M., 'Coutances: cathédrale Notre-Dame', *L'architecture normande*, vol. 2, 43–4

Baylé, M., 'Graville-Saint-Honorine: église Sainte-Honorine', *L'architecture normande*, vol. 2, 114–17

Baylé, M., 'Jumièges: abbatiale Notre-Dame', *L'architecture normande*, vol. 2, 32–6

Baylé, M., 'Jumièges: église Saint-Pierre', *L'architecture normande*, vol. 2, 14–15

Baylé, M., 'Lessay: abbatiale de La Trinité', *L'architecture normande*, vol. 2, 97–100

Baylé, M., 'Lonlay-l'Abbaye: abbatiale Notre-Dame', *L'architecture normande*, vol. 2, 91

Baylé, M., 'La Lucerne: abbatiale de La Trinité', *L'architecture normande*, vol. 2, 138–41

Baylé, M., 'Montaure: église Notre-Dame', *L'architecture normande*, vol. 2, 20–1

Baylé. M., 'Montivilliers: abbatiale Notre-Dame', *L'architecture normande*, vol. 2, 118–21

Baylé, M., 'Mont-Saint-Michel: abbatiale romane', *L'architecture normande*, vol. 2, 45–7

Baylé, M., 'Mont-Saint-Michel: église Notre-Dame-sous-Terre', *L'architecture normande*, vol. 2, 12–13

Baylé, M., 'Rouen: abbatiale Saint-Ouen', *L'architecture normande*, vol. 2, 192–5

Baylé, M., 'Saint-Martin-de-Boscherville: abbatiale Saint-Georges', *L'architecture normande*, vol. 2, 126–9

Baylé, M., 'La Trinité de Caen', *Congrès archéologique de France*, (1978), 22–58

Baylé, M., *La Trinité de Caen. Sa place dans l'histoire de l'architecture et du décor roman*, Bibliothèque de la Société Française d'Archéologie 10 (Paris, 1979)

Beaudette, P., '"In the World but not of it": Clerical Celibacy as a Symbol of the Medieval Church', *Medieval Purity and Piety: Essays on Medieval Clerical Celibacy and Religious Reform*, ed. M. Frassetto, Garland Medieval Casebooks 9 (New York and London), 23–46

Beck, B., 'Hambye: abbaye Notre-Dame', *L'architecture normande*, vol. 2, 142–5

Beck, B., 'Recherches sur les salles capitulaires en Normandie et notamment dans les diocèse d'Avranches, Bayeux et Coutances', BSAN, 58 (1965–6), 7–118

Becoming Male in the Middle Ages, ed. J. J. Cohen and B. Wheeler, The New Middle Ages (New York and London, 1997)

Bell, D. N., 'Chambers, Cells and Cubicles: the Cistercian General Chapter and the Development of the Private Room', *Perspectives for an Architecture of Solitude*, ed. Kinder, 187–98

Bell, D. N., 'The Siting and Size of Cistercian infirmaries in England and Wales', *Studies in Cistercian Art and Architecture vol. 5*, ed. Lillich, 211–37

Bennet, M., 'Virile Latins, Effeminate Greeks and Strong Women: Gender Definitions on Crusade?' *Gendering the Crusades*, ed. Edgington and Lambert, 16–30

Bériac, F., *Des lépreux aux cagots: recherches sur les sociétés marginales en Aquitaine médiévale* (Bordeaux, 1990)

Bériac, F., *Histoire des lépreux au Moyen Âge une société d'exclus* (Paris, 1988)

Bériou, N. and F.-O. Touati, *Voluntate dei leprosus: les lépreux entre conversion et exclusion aux XIIe et XIIIe siècles*, Testi, Studi, Strumenti 4 (Spoleto, 1991)

Berkhofer III, R., *Day of Reckoning: Power and Accountability in Medieval France* (Philadelphia, 2004)

Berman, C., *The Cistercian Evolution: the Invention of a Religious Order in Twelfth-Century Europe* (Philadelphia, 2000)

Bienvenue, J.-M., 'L'order de Fontevraud et la Normandie au XII siècle', AN, 35 (1985), 3–15

Binski, P., *Medieval Death: Ritual and Representation* (London, 1996)

Bodies and Disciplines: Intersections of Literature and History in Fifteenth-Century England, ed. B. A. Hanawalt and D. Wallace, Medieval Cultures 9 (Minneapolis and London, 1996)

Boelens, M., *Die Klerikerehe in der Gesetzgebung der Kirche unter besonderer Berücksichtigung der Strafe: eine rechtsgeschichtliche Untersuchung von den Anfängen der Kirche bis zum Jahre 1139* (Paderborn, 1968)

Bolton, B., 'Mulieres sanctae', *Sanctity and Secularity the Church and the World*, ed. D. Baker, Studies in Church History 10 (Oxford, 1973), 77–95

Bonde S. and C. Maines, 'A Room of One's Own: Elite Spaces in Monasteries of the Reform Movement and an Abbot's Parlour at Augustinian St-Jean-des-Vignes, Soissons (France)', *Religion and Belief in Medieval Europe*, ed. G. de Boe and D. Verhaeghe, Papers of the Medieval Europe Brugge 1997 Conference 4 (Zellik, 1997)

Bouet, P. and M. Dosdat, 'Les évêques normands de 985 à 1150', *Les évêques normands du XIe siècle*, ed. P. Bouet and F. Neveux (Caen, 1995), 19–35

Bouet, P., 'Le patronage architectural des ducs de Normandie', *L'architecture normande*, vol. 1, 349–67

Bourdieu, P., *Outline of a Theory of Practice* (Cambridge, 1977)

Bouvris, J.-M., 'En marge de l'année des abbayes normandes: la date de la restauration de l'abbaye d'Almenèches', *Bulletin de la société historique et archéologique de l'Orne*, 98 (1980), 113–41

Boynton, S., 'The Liturgical Role of Children in Monastic Customaries from the Central Middle Ages', *Studia Liturgica*, 28 (1998), 194–209

Boynton, S., 'Work and Play in Sacred Music and its Social Context, c.1050–1250', *The Use and Abuse of Time in Christian History*, ed. R. N. Swanson, Studies in Church History 37 (Woodbridge, 2002), 57–79

Brody, S., *The Disease of the Soul: Leprosy in Medieval Literature* (Ithaca and London, 1974)

Brooke, C. N. L., *Churches and Churchmen in Medieval Europe* (London, 1999)

Brooke, C. N. L., 'Gregorian Reform in Action: Clerical Marriage in England 1050–1200', *Cambridge Historical Journal*, 12 (1956), 1–21

Brooke, C. N. L., *The Medieval Idea of Marriage*, (Oxford, 1989)

Brooke, C. N. L., 'Priest, Deacon and Layman from St Peter Damian to St Francis', in Brooke, *Churches and Churchmen*, 233–53

Brooke, C. N. L., 'Reflections on the Monastic Cloister', *Romanesque and Gothic: Essays for George Zarnecki*, ed. N. Stratford, 2 vols (Woodbridge, 1987), vol. 1, 19–25

Brown, P., *The Cult of Saints: its Rise and Function in Latin Christianity* (Chicago and London, 1981)

Brown, P., *Society and the Holy in Late Antiquity* (London, 1982)

Brundage, J., *Law, Sex and Christian Society in Medieval Europe* (Chicago and London, 1987)

Burton, J., *The Monastic Order in Yorkshire 1069–1215*, Cambridge Studies in Medieval Life and Thought, 4th series 40 (Cambridge, 1999)

Burton, J., *The Yorkshire Nunneries in the Twelfth and Thirteenth Centuries*, Borthwick Papers 56 (York, 1979)

Bynum, C. W., *Fragmentation and Redemption: Essays in Gender and the Human Body in Medieval Religion* (New York, 1991)

Bynum, C. W., *Holy Feast and Holy Fast: the Religious Significance of Food to Medieval Women* (Berkeley and London, 1987)

Camille, M., 'Signs of the City: Place, Power and Public Fantasy in Medieval Paris', *Medieval Practices of Space*, ed. Hanawalt and Kobialka, 1–36

Carroll-Clark, S. M., 'Bad Habits: Clothing and Textile References in the Register of Eudes Rigaud, Archbishop of Rouen', *Medieval Clothing and Textiles 1*, ed. Netherton and Owen-Crocker, 81–103

Caspri-Reisfeld, K., 'Women Warriors during the Crusades, 1095–1254', *Gendering the Crusades*, ed. Edgington and Lambert, 94–107

Cassidy-Welch, M., 'Incarceration and Liberation: Prisons in the Cistercian Monastery', *Viator*, 32 (2001), 23–42

Cassidy-Welch, M., *Monastic Spaces and their Meanings: Thirteenth-Century English Cistercian Monasteries*, Medieval Church Studies 1 (Turnhout, 2001)

Certeau, M. de, *The Practice of Everyday Life* (Berkeley, 1984)

Cheney, C. R., *Episcopal Visitation of Monasteries in the Thirteenth Century*, 2nd edn (Manchester, 1983)

Chibnall, M., *The Debate on the Norman Conquest*, Issues in Historiography (Manchester, 1999)

Chibnall, M., 'Ecclesiastical Patronage and the Growth of Feudal Estates at the Time of the Norman Conquest', *AN*, 4 (1958), 103–18

Chibnall, M., 'The Empress Matilda and Bec-Hellouin', *ANS*, 10 (1987), 35–48

Chibnall, M., *The Empress Matilda: Queen Consort, Queen Mother and Lady of the English* (Oxford, 1991)

Chibnall, M., 'Liens de *fraternitas* entre l'abbaye de St-Évroult et les laics (XIe–XIIe siècles), *Les mouvances laïques des orders religieux*, 235–9

Chirol, E., 'Crosses de deux abbesses de Saint-Amand mises au jour à Rouen, le 29 mai 1964', *Bulletin de la Commission départementale des Antiquités de la Seine-Maritime*, 25 (1964–5), 209–21

'Chronique des fouilles médiévales', *Archéologie médiévale*, 22 (1992), 447

'Chronique des fouilles médiévales', *Archéologie médiévale*, 24 (1994), 431–2 and 465–7

Conflicted Identities and Multiple Masculinities: Men in the Medieval West, ed. J. Murray, Garland Medieval Casebooks 25 (New York and London, 1999)

Constable, G., *Letters and Letter Collections*, Typologie des Sources du Moyen Âge Occidental 17 (Turnhout, 1976)

Cottineau, J., *Répertoire topo-bibliographique des abbayes et prieurés*, 3 vols (Macon, 1939)

Coulet, N., *Les visites pastorales*, Typologie des Sources du Moyen Âge Occidental 23 (Turnhout, 1977)

Coutan, [no initial], 'Description archéologique du prieuré de Tous-les-Saints près de Bellencombre', *Bulletin de la Commission des Antiquités de la Seine-Inférieure*, 19 (1939), 198–9.

Cowdrey, H. E. J., *Pope Gregory VII 1073–1085* (Oxford, 1998)

Cownie, E., *Religious Patronage in Anglo-Norman England 1066–1135*, Studies in History, new series (Woodbridge, 1998)

Cresswell, T., *In Place/Out of Place: Geography, Ideology and Transgression* (Minneapolis and London, 1996)

Crises et réformes dans l'église de la réform grégorienne à la préréforme, Actes du 115e congrès national des sociétés savantes (Paris, 1991)

Crouch, D., *The Beaumont Twins: the Roots and Branches of Power in the Twelfth Century*, Cambridge Studies in Medieval Life and Thought, 4th series 1 (Cambridge, 1986)

Davis, A., *The Holy Bureaucrat: Eudes Rigaud and Religious Reform in Thirteenth-Century Normandy* (Ithaca and London, 2006)

Day, G., 'Juhel III of Mayenne and Savigny', *Analecta Cisterciensia*, 34 (1980), 103–28

Deck, S., 'Le temporal de l'abbaye cistercienne de Beaubec I. Du XIIe a la fin du XIVe siècle', *AN*, 24 (1974), 131–56

Delabarre, E., 'L'abbaye de Saint-Amand', *Bulletin des Amis des Monuments Rouennais*, (1906), 51–98

Delsalle, L.-R., 'Un monument oublié; l'abbaye de Saint-Amand', *Bulletin de la Société des Amis des Monuments Rouennais*, (1979–80), 31–57

Des clercs au service de la réforme. Études et documents sur les chanoines réguliers de la province de Rouen, ed. M. Arnoux, Biblioteca Victorina 11 (Turnhout, 2000)

Desmarchelier, M., 'L'architecture des églises de moniales cisterciennes, essai de classement des différents types de plans (en guise de suite)', *Mélanges à la mémoire du père Anselme Dimier, vol. 5*, ed. B. Chauvin (Arbois, 1982), 79–121

Deshayes, J., 'Le pavement roman de l'ancienne abbatiale Notre-Dame-du-Pré à Saint-Désir de Lisieux et le problème de la sépulture de l'évêque Hugues d'Eu', *Chapitres et cathédrals en Normandie*, ed. S. Lemagner et al., Annales de Normandie Série des Congrès des Sociétés Historiques et Archéologiques de Normandie 2 (Caen, 1997), 469–78

Dixon-Smith, S., 'The Image and Reality of Alms-giving in the Great Halls of Henry III', *Journal of the British Archaeological Association*, 152 (1999), 79–96

Dortel-Claudot, M., 'Le prêtre et le mariage: evolution de la législation canonique dès origines aux XIIe siècle', *L'année canonique*, 17 (1973), 319–44

Ducarel, A. C., *Anglo-Norman Antiquities Considered in a Tour Through Part of Normandy* (London, 1767)

Dunbabin, J., *Captivity and Imprisonment in Medieval Europe, 1000–1300*, Medieval Culture and Society (Basingstoke, 2002)

Duprey, C., J. Guez and L. Lefebvre, 'Histoire de l'hôpital de Montivilliers de la fondation de l'hôtel-Dieu (1241) au transfert de l'hospice (1924)', *Montivilliers hier, aujourd'hui et demain*, 4 (1991), 29–74

Duval-Arnould, L. 'Les dernières années de comte lépreux Raoul de Vermandois', *Bibliothèque de l'École des Chartes*, 142 (1984), 81–92

Elliott, D., *Fallen Bodies: Pollution, Sexuality and Demonology in the Middle Ages*, The Middle Ages (Philadelphia, 1999)

Elliott, D., *Spiritual Marriage: Sexual Abstinence in Medieval Wedlock* (Princeton, 1993)

Erlande-Brandernburg, A., 'L'architecture gothique en Normandie', *L'architecture normande, vol. 1*, 127–36

Exile in the Middle Ages, ed. L. Napran and E. van Houts, International Medieval Research 13 (Turnhout, 2004)

Farmer, S., *Surviving Poverty in Medieval Paris: Gender, Ideology and the Daily Lives of the Poor* (Ithaca and London, 2002)

Fauchon, M., 'Les maladreries ou léproseries dans l'Avranchin et le Mortainais', *Revue de l'Avranchin*, 73 (1996), 71–4

Flint, V., 'Spaces and Discipline in early Medieval Europe', *Medieval Practices of Space*, ed. Hanawalt and Kobialka, 149–66

Foot, S., *Veiled Women, Studies in Early Medieval Britain*, 2 vols (Aldershot, 2000)

Fossier, R., 'The Feudal Era (Eleventh–Thirteenth Century)', *A History of the Family vol. 1: Distant worlds, Ancient Worlds*, ed. A. Burguière et al. (Cambridge, 1996), 407–29

Fouré, A., 'Rouen, abbatiale St-Ouen', *Bulletin de la commission départementale des antiquités de la Seine-Maritime*, 32 (1978–79), 193–202

Fournée, J., *Abbaye de Fontaine-Guérard, Abbayes* et Prieurés de Normandie 19 (Rouen, 1979)

Fournée, J., 'L'abbaye du Trésor', *Annuaire des Cinq Départements de Normandie*, (1981), 89–97

Fournée, J., 'Contribution à l'histoire de la lèpre en Normandie: les maladreries et les vocables de leurs chapelles', *Lèpre et lépreux en Normandie, Cahiers Léopold Delisle*, 46 (1997), 49–142

Fournée, J., '*Deux abbayes* cisterciennes de la région de l'Andelle', *Annuaire des Cinq Départments de Normandie*, (1986), 79–89

Framing Medieval Bodies, ed. S. Kay and M. Rubin (Manchester, 1994)

Franklin, J. A., 'The Romanesque Sculpted Arch at Montivilliers: Episodes from the Story of David', *Medieval Art, Architecture and Archaeology at Rouen*, ed. Stratford, 36–45,

Gallia Christiana in provincias ecclesiasticas distributa, ed. D. De Ste.-Marthe, 16 vols (Paris, 1715–1874, repr. Farnborough, 1970)

Gazeau, V., 'Les chanoines réguliers de Corneville et de Bourg-Achard au XIIe siècle', *Des clercs au service de la reform*, 198–206

Gazeau, V., 'Le domaine continental de l'abbaye de Notre-Dame et Saint-Léger des Préaux au XI siècle', *Aspects de la société et de l'économie dans la Normandie médiévale (X–XIII siècles)*, ed L. Musset et al., Cahiers des Annales de Normandie 22 (Caen, 1988), 165–83

Gazeau, V., 'Guillaume de Volpiano et le monachisme normand' *Normandie vers l'an mil*, ed. F. de Beaurepaire and J.-P. Chaline (Rouen, 2000), 132–6

Gazeau, V., 'Le temporal de l'abbaye de St-Pierre de Préaux au XIe siècle', *Recueil d'études en homage à Lucien Musset*, Cahiers des Annals de Normandie 23 (Caen, 1990), 237–53

Geary, P., *Living with the Dead in the Middle Ages* (Ithaca and London, 1994)

Gender in Debate from the Early Middles Ages to the Renaissance, ed. T. S. Fenster and C. A. Lees, The New Middle Ages (New York and Basingstoke, 2002)

Gendering the Crusades, ed. S. B. Edgington and S. Lambert (Cardiff, 2001)

Gendering the Middle Ages, ed. P. Stafford and A. B. Mulder-Bakker (Oxford, 2001), special issue *Gender and History*, 12 (2000)

Germain, M., *Le monasticon Gallicanum*, 2 vols (repr. Paris, 1882)

Gilchrist, R., 'Christian Bodies and Souls: the Archaeology of Life and Death in Later Medieval Hospitals', *Death in Towns: Urban Response to the Dying and the Dead, 100–1600*, ed. S. Bassett (London, and New York, 1992), 101–18

Gilchrist, R., *Contemplation and Action: the Other Monasticism*, The Archaeology of Medieval Britain (London, 1995)

Gilchrist, R., *Gender and Material Culture: the Archaeology of Religious Women* (London, 1994)

Gilchrist, R., 'Medieval Bodies in the Material World: Gender Stigma and the Body', *Framing Medieval Bodies*, ed. Kay and Rubin, 43–61

Gilchrist, R., *Norwich Cathedral Close: the Evolution of the English Cathedral Landscape*, Studies in the History of Medieval Religion 26 (Woodbridge, 2005)

Gilchrist, R. and B. Sloane, *Requiem: the Medieval Monastic Cemetery in Britain* (London, 2005)

Gold, P. S., 'The Charters of Le Ronceray d'Angers: Male/Female Interaction in Monastic Business', *Medieval Women and the Sources of Medieval History*, ed. J. T. Rosenthal (Athens, GA, 1990), 122–32

Gold, P. S., *The Lady and the Virgin: Image, Attitudes and Experience in Twelfth-Century France* (Chicago and London, 1990)

Golding B., 'Anglo-Norman Knightly Burials', *The Ideals and Practice of Medieval Knighthood*, ed. C. Harper-Bill and R. Harvey (Woodbridge, 1986), 35–48

Golding, B., 'Burials and Benefactions: an Aspect of Monastic Patronage in Thirteenth-Century England', *England in the Thirteenth Century: Proceedings of the 1984 Harlaxton Symposium*, ed. W. M. Ormrod (Woodbridge, 1985), 64–75

Golding, B., 'Robert of Mortain', *ANS*, 13 (1990), 119–44

Gonthier, D. and C. Le Bas, 'Analyse socio-économique de quelques recueils de miracles dans la Normandie du XIe au XIIIe siècles', *AN*, 24 (1974), 3–36

Gosse-Kishinewski, A., 'Lisors: Abbaye Notre-Dame de Mortemer', *L'architecture normande*, vol. 2, 146–50

Grant, L., *Architecture and Society in Normandy, 1130–1270* (New Haven, 2005)

Grant, L., 'Caen: abbatiale Saint-Étienne', *L'architecture normande*, vol. 2, 156–8

Grant, L., 'Savigny and its Saints', *Perspectives for an Architecture of Solitude*, ed. Kinder, 109–14

Grenville, J. *Medieval Housing*, The Archaeology of Medieval Britain (London, 1997)

Hagger, M., 'Kinship and Identity in Eleventh-Century Normandy: the Case of Hugh de Grandmesnil, c. 1040–1098', *JMH*, 32 (2006), 212–30

Hall, E. and J. Sweeney, 'The *Licentia de Nam* of the Abbesses of Montivilliers and the Origins of the Port of Harfleur', *Bulletin of the Institute of Historical Research*, 52 (1979), 1–8

Hall, E. and J. Sweeney, 'An Unpublished Privilege of Innocent III in Favour of Montivilliers: New Documentation for a Great Norman Nunnery', *Speculum*, 49 (1974), 662–79

Hallam E. M. and J. Everard, *Capetian France 987–1328*, 2nd edn (Harlow, 2001)

Halpin, P., 'Women Religious in Late Anglo-Saxon England', *Haskins Society Journal*, 6 (1994), 97–110

Hamilton, S., *The Practice of Penance 900–1050*, Studies in History, new series (Woodbridge, 2001)

Hanawalt, B., 'At the Margin of Women's Space in Medieval Europe', *Matrons and Marginal Women in Medieval Society*, ed. R. Edwards and V. Ziegler (Woodbridge, 1995), 1–17

Harevan, T. K., 'The History of the Family and the Complexity of Social Change', *American Historical Review*, 96 (1991), 95–124

Harrison, D., *Medieval Space: the Extent of Microspatial Attitudes in Western Europe during the Middle Ages*, Lund Studies in International History 34 (Lund, 1996)

Harvey, B., *Living and Dying in England 1100–1540: the Monastic Experience* (Oxford, 1993)

Haskins, C. H., *Norman Institutions* (New York, 1918; repr. 1960)

Hayes, D. M., *Body and Sacred Place in Medieval Europe, 1100–1389*, Studies in Medieval History and Culture 18 (New York and London, 2003)

Henderson, J., *Piety and Charity in Late Medieval Florence* (Oxford, 1994)

Henry, J., 'L'abbaye de Notre-Dame de Cormeilles', *La Normandie Bénédictine*, ed. Daoust, 305–21

Henry, J., 'Les abbayes de Préaux', *La Normandie Bénédictine*, ed. Douast, 191–227

Herschman, J., 'The Eleventh-Century Nave of the Cathedral of Coutances: a New Reconstruction', *Gesta*, 22 (1983), 121–34

Herval, R., 'L'abbaye de Lessay', *La Normandie Bénédictine*, ed. Daoust, 287–303

Hicks, L., 'Exclusion as Exile: Spiritual Punishment and Physical Illness', *Exile in the Middle Ages*, ed. Napran and van Houts, 146–55

Hillier, B. and J. Hanson, *The Social Logic of Space* (Cambridge, 1984)

Hochstetler, D., 'The Meaning of the Cloister for Women According to Caesarius of Arles', *Religion, Culture and Society in the Early Middle Ages: Studies in Honor of Richard E. Sullivan*, ed. T. Noble and J. S. Cantreni (Kalamazoo, 1987), 27–40

Hockey, S. F., 'William fitz Osbern and the Endowment of his Abbey of Lyre', *ANS* 3 (1980), 95–105

Hope, W. H. St. J. and H. Brakspear, 'The Cistercian Abbey of Beaulieu in the County of Southampton', *Archaeological Journal*, 63 (1906), 129–86

Hughes, D. O., 'Regulating Women's Fashions', *A History of Women in the West. Vol. 2: Silences of the Middle Ages*, ed. C. Klapisch-Zuber (Cambridge, MA and London, 1992), 136–58

Huneycutt, L. L., *Matilda of Scotland: a Study in Medieval Queenship* (Woodbridge, 2003)

Hunt, N., *Cluny under Saint Hugh, 1049–1109* (London, 1967)

Imbert, J., *Les hôpitaux en droit canonique* (Paris, 1947)

Izbicki, T. M., 'Forbidden Colors in the Regulation of Clerical Dress from the Fourth Lateran Council (1215) to the Time of Nicholas of Cusa (d. 1464)', *Medieval Clothing and Textiles 1*, ed. Netherton and Owen-Crocker, 105–14

Jansen, V., 'Architecture and Community in Medieval Monastic Dormitories', *Studies in Cistercian art and architecture vol. 5*, ed. Lillich, 58–94

Jean-Marie, L., *Caen aux XIe et XIIe siècles: espace urbain, pouvoirs et société* (Condé-sur-Noireau, 2000)

Jeanne, D. 'Les lépreux et le léproseries en Normandie moyenne et occidentale au Moyen Âge orientations des recherches', *Lèpre et lépreux en Normandie, Cahiers Léopold Delisle*, 46 (1997), 19–48

Jeanne, D., 'Quelques problématiques pour la mort du lépreux? Sondages archéologiques du cimetière de Saint-Nicolas de la Chesnaie, Bayeux, AN, 47 (1997), 69–90

Johnson, E., 'The Process of Norman Exile into Southern Italy', *Exile in the Middle Ages*, ed. Napran and van Houts, 29–38

Johnson, P. 'The Cloistering of Medieval Nuns: Release or Repression, Reality or Fantasy', *Gendered Domains: Rethinking Public and Private in Women's History*, ed. D. O. Helly and S. M. Reverby (Ithaca, 1992), 27–39

Johnson, P., *Equal in Monastic Profession: Religious Women in Medieval France*. Women in Culture and Society (Chicago, 1991)

Johnson, P., 'Pious Legends and Historical Realities: the Foundations of La Trinité de Vendôme, Bonport and Holyrood', *Revue Bénédictine*, 151 (1981), 184–93

Jones, S. E., 'The Twelfth-Century Reliefs from Fécamp: New Evidence for their Dating and Original Purpose', *Journal of the British Archaeological Association*, 138 (1985), 79–88

Jong, M. de, *In Samuel's Image: Child Oblations in the Early Medieval West*, Brill's Studies in Intellectual History 12 (Leiden, 1996)

Jong, M. de and F. Theuws, 'Topographies of Power: Some Conclusions', *Topographies of Power in the Early Middle Ages*, ed. M. de Jong and F. Theuws, The Transformation of the Roman World 6 (Leiden, 2001), 533–45

Jumièges: congrès scientifique du XIIIᵉ centenaire, 2 vols (Rouen, 1955)

Karras, R. M., *Common Women: Prostitution and Sexuality in Medieval England*, Studies in the History of Sexuality (Oxford, 1996)

Kealey, E. J., *Medieval Medicus: a Social History of Anglo-Norman Medicine*, (Baltimore and London, 1981)

Kelleher, M. A., '"Like Man and Wife": Clerics' Concubines in the Diocese of Barcelona', *JMH*, 28 (2002), 349–60

Kerr, J., 'Monastic Hospitality: the Benedictines in England, c.1070–1245', *ANS*, 23 (2000, 2001), 97–114

Kienzle, B. M., *Cistercians, Heresy and Crusade in Occitania, 1145–1229: Preaching in the Lord's Vineyard* (Woodbridge, 2001)

Kinder, T. N., *Cistercian Europe: Architecture of Contemplation*, Cistercian Studies 191 (Kalamazoo, 2002)

Knowles, D., *The Monastic Order in England*, 2nd edn (Cambridge, 1963)

Kobialka, M., *This is My Body: Representational Practices in the Early Middle Ages* (Ann Arbor, 1999)

Langlois, P., *Histoire du prieuré du Mont-aux-Malades-lès-Rouen et correspondance du prieur de ce monastère avec saint Thomas de Cantorbéry 1120–1820* (Rouen, 1851)

Laven, M., *Virgins of Venice: Enclosed Lives and Broken Vows in the Venetian Convent* (London, 2002)

Lawrence, C. H., *Medieval Monasticism: Forms of Religious Life in Western Europe in the Middle Ages*, 3rd edn (Harlow, 2001)

Le Cacheux, M.-J., 'Histoire de l'abbaye de Saint-Amand-de-Rouen des origines à la fin du XVIe siècle', *BSAN*, 44 (1937), 5–289

Le Cacheux, P., 'La date de la fondation de l'Abbaye Blanche de Mortain', *Revue catholique de Normandie*, 10 (1900–01), 309–23

Le Cacheux, P., *L'exemption de Montivilliers* (Caen, 1929)

Léchaudé d'Anisy, M. A., 'Recherches sur les léproseries et maladreries dites vulgairement maladreries qui existaient en Normandie', *MSAN*, 17 (1847), 149–212

Leclercq, J., 'La clôture points de repère historiques', *Collectanea Cisterciencia*, 43 (1981)

Lee, B. R., 'The Purification of Women after Childbirth: a Window into Medieval Perceptions of Women', *Florilegium*, 14 (1995–96), 43–55

Lefebvre, H., *The Production of Space* (Oxford, 1991)

Lekai, L. J., *The Cistercians: Ideal and Reality* (Kent, OH, 1977)

Le Maho, J., 'Autour de la foundation de l'abbaye de Boscherville (début du XIIe siècle) quelques observations historiques et archéologiques', *Bulletin de la commission départementale des antiquités de la Seine-Maritime*, 43 (1995), 129–42

Le Maho, J., 'Une collégiate normande au temps de Guillaume le Conquérnat: St-Georges-de-Boscherville, d'après les fouilles de 1981', *Les mondes normands (VIIIe–XIIe s.)*, ed. H. Galiné (Caen, 1989), 103–11

Le Maho, J., *Jumièges Abbey* (Paris, 2001)

Le Maho, J., 'Recherches sur les origines de quelques églises de Rouen (VI–IX siècles)', *Bulletin de la Commission départementales des Antiquités de la Seine-Maritime*, 43 (1995), 143–205

Le Maho, J., 'Saint-Martin-de-Boscherville: collégiale Saint-Georges', *L'architecture normande*, vol. 2, 122–5

Linehan, P., *The Ladies of Zamora* (Manchester, 1997)

Logan, F. Donald, *Runaway Religious in Medieval England c. 1240–1540*, Cambridge Studies in Medieval Life and Thought, 4th series 32 (Cambridge, 1996)

Mabillon, J., *Annales ordinis s. Benedicti occidentalium monachorum patriarchae*, 6 vols (Paris, 1703–39)

MacKenzie, K., 'Boy into Bishop', *History Today*, 37 (December, 1987)

Maillefer, J.-M., 'Une famille aristocratique aux confins de la Normandie les Géré au XIe siècle', *Autour du pouvoir ducal Normand Xe–XIIe siècles*, ed. Musset, Bouvris and Maillefer, 175–206

Makowski, E., *Canon Law and Cloistered Women: 'Periculoso' and its Commentators 1298–1545*, Studies in Medieval and Early Modern Canon Law 5 (Washington, 1997)

Mansfield, M. C., *The Humiliation of Sinners: Public Penance in Thirteenth-Century France* (Ithaca and London, 1995)

Martin, J.-C., 'Un couvent des femmes, le prieuré de la Chaise-Dieu', *La femme en Normandie. Actes du XIXe congrès des sociétés historiques et archéologiques de Normandie* (Caen, 1986), 287–96

Martindale, A., 'Patrons and Minders: The Intrusion of the Secular into Sacred Spaces in the Late Middle Ages', *The Church and the Arts*, ed. D. Wood, Studies in Church History 28 (Oxford, 1992), 143–78

Masculinity in Medieval Europe, ed. D. Hadley, Women and Men in History (Harlow, 1999)

McLaughlin, M., 'Secular and Spiritual Fatherhood in the Eleventh-Century', *Conflicted Identities and Multiple Masculinities*, ed. Murray, 25–43

McNamara, J. A., 'The *Herrenfrage*: the Restructuring of the Gender System, 1050–1150', *Medieval Masculinities*, ed. Lees, 3–29

McNamara, J. A., *Sisters in Arms: Catholic Nuns through Two Millenia* (Cambridge, MA and London, 1996)

McNamara, J. A., 'An Unresolved Syllogism: the Search for a Christian Gender System', *Conflicted Identities and Multiple Masculinities*, ed. Murray, 1–24

Medieval Art, Architecture and Archaeology at Rouen, ed. J. Stratford, British Archaeological Association Transactions 12 (Leeds, 1993)

Medieval Clothing and Textiles 1, ed. R. Netherton and G. R. Owen-Crocker (Woodbridge, 2005)

Medieval Masculinities: Regarding Men in the Middle Ages, ed. C. A. Lees, Medieval Cultures 7 (Minneapolis and London, 1994)

Medieval Memories: Men, Women and the Past 700–1300, ed. E. van Houts, Women and Men in History (Harlow, 2001)

Medieval Practices of Space, ed. B. Hanawalt and M. Kobialka, Medieval Cultures 23 (Minneapolis and London, 2000)

Mesmin, S. C., 'Du comté la commune: la léproserie de Saint-Gilles de Pont-Audemer', *AN*, 37 (1987), 235–68

Mesmin, S. C., 'Waleran, Count of Meulan and the Leper House of St-Gilles de Pont-Audemer', *AN*, 32 (1982), 3–19

Methuen, P. A., *Normandy Diary* (London, 1952)

Millénaire monastique du Mont-St-Michel, 5 vols (Paris, 1966–71)

Mollat, M., *The Poor in the Middle Ages: an Essay in Social History* (New Haven and London, 1986)

Moore, R. I., *The Formation of a Persecuting Society: Power and Deviance in Western Europe* (Oxford, 1987)

Morrison, K. A., 'The Figural Capitals of the Chapterhouse of Saint-Georges-de-Boscherville', *Medieval Art, Architecture and Archaeology at Rouen*, ed. Stratford, 46–50

Les mouvances laïques des orders religieux, Actes du troisième colloque international du C.E.R.C.O.R. (St-Etienne, 1996)

Mundy, J., 'Hospitals and Leprosaries in Twelfth- and Early Thirteenth-Century Toulouse', *Essays in Medieval Life and Thought*, ed. J. H. Mundy, R. W. Emery and B. N. Nelson (New York, 1965), 181–205

Murray, A., *Suicide in the Middle Ages vol. 1: the Violent Against Themselves* (Oxford, 1998)

Musset, L., 'Les abbayes normandes au moyen âge: position de quelques problèmes', *Les abbayes de Normandie, actes du XIIIe congrès des sociétés historiques et archéologiques de Normandie*, ed. L. Andrieu et al. (Rouen, 1979), 13–26

Musset, L., 'Ce qu'enseigne l'histoire d'un patrimoine monastique: St-Ouen de Rouen du IXe au XIe siècle', *Aspects de la société et de l'économie dans la Normandie médievale*, eds. L. Musset, J.-M. Bouvris and V. Gazeau, Cahiers des Annales de Normandie 22 (Caen, 1988), 115–30

Musset, L., 'Un document americain sur l'abbaye de Montivilliers', *AN*, 27 (1977), 119–20

Musset, L., *La Normandie romane*, 2 vols (Saint-Leìger-Vauban, 1967–74)

Musset, L., 'Les origines du prieuré de St-Fromond: un acte negligee de Richard II', *BSAN*, 53 (1957), 475–89

Musset, L., 'Les origins et le patrimoine de l'abbaye de St-Sever', *La Normandie Bénédictine*, ed. Daoust, 357–73

Musset, L., 'Les premiers temps de l'abbaye d'Almenèches des origines aux XIIe siècle', *L'abbaye d'Almenèches-Argentan et Ste. Opportune*, ed. Chaussy, 11–36

Musset, L., 'Les sépultures des souverains normands: un aspect de l'idéologie du pouvoir', *Autour du pouvoir ducal normand Xe–XIIe siècles*, Musset, Bouvris and Maillefer, 19–44

Napran, L., 'Marriage and Excommunication: the Comital House of Flanders', in *Exile in the Middle Ages*, ed. Napran and van Houts, 69–80

Neveux, F., 'L'urbanisme au moyen âge dans quelques villes de Normandie', *L'architecture normande*, vol. 1, 271–87

Noell, B., 'Expectation and Unrest Among Cistercian Lay Brothers in the Twelfth and Thirteenth Centuries', *JMH*, 32 (2006), 253–74

La Normandie bénédictine au temps dè Guillaume le Conquérant (XIe siècle), ed. J. Daoust (Lille, 1967)

Oury, G.-M., *Abbaye Notre-Dame d'Almenèches-Argentan*, Abbayes et Prieuriés de Normandie 8 (Rouen, 1979)

Parisse, M., 'Des veuves au monastère', *Veuves et veuvage dans le haut moyen âge*, ed. M. Parisse (Paris, 1993), 255–74

Perspectives for an Architecture of Solitude: Essays on Cistercian Art and Architecture in Honour of Peter Fergusson, ed. T. Kinder, Medieval Church Studies 11 (Turnhout, 2004)

Pestell, T., *Landscapes of Monastic Foundation: the Establishment of Religious Houses in East Anglia, c.650–1200*, Anglo-Saxon Studies 5 (Woodbridge, 2004)

Peyroux, C., 'The Leper's Kiss', *Monks and Nuns, Saints and Outcasts: Religion in Medieval Society*, ed. S. Farmer and B. H. Rosenwein (Ithaca and London, 2000), 172–88

Piponnier, F., and P. Mane, *Dress in the Middle Ages* (New Haven and London, 2000)

Platelle, H., 'Les relations entre l'abbaye Saint-Amand-de-Rouen et l'abbaye Saint-Amand-d'Elnone', *La Normandie bénédictine*, ed. Daoust, 83–106

Pobst, P. E., 'Visitation of Religious and Clergy by Archbishop Eudes Rigaud of Rouen', *Religion, Text and Society in Medieval Spain and Northern Europe: Essays in Honour of J. N. Hillgarth*, ed. T. E. Burman, M. D. Meyerson and L. Shopkow, Papers in Medieval Studies 16 (Toronto, 2002), 223–49

Pommeraye, Dom., *Histoire de l'abbaye de Saint-Amand* (Rouen, 1662, following *Histoire de l'abbaye royale de Saint-Ouen*)

Porée, A., *Histoire de l'abbaye du Bec*, 2 vols (Évreux, 1901)

Potter, J., 'The Benefactors of Bec and the Politics of Priories', *ANS*, 21 (1998, 1999), 175–92

Potts, C., *Monastic Revival and Regional Identity in Early Normandy*, Studies in the History of Medieval Religion 11 (Woodbridge, 1997)

Poulle, B., 'Les archives et la dédicace de l'abbatiale de l'abbaye Blanche', *Revue de l'Avranchin*, 67 (1989), 253–63

Power, D., *The Norman Frontier in the Twelfth and Early Thirteenth Centuries*, Cambridge Studies in Medieval Life and Thought, 4th series 62 (Cambridge, 2004)

Prat, H. de, 'Le prieuré royal des bénédictines de Moutons à Saint-Clément', *Revue de l'Avranchin*, 74 (1997), 135–46

Priem, G., *Abbaye royale de Montivilliers*, Abbayes et Prieurés de Normandie 14 (Rouen, 1979)

Priem, G., 'L'église Ste-Honorine de Graville au Havre', *La Normandie Bénédictine*, ed. Daoust, 375–97

'Procès-verbaux des séances du 5 mai 1939', *BSAN*, 47 (1939), 287–8

Quirk, K., 'Men, Women and Miracles in Normandy, 1050–1150', *Medieval Memories*, ed. van Houts, 53–71

Racinet, P., 'Familiers et convers, l'entourage des prieurés bénédictines au moyen âge', *Les mouvances laïques des orders religieux*, 19–34

Rawcliffe, C., 'Learning to Love the Leper: Aspects of Institutional Charity in Anglo-Norman England', *ANS*, 23 (2001), 231–50

Rawcliffe, C., *Leprosy in Medieval England* (Woodbridge, 2006)

Rawcliffe, C., 'Women, Childbirh and Religion in Later Medieval England', *Women and Religion in Medieval England*, ed. D. Wood (Oxford, 2003), 91–117

Renault, M., 'Nouvelles recherches sur les léproseries et maladreries en Normandie', *MSAN*, 28 (1871), 106–48

Renoux, A., *Fécamp: du palais ducal au palais de Dieu. Bilan historiques et archéologiques des recherchements sur le site du château des ducs de Normandie* (Paris, 1991)

Richards, P., *The Medieval Leper and his Northern Heirs* (Cambridge, 1977)

Robinson, I. S., 'Church and Papacy', *The Cambridge History of Medieval Political Thought c.350–c.1450*, ed. J. H. Burns (Cambridge, 1988), 252–305

Rocher, P., *Abbaye de Villers-Canivet: sauvons les dernières pierres!* (Alençon, 1995)

Rosenwein, B., *Negotiating Space: Power, Restraint and Privileges of Immunity in Early Medieval Europe* (Manchester, 1999)

Rouet, D., 'Une dépendance de l'abbaye St-Pierre de Préaux: le prieuré Ste-Radegonde de Neufchâtel-en-Bray d'après les sources de l'abbaye de Préaux', *AN*, 49 (1999), 515–38

Rouet, D., 'Le patrimoine anglais et l'Angleterre vus à travers les actes du cartulaire de St-Pierre de Préaux', *La Normandie et l'Angleterre au moyen âge*, ed. P. Bouet and V. Gazeau, (Caen, 2003), 99–116

Rubin, M., *Charity and Community in Medieval Cambridge*, Cambridge Studies in Medieval Life and Thought, 4th series 4 (Cambridge, 1987)

Rushton, N., 'Monastic Charitable Provision in Tudor England: Quantifying and Qualifying Poor Relief in the Early Sixteenth Century', *Continuity and Change*, 16 (2001), 9–44

Schulenburg, J. T., 'Strict Active Enclosure and its Effects on the Female Monastic Experience (ca. 500–1100)', *Medieval Religious Women vol. 1: Distant Echoes*, ed. J. A. Nichols and L. T. Shank, Cistercian Studies 71 (Kalamazoo, 1984), 261–92

Shahar, S., 'The Boy Bishop's Feast: a Case-study in Church Attitudes towards Children in the High and Late Middle Ages', *The Church and Childhood*, ed. D. Wood, Studies in Church History 31 (Woodbridge, 1994), 243–60

Shahar, S., *Childhood in the Middle Ages* (London and New York, 1990)

Shahar, S., *Growing Old in the Middle Ages* (London and New York, 1997)

Sigal, P.-A., *L'homme et le miracle dans la France médiévale (XIIe et XIIIe siècles)* (Paris, 1985)

Simon, G. A., 'L'abbaye de Saint-Désir de Lisieux et ses églises successives', *Annuaire des Cinq Départments de la Normandie* (1927), 28–45

Simon, G. A., *L'abbaye de Saint-Désir de Lisieux et ses fondateurs avec la liste des abbesses* (Lisieux, 1925)

Skinner, P., *Women in Medieval Italian Society 500–1200*, Women and Men in History (Harlow, 2001)

Sørensen, M. L. S., *Gender Archaeology* (Cambridge, 2000)

Sørensen, M. L. S., 'Is there a Feminist Contribution to Archaeology?', *Archaeological Review from Cambridge*, 7 (1998), 9–20

Southern, R. W., *St Anselm and his Biographer: a Study of Monastic Life and Thought 1059–c.1130* (Cambridge, 1963)

Stafford, P., 'The Meaning of Hair in the Anglo-Norman World: Masculinity, Reform and National Identity', *Saints, Scholars and Politicians: Gender as a Tool in Medieval Studies*, ed. M. van Dijk and R. Nip (Turnhout, 2005), 153–71

Stein-Kecks, H., '*Claustrum* and *Capitulum*: Some Remarks on the Façade and Interior of the Chapter House', *Der mittelalterliche Kreuzgang–the Medieval Cloister–le Cloître au moyen age. Architecktur, Function und Programm*, ed. P. K. Klein (Regensburg, 2004), 157–89

Strayer, J. R., *The Administration of Normandy under Saint Louis* (Cambridge, MA, 1932)

Strayer, J. R., 'A Forged Charter of Henry II for Bival', *Speculum*, 34 (1959), 230–7

Studies in Cistercian Art and Architecture vol. 5, ed. M. P. Lillich, Cistercian Studies 167 (Kalamazoo, 1998)

Suydam, M., 'Origins of the Savignac Order: Savigny's Role within Twelfth-century Monastic Reform', *Revue Bénédictine*, 86 (1976), 94–108

Swanson, R. N., 'Angels Incarnate: Clergy and Masculinity from Gregorian Reform to the Reformation', *Masculinity in Medieval Europe*, ed. Hadley, 160–77

Swietek, F. R., 'King Henry II and Savigny', *Cîteaux*, 38 (1987), 14–23

Tabbagh, V., *Diocèse de Rouen*, Fasti Ecclesiae Gallicanae 2 (Turnhout, 1998)

Tabuteau, B., 'De l'expérience érémitique à la normalisation monastique: étude d'un processus de formation des leprosaries aux XIIe–XIIIe siècles. Le cas d'Évreux', *Fondations et oeuvres charitables au moyen âge*, ed. J. Dufour and H. Platelle (Paris, 1999), 89–96

Tabuteau, E. Z., *Transfers of Property in Eleventh-Century Norman Law* (Chapel Hill and London, 1998)

Taglia, K. A., '"On Account of Scandal ...": Priests, their Children, and the Ecclesiastical Demand for Celibacy', *Florilegium*, 14 (1995–96), 57–70

Thibout, M., 'L'abbaye de Lonlay', *Congrès archéologique de France* (1953 for 1954), 262–76

Thiron, J., 'L'abbaye de St-Évroul', *Congrès archéologique de France*, 157 (1954), 356–84

Thompson, K., 'Family and Lordship to the South of Normandy in the Eleventh Century: the Lordship of Bellême', *JMH*, 11 (1985), 215–26

Thompson, S., 'The Problem of Cistercian Nuns in the Twelfth and Early Thirteenth Centuries', *Medieval Women*, ed. D. Baker, Studies in Church History, subsidia 1 (Oxford, 1978), 227–52.

Thompson, S., *Women Religious: the Founding of English Nunneries after the Norman Conquest* (Oxford, 1991)

Touati, F.-O., 'Les groups de laics dans les hôpitaux et les leprosaries au moyen âge', *Les mouvances laïques des orders religieux*, 137–62

Touati, F.-O., *Maladie et société au Moyen Âge. La lèpre, les lépreux et les léproseries dans la province ecclésiastique de Sens jusqu'au milieu du XVI siècle*, Bibliothèque du Moyen Âge 11 (Paris and Brussels, 1998)

Tuan, Y.-F., *Space and Place: the Perspective of Experience* (Minneapolis, 1977)

van Houts, E., *Local and Regional Chronicles*, Typologie des Sources de Moyen Âge Occidental 74 (Turnhout, 1995)

van Houts, E., *Memory and Gender in Medieval Europe 900–1200*, Explorations in Medieval Culture and Society (Basingstoke, 1999)

Vauchez, A., *The Laity in the Middle Ages: Religious Beliefs and Devotional Practice*, ed. D. E. Bornstein (Notre Dame, IN and London, 1993)

Vaughn, S. N., *The Abbey of Bec and the Anglo-Norman State 1034–1136* (Woodbridge, 1981)

Vaughn, S. N., *Anselm of Bec and Robert of Meulan: the Innocence of the Dove and the Wisdom of the Serpent* (Berkeley, 1987)

Vaughn, S. N., *St Anselm and the Handmaidens of God: a Study of Anselm's Correspondence with Women*, Utrecht Studies in Medieval Literacy 7 (Turnhout, 2002)

Vaughn, S. N., 'St Anselm and Women', *Haskins Society Journal*, 2 (1990), 88–91

Venarde, B., '*Praesidentes negotiis*: Abbesses as Managers in Twelfth-Century France', *Portraits of Medieval and Renaissance Living: Essays in Memory of David Herlihy*, ed. S. K. Cohen and S. A. Epstein (Ann Arbor, 1996), 189–205

Venarde, B., *Women's Monasticism and Medieval Society: Nunneries in France and England. 890–1215* (Ithaca and London, 1997)

Waddell, C., 'One Day in the Life of the Savigniac Nun: Jehanne de Deniscourt', *Cistercian Studies Quarterly*, 26 (1991), 135–51

Walmsley, J., 'The Early Abbesses, Nuns and Female Tenants of the Abbey of Holy Trinity, Caen', *Journal of Ecclesiastical History*, 48 (1997), 425–44

Ward, B., *Miracles and the Medieval Mind: Theory Record and Event 1000–1215*, revised edn (Aldershot, 1987)

Ward, J. C., 'Fashions in Monastic Endowments: the Foundations of the Clare Family 1066–1314', *Journal of Ecclesiastical History*, 32 (1981), 427–51

Warren, N. B., *Spiritual Economies: Female Monasticism in later Medieval England*, The Middle Ages (Philadelphia, 2001)

Wemple, S., *Women in Frankish Society: Marriage and the Cloister 500–900* (Philadelphia, 1985)

Williams, D. H., *The Cistercians in the Early Middle Ages* (Leominster, 1998)

Williams, D. H., 'Cistercian Nunneries in Medieval Wales', *Cîteaux*, 26 (1975), 155–74

Williams, D. H., 'Layfolk within Cistercian Precincts', *Monastic Studies II: the Continuity of Tradition*, ed. J. Loades (Bangor, 1991), 87–118

Yvernault, F., 'Les bâtiments de l'abbaye de Montivilliers au moyen âge', *Montivilliers, hier, aujourd'hui, demain*, 9 (1997), 41–51

Index

Note: As entries in the appendices appear in alphabetical order, information found there (names of founders, etc.) is not indexed, though page references are given to the appendices for religious houses that are not directly referred to in the text.

Other volumes in
Studies in the History of Medieval Religion